THE CLASSICS
OF **WESTERN**
SPIRITUALITY

THE CLASSICS OF WESTERN SPIRITUALITY
A Library of the Great Spiritual Masters

President and Publisher
Kevin A. Lynch, C.S.P.

EDITORIAL BOARD

Jean Gerson
EARLY • WORKS

TRANSLATED AND INTRODUCED BY
BRIAN PATRICK McGUIRE

PREFACE BY
BERNARD McGINN

PAULIST PRESS
NEW YORK • MAHWAH

Cover art: DAISY DE PUTHOD, an illustrator and portrait painter living in Hopewell Junction, New York, was born in Paris, France, to an artistic family. Her watercolor of Jean Gerson as a pilgrim was inspired both by an early sixteenth-century engraving attributed to Albrecht Dürer and by watercolors of the medieval period during which Gerson lived. The symbols depicted on the shield in the illustration are first referred to by Gerson in one of his letters, in which he describes his personal seal, explaining it in terms of his life and quest for truth and meaning.

Copyright © 1998 by Brian Patrick McGuire

Library of Congress Cataloging-in-Publication Data

Gerson, Jean, 1363–1429.
    [Selections. English. 1998]
    Jean Gerson : early works / translated and introduced by Brian Patrick McGuire.
        p.   cm.–(Classics of Western spirituality ; #92)
    Includes bibliographical references and indexes.
    ISBN 0-8091-0498-9 (alk. paper).–ISBN 0-8091-3820-4 (pbk. : alk. paper)
    1. Mysticism–Catholic Church–Early works to 1800. 2. Christian life–Catholic authors–Early works to 1800. 3. Catholic Church–Doctrines–Early works to 1800. I. McGuire, Brian Patrick. II. Title. III. Series.
BX4705.G45A25   1998
230′.2–dc21   98–19127
                                                                              CIP

Published by Paulist Press
997 Macarthur Boulevard
Mahwah, New Jersey 07430

www.paulistpress.com

Printed and bound in the United States of America

Contents

Translator of This Volume

BRIAN PATIRICK McGUIRE was born in Honolulu, Hawaii, and received his B.A. in history from the University of California at Berkeley in 1968. A Fulbright scholar at Balliol College, Oxford, he did his D.Phil under Sir Richard Southern. Since 1971 he has been teaching in Denmark, where he helped found the Centre for Medieval Studies at Copenhagen University. In 1996 he became the first occupant of a new chair in medieval history at Roskilde University, outside of Copenhagen. He has published widely on subjects associated with medieval monasticism and spirituality.

Author of the Preface

BERNARD McGINN is the Naomi Shenstone Donnelley Professor of Historical Theology and the History of Christianity at the Divinity School of the University of Chicago. He received a licentiate in sacred theology from the Pontifical Gregorian University in 1963 and a Ph.D. in history of ideas from Brandeis University in 1970. He is the Editor-in-Chief of the Classics of Western Spirituality series and has written extensively on the areas of spirituality and mysticism. Dr. McGinn is nearing completion of his four-volume series, *The Presence of God: A History of Western Christian Mysticism.*

Foreword

*J*ean Gerson has been almost a daily companion for me in the last five or six years. I discovered him long ago in the somber pages of Johan Huizinga's *The Waning of the Middle Ages*, but I would contend today that Huizinga does not do justice to the nuances of Gerson's thought and its message of Christian hope. I hope that this volume will make Gerson's writings better known, for as I will show in the introduction to this volume, Gerson is a theologian and spiritual writer who is eminently worth knowing. Until now, however, he has been reserved for specialists. A few days ago I tried to find works on Gerson at one of the best religious bookstores in Paris. Perhaps because of my accent, or perhaps because of the obscurity of the author, a kind clerk led me to books by Georges Sand. When I spelled out the name I wanted, the computer revealed that nothing at all was available.

In translating Gerson I have turned time and again to the expertise of the dean of Gerson studies, Gilbert Ouy, emeritus *directeur de recherches* at the Centre National de la Recherche Scientifique in Paris. Years ago Gilbert Ouy responded warmly to a query about Gerson, and he has been totally unselfish in sharing his knowledge and insights. Recently he carefully reviewed my version of *The Mountain of Contemplation*. It has been a privilege to work with him, and I am grateful to Gilbert Ouy for his attention and the warm hospitality he and his wife and the members of his former *équipe* have shown me.

In Copenhagen I have received assistance with the French letters of Gerson from my colleague Jonna Kjær at the Institute for Romance Studies. My former colleagues at the Institute for Greek and Latin in Copenhagen, Christian Troelsgaard, Sten

Ebbesen, and Karsten Friis-Jensen have been available for my questions about Gerson's sources. Here I also had invaluable aid from my former student Signe Strecker, whose tireless poring over obscure tomes saved me many hours. Other students, especially in my Latin class, have also made contributions. My friends and fellow medievalists Kirsten Grubb Jensen and Oluf Schönbeck have added valuable comments. My new colleagues at the Department of History and Social Theory, Roskilde University, thirty kilometers and generations away from Copenhagen, have responded positively to my work on Gerson and offered many good insights.

Thanks to the Internet and email, I have at times almost daily assaulted my colleague and friend Mark F. Williams at Calvin College in Grand Rapids, Michigan, with queries especially about Gerson's classical references. When Professor Williams himself was not able to provide answers, he turned to colleagues on some of the classical networks. The results, however incomplete, provide much more information about Gerson's intellectual background than anything found in Glorieux's frustrating standard edition of Gerson.

My closest friend from childhood, Michael Oborne, took time off from his duties at a Paris-based international organization and drove me to the site of Gerson's disappeared village north of Rheims. Michael's enthusiasm for medieval life and spirituality has been with me in a bond that goes back to the age of nine years.

My wife, Ann Kirstin Pedersen, and my son, Christian Sung Dan Pedersen, have patiently listened to my thoughts about Gerson for most of the 1990s, and I am grateful to them for being there. Many thanks also are due to my Cistercian friends in the United States for their support and inspiration, and especially to E. Rozanne Elder of the Cistercian Institute at Western Michigan University. Likewise, I acknowledge a Carthusian bond with James Hogg of Salzburg, Austria, and Dennis Martin of Loyola University, Chicago.

I am especially indebted to the general editor of the Classics of Western Spirituality series, Bernard McGinn of the University of Chicago. Professor McGinn and his wife, Patricia, have shown me every kindness in making this volume possible. At the same time I am grateful to the Paulist Press and especially to Maria Maggi with their help in preparing this work.

This volume I want to dedicate to two persons: First, to my Gersonian master, Gilbert Ouy, who has taught me so much and whose knowledge of our common master is both vast and humanistic. Second, to the memory of my sister Sharon Ann McGuire, who died tragically at the age of fifty-seven on 2 November 1997. Sharon was my first intellectual mentor and showed me the way to medieval spirituality. I will always miss her and be thankful for the riches with which she endowed me.

Præstemarken, Svallerup, Denmark
The Feast of Saint Ambrose, 1997

Preface

There are some towering figures in the history of Christianity who not only are representative of the era in which they lived, but who also have a perennial message, one equally challenging and applicable for every age. One thinks especially of Augustine of Hippo in this connection, but the same is true for Origen, Thomas Aquinas, Luther, and Teresa of Avila. Jean Gerson (1363–1429) is not to be numbered among this select group. Few figures, however, sum up their era more perfectly than does Gerson. More than anyone else, Gerson's life and writings reveal to us the complex and often contradictory world that was at once the late Middle Ages and the early spring of the Northern Renaissance.

Gerson not only illuminates this world; he also helped form it. Born in modest circumstances, his rise to a position of influence and power (like many others in the Middle Ages) was a result of academic brilliance in the service of the church. The young Gerson received his doctorate in theology in 1394 and a year afterwards was made chancellor of the University of Paris—the foremost academic post in Western Christendom. Gerson's career as academic, polemicist, church reformer, and politician between 1395 and 1419, when he retired from public life, placed him in the forefront of the great issues and debates of the day. The most notable was the crisis of the Great Schism (1378–1417), which pitted a pope at Rome against a pope at Avignon and divided Europe. Gerson was one of the most able voices arguing that a general council had the power to settle the dispute and restore order to the church. But Gerson was more than a leading conciliarist. He was also a staunch opponent of heresy, a proponent of the liberties of the French church, a first-rate administrator—the list could go on.

PREFACE

Gerson's ecclesiastical success story, however, tells only half
the tale. As Brian Patrick McGuire stresses in the rich introduction that follows, the chancellor was often ambivalent about
church politics and his role in it. The remarkable letter that he
wrote in 1400, when he wished to lay down his responsibilities at
the university, reveals how troubled his soul was over its involvement in a world of compromise, lies, backbiting, hypocrisy, and
deceit. Although Gerson uses the language of compulsion
thoughout the early part of the letter to indicate his aversion to
the life he was leading, he is aware of his own inner complicity in
so much of what he does—"I am rightly called a two-headed monster and am also considered to be an example of ambition,
indeed of perjury." In his inner conflicts, as much as in his
remarkable achievements, Jean Gerson mirrors his anxious age.

Part of Gerson's inner ambivalence sprang from his strong
preference for the quiet of contemplation over the hurly-burly of
the life of action. (It was only in his final decade that he was able
to devote himself to full-time cultivation of the inner life.) The
tension between action and contemplation had a long history in
Christian spirituality. While some spiritual leaders seem to have
been able to combine action and contemplation without much
strain, others, including figures like Gregory the Great and
Bernard of Clairvaux (two of Gerson's favorite authors),
poignantly wrote about their divided existence in ways that must
have resonated deeply with the chancellor.

Gerson's devotion to the ideal of contemplation was expressed
in many of five hundred or so works that make up his large oeuvre. These writings give him an important, if sometimes
neglected, place in the history of Christian spirituality. His capa-
cious mind had absorbed a wide range of earlier ascetical and
mystical literature, not just for learning's sake, but for the benefit
of all who wished to pursue the path of loving devotion to God.
Gerson's writings show that he was an eager contributor to the
late medieval movement of spiritual and mystical literature into
vernacular forms that could be read by pious lay Christians, as *The
Mountain of Contemplation* and the *Treatise against "The Roman de
la Rose"* translated here demonstrate. Gerson is typically late

medieval in his desire to make mystical contemplation available to all.

If mystical contemplation was spreading outside the cloister in the later Middle Ages, it is important to note that this dissemination, or at least some aspects of it, were also controversial. Some forms of visionary experience, as well as certain modes of expressing mystical union with God, were considered questionable and even dangerous to sound faith and proper piety. Gerson took an important role in this debate. The treatise *On Distinguishing True from False Revelations* and parts of the *Speculative Mystical Theology* contain many penetrating contributions to the discussion about true versus false forms of mysticism during the last centuries of the Middle Ages.

Finally, we should also note that the late medieval period saw a proliferation of handbooks and summas of ascetical and mystical teaching designed to clarify and organize traditional teaching and to provide material for confessors and spiritual directors. This endeavor, which can be traced back well into the thirteenth century, found one of its most complete expressions in the chancellor's joint treatises on *Practical Mystical Theology* (fully translated here) and *Speculative Mystical Theology* (partly translated). It is in this latter work that Gerson first put forth his definition of mystical theology as *cognitio experimentalis Dei*, that is, "experiential knowledge of God"—one of the most influential definitions of the term ever made.

Gerson's role in the history of spirituality and mysticism was primarily that of an organizer and an educator, someone who sought to summarize more than a millennium of spiritual wisdom for a broad audience. His success in this endeavor is testified to by the wide dissemination and influence of his works for several centuries after his death. (This fame helps explain why *The Imitation of Christ,* the most influential of all popular handbooks of Christian devotion, was often ascribed to him in later times.) Although Gerson's spiritual writings have not received as wide a readership in recent years, the present volume, with its expert selection of key texts and sensitive translations, amply demonstrates that Jean Gerson is, indeed, a "classic" of Christian spirituality. When we read him we gain a unique insight into one of the most fascinating eras in the history of Christianity. What is more, we are given the opportunity, under his sure footed and careful guidance, to immerse ourselves in the riches of the Christian spiritual tradition.

Introduction

WHY READ GERSON?

Jean Gerson (1363–1429), chancellor of the University of Paris from 1395, is one of the greatest theologians and mystical writers of the Middle Ages. In the breadth of his interests and the depth of his insights he sums up a thousand years of efforts to understand the content of the Christian religion and to bring people to God through the right functioning of the church. Gerson was concerned both with rational explanation and with mystical experience. In Gerson's more than five hundred works one can find a summation of the medieval search for a rational basis for faith and an affective meeting with God.

Gerson's writings—and his very name—are nevertheless hardly known outside specialist circles. This situation has prevailed since the eighteenth century. More than a hundred years ago, an article on Gerson in a French encyclopedia claimed that this theologian, church leader, and mystic had become nothing but a name, for no one ever read him any longer.[1] The remark caused a small intellectual controversy in a France then torn apart by dissension between a conservative Catholic intelligentsia and an anticlerical party. Nineteenth-century France was a place where one either demonized medieval churchmen or made heroes of them.[2] There was no room for real discussion, and Gerson suffered greatly from both his admirers and his detractors.[3]

For Roman Catholics who saw themselves as defending truth, Gerson had chosen the wrong side. In the aftermath of the declaration of papal infallibility in 1870, Gerson's discussions of the superiority of council over pope were no longer politically or theologically correct.[4] A few French Catholic writers, however,

1

did their best to submerge this aspect of his career and emphasize his work as a preacher and educator.[5]

There is something of provincial patriotism in such treatments of Gerson, and it is only since the 1960s that he has been rescued from this oblivion in France by the careful studies of the outstanding philologist Gilbert Ouy. He has shown how Gerson contributed to the first great wave of northern humanism in the late fourteenth and early fifteenth century.[6] Outside the French-reading world, however, Gerson has remained a name that regularly appears in standard histories of the period but until quite recently has not aroused much interest. Once his contribution to efforts to solve the great papal schism of 1378–1414 is named, historians can move on to other, more controversial figures.[7] Historians of theology in the Lutheran tradition have looked carefully at Gerson in terms of his being a "forerunner" of Luther.[8]

Since the 1970s, Gerson nevertheless has become more visible in terms of his contribution to the theological debate and church life of his own time.[9] The Canadian historian D. Catherine Brown's *Pastor and Laity in the Theology of Jean Gerson* has provided a sober, well-structured introduction to Gerson's ideas for reforming the life of the church in terms of clergy and laity.[10] The book encourages the reader to take a closer look at some of Gerson's own writings.

In a series of articles over the past few years, I have considered Gerson in terms of links between his personal and spiritual life, on the one hand, and his public and academic life, on the other.[11] In this interest, I have followed the inspiration of the only writer about Gerson in this century who has tried to give a complete portrait of the man, his life and times. James L. Connolly's *John Gerson: Reformer and Mystic* remains after more than seven decades the best general introduction to Gerson in English.[12] At times I think Connolly idealizes Gerson's life and thinking, and certainly recent advances in the intellectual history of the later Middle Ages date this work. But Connolly read all of Gerson, as few have done, and his familiarity with these texts makes his book a pleasure to read.

At the end of the twentieth century and the opening of a new millennium, Gerson himself is worth reading because of his commitment to the unity of intellectual discourse and emotional involvement in the pursuit of lasting truths and genuine loves. For Gerson there could be no final division between the rational and the affective life. His writings can be looked upon as contributions to an ongoing discussion about the interpretation of God's revelation in terms of the daily lives of men and women. Gerson dedicated himself to describing, in both clerical Latin and popular French, the interior life of the person searching for God. James Connolly was right in calling him reformer *and* mystic. But as Catherine Brown has added, Gerson also was concerned with the life of the church, in terms of the duties of its pastors and the situation of its lay members.

Gerson's works touch on almost all aspects of the Christian faith. He is a theologian who sought to interpret human experience rather than one concerned with models for abstract analysis. Yet Gerson's training and desire for intellectual order made him unwilling to shed the discipline of scholastic theology. Gerson's presentation of what he calls mystical theology is characterized by careful definitions and references to scholastic writers.

The reader looking for uplifting thoughts and soaring prose will not find much material here, for Gerson kept himself from such flights. But in his very self-restraint, Gerson communicates a yearning for intimacy with God that spills over the boundaries of scholastic terminology and recalls the great mystical writers of the church, from Pseudo-Dionysius to Augustine, Bernard, and Richard of Saint Victor. Gerson knew and meditated on all of them, and the careful reader will be surprised by the degree to which he absorbed their terms and images into his own synthesis. Gerson was faithful to an old tradition of mystical writings, but he communicated it in terms of much more recent scholastic language.

Reading Gerson can be both inspiring and frustrating—inspiring because the man's brilliance and sense of style illuminate whole intellectual landscapes; frustrating because he can fail to deliver the insights that he seems to promise. In his writings on the mystical life, Gerson offers instruction in reaching the very threshold of God's presence, and yet the closer he comes, the more reservations he has. He insists, as we shall see, that uneducated lay people can have direct experience of God, even more so than overeducated clerics, and yet he can be scathingly critical of the language used by those who try to describe their immediate perceptions of God.

At times Gerson, who outwardly reached the pinnacle of success in church and university, seems to have been a very confused and unhappy human being. But usually he also conveys himself as deeply insightful and disarmingly honest. In his hopes and fears, desires and passions, traumas and complexes, Jean Gerson made himself approachable and understandable. A late medieval Christian and a priest, he can speak to those who seek God not in pop religion but in the experience of communities of learning, discipline, and authority.

Gerson's mental vitality and ever-active personal dimension make it hard to characterize him in terms of the intellectual currents of his time. In his works he is less of a synthesizer than a problem solver, caught up in the questions of his day and relating them to practical concerns. He may have been a lonely and worried man, but in maintaining integrity of belief and a commitment to the care of other people, he blazed his own trail to the presence of God. Gerson is worth reading because he devoted himself to the intellect without forgetting the importance of the affective life. His synthesis of understanding and emotion is a monument to dedication and concentration amid the difficult times in which he lived.

THE LIFE OF JEAN GERSON

Formation Years

In the late summer of 1377 a fourteen-year-old youth left home and headed for Paris.[13] He was like thousands of boys before him in medieval Europe who had gone to Paris in order to follow a course in humanities that was the gateway to higher learning and good positions in the church.[14] Unlike most of his predecessors, however, Jean Gerson would get to the very top of the University of Paris. By 1395, eighteen years later, he possessed the highest degree the University gave: the doctorate in theology. In the same year he was made chancellor of the University, a post that made him head of the faculty of theology and the person responsible for the granting of degrees.[15]

The physical distance is not great, about 200 kilometers or 125 miles as the crow flies, from Gerson's birthplace, the now disappeared hamlet of Gerson-lès-Barby, to the left bank of the Seine and the site of the medieval University of Paris. But in social and intellectual terms, Jean was not the most likely person to succeed. His father, Arnoul le Charlier, may have been at most a skilled craftsman who owned a little land and rented a bit more near the hamlet.[16] His mother, Elisabeth la Chardenière, came from one of the hamlet's oldest families but certainly cannot be called more than the daughter of a rural clan. Jean was the firstborn, and after him came a procession of other children who required care and attention: the oldest girl Marion (the only girl who apparently ever married); another Jean, whom we can call Jean the Benedictine, for he eventually became monk of St. Rémi, a great monastic foundation at Reims, about 40 kilometers or 25 miles to the southwest. The abbey of Saint Rémi, the great romanesque facade of whose church can still be seen in restored form at Reims, was the great landowner of the area and had a priory at Rethel, a few miles from the hamlet of Gerson. It is here that the two Jeans may have gotten their first training in how to read and write Latin.

Two more girls were born at the end of the 1360s, Jabina and Raulina. Agnes and Pierre died as infants.[17] Then came two girls whose names we do not know. In 1382, five years after Jean had left for Paris, Nicolas was born. In the later 1390s he was to join his oldest brother in Paris for a time, before he in 1400 entered the Celestine Order.[18] The last boy was also called Jean, born in 1383, and since he was also to become a Celestine monk, we can call him Jean the Celestine. The last girl and the twelfth child born to Elisabeth la Chardinière may have been the Poncete named as the writer of a letter dated to 1395–96 and dictated by the mother.[19]

There is no trace today of the hamlet of Gerson, and the original parish church at nearby Rethel, where Gerson and his siblings were baptized, has long since disappeared. Only a monument to Gerson in the church built in the 1880s bears witness to the origins of one of the greatest theologians of the Middle Ages.[20] We will never know why Gerson's parents were willing to make the economic sacrifices necessary to send their oldest son to Paris. But Jean Gerson was fortunate to be born within the boundaries of Champagne and so was eligible to receive a scholarship to the College of Navarre, founded at Paris in 1304 by Joanna of Navarre, queen of Philip the Fair.[21]

Gerson's story is by no means unique in the medieval university: the scholarship boy who takes advantages of the contacts he makes at school and works hard, so he reaches the top.[22] Later in life, Gerson was acutely aware of the personal sacrifices he had to make in order to attain the heights. As he wrote to his colleagues at the College of Navarre, he had no time to waste on idle conversations or even on the enjoyment of friendships. He described himself as something of a loner, keen on getting ahead in the university and making his mark:

> And I glory in this one thing in the Lord, that the college made it possible that there were few opportunities for such confabulations. I rarely had a chance to talk and to experience leisure, since it was so rare that there was someone else with whom I could enjoy engaging in the exchange of words, for so great among us was the difference of background and studies.[23]

Gerson may seem to us to have been the fortunate oldest son who received the lion's share of the family's surplus in order to make possible his education, but he looked at the matter differently. In an almost bitter passage to one of his brothers, he described the responsibility he bore in getting an education and hinted that he might have preferred to join a monastery, as his brother was able to do:

> God showed great mercy on you, since you had no relatives or friends who wanted you to become something great in the world

and so would have been opposed to your intention. It is, and always has been, quite different for me, as well as for countless other people who read in the book of experience that one's enemies are the members of one's own household (Mt 10:36).[24]

For all his ambiguity about his upbringing, Jean Gerson still seemed deeply devoted to his parents, whom he described as pious Christians. Gerson tells an anecdote about how his father once stretched out his arms to him in order to emphasize the sufferings of Christ on the cross.[25]

The appearance of a family grounded in its faith cannot remove the impression one gets from scattered references in Gerson's writings that his early life was not easy. In economic and social relationships he may well have felt inferior to the privileged sons of nobles who also frequented the College of Navarre. On paper, however, everything went according to schedule for the young Gerson at the University of Paris. By 1381 he had completed the humanities course and was bachelor of arts.[26] He listened to lectures on the Bible until 1385 and then for two years endured expositions of Peter Lombard's *Sentences*, the comprehensive twelfth-century collection of texts that long had been the theological textbook of Paris University. As a bachelor of theology in 1387 Gerson gave mandatory lectures on the Bible and then himself lectured on the *Sentences*. By 1390 he had finished his first training in theology and was *baccalarius formatus*. In 1392 came the licentiate in theology, and soon after, probably in 1394, the crowning glory, the doctorate.

The licentiate and the doctorate were awarded not for a piece of research, as is the custom today, but in recognition that the candidate was able to participate and show skill in the formal debates, disputations, that were the culmination of scholastic discourse.[27] The theological student had to have a vast knowledge of previous masters and had to convince his listeners that he both was orthodox in his views and able to add something to the debate, instead of merely repeating what earlier masters had asserted. The requirements of originality and orthodoxy made the path to the theological doctorate a narrow and even treacherous one.

Gerson would never have been able to reach this far at the age of thirty-two without the help of his contacts at the University. However much the young theologian may have felt isolated from his contemporaries at the College of Navarre, he had some able helpers and protectors. Most important of them was Pierre d'Ailly, who was only a few years older than Gerson, but who was both a respected theologian and a politically central figure at Paris. Pierre d'Ailly spearheaded a movement to reform the workings of the University in the face of a corrupt chancellor, Jean Blanchard.[28] D'Ailly's efforts were crowned with the chancellorship, an office that he more or less handed over to Gerson in 1395. At the age of thirty-two, when many late-twentieth-century continental Europeans are just finishing their course of university studies, Jean Gerson became chancellor of the faculty of theology and thus honorary head of the entire University.

Gerson and d'Ailly may have reached the top at such an early point in their lives partly because competition was not great. The Europe they inhabited was still marked by the ravages of the Plague, not just the initial episode in 1349–51, but also its return in the 1360s and later. The Plague took with it both the very young and the very old, and Gerson grew up in a world with a third fewer people than the childhood world of his parents.[29]

It has long been fashionable to describe this world in terms of crisis and conflict, centering on the Hundred Years' War and the Great Western Schism. Certainly the unsettled political situation between England and France affected life in Paris during these decades. But the war was an intermittent affair and from about 1380 did not burden the north of France in the way it did after 1415, when the English allied themselves with the Burgundians and were able to conquer Paris.[30]

A world that to us looks so unstable was actually full of opportunities for an intelligent, ambitious, and well-connected young theologian such as Gerson. In July of 1388 he accompanied his mentor and friend, chancellor Pierre d'Ailly, to the papal curia at Avignon. The University delegation was not sent this time to end the schism but to get the pope to accept the University's decision to condemn the teaching on the Immaculate Conception of Mary by the Dominican John of Monzon.[31] From this time onward, however, Gerson involved himself in efforts to end the schism and was a regular visitor at the Avignon court. Later, he also met the Roman pope in Italy.

Crisis Years (1397–1401)

The end of the fourteenth century was a period of social unrest, military insecurity, and political instability in France. The king, Charles VI, was after 1392 intermittently subject to attacks of insanity and so could not rule consistently.[32] Gerson seemed to sense the instability of the situation, for after preaching a number of well-received sermons at court, he may have accepted the chancellorship of the University partly in order to distance himself from royal intrigues.[33] His political champion was the duke of Burgundy, Philip the Bold, whose chaplain he became in 1393.[34] Philip had literary and intellectual interests and did his best to see that the young theologian and popular preacher acquired an economic basis for his activities. As Gerson himself complained, the prestigious post of chancellor did not bring in an equally impressive income.[35] He was given a benefice at the church of Saint Donatien in Bruges, a rich city that belonged to the duke.[36] Years of controversy over Gerson's right to the income of the position followed, and the same was the case with a position at the Paris right-bank church of Saint Jean-en-Grève.[37] Gerson took such preferments as more than an income: he did his best to reform Saint Donatien, much against the will of the locals, and some of his finest sermons to the laity were preached at Saint Jean.[38]

Weaving his way through church and court scandals of the time, Gerson became known as a man of integrity. He was bold enough to write a treatise on the moral necessity that prisoners condemned to death be allowed to receive a priest and make a last confession, something that they previously had been denied.[39] Gerson indicated that any secular power, even the king, who defended the old practice was in danger of losing his soul and going to hell. At such times Pierre d'Ailly may have held his hand over Gerson, but in general the promising young theologian seems to have found his own way through the mazes of academic and political life.

Between 1398 and 1400, however, Gerson underwent a personal crisis in which he questioned everything that he had learned and achieved. He went to Bruges to take possession of his benefice and decided that he was obliged by conscience to drop his position at the University of Paris. In a remarkable letter, probably sent to his colleagues at the College of Navarre, Gerson described the moral and emotional compromises he had to make in order to carry out the office of chancellor.[40] Starting almost every individual point in his complaint with the passive verb *cogor* ("I am forced"), he objected that he had to prefer candidates for degrees not because of their learning but because of their patrons. He had to interrupt his teaching and administrative duties in order to entertain nonentities who were politically or socially important for the University. He had to rush around to such an extent that he could not find inner peace to pray or say the mass in a proper manner.

Gerson's blatant description of the hypocrisy of academic life makes this letter one of the most remarkable we have from any medieval collection. I find it far more open in what it reveals about the inner life of a human being than twelfth-century Peter Abelard's rhetorical *tour de force* in his letter known as *The Story of His Misfortunes*.[41] Abelard's sense of audience and ability for dramatizing his situation make it difficult to see his complaint as a personal statement, while Gerson's directness and relative lack of polish are much more convincing.

Gerson, of course, knew about the rules of rhetoric and the means to appeal to an audience. As Gilbert Ouy time and again has shown, Gerson's contemporaries at the College of Navarre include some of the first great French humanists, and he certainly shared with them an appreciation of classical texts and references.[42] But in the letters from Bruges, Gerson restrained to a great extent the literary gifts with which he could excel and expressed his doubts about what he had become. Years before, in the first letter we have from Gerson's hands, he conveyed himself to a patron, probably Pierre d'Ailly, as an almost over-clever manipulator of classical and Christian literary references.[43] Now, in the crisis of his life, Gerson stepped out of such fine clothes and gave the world a look into a troubled mind.

In the Middle Ages it was common for churchmen to claim hesitation about taking high office and to provide at least a token show of resistance.[44] It is not clear whether Gerson fitted this mold when he first took office, but in trying to resign his position after a few years, he was acting more like the Brethren of the Common Life than like a distinguished theologian of the University of Paris. He may have been in the midst of a mental and nervous breakdown. Emotionally starved and intellectually exhausted, he was coming to grips with the person he had become in his lightning career rise at Paris.

Gerson's attack on academia provides one of the most intelligent descriptions of the pride and self-indulgence that can characterize university academics. Gerson may have been on the verge of mental illness, but his breakdown enabled him to cut through the cant of official language and to confront his own academic cowardice:

> I am forced to follow the crowd in doing what I do not want or what is not permitted, just as one who is an enemy or is suspected of having ambition. It is not enough to hide this fact or to flee it or to be silent.[45]

Gerson recovered and the tone of his letters changed. Soon he was drawing up reform programs for the faculty of theology and the University as a whole. But he never forgot the lesson of his breakdown: the realization that the great academic sin is *superbia*, an arrogant sense of being superior to others and a belief that one deserves to live in a special, privileged world because of one's own outstanding merits.

Gerson from now on insisted on a university that existed in order to serve the church and its members. In the language of our time, it was not enough to have a university whose members spoke an esoteric research language.[46] It was essential that the learning of the different faculties, especially theology, be made available for ordinary people, the *gens simples* to whom Gerson regularly referred. Good theologians were obliged to be good preachers, both in Latin to their colleagues and students, and in the vernacular for parishioners. Gerson's university vision remains with us to this very day as a challenge to do research on the highest level and to convey its fruits to people who thirst for truth and enlightenment but do not have time or opportunity to enter directly into university discourse.

Fruitful Years (1401–1408)

Gerson's stay at Bruges was extended by an illness that confined him to bed for several months. During his recovery he reflected on the character of mystical experience. The first fruits of his thoughts are contained in *The Mountain of Contemplation*, a guide for lay people to the mystical life, written primarily for his sisters, who were still at home with Gerson's parents.[47] Like Chaucer and Boccaccio a few decades earlier, Gerson realized that there was a lay audience, especially of women, thirsty for new forms of literature and learning.[48] He conceded that his exposition of mystical theology was to a great extent already available in Latin, but there was a lack of writings on the subject in French.

So began a series of treatises on religion dedicated to his sisters but intended for a larger lay audience.[49] Gerson discovered at Bruges that his call went far beyond the court and the university, for he felt a pastoral concern for the entire laity. Gerson returned to Paris in September of 1400[50] and resumed what became one of the most productive and fruitful careers of any Parisian master. He continued writing moral treatises in French, while he resumed his lectures and university sermons. Long letters or brief treatises in Latin on a number of subjects poured forth from his pen[51]: on the schism and the reconciliation of the church; on the Carthusians' abstention from the eating of meat; on the dangers of John Ruusbroec's teaching on the union of the soul with God in the mystical vision in this life. In French, Gerson attacked Jean de Meun's learned poem, *The Romance of the Rose*. In a sermon, probably to the Cistercians at the College de Saint Bernard in Paris on the feast day of their saint, Gerson praised Bernard's attachment to the contemplative life and saw him as a great, solitary mystic.

On 8 and 9 November 1402 Gerson gave two lessons to his students, *Against the Vain Curiosity of Students*, in which he made a frontal attack on the penchant of students to celebrate what appeared to be new learning at the cost of the traditional curriculum.[52] Here and elsewhere in his work, Gerson called for the study of established texts rather than the pursuit of esoteric interests. He even insisted that he would rather his students read thirteenth-century scholastics instead of his own works, which were being grabbed up in incomplete form.[53]

During this period Gerson was lecturing on the Gospel According to Saint Mark, a work only available to us in a fragment.[54] But we do have the revised text of another set of lectures, on mystical theology.[55] Gerson's *Speculative Mystical Theology* in many ways sums up his attempt to reconcile personal experience and theological knowledge. Looking at the entire tradition of mystical theology from Pseudo-Dionysius to contemporary writers, Gerson attempted to provide for his students a guide to questions on the soul and its powers in the search for the presence of God. Gerson thus conveyed in Latin and in terms of learned discourse what he had earlier provided in French for his sisters and a non-university audience. A few years later, in the autumn of 1407, Gerson completed this work with *Practical Mystical Theology*, a practical guide, as it were, to the mystical life in terms of possibilities and pitfalls, going so far even as discussing bodily posture and positions that could be best for the practice of meditation and in the pursuit of contemplative experience.[56]

It is almost impossible to imagine the intensity of Gerson's involvement in the debates of his time during these productive years. The chancellor was everywhere, giving sermons on penance, on humility, and on chastity. He assembled the parts of his *Opus Tripartitum* or *Doctrinale*, which would become his best-known guide to the Christian life, with its *Mirror of the Soul, Examination of Conscience*, and *Medicine of the Soul*.[57] Gerson's concern for the sacrament of confession was summarized in his *On the Art of Hearing Confessions*.[58] His involvement in the teaching of the young, as at the cathedral school of Notre Dame, is evident in his *On Bringing Youth to Christ*, probably from 1406.[59] Gerson's penchant for writing "tracts for the times" was fairly unusual for a university teacher, but he preferred to make an immediate contribution to debates about faith and morals instead of limiting himself to learned scholastic discussions.

A Lifelong Family Commitment

On 8 June 1401 Gerson's mother died. Aside from the epitaph he composed for her, we know little about his reactions to his loss.[60] We are better informed about Gerson's feelings on saying goodbye to his brother Nicolas, who on 11 November 1401 entered the Celestine Order.[61] Nicolas had been living with his oldest brother at Paris. Three weeks after Nicolas had left for the house of the Trinity at Villeneuve-lez-Soissons, Gerson wrote a remarkable letter in which he described his own situation.[62] A sense of emptiness had overtaken him, and he had felt his everyday life in a shambles, until he managed to recall the meaning of Nicolas's vocation and to rejoice in his brother's offering of himself to God.

I am not convinced by the ending of this letter, which is almost too much in conformity with the requirement of Christian selflessness to be an accurate reflection of the state of mind of a man whose isolation from all other human bonds made his family links central throughout his life. Gerson was perhaps expressing a hope and desire that he would come to accept Nicolas's choice. Here, just as in letters concerning the youngest brother, Jean the Celestine, we can see how the older Gerson insisted on maintaining contacts with the two brothers who for a period lived with him at Paris and then chose to leave the academic milieu and become monks.

In one letter, which unfortunately is lost to us, Nicolas seems to have accused Jean Gerson of giving young Jean nightmares because of his too strict advice. In his reply, Gerson defended his concern and refused to relent.[63] Whatever family misunderstandings may have been behind Gerson's involvement, Gerson's letter reveals a continuing involvement with the spiritual and mental condition of his family members. In the period up to about 1408, he continued to write letters and treatises of advice to his sisters, who remained at home with their father after their mother's death.[64] The psychological implications of Gerson's hold on his sisters may be disturbing, especially in his admission to his oldest sister, Marion, that he had never liked her husband or really approved of the marriage. Marion had returned to the family together with her child, and Gerson hoped she would remain there. Apparently she did not, but the other sisters did form a kind of informal religious community and continued to live together after the death of their father in 1404.

One more indication of continuing family bonds is the fact that in 1419, after his exile in Germany and Austria, Gerson was able to return to France and live at Lyon in the religious house where his youngest brother, Jean the Celestine, had become prior.[65] Jean not only provided lodging for his brother, but was with him at the end of his life and became his literary executor, making sure that Gerson's treatises were accounted for.[66] One senses the loyalty and love of Jean the Celestine in the ending he attached to Gerson's last work, *Treatise on the Song of Songs*:

> The learned doctor completed this outstanding work...at Lyon in France in the year of the Lord 1429, on Saturday 9 July. On the twelfth day of the same month, in the sixty-sixth year of his life, amid words of prayer, he devoutly handed over his spirit to God. Now, as one can piously believe, he can enjoy the embraces and kisses of the beloved spouse.[67]

Jean the Celestine was certain that his older brother could now experience firsthand the joys of which he had previously written in his commentary on the Song of Songs.

To the very end, Jean Gerson identified his religious yearnings with a deep family commitment and presence. With few friends in his life, except perhaps Pierre d'Ailly, and with none of the spiritual bonds with holy women that were so common for medieval clerical or monastic men, Gerson clung to his brothers and sisters in the flesh.

A Consummate Politician

Jean Gerson was so versatile in his life and writings that it would be unjust to see him only as a successful theologian and preacher who remained emotionally close to his biological family. After his return to Paris in the autumn of 1400, he learned to live with the administrative and political burdens of office. He did not again betray the fatigue and depression that overcame him in 1398–99. Just as Gerson in the 1390s risked his career by complaining to the court about the treatment of prisoners condemned to death, he spoke out regularly about what he considered to be other abuses of his time.[68]

In 1403 Gerson consolidated his attachment to his new life in Paris by purchasing a residence within the cloister of the cathedral of Notre Dame.[69] Here he also took on the supervision of the youths attending the school, as well as the hospital (Hôtel-Dieu) belonging to the cathedral chapter.[70] Several other schools were under his nominal care, and his treatises on education show that he took this obligation quite seriously.

In 1404 Gerson reacted in shock to an outrage committed against the students of the University. Under the leadership of the king's chamberlain, Charles de Savoisy, a procession of students and teachers to the church of Saint Catherine had been attacked, and several persons had been wounded. The University went on strike and a few days later Gerson addressed the Senate of the realm.[71] Here he described the University as the innocent "daughter of the king," whose members had gone into procession in order to pray for peace and for the king's health. Instead, they had been met on the street with horsemen and blows, and the attack had continued even into the interior of the church. In this address, known as *Estote misericordes* ("Be Merciful"), from the text of Luke 6:36, Gerson described a vision of the University

16

as founded in Paris by Charlemagne himself.[72] This institution, the king's daughter by adoption, had now been brutalized in a way that went beyond what the Goths in 410 had done in attacking the city of Rome. Recalling Augustine's words in *The City of God*, Gerson points out how the barbarians had spared the Christians who took refuge in churches.[73] Now the supposedly Christian troops did not even spare those in church: "This crime has taken place next to the residence of the king, next to the fountain of royal justice, the Parlement and the Châtelet, in the main city of all France."[74] After such an incident, how could parents in the future dare to send their sons to Paris to study? Thus the clergy will suffer, for it will not be properly educated, and "when there is a lack of clergy, then the chivalry will not last for long."[75]

Gerson saw civil discord as a threat not just to the University but to the very fabric of society. He demanded restitution and punishment of the guilty, and he apparently got what he wanted. Three days later, on 22 August 1404, Charles de Savoisy was condemned and removed from office.[76] But the causes of dissension remained, so long as the king was weak. His brother, Louis of Orléans, was locked in a poisonous rivalry with the duke of Burgundy, John the Fearless.[77] Gerson was on one of his many missions to Avignon and Rome to end the schism when on 23 November 1407 the duke of Orléans was cut down in the street by the duke of Burgundy. The latter fled Paris, but soon after Gerson's return in February 1408, the duke of Burgundy dared to show his face again. He had a master of the University of Paris, Jean Petit, write a treatise defending his act as justifiable tyrannicide. Gerson refused to accept the intellectual and theological bases for Petit's argument. On many occasions in the coming years, Gerson wrote against this teaching and its consequences.[78]

For a theologian like Gerson, whose career had been dependent on the generosity of the duke of Burgundy, such a declaration was by no means prudent. Eventually he lost his preferment at Bruges.[79] In the same years that Gerson was fighting to keep his position at Bruges, he was also unable to enjoy any income from his benefice in Paris at the church of Saint Jean-en-Grève, where the abbot of Bec until 1409 pressed claims.[80] Here, as in much else in Gerson's life, his everyday existence must have been infinitely complicated by legal quarrels and political problems. One wonders how he had the mental and physical energy to keep up his steady stream of treatises and sermons in the midst of such depressing and distressing distractions.

At times in these years, when the Armagnacs (the partisans of the deceased Louis of Orléans) and the Burgundians were at each other's throats, Gerson may have been physically in danger. He was absent from the deliberations of the chapter of Notre Dame from October 1410 to February 1411, but apparently because of illness.[81] In July of 1411 the Burgundians took political control in Paris, and a civil war began, with factions in the middle class, especially including the butchers, allying with the duke of Burgundy. Gerson did his best to intervene, and for a period during 1412 and 1413 the life of the city and the University resumed some normality. But in April came what is known as the revolution of the Cabochiens, a name taken from one of the leaders of the Paris butchers, Simon Caboche.[82] The butchers, allied with the Burgundians, took power and began to terrorize the rest of the population. According to a contemporary chronicler, Gerson's residence was invaded, and he had to seek refuge in the vaults above the cathedral of Notre Dame.[83]

This state of affairs continued through April, May, and June, until Duke John the Fearless fled and his Parisian butchers were expelled. A shaky peace returned to Paris, but Gerson's thoughts were already elsewhere, on the convocation of a general council at Constance, which once and for all was to end the Great Schism. Gerson had not attended the previous council at Pisa (1408), which, instead of reducing the number of popes from two to one, inadvertently had increased them to three. Now Gerson threw all of his intellectual resources into efforts to make the new council successful.

Gerson's role at Constance has been much discussed in historical literature.[84] He was active in the condemnation and burning of John Hus, the Bohemian heretic who was promised safe conduct to the council and then betrayed. Gerson continued to speak out against Jean Petit's doctrine of tyrannicide, and he is also remembered for his statement on the authenticity of the revelations of Birgitta of Vadstena.[85] He was now being consulted as one of the great theological authorities of the Western church, and his moral leadership was especially important when the church fathers woke up to find that one of the popes, who supposedly had arrived in order to resign, had fled Constance. Gerson preached a central sermon that day in order to calm people's nerves, and in the end his predictions of a solution to the dilemmas of the schism were realized.[86]

Gerson had long clung to the solution of the *via cessionis* (the procedure of voluntary abandonment of office), the hope that each of the popes would give way and yield power to a new conclave and election. In the end, this method of compromise failed, and Gerson adopted the more radical conciliarist position that a general council has the right to depose a pope and elect his successor. The new pope, Martin V, studiously ignored the fact that his position was the result of precisely such a procedure, and the first half of the fifteenth century was characterized by futile debates about who runs the church and who has the last word, pope or council or pope in council.[87]

A Pilgrim in a Troubled Age

Sometime between 23 and 28 January 1415, Jean Gerson left Paris, never to return.[88] In the years to come, he continued to insist on his title of chancellor, but the political situation in Paris, with the English alliance with the Burgundians, made it impossible for an enemy of the duke of Burgundy to return to the University. In more than one place in his writings, Jean Gerson referred to the Hebrew word for pilgrim or wanderer and its closeness to the name of the hamlet of his birth. To be a Gerson was to be a *peregrinus* or a *viator*, a wayfarer on his way to the only true home in heaven.[89]

In such a statement, Gerson naturally asserted what many medieval people believed about their state in life, that they were pilgrims on the way to God. But in these years after 1415 Gerson especially experienced physical alienation from his surroundings. First at Constance, then at the great abbey of Melk, and afterward in Vienna, where the Duke of Austria tried to get him to teach at the newly founded university, Gerson had to accept asylum in German-speaking parts of Europe. His beloved France was too dangerous a place for such a political refugee. Gerson could engage in discourse in the international language of his day, Latin, but we know from his French sermons and treatises how much he loved and used his own vernacular. He probably missed not only the academic milieu of Paris but also the children and adults who had looked to him for advice and guidance.

Gerson's sense of exile is reflected in his writing in 1418 of *Consolation of Theology*, based on Boethius's *Consolation of Philosophy* from the sixth century. This work has recently been reevaluated and is now seen as a theological breakthrough in terms of its language and approach. According to the intellectual historian Mark Burrows, the theology of the later Gerson is still in a process of development, an indication of the great vitality of a man who remained in touch with his own inner life and the life of the church.[90]

After the death of the duke of Burgundy in 1419, Gerson was able to return to what was left of France: the area south of the Loire that the English had not taken. It was safe for him to move in with his brother Jean the Celestine at Lyon, until in 1425 he moved across the Saône River into a residence provided by the archbishop of Lyon in return for teaching the youth attached to the choir school at the collegiate church of Saint Paul.[91] Gerson was again a teacher, not at the university level, but in contact with one of the age groups to which he also had dedicated himself in his Paris years. In 1879 a statue of Gerson with a schoolboy was placed before the door of the church of Saint Paul in Lyon and rightfully indicates the old curé's last pastoral concern.[92]

The stream of letters and treatises continued. Gerson was consulted by many monks and priests who needed advice on the spiritual life. The Carthusian hermits of La Grande Chartreuse wrote to him regularly with lists of questions, and Gerson answered all of them.[93] His style in these years lacks the personal quality of his early letters, but the same spiritual intensity can be seen elsewhere, as in his last work, *Treatise on the Song of Songs*.[94] Here he guarded himself from indicating directly whether he himself had had mystical experience. The French historian of theology André Combes spent hundreds of pages in trying to prove that Gerson indeed did have a mystical experience in 1425 that changed his life.[95] I cannot concur in this attempt to turn a single sentence in Gerson into an indication of a total transformation of his theology and interior life.[96] I think that Gerson from his early Paris days was looking for the total experience of the love of God and at moments did stand on the threshold of mystical experience. But what mattered was not the actual taste of mysticism; it was the effort of putting himself into God's presence and letting God do the rest.

In the last few months of his life Gerson became aware of the extraordinary role of Jeanne d'Arc in gathering political and military forces to liberate the north of France. After her victory at Orléans in May, Gerson was asked to respond to challenges to the authenticity of the revelations Jeanne claimed to receive. His answer, *On the Maid of Orléans*, largely accepts Jeanne as divinely inspired.[97] Gerson's own love for France led him to believe that the girl who was restoring his country had to reflect the voice of God and not the devil.

As is well known, the English and the Burgundians thought differently and arranged for Jeanne d'Arc to be burned as a witch. Gerson did not live to experience this misuse of political and ecclesiastical power, but his writings on the veracity of revelations were later used in collections dealing with the danger of witches.[98] Here, as in so much else, Gerson's writings anticipated debates of the coming decades and even centuries. Who rules the church? What can the individual do in order to contribute to his or her own salvation? How can we know that a vision comes from God? How can the reformation of the church (Gerson's own term) be achieved? The answers that the coming age would provide are hardly Gerson's, but his contribution to the debate would be recognized in the printed editions of his work available already by 1500.[99]

INTRODUCTION

Gerson's Spirituality and Sexuality

It is my intention in choosing a few of the myriad works of Jean Gerson to give the reader an opportunity to get his or her own impression of the interior life of the great chancellor and theologian. I have not limited myself to works of mystical theology because I think that the term *spirituality* includes the totality of a person's human expression in relation to his or her search for love. From his early Paris years Gerson sought the embrace of God and occasionally experienced the tenderness and warmth he sought. At the same time, however, he was very much afraid of his own physical warmth and bodily need for other human beings.

From the time Gerson left home for Paris in 1377, and perhaps already earlier, he cut himself off from intimate bonds with other persons. He took deadly seriously the sexual morality developed by church theologians since the time of Augustine and considered all genital expression of sexuality outside of marriage as mortal sin. At the same time, Gerson was acutely aware that nobles, priests, and even nuns and monks did not live up to church requirements, and his writings reflect a lifelong campaign to warn lay and church people against many different forms of sexual behavior.[100]

Here Gerson was ruthlessly honest and even admitted that he had fallen in love with a nun and desired her sexually after believing that his attachment was purely spiritual.[101] As a consequence, Gerson ruled out the possibility of the sentimental and spiritual friendships that for centuries had been acceptable in the church. Gerson was a pessimist about human behavior: he saw every form of spiritual love as "quickly descending into naked carnal love."[102]

What does this view of sexual guilt and sin have to do with the spirituality of Jean Gerson? A great deal, if *spirituality* and *sexuality* are two words expressing aspects of the same human need for union and intimacy. Gerson himself tried to divorce physical from spiritual love and refused in his treatises to make any comparisons between the two types.[103] The matter was too dangerous and explosive for Gerson, but his passionate insistence on chastity of the clergy reflects a lifelong battle with his own thoughts and fantasies. I think it is no accident that Gerson wrote the most specific treatise on masturbation we have from a medieval theologian.[104] He himself would have had to deal with the problem in his own life.

At times I find his solutions and advice almost embarrassing, as when he says it is acceptable for a confessor to give his penitents ideas about types of sexual activity in order to make sure that the confessor can determine what a penitent actually has been doing.[105] For Gerson, the need for precise information about sexual acts can seem to verge on an obsession. Gerson's demand that the penitent go into detail, even if it brings on involuntary sexual titillation to the priest, can lead the modern reader to ask what psychological mechanisms were at work in the theologian's own mind.[106]

Once this shadow side of Gerson is admitted, one can return to the positive achievement of his life. He was faithful to his ideals. Whether it was a question of teaching the young or defending university freedom, Gerson refused to compromise. He stuck to his commitments and insisted that the rights of the university and its scholars be respected. In the midst of Paris anarchy, he appealed to peace and reason. Negotiating endlessly with first two and then three popes, he maintained calm and worked consistently toward a solution.

Gerson's productivity and patience are connected to the depth of his inner life. He would burn the midnight oil in writing to his sisters and lecture the next day to his students because he felt committed both to family and to university.[107] At the same time he would describe himself as a simple parish priest, providing advice and guidance in the moral dilemmas of everyday life.

Gerson's tireless involvement in the details of political, pastoral, and legal controversies does not seem to have detracted from the depth of his thinking and the clarity of his writing. He dedicated his life to others and yet himself remained a man distant from most other people. Monastic community never quite convinced him, and he kept to himself as a lonely intellectual providing light and inspiration for his generation and the ones to come. As teacher, confessor, preacher, and administrator, Jean Gerson managed not only to survive but also to thrive.

In view of the instability of his age, its violence and irrationality, the serenity evident in many of his writings is extraordinary. I find the source of that serenity in Gerson's deep faith and trust in a loving God to whom he was returning after a long exile on earth. Gerson lived his life in pain and resignation, but also in intellectual ferment. A pilgrim, he patiently found his way across a treacherous landscape and headed for home.

The Mountain of Contemplation

A few years before he wrote the *Speculative Mystical Theology*, Gerson anticipated this treatise in his *Mountain of Contemplation*. Here he chose to write "in French rather than in Latin, and more to women than to men."[108] It is significant that Gerson's first full statement on the mystical life was written in the vernacular and intended for women. He responded to what he felt was a need to convey learning in a digestible form to a new audience that had grown up in the previous century: women with some education who wanted to share the Christian life not only in practice but also in terms of its theoretical background. For Gerson, these women were represented by his sisters, whom he encouraged to stay together on the family homestead, not to marry, and to pray and work in an informal religious community.[109] *The Mountain of Contemplation* was intended for Gerson's sisters, as well as for other women, and men, who had no scholastic training but desired to structure their spiritual lives.

Gerson deals here with the same problems of knowledge and experience that he would address in Latin in the *Speculative Mystical Theology*, but in faithful awareness of his vernacular audience, unfamiliar with scholastic terms. Many of his recommendations from the *Practical Mystical Theology* are also present here, such as the requirement for penance and the necessity of solitude.[110] But there are also fresh images not present in the Latin texts. Gerson develops the idea, for example, that we are like hunting dogs who must go after the scent of God's good odor![111] He also goes into detail concerning the image of a ladder of contemplation, and here refers to the teaching of Bernard of Clairvaux.[112] We start with humble penance in a process of mortification, go from there to a secret place of silence and solitude, where we experience a state of languishing for God. Here Gerson dwells on the question of bodily posture, suitable places for prayer, and other practical questions.

The third level of contemplation is that of perseverance, where the distractions that pursue us like flies have been driven off and we come to the love of God (§35, Gl 7.1.42). Gerson lists some of the hindrances that make progress difficult and warns against overconfidence or the desire to proceed too fast (§36, Gl 7.1.45). Throughout this ascent of the mountain of meditation, Gerson emphasizes a need for the practice of prayer (§41, Gl 7.1.50–51). Tears and a sense of devotion might come, but they do not exist for our own pleasure (§43, Gl 7.1.52–3). Sometimes the soul will feel something like a spiritual drunkenness. "It will sometimes seem that everything is full of the glory and praise of God" (cf. Ps 150:6)(§45, Gl 7.1.55).

Here Gerson ends, choosing not to describe the union that Saint Paul and others experienced. He may have wanted to avoid giving his sisters and other readers the sense that the final experience of union was something that everyone could expect when he or she followed his method and ascended the heights. But the very fact of writing about the ascent to God in the vernacular instead of in Latin was a bold step. Gerson was extending the boundaries of learned discourse. He insisted that his sisters and other women, as well as men, could seek contemplative experience through a form of discipline that started with penance, continued in meditation, and made possible a steadfast pursuit of the presence of God.[113] Gerson was devoted to *gens simples sans lettres*, ordinary people who had no Latin. They deserved a method and a language in which to seek a way to God. This process ended in a form of prayer that opened the person to God's love and grace.

INTRODUCTION

Sermon on the Feast of Saint Bernard

The language of contemplation is very much present in Gerson's sermon on the feast of Saint Bernard, probably preached at the Cistercian College de Saint Bernard in Paris, perhaps on 20 August 1402.[114] I have chosen this sermon instead of any other because it gives a sense of how Gerson addressed an audience that shared with him an interest in the mystical life of the soul. We should not think of the Cistercian monks as completely different from the students for whom Gerson wrote his *Mystical Theology*. The monks who heard Gerson's sermon were attending the University and learning theology. In the middle decades of the thirteenth century the Cistercian General Chapter had decided that the brightest young monks should attend the University.[115] For them, as for Gerson, the goal was to combine the learning of scholastic theology with the experience of affectivity. For both the Cistercians and for Gerson, one of the finest sources of affective knowledge was to be found in the writings of Saint Bernard.

Elsewhere I have analyzed the contents of this sermon and shown how Gerson made good use both of Bernard's own writings and of hagiographical sources about him.[116] The theme of the sermon is a line from the Song of Songs: "Sustain me with flowers, refresh me with apples, because I am languishing with love" (2:5). Gerson used these words as a summation of Bernard's life and desire to experience the love of God.

The chancellor knew Bernard's *Sermons on the Song of Songs* sufficiently well to realize that the abbot of Clairvaux was a master of the language of love. Instead of reviewing one or more of these sermons, however, Gerson provided a thematic summary of Bernard's life in terms of his movement from a school of contrition and penance to a school of sanctity and meditation, ending in a school of intimate solitude and contemplation. Thus the steps toward the contemplative life, described in abstract form in the *Mystical Theology*, are seen here as reflected in Bernard's experience.

In order to make Bernard all the more present for the audience, Gerson as preacher took on the persona of the saint and had him speak in the first person (Gl 5.326). Gerson has his Bernard remember a sense of fatigue before he discovered the school of penance and discipline:

> In this way the soul truly languishes when it aspires constantly to its God. I experienced so great a weariness that I became wholly feeble and faint. I was not content with anything I did, or anything I saw in the world. And I said to my soul: "Surely you are still untrained in love and not very learned, my soul. Can this not be the reason why your beloved has not come to you"(Gl 5.327)?

By means of such striking, immediate, personal language, Gerson in the person of Bernard summarized the experience of a lifetime and hammered in his point that the purely academic school is a place where one is starved and dried up. Gerson used just enough examples from Bernard's life to make his message concrete, as when he mentioned the saint's sexual temptations in youth. But he did not try to recount all of what the monks easily could have found in the *Vita Prima*, the standard hagiography of their saint.

Gerson also made use of Bernard's language and life in order to lash out at teachers who corrupt their pupils, even sexually, and to lament the disunity of the church (Gl 5.331). Reminding his listeners of how Bernard once helped heal a schism, Gerson called for a new Bernard to step forward. At the end of the sermon Gerson summarized the qualities in Bernard that prepared him for his special work. Gerson especially emphasized the saint's love of solitude, which kept him from wasting time on empty conversations (Gl 5.338).

Gerson's view of Bernard's apartness does not agree with the way he has been looked upon in our time, as a man who was deeply beholden to his friendships and who made his monastery into a home for his friends and relatives. Gerson ignored this side of Bernard, which is visible not only in his letters but also in his *Sermons on the Song of Songs*. In other areas, however, the university chancellor showed great awareness and insight into the language, imagery, and spirituality of Bernard. Gerson was rightly famed for the quality of his sermons, which apparently could touch the hearts and minds of his audiences. We have no evidence concerning the Cistercian response to Gerson's sermon, but its contents reveal great concern and awareness for the meaning of the monastic vocation.

The Letters (c. 1385–1408)

Gerson apparently made no special attempt to collect his letters. We can be grateful to his youngest brother, Jean the Celestine, for the respect he showed for practically everything Gerson wrote. It is only recently, however, that the letters have taken their rightful place as a distinct part of Gerson's work. Until the edition of Gerson's works by Palemon Glorieux in the 1960s and 1970s, the letters were still spread about in editions of Gerson. Now we can look at them as a whole in terms of the chronology of the chancellor's life.

The very first letter (1) in the collection is a result of the detective work of Gilbert Ouy of Paris. In the 1950s he found this text and recognized it as being from the hand of a very young Gerson, whose style and images reflect the attempt of an immature writer to make his mark on his surroundings.[117] The result is an almost untranslatable piece of prose, with an extended image of ships, the sea, storms, and wrecks, in order to reflect the writer's own perilous situation. The personal references to Gerson's own financial situation are obscure. At moments, however, the text betrays a sense of insecurity, as when Gerson refers to his parents, who could not support their son any longer: "I fear, may God forbid, that they will become a parable for the neighbors (cf. Ps 68:12), a source of ridicule for strangers and a ribald refrain for base people" (Gl 2.3).

Gerson wanted to impress his patron, who may have been Pierre d'Ailly, that he was a hard worker and that a further investment in his studies would indeed be worth his while. His appeal lacks any extended religious imagery. He expressed himself in terms of a new language of humanism, perhaps in response to the currents in which he involved himself at the College of Navarre. Gerson's combination of arrogant self-assertion and classical learning indicates that the young Gerson of 1385 may have been a much less convinced Christian than the man who later tried to abandon the chancellorship.

The next letter (Letter b) was written by Gerson's mother, Elisabeth la Chardinière, to her sons Nicolas and Jean, assumedly in 1396–97, while they were living at Paris with their older brother. The authenticity of the letter was once in doubt, and it has even been claimed that Elisabeth could not have written the letter herself, that the real author must have been her husband, Arnoul![118] The writer conveys herself as a mother who misses her sons but wants them to do well, especially in terms of their moral and religious lives. She goes so far as to echo the saying of Saint Louis's iron mother, Blanche of Castile, that she would prefer to see her son physically dead rather than alive and guilty of mortal sin.[119]

In this letter the entire family is bound together in a community of prayer and mutual caring. We meet here one of the probable sources for Gerson's religious life: the presence of a strong woman who remained spiritually with him long after he had left for Paris. Her faith was perhaps the point of departure for Gerson's lifelong pursuit of Christian truth.

We have just a fragment of a corresponding letter from Gerson's father to him in Paris (Letter e) concerning the situation of his sisters, whose religious guidance he had taken upon himself.[120] Gerson's role is more apparent in a letter he wrote his sisters from Bruges (Letter 1*), probably in the winter of 1399–1400. Gerson is very concrete here, describing how he divides up his week according to religious devotions to the Trinity, the angels, the saints, and so on. It is hard to believe that the author of this letter, with its appeal to an accessible lay spirituality, is the same person who a decade earlier had studded his writing with erudite classical references. But Gerson was both a learned humanist and a popularizer of religious devotion.

Gerson's Letter 2, to an unknown person, is his list of reasons for resigning the chancellorship of the University, written from Bruges, perhaps in early 1400. Gerson here set out to show how repulsive his way of life had become in the chancellorship. There are almost no learned references, only some biblical reminiscences.

INTRODUCTION

This letter may be among the most personal and direct statements of Gerson's life. It provides rare insight into how a medieval intellectual at moments could lose faith in the meaning of what he was doing. As he wrote: "It is my nature and custom in terms of action to be wholly inept and inert, full of scruples and fear, most easily upset, so that I continually mull over something more than a thousand times"(Gl 2.21).

The next letter we have (3) is from Bruges, dated to the first of April 1400. It has a wholly different tone. Self-pity and commiseration are replaced by a sense of moral outrage. Addressing himself to Pierre d'Ailly, Gerson again describes his troubles and difficulties in office at Paris and then makes a strong statement on the terrible state of the church. Appended to the letter is a list of proposals for the reform of the teaching of theology. Gerson uses a word that will become one of his favored terms in expressing what needs to be done: reformation *(reformatio)* (Gl 2.26).

Gerson's new hope in change and improvement is also reflected in the next letter (4) from Bruges on 27 April 1401, probably to Gerson's colleagues at the College of Navarre. Here he indicates that the Duke of Burgundy is responsible for his return to duties of the chancellorship. To the same colleagues he two days later wrote at much greater length (Letter 5), conveying his fear that so many books were written and never read and that the faculty of theology was neglecting the learning amassed by past masters. Scholastic theology must lead to edification and preaching. Otherwise there is no meaning in all its knowledge.

Gerson was looking for a way of life in which learning would not be a goal in itself but would contribute to the life of the church. For himself, however, Gerson refused to acknowledge a need for friendships or emotional attachments (Gl 2.25). He refused to admit that good conversations might be a way for people to form emotional bonds that could help them in their intellectual and religious lives.

The next letter from Bruges (6), written between May and September 1400, was also addressed to colleagues at the College of Navarre. Here Gerson reviewed in detail what he considered to be the problems and limitations of both students and teachers at

Paris. He lamented the lack of sermons preached for University members and called for the return of the Dominicans, for whose removal he a few years earlier had campaigned.[121] Peace and reconciliation with the friars would be a point of departure for a new period of harmony and reform at the University.

The final letter from Bruges (7), from this same period, the summer of 1400, repeats Gerson's conviction that it is more important to familiarize oneself with traditional learning than to engage in the newest fads. The eagerness of students for whatever was new had led to the dispersion of some of Gerson's own writings in incomplete form.

A reflection of Gerson's new polemic once he returned to Paris is his treatise defending the Carthusians, with an introductory letter (8).[122] But the return to Paris also brought separation from his brother Nicolas, whose departure for the Celestines evoked one of the most remarkable and self-revelatory letters we have from Gerson (Letter 9).[123] Gerson seems almost awkward and embarrassed in a letter (10) he wrote two days later, 7 December 1401, to Nicolas's superior, more or less asking the man not to be too harsh on Nicolas and to look after his needs, "even his bodily ones" (Gl 2.48).

Gerson's continuing concern for Nicolas is reflected in the fact that he wanted to share with him his thoughts on contemplation, based on his reading of sermons on the Song of Songs. Writing Nicolas (or his superior, but then indirectly Nicolas) on 13 April 1402, Gerson expressed how delighted he had been to find in what he thought were the writings of Bernard of Clairvaux (actually Gilbert of Hoyland) a threefold division of contemplation into contrition, solitude, and perseverance.[124] This distinction was very close to what Gerson had written a few years earlier at Bruges in his *Mountain of Contemplation.*

By early 1402 we leave behind what might be called the personal letters of Gerson and find a more formal mode of expression. The letters that follow in the rest of Glorieux's collection are for the most part small treatises that use the letter form in order to provide a context for Gerson's thoughts. Writing to the Carthusian Barthélemy Clantier, Gerson explained at length his hesitations and concern about the third book of John Ruus-broec's *The Spiritual Espousals* (Letter 13, Paris, March 1402).[125] It should be noted how careful Gerson was in his evaluation of Ruusbroec's way of expressing himself. He had grave doubts, but he did not outrightly condemn Ruusbroec. And he makes a point at the end that learned theologians should not be puffed up. They can err out of a lack of affectivity.

In 1402 Gerson sent a treatise, *On the Spiritual Life of the Soul*, to Pierre d'Ailly and used the occasion to write a covering letter (14) in which he summarized his lifelong devotion to his former teacher.[126] In the same year he wrote the *Treatise Against "The Romance of the Rose,"* attacking its author Jean de Meun for errors in faith and morals and for corrupting youth.[127] Pierre Col, one of the supporters of Jean de Meun's work, wrote back to Gerson and warned him that he, like others before him who had denied their sexuality, would probably end up succumbing to love and going mad.

Gerson's reply came in October of 1402 (Letter 15)(Gl 2.65–70). His central point is that any writings, just as any pic-tures, that "are provocative, lustful, and prurient are to be cursed and banned from the commonwealth of Christian religion." This long letter can be looked upon as a postscript to Gerson's origi-nal treatise. His message is clear: such books should be burned. Even if Gerson were offered more than a thousand pounds for *The Romance of the Rose*, he would rather consign the last extant copy to the flames (Gl 2.70).

For Gerson, the secular power was obliged to intervene in order to rid the land of all obscene forms of expression. Here we see the faint outline of an absolute state demanding conformity with moral standards and emerging from the fanaticism of Reformation and Counter Reformation.

Gerson's longstanding involvement with efforts to end the papal schism is reflected in a letter from the south of France, Tarascon, on 5 January 1404, to the duke of Orléans (Letter 16)(Gl 2.71–72). Here he tries to explain the content and meaning of a sermon he had given a few days earlier and that he insists had been misunderstood and misinterpreted. "I did not conclude the necessity of withdrawal of obedience [to the pope], even though I did not presume to attack this conclusion." Gerson was hoping that the Avignon pope, Benedict XIII, would himself resign, and he was leaving open the possibility that Benedict might later be restored to office. Whatever Gerson actually had said, Benedict had not been pleased, and the chancellor also had to defend himself to his former teacher and mentor, Pierre d'Ailly, in a letter from Paris in 1405 (Letter 20)(Gl 2.78–80).

Gerson's irritation is evident, for he ends with a sour citation from Ecclesiastes (1:15): "The number of fools is infinite!" He appealed to d'Ailly's better judgment, and we find here a taste of the earlier Gerson breaking through an intellectual facade and making a personal statement: "You most wise teacher, before whose eyes I am totally open, you know me within and without."

Most of Gerson's epistolary efforts, however, remained in a more traditional mold. He wrote to an unnamed bishop, prior to March 1404, in sending a treatise on the ten commandments (Letter 17).[128] To an unknown person he sent his *Threefold Work* (*Opus Tripartitum*), "concerning the commandments, confession, and the science of dying, treating them in all possible brevity" (Letter 18)(Gl 2.74–76). Here, as in many other of his French-language treatises, Gerson was doing his utmost to make the essential teachings of the church evident and clear for non-experts. Gerson first wrote his prescriptions in Latin and then repeated them in French. He is thinking of parish priests (*simples curés*), young girls and boys who need to be educated (*pour les josnes escoliers soient filz ou filles*), and of their parents (*les peres et les meres pour leurs enfans*). Gerson seems here as elsewhere to have translated a personal concern for the religious instruction of the members of his biological family into a general commitment to providing education for all members of the laity.

Wholly in French is Gerson's letter of advice to a dying man (Letter 19, Paris, probably 1403–1404).[129] Once again the letter accompanies a short treatise, *The Science of Dying Well*. Gerson refers to stories from the *Lives of the Fathers* and perhaps also from James of Voragine's *Golden Legend*.[130]

To a hermit named Antoine or Anthony, Gerson also sent a

letter of advice (21), to which he added a rule for daily life (Gl 2.81–84). This warned against getting involved in pastoral cares or in receiving anyone who might come to him for help and advice: "Do not burden your mind with superfluous cares under the pretense of saving other people." Some of the provisions remind the reader of Aelred of Rievaulx's *Rule of Life for a Recluse*, which Gerson probably did not know.[131] Here, as elsewhere in his writings, Gerson was deeply suspicious of any unusual religious experiences, which are normally to be looked upon as a sign that something is wrong in one's way of life. Gerson insisted on balance and warned against extreme forms of asceticism. He was probably describing the kind of life he sought for himself. As a teacher, administrator, preacher, and parish priest, he could not allow himself the solitude Antoine sought. But a part of Gerson, nevertheless, kept a distance from other people and sought salvation in interior solitude.

Gerson's sense of duty, however, did not allow him much solitude. We find him on the road, together with perhaps the one friend of his life, Pierre d'Ailly, in the tedious and harrowing attempt to end the schism. They jointly composed a letter (22) from Genoa on 15 September 1407 to "the Lord Angelo, who at Rome has himself called Gregory XII" (Gl 2.84–86). Gerson and d'Ailly felt betrayed that Gregory, after indicating that he would follow the "way of cession" and yield his title, had clung to it. Gerson's diplomatic language is balanced on a knife edge: the Roman pope is to be aware of the gravity of the situation and is encouraged to follow his own appeal to humility.

Apparently on the same journey south to heal the schism, Gerson and Pierre d'Ailly visited the Celestine house where Nicolas the Celestine was a professed monk and where the youngest brother, Jean, now had become a novice. Gerson was shocked by the condition of his youngest brother and in a letter (23) composed back in Paris, perhaps early in 1408, he expressed concern that Jean could not survive the ascetic program he had imposed on himself (Gl 2.86–90).

This is the last letter in the collection with a great deal of personal content, and it is no accident that it is addressed to a member of Gerson's immediate family. Nicolas had apparently complained that Gerson's letters disturbed and upset their youngest brother. Gerson replied by insisting on a need for taking into account the differences among people in a monastery. Any community must consider the situation of its individual members. Gerson promised that if it helped Jean to stop his letters, then he would write no more. Brother Nicolas was asked to do whatever he could in order to watch over young Jean.

Considering the common ideal based on entrance into a monastic community as abandonment of biological family and all ties outside the cloister, Gerson here, as in earlier letters, indicated a refusal to let go![132] Just as he had had difficulty in saying goodbye to Nicolas in 1401, he again was afraid about what might happen to one of his brothers in a strict monastic life. To the hermit Antoine Gerson warned against involvements with other people, but with his own biological brothers he continued to be involved, regardless of their monastic commitment.

A much more magisterial side of Gerson is visible in a letter-treatise he wrote, perhaps about the same time, to a bishop concerning the types of sins that were considered reserved cases, normally absolved by a prelate instead of by a parish priest (Letter 24).[133] Gerson here argued that women and children had little or no possibility of leaving husbands or parents and traveling to the nearest episcopal seat in order to obtain absolution. Instead of doing so, they would continue to live in sin and be deprived of the sacrament of penance (Gl 2.90).

Such considerations earned Gerson the title that was given to him a few decades after his death, *doctor consolatorius*, the consoling doctor,[134] concerned with the healing of sick souls by taking into account the circumstances of the penitents. Gerson insisted that there could be no reserved cases for youths under the age of fourteen. The end of the letter provides a full list of the reserved cases that should be handed over to the discretion of the parish confessor. These are for the most part sexual acts, from solitary masturbation to incest.

Just as Gerson was concerned with the sexual activities of ordinary people, he wanted to be in contact with their visionary experiences. Besides writing two treatises on the contents of visions, one of which is translated below, he wrote a response to a canon of the cathedral of Reims, Jean Morel, concerning the revelations of a local woman named Ermine (Letter 25)(Gl 2.93–96). She had a series of visions from November 1395 until her death in August 1396. These were written down and sent to Gerson, as a recognized theological expert who might be able to determine whether the visions came from God or from the devil. Gerson's answer is calm and clear: since there is nothing of heretical or other dubious content in the visions, and since God has the power to provide new visionary experiences, there is no a priori reason to reject their veracity.

Ermine's penitential way of life could be a model for others. She had manifested the humility that is the true sign of those chosen by God. As two decades later with the visions of Jeanne d'Arc, Gerson was willing to believe in the possibility that an unlettered woman could utter the secrets of God. His positive judgment may have been encouraged by local loyalties toward Reims, where he may have gone to school and where his brother had become a monk. One detects, however, a certain awkwardness and hesitation about accepting Ermine's visions wholeheartedly, just as Gerson later indicated in dealing with the visions of Birgitta of Vadstena.

At the end of this letter Gerson excused himself for lack of time and promised to return to the matter at some future date. As ever, Gerson was jumping from one pressing project to another. Sometimes Gerson did return to earlier concerns, as in a second letter to Barthélemy Clantier (Letter 26, Paris, April-June 1408), again concerning Ruusbroec (Gl 2.97–103). However much he may have been attracted to flights of mystical revelation, Gerson usually kept himself to the discipline of scholastic analysis. This letter with its eight careful points provides a model of such thinking.[135]

Gerson was suspicious of the use of images in order to describe the union of the soul with God. There could be no total assimilation of human and divine nature. In meeting God, the soul reaches a state of perfection, not of annihilation. The latter teaching Gerson thought he found in Ruusbroec's work, but this letter is not so much a direct response to his treatise *The Spiritual Espousals* as an answer to Ruusbroec's defenders.

The defense of orthodoxy was also very much in Gerson's mind when he wrote to the abbot of Saint Denis on 8 October 1408 (Letter 27)(Gl 2.103–5). The monks of this great abbey church where the French kings were buried had commissioned or bought a painting or altar panel that challenged the veracity of a relic of Saint Denis that the cathedral church of Notre Dame claimed to have. As chancellor of Notre Dame, Gerson was obliged to defend his church. Saint Denis was not just the patron saint of Paris; in Gerson's time he was still confused with the great mystic Pseudo-Dionysius, whose writings were so important as a point of departure for Gerson's own mystical theology.[136]

It was necessary to champion Saint Denis's relic at Notre Dame not only for reasons of local patriotism but also because the cult of relics was under attack. Gerson admitted at the end of the letter that there could be doubt about the veracity of some relics. But it was better to give them the benefit of the doubt than to challenge the sincere beliefs of the faithful.

In view of the avalanche of protest against the cult of relics that would come in the next century, Gerson's arguments can seem almost disingenuous. His central concern, however, was the religious life of the laity and a fear of undermining its contents. Elsewhere Gerson did protest against practices that he thought were unfit for Christians, such as the feast of fools and other travesties of religion.[137]

A final indication of Gerson's long attachment to Pierre d'Ailly is a letter sent to him. It is dated 11 October and could be from 1408 or 1411 (Letter 28)(Gl 2.105–7). Gerson was replying to two letters of d'Ailly, which we do not have, but this letter shows how the two theologians remained in contact with each other after their frustrating mission of 1407. Gerson was caught up in writing a sermon for the feast of All Saints[138] and encouraged his friend to look at Pseudo-Dionysius's eighth chapter in *On the Divine Names*. He conveys a sense of detachment and distance to what was happening around him.

I have reviewed in some detail the contents of the individual letters because I want to give the reader a sense of the riches they contain. Gerson was involved in so many different aspects of the church politics of his day that it is almost impossible to gain a complete sense of his life and writings. The letters are an invaluable and usually neglected expression of his identity as intellectual and church reformer. Here we find the imprint of his personality in clearer form than anywhere else. In his mid-forties, in 1408, Gerson was still a brother involved with the lives of his family members, a priest dedicated to his duties as preacher and confessor, an educator concerned with standards of teaching and lecturing at the University of Paris, and a church reformer determined to bring the schism to an end. He believed it possible to save the unity of Christendom through a church that was devoted to the pastoral care of its people.

However much one can question the harmony of Gerson's interior life and wonder if his reforming ideas were feasible, he was aware of his own limitations and usually showed generosity toward those whose opinions were different from his own. In the end, however, he believed in absolute and uncompromising truth and insisted that the scholastic method of question and answer was the best way to reach such insight. Those who departed from right thinking, such as the Jean de Meun who praised fornication, or the mystical writers who believed in total absorption of one's being in God, were to be opposed and rejected for their errors.

SPECULATIVE AND PRACTICAL FORMS OF MYSTICAL THEOLOGY

Mystical theology may seem today to be almost a contradiction in terms.[139] Theology is conceived as an intellectual discipline, even a form of science, which primarily investigates the relationship of the human person to God. Theology thus requires a language and a set of concepts on which there is some agreement, in order to carry out the investigation and to provide a common discourse. Mysticism, on the contrary, goes beyond words and dialogue and refers to an experience that almost always remains hidden and inaccessible. Some mystics describe the experience of God, and describe conversations with the deity or with Christ or the saints. Their claims cannot be rationally investigated and analyzed, as we do with discussions in church fathers about the meaning of the gospels.

For Gerson, there was a distance between the discursive, scholastic theology of his own day and a mystical theology, which he conceded was based on an essentially hidden knowledge.[140] But Gerson approached mystical theology not in terms of God's private revelations to individuals but as the knowledge of God obtained through what he called "repentant affectivity."[141] Thus what mattered for Gerson was not the end result in reaching or describing God's presence in the soul. The central goal was wisdom or understanding reached through penance and love rather than through analysis and reason.

Mystical theology thus involves an affective approach to the mystery of God's presence in our lives. This theology has its own language, which Gerson uses with great care and skill. Gerson's division between the speculative and the practical, however, does not always work. Toward the end of the *Practical Mystical Theology* (PMT), Gerson admitted that he had gotten bogged down in theoretical considerations.[142] Similarly, there are moments in the *Speculative Mystical Theology* (SMT) when Gerson asked very practical questions about how the senses function and how we perceive light. To a large extent, however, Gerson keeps the two aspects of mystical theology separate and succeeds in providing a language that is understandable.

Gerson invested great care in developing his theses, and he revised the text a number of times, as late as the 1420s at Lyon.[143] It was important for him to be quite clear in his presentation, and I have tried to make an English version of his thought that is equally comprehensible. Because of the requirement of space, however, I have had to leave out a large part of the SMT. Here, however, I summarize both works.

Mystical theology, Gerson begins, is more perfect and more certain than scholastic theology because it is based on experiences known with a more complete certitude (SMT 3:1, Combes, p. 11). Experience is thus essential, but an experience that is derived from a foundation of faith: in the Anselmian phrase, we must believe in order to understand. The saints believed and came to understand. They had no ulterior motives of gain or fame from making known their perceptions (SMT 5:3, Combes, pp. 14–15).

The problem, of course, is that interior forms of affectivity cannot be expressed in words. But words are necessary, and a less learned person can sometimes better express the content of affectivity than a scholastically trained teacher. At the same time, however, mystical theology can be discussed by those who do not have direct experience of God. Scholastic discourse, however, is necessary to protect us from errors that come through ignorance and, worse, through pride (SMT 8:5, Combes, pp. 20–21).

Gerson felt most comfortable with those who had shown both kinds of learning, both in intellect and in affectivity. These included theologians such as Augustine, Hugh of Saint Victor, Bonaventure, William of Auvergne, and Thomas Aquinas. Gerson put himself at the end of a thousand-year tradition that favored rational analysis in order to reach an understanding of the content and meaning of mystical expression.

In a new section Gerson considers the rational soul and its powers. Here he speaks of the necessity of making formal distinctions without there being real distinct entities in the soul. This section provides in my mind the best answer to the question whether Gerson was a "realist" or a "nominalist" in the conventional medieval sense of those who believed that ideas or concepts have real existence or are "merely" names. In order to understand the soul, which basically is indivisible, we must intellectually divide it up according to powers and functions. These distinctions are more than names, but they do not indicate "real" separate compartments in the soul. If my interpretation is correct, then Gerson was a moderate nominalist, for he assumed the reality of intellectual concepts in the mind but not outside the mind. As he wrote: "There is nothing wrong...in seeking abstractions, if objects in their natures are such that the intellect in dealing with them can use such abstractions in order more easily to reach understanding" (SMT 9:5, Combes, p. 23).

Gerson refused to consider the question further and relegated it to the province of the arts masters, instead of letting it overshadow his theology (SMT 9:6, Combes, p. 24). The rational soul has distinct functions and actions, not in terms of the soul's essence but according to the names of its properties. The soul is in possession of a simple intelligence that draws from God "a certain natural light" (SMT 10:1, Combes, p. 16). This light enables the soul to know first principles or basic conceptions in terms of affirmation or negation or hierarchies of values. Turning to Pseudo-Dionysius, Gerson saw a great chain of being in a progression from God's being to lesser beings.[144]

Reason, the cognitive power of the soul, has a dual use: superior principles are known to it in the light of simple intelligence; inferior ones are known through experience. The cognitive power of the senses makes use of bodily organs (SMT 12:1, Combes, p. 30). To each cognitive power there is a proportional affective power.

Gerson's psychology, as we can call this section of his *Speculative Mystical Theology*, ends with a description of the affective powers of the soul. These are divided into synderesis, will or rational appetite, and the sensitive appetite. Synderesis is a central concept for Gerson, for it is a power of the soul coming directly from God and providing us with a natural inclination to do what is good (SMT 14:1, Combes, p. 33). Gerson is always on the lookout for Pelagianism and its optimistic assertion of the individual's ability to obtain salvation.[145] Synderesis has nothing to do with the Pelagian teaching. It is a power of the soul to follow what it perceives as being right. Synderesis is called other names, such as "a spark of intelligence" bringing us toward what is good.[146]

Gerson continues with his definitions of the soul's powers. The rational appetite or will inclines us to make choices on the basis of the reason (SMT 15:2, Combes, p. 35). The animal or sensual appetite is a power of the soul dependent on the information that the senses give it. The cognitive and affective powers of the soul are then described in terms of light and heat, in language partly borrowed from Dionysius.

Gerson was striving to express the inexpressible in terms of how we think and feel. He was dependent on a discussion that goes back to Aristotle and Plato and which was developed by Islamic thinkers such as Avicenna, who posited a whole hierarchy of intelligences between God and the human person.[147] Gerson avoids easy solutions that would be heretical in attributing innate knowledge to the soul (SMT 18:4–5, Combes, pp. 42–43). The powers of the soul are compared to six mirrors that are joined together and made to reflect each other (SMT 19:3, Combes, p. 47).

The next major section describes the process of contemplation, which Gerson considers to be present "in the cognitive power of intelligence," just as mystical theology "reposes in the affective power of synderesis" (SMT 21:1, Combes, p. 51). Gerson distinguishes among cogitation, meditation, and contemplation. In the first our thought processes meander from one image to another. In the second we are able to concentrate on one train of thought, while in the third we attain a state of wonder. Cogitation is easy and effortless, while meditation is not. Gerson referred to his own difficulty with concentrating on study to show how "cogitation turns into meditation" (SMT 23:2, Combes, p. 55). He also drew on images from classical mythology to describe this struggle for meditation. This mind is "burdened with a great stone of earthly curiosity, as was Sisyphus" (SMT 23:10, Combes, p. 58). Amid a host of allusions here, Gerson shows how he had not forgotten the classical knowledge he had acquired in his youth.

The practice of meditation can lead to contemplation, when sense impressions are sorted out and we open ourselves to the illumination that comes from divine grace (SMT 24:1–2, Combes, p. 60). Gerson borrows Augustine's image of being on the summit of a high mountain, where there are no wind or clouds. Here one can lift up one's eyes and perceive the divine. Contemplation is to be found in the superior cognitive power of the soul, called intelligence (SMT 24:8, Combes, p. 63). Gerson thus took sides in a perennial debate about affectivity and understanding: he saw the contemplative experience as deriving from intelligence, not feeling. Later fifteenth-century writers would criticize him harshly for such a definition.[148]

Once contemplation takes place, however, it is not just a function of the reason or the imagination. A person lapses into error if he does not reach a spiritual form of knowing (SMT 25:3, Combes, p. 65). This knowledge corresponds to a degree of affectivity based on an ecstatic love, which "rises above and seizes the divine" (SMT 27:1, Combes, pp. 67–68). In the final analysis, cognition alone cannot complete the process begun on the contemplative heights. There remains the grasp of love that Gerson also calls jubilation. Here all difficulties from the lower stages disappear, and the person experiences a "free, pure, unimpeded and abstract love" (SMT 27:5, Combes, p. 69).

Once this process is understood, Gerson can return to the point of departure for the entire treatise: the knowledge of God that comes through mystical theology is better available through penitent affectivity than through the inquiring intellect (SMT 28:1, Combes, p. 70). Mystical theology in the end is superior to what Gerson calls speculative theology, just as love is superior to cognition. Thus penance is necessary for the ascent to God. Only the purified human being can reach out to grasp the love of God that is here offered.

Gerson continues in this vein, distinguishing mystical from speculative theology. In speculative theology, one pursues truth; in mystical theology, the goal is the good (SMT 29:3, Combes, pp. 73–74). In the act of sensing, a person desires the whole object. In seeking God, the spirit surpasses itself, like water that boils and turns to steam. Mystical theology does not need the school of intellect; it is acquired through the school of affectivity. Without dismantling the structure of scholastic reasoning, Gerson simply points to the need for something more.

Referring to Bernard's teaching (actually it is that of William of Saint Thierry), Gerson concludes that any speculative theology is incomplete without mystical theology. Thus it is not enough to read the Bible and the Fathers and know what they say; we are obliged to take upon ourselves the affectivity of these authors.

Otherwise we are like blind men who have heard of colors and perhaps dictate learned treatises on them but have only a limited idea of what we are talking about (SMT 30:6, Combes, p. 79)!

Gerson uses a number of other comparisons from everyday life in order to clarify the difference between the two theologies: the speculative theologian is like the craftsman who has theoretical knowledge of his trade, while the mystical theologian resembles the expert who is skilled in both theory and act (SMT 33:1, Combes, p. 85). Similarly the spiritual sailor can never reach the stability of God's safe harbor if he only has knowledge of the intelligible sea (SMT 33:5, Combes, p. 87). Sensuality is changeable, restless, prone to movement; each of the passions of the soul is similarly driven in different directions.

In the next major section Gerson considers the workings of the love of God, which is absolutely necessary for the spiritual sailor. Love captures the beloved and leads to ecstasy, a rapture of the mind in which all inferior powers cease to function (SMT 36:4, Combes, pp. 96–97). It is affection and not cognition that causes rapture, and yet rapture can be present in the reason, as with those who study (SMT 38:2, Combes, pp. 101–2). In trying to define mental rapture, Gerson is closely dependent on the language of Richard of Saint Victor, a major source for this part of the *Speculative Mystical Theology*. But in order to describe the union of the lover with the beloved, Gerson also recalls Aristotle's *Ethics*, where the friend is alter ego (SMT 40:4, Combes, p. 104).

In defining the state of union achieved, Gerson is careful to put a distance between himself and those who would speak of a transformation of the soul into God. To say that the soul loses its own being and takes on God's being is a "mad teaching" that the church several times has condemned (SMT 41:3–4, Combes, pp. 105–6). Even Peter Lombard's terminology receives Gerson's criticism here. Lombard lacked precision, though he was by no means heretical. Gerson carefully makes his way through a treacherous landscape of seemingly attractive resolutions to the question of the bond between God and the human person. Gerson was fascinated and appalled by what can happen to those who actively seek the experience of this union, as with a woman who died after she "became so fervent...that she was not able to contain herself....The bonds of her blood and nerves were torn away" (SMT 41:8, Combes, p. 108). Gerson turned to various comparisons from nature to show that the soul does not lose its being in union. It fulfills itself in this union and becomes complete (SMT 41:17–18, Combes, pp. 111–12). Mystical theology ends as perfect prayer: the union of the body, mind, and heart with God (SMT 43:2, Combes, pp. 116–17). The perfection of the rational mind lies more in perfect prayer or mystical theology than in intellectual contemplation, which by itself is arid. The *Speculative Mystical Theology* thus ends with a consideration of the meaning of prayer and its benefits (SMT 44:6, Combes, p. 121).

Instead of completing his treatise with lofty promises of joy in the vision of God, Gerson chose to talk about the necessity of prayer as the basis for any union. He recommended treatises by Hugh of Saint Victor and William of Auvergne. The first is fairly widely known today for his writings on affective theology,[149] while the *Divine Rhetoric* is only available in a seventeenth-century edition and may just be in the process of being rediscovered.[150]

Gerson made frequent use of William of Auvergne's work because the early-thirteenth-century theologian and bishop of Paris was very much concerned with the pastoral side of theology. Like Gerson, William insisted that theological learning had to lead to greater devotion among Christians. Otherwise it was a waste of time. At the same time, William in his *Divine Rhetoric* asked how the Christian could learn to pray, for all good theology had to end in the act of prayer.

The *Speculative Mystical Theology* is based on a tradition of writings about prayer, affectivity, and the contemplative life, from Pseudo-Dionysius through Augustine, the twelfth-century Victorines, Thomas Aquinas, Bonaventure, and other Franciscan theologians. Gerson drew on a strand in academic theology that combined intellectual discipline with affective experience. He made use of the most precise definitions about the soul in Aquinas, ultimately derived from Aristotle. Gerson wove this complex fabric into a whole that only now is becoming apparent to us. For the greatest historian of medieval thought in the twentieth century, Etienne Gilson, the truth about scholasticism could be summarized in the work of Thomas Aquinas. For an active theologian in the fifteenth century like Jean Gerson, scholasticism's method led inevitably from speculative to mystical theology. Gerson by no means abandoned Thomas, for he knew his predecessor's work well. But Thomas was not the whole answer.

The *Practical Mystical Theology* continues in this vein but concentrates on how the individual is to attain the experience of mystical theology. Everyone is obliged to seek perfection. If we do not make progress toward it, then we automatically regress (PMT 4:1, Combes, p. 144). But not everyone can engage in the contemplative life. Prelates of the church especially have little time for contemplation, and if they take such time by neglecting their active duties, then they are misusing contemplation (PMT 3:3, Combes, p. 141).

As in the first treatise, Gerson addressed a mainly clerical audience. He expected his students to attain positions of pastoral responsibility in the church, and he did not want them to think that the contemplative way of life was the only really desirable one. A central point in his considerations here is that the affective experience of God is not something that can be learned or merited through effort. God's gift is freely given (PMT 6:16, Combes, pp. 160–61). Gerson was ever on his watch against any indication that the individual person can merit God's grace. At the same time, however, he was a firm believer in the virtue of working hard and striving for a goal, so he insists that a sense of aridity is no excuse for giving up. Blow on the fire, give it life, he says; do not give up spiritual readings when they lead nowhere (PMT 7:1, Combes, pp. 165–66). If devotion finally comes, then be careful of arrogance, for we can quickly sacrifice all that we have gained.

Sometimes this advice might seem almost banal, but Gerson's purpose is to describe what can happen in the person who sets out in pursuit of the experience of the mystical life. How can one know, for example, if strong feelings are good or evil (PMT 7:8, Combes, p. 170)? There is always the danger that our fantasies or imagination will carry us off in an undisciplined manner. Each person must find the circumstances suitable for making progress in the interior life. One person selects a public place, another a secret one. Gerson discusses various positions of the body that are best for prayer (PMT 9:2, Combes, pp. 182–83). Some hours of the day or night are better than others, but again this is an individual matter. In this effort the body needs nourishment (PMT 10:4, Combes, p. 193). There is no virtue in destroying the body for the mind's sake.

It is not always good to be dependent on reading a book in order to be open to the grace of contemplation. One must sometimes await God in silence (PMT 11:2, Combes, pp. 197–99). A person should grow accustomed to praying in spirit and in mind (1 Cor 14:15), so that both the disturbance of talking and the need to look at a book are eliminated. Few people, however, can stand being alone with themselves. Instead of letting their minds be receptive, they flee to the comfort of reading or conversation (PMT 11:5, Combes, p. 199).

In such passages Gerson comes close to an attitude toward solitude and silence prominent in the late medieval *Imitation of Christ*. In the nineteenth century many French historians believed that Gerson was the author of this tract.[151] Hardly anyone would make such a claim today, even though the authorship by Thomas à Kempis continues to be discussed. In any case, Gerson here shows attachment to a tradition that was very much alive in the Brethren of the Common Life, with their emphasis on seeking stillness and solitude.[152] Ultimately this attitude goes back to the desert fathers of Late Antiquity and their fierce desire to be alone in order to make room for the presence of God.

The love we seek in God, Gerson adds, will be combined with fear and trembling. Here he refers to the Franciscan writer Hugh of Balma's *The Roads to Zion Weep*, one of his major sources of inspiration.[153] Like William of Auvergne's *Divine Rhetoric*, Hugh's work has only recently been recognized in terms of its centrality in later medieval discussion about the spiritual life. Even as late as the nineteenth century, this work was thought to have been by Bonaventure and was generally ignored.

Gerson, in his concern to give his readers practical instruction, developed at length an image of the feathers on the mystical dove that is the soul (PMT 11:12–14). These feathers are different types of meditations concerning God's judgments, the fear of damnation, the hope of salvation, trust in the help of others, and so on. The feathers enable the wings of the soul to take flight and come to God.

Here Gerson returned to the intellectual world and considered more fully how creation seeks to return to its Creator. The return of the soul to God makes use of the language of Pseudo-Dionysius and other mystical writers, but now in a strict scholastic form. In the midst of these considerations, Gerson admitted that he had reverted to speculative theology (PMT 12:10, Combes, p. 213). The time had come to end his treatment, in admitting that the person who seeks mystical experience will run into "a great crowd of phantasms" (PMT 12:12, Combes, p. 214). In our striving to see the face of God, we often find nothing but darkness. Thus Gerson returned to the necessity of penance, of cleansing our lives so that the renewed spirit can be open to the grace of God.

In the very last paragraph of his work Gerson suggests the joy that the soul will receive in its final union, and he allows himself a citation from the Song of Songs, "My beloved is mine, and I am his" (Sg 2:16). Caution had until now kept Gerson from such language. Gerson's intention was to teach a method, not to convey the contents of his own experience or that of others. His sobriety underlines his integrity as an intellectual and a teacher. Gerson wanted his students to understand that their lives and studies were not complete without an awareness of the tradition and practice of mystical theology. As the good teacher who refers his students to relevant literature, Gerson at some point added to his treatises a "list of some teachers who have spoken of contemplation" (Combes, p. 220).

Gerson was basically an optimist about the possibility for the Christian, whether learned or not, to attain mystical knowledge of God. God's grace was a prerequisite, but the individual's own efforts mattered. The union of love could come to anyone. Its greatest enemy was intellectual pride. Gerson never lost sight of his student audience, prone to admire abstruse intellectual constructions and to forget that the faculty of theology existed not for the sake of abstract gymnastics but for the enrichment of the Christian life.

ON DISTINGUISHING TRUE FROM FALSE REVELATIONS

The question of mystical experience, so essential in the *Mystical Theology* and in the *Sermon on the Feast of Saint Bernard*, is also important in Gerson's *On Distinguishing True from False Revelations*, from early 1402.[154] The treatise was sent to Gerson's brother Nicolas, who had just left Paris to join the Celestines, and who was very much in his older brother's thoughts. It reflects Gerson's simultaneous fascination and suspicion toward those who claimed to have firsthand experience of God, especially in visions. The treatise's central image is that of a coin, whose appearance and other qualities need to be carefully investigated in order to determine whether it is genuine or counterfeit. Following a passage in Paul on the necessity to distinguish whether spirits are from God or from the devil (1 Cor 12:10), Gerson asks how one can do so in a proper and convincing way. How can we know, for example, that the prophecy given to Zechariah concerning the name of his son, John, "was an angelic act rather than a diabolical illusion" (Gl 3:37)?

This problem of discernment of spirits is particularly acute now, says Gerson, in the final age of the world, when so many people indulge in fantasies and illusions. The test of examination for the coin of revelation requires humility, discretion, patience, truth, and charity. The first quality is one that Gerson also emphasized in his *Mystical Theology* and *Mountain of Contemplation*. Anyone who thinks he deserves revelations "deserves to be fooled," for no one can merit such a privilege (Gl 3.39). The first response to what can seem to be revelations from God should be rejection, as an indication that one is "insane, manic, or depressive" (Gl 3.40). This reaction is an indication of humility of the type found in Mary, who kept all matters in her heart (Lk 2:19), and even in Paul, who often admitted that he did not know what happened to him when he received visions.

The second sign of a genuine spiritual coin is discretion, which requires those who receive revelations to follow the counsel or advice they get from people in authority (Gl 3.42). As an example of lack of discretion Gerson describes a married woman with children whom he recently had met at the town of Arras. She went without food for days at a time and then had bulimic periods of overeating. When Gerson asked her why she behaved in such a manner, she replied that she was unworthy to take in food. For more than six months, she had refused to go to confession and ask for advice on the matter, and she would not listen to her husband, whom Gerson described as being "upset" by her behavior.[155]

For Gerson as a man of authority it was absolutely essential that lay people, especially women, who claimed to have special experiences and revelations, submitted themselves to the judgment of the church. If they refused to do so, this was a sign that their visions came not from God but from demons. As a trained theologian, Gerson believed that only people like himself could judge the veracity of what people were asserting. In his reaction to the woman of Arras, the reader can sense Gerson's combined attraction and repulsion toward the unlearned who believed they heard the voice of God.

In this case, as in others, Gerson chose to dismiss such people as suffering either from the attacks of the devil or from some form of mental illness (Gl 3.44). Gerson and his fellow clerics were not naïve believers in anything they heard. On the contrary, he almost seems to prefer to think that many such revelations are the products of sick minds. He worried that extreme forms of asceticism could harm people, and he remembered Benedict's warning that monks are to be careful about choosing the life of the hermit: "Not every inexperienced novice can bear the blows of the spiritual struggle, and so how can he safely hand himself over to a more serious match with a giant?"[156]

A third sign of the genuineness of spiritual coin is patience, which is not the same as the obstinacy shown by people like the woman of Arras. A fourth sign is truth, which means that the

50

person is willing to let his or her writings or sayings be investigated carefully by trained theologians (Gl 3.46). These will look for anything that might be in conflict with good morals or sincere faith. We must always be on our lookout, as Augustine tells of his mother, Monica, who at night distinguished true from false visions.[157] As an example of our need to determine what is true from false, we can take the banal case of how to know whether we are sleeping or awake. Some dreams can be so vivid that we can believe we are really experiencing them in wakefulness.

Gerson returns to the necessity of humility as the most important criterion for finding true revelations. We have nothing to fear if we place ourselves in the presence of God and expect or require nothing from him.[158] Pride has to be totally removed, or else it will rear its ugly head again, like the Hydra in poetry. As far as the truth of revelation is concerned, however, we have no reason to worry that God in his omnipotence will show himself in a manner that is absurd. For Gerson, there is a basic reasonability in the world, an order that he trusts will prevail, even in maintaining a sense of God's absolute power. Thus it is possible to reject the visionaries who appear with wild demands. The final sign that can determine authenticity is charity. Rightful love can be distinguished from forms of love that lead to sexual enjoyment outside of marriage. Gerson recalls what he heard about a magnate who delighted in fornication and said that it brought him closer to God. Gerson rejects the possibility that this could have been a love of which God approved. Then he speaks of what probably was his own experience: a spiritual bond to a nun that could have turned into sexual involvement. His conclusion is clear: "All passionate feeling is a most dangerous companion for virtue."[159] The passions are to be kept under careful control. Gerson shows awareness here of the pitfalls present for those who seek the intensity of mystical experience and want to share it with others. The bonds of spiritual friendship can easily change into something carnal. In Gerson's mind, the individual must remain at a distance from other people in order to hear the still, clear voice of God. He is again probably speaking of himself when he describes a person who experienced a crisis of faith and then reached a great calm (Gl 3.54).

Gerson, like us, lived in an age with prophets on every corner. He felt obliged to provide his readers and listeners with ways to deal with what they heard. As a good churchman, he appealed to the authority of the church. But he also believed in the good sense of people, in their humility, discretion, patience, and charity. The Christian faith did not ask for blind commitment. Its content was in harmony with common sense and human affections.

Years later, at the Council of Constance, Gerson made a similar treatise on the truth of visions, but this does not have the personal element of his earlier work.[160] The older Gerson was more a universal teacher who had distanced himself from his own crises of faith and now spoke not to the students of Paris or to his sisters but to the whole of Christendom. In both treatises, however, Gerson conceded that it was possible to find methods to distinguish truth from falsity amid a cacophony of voices claiming to speak God's word.

ON THE ART OF HEARING CONFESSIONS

Another treatise that casts light on Gerson and the spiritual life is his *On the Art of Hearing Confessions*. This work can only be roughly dated, to about 1406 (Gl 8.10–17). It clearly belongs, however, to the period of explosive creativity that characterized the years from Gerson's return to Paris in 1400 until his temporary departure south in 1407.

Here, as in parts of the treatises on mystical theology and on visions, Gerson reveals a practical, almost do-it-yourself interest. He considered what was necessary for an examination of the penitent to be thorough and fair. The priest should not rush through the confessions of all in his parish. If necessary he should even delay some confessions until after Easter, so that he could have the time to talk to the individual penitents at length. As in his treatment of reserved cases in Letter 24, Gerson was particularly concerned with sins of the flesh. He described in detail his technique for getting the penitent to reveal everything about such matters. From the start the confessor must be affable and friendly, giving the penitent little or no sense of the enormity of his sins (Gl 8.12).

Gerson preferred that the priest almost trick the penitent into bragging about his sexual behavior instead of making it clear from the start that such acts are condemned by the church. The method that Gerson describes is really a kind of entrapment:

> And let such things be said sufficiently slowly, and as if they were foreknown, or not considered to be so grave. The confessor is not to stare into the face of the sinner but to look away, as if he were not worried, or almost as if he were telling a story. He should say: I can well see that you did such and such. Consequently tell everything in the Lord's name. I will be indulgent to you (Gl 8.14).

I have translated this treatise rather than Gerson's much more specific one concerning the confession of masturbation because I think the consoling doctor's procedure needs to be seen in the context of more than his pursuit of one form of sexual behavior that was forbidden by the medieval church.[161] It is important not to sensationalize Gerson's terms or to misunderstand the honesty and directness with which he uses language. He was here writing in Latin for a clerical audience that must have regularly heard about sexual acts that, however interesting they might be for us, were banal facts which confessors like Gerson felt obliged to unearth. What can seem almost prurient to us was to Gerson and his colleagues simply one more manifestation of the gap between God's law and human behavior.

Gerson's desire for the truth, however, sometimes verges on an obsession, which may reflect his own lonely sexuality. But there is no reason to try to put Gerson on the couch of late-twentieth-century popularized Freudian psychology and judge him according to the vulgarized knowledge of our age. For Gerson, the sacrament of confession was essential for human beings to reach salvation. For the medieval church and its priests, God's forgiveness had to be communicated through the priest. Otherwise most people did not have a chance of salvation.

There is always a fine line between prurient interest and genuine concern with the hidden lives of other people. Gerson did his best to remind the confessor of his duty. Whatever doubts I have about Gerson's emotional makeup, I have no reservation about the man's commitment to the sacrament of confession as a way to heal the spiritual illnesses he detected in other people.

TREATISE AGAINST THE ROMANCE OF THE ROSE

As we have seen, Gerson was strongly concerned with the expression of human sexuality. In returning to Paris in 1400 he became aware of the attraction of a French poem about the pursuit of a woman and the final enjoyment of her favors. *The Romance of the Rose* begins ever so innocently with William de Lorris's twelfth-century wordplay, but its continuator in the thirteenth century, Jean de Meun, was far more specific in his sexual imagery and shook up a longstanding courtly debate on marriage and morals.[162] In the early fifteenth century a new generation of poets celebrated the art of *The Romance of the Rose*.[163]

Gerson decided in 1402 to reply to this debate by using its own language of allegory.[164] He attacked the *Romance* by describing how he had woken up on 18 May that year to find himself in the court of Christianity, where Lady Chastity was making charges against the Fool of Love, who had guided readers through the *Romance*. Since the author, Jean de Meun, was long since dead, only the Fool remained to be accused of corrupting the morals of the young through his poem.

In terms of literary genre, this little treatise is different from anything else in this collection of Gerson's writings. Some readers might wonder what it has to do with his spirituality. The *Treatise* deserves inclusion here because it reflects one of the major concerns of Gerson's life: how to make sure that Christian people lived in harmony with the gospels. For Gerson, it was not possible to reconcile courtly interest in physical love with the message of Christ. For his opponents, the opposition between courtly love and Christian teaching was not so obvious.

Gerson got involved in a debate where he can easily appear as a puritanical Christian out to burn books that we today value for their literary quality, subtlety, and humor. Gerson also loses out in today's discussions about women, for he generally ignored the contribution made to the debate by his contemporary, Christine of Pizan, who anticipated late-twentieth-century feminist views in criticizing a literature that turned women into objects for men's sexual titillation.[165] Gerson thus showed neither literary appreciation nor gender sensitivity; he can be made out to be a reactionary who wanted to turn back the clock to an age of innocence that perhaps never had existed!

Here, as elsewhere, Gerson can be read in a one-dimensional manner unfavorable to him and the reforming efforts of the later medieval church. But if one believes in marriage as a sacrament and the only proper and right context for sexual union, as Gerson did, then *The Romance of the Rose* is indeed a questionable work. Its very cleverness and intelligence hide what it is all about: the naked physical conquest of a woman by a man, popularly known in late-twentieth-century America as "scoring," and perhaps even rape.

Instead of writing a vitriolic sermon against this work, Gerson decided to confront it in its own language. He entered its allegorical world, but instead of presenting the secular court of Love, he set up a court of Christianity. In such a context, the *Romance* had to be condemned as a piece of subtle deception. Gerson involved himself in the behavior of other people and their language of moral expression because he was concerned with what was going on around him. His goal was not regulation of behavior for the sake of the church hierarchy's power. As a priest and a teacher, he had to convey the truth as he perceived it in God's church. Gerson worked at the University, in his parish, and at court for the unity of the church and the maintenance of standards he considered to be absolute. Whether he was teaching young scholars, administering a hospital, or writing against what he considered to be salacious literature, Gerson was asserting a belief in the wholeness of Christian society, where mutual care and concern are the foundation of life.

In the century after Gerson's death in 1429, consoling and reforming doctors of the church were generally replaced by

university professors out of contact with the world around them
and churchmen who were more interested in great buildings
than in parish work. This is an old story in the history of Christianity: one wave after another of reform and renewal followed
by periods of conformity and indifference, and then breakouts of
radical religion. In comparison to some of the rabid preachers of
his own day and of the sixteenth century, Gerson was a reasonable, careful church reformer. His honesty in searching for
authentic mystical theology makes him more than an intellectual
figure. His spirituality in all its pain reaches far beyond his time.
In rediscovering Gerson, we find ourselves.

ON TRANSLATING GERSON

In terms of translations, Gerson has been, to continue the language of sexuality, almost virgin territory. Part of his treatise
against the curiosity of students and fragments of his sermons
were rendered into English in 1969.[166] In 1976 a University of
South Carolina Ph.D. thesis made available some of his French
works, including his *Treatise Against "The Romance of the Rose."*[167]
In French, a collection of documents concerned with this debate
included modern translations of Gerson's Latin work, together
with invaluable notes.[168]

The most complete translation of Gerson in English until now
has been Paschal Boland's Catholic University of America disser-
tation from 1959: *The Concept of "Discretio Spirituum" in John Gerson's "De Probatione Spirituum" and "De Distinctione Verarum
Visionum a Falsis."* Since Boland's translation would only be available at major university libraries, I retranslated the earlier of the
two treatises. Boland left out a part of Gerson's text, while I have
done all of it. His notes are incomplete and sometimes incorrect.
I may, nevertheless, also have overlooked some of Gerson's
sources, and his Latin is not easy.

Except for André Combes's formidable edition of the *Mystical
Theology*, we lack a critical edition of Gerson.[169] Any translation
reflects the pitfalls of Glorieux's edition. Most of the time, Glorieux did not give himself the time to look for the references to

works of other authors with which Gerson is so rich. Glorieux is best when he was able to use a text provided him by outstanding researchers such as André Combes or Louis Mourin. I would have never been able to get to the sources of the *Mystical Theology* without Combes's sometimes overcopious notes and references. Other scholars will have to improve on my work, as I have expanded the work of earlier generations.

I have done my utmost to make Gerson's text accessible for the reader who is interested in medieval spirituality but does not have the time or the skill to turn to the Latin. Thus I have sacrificed the integrity of many of Gerson's long sentences for the sake of clarity. I have perhaps in places made his thought more simple and understandable than it really is. Sometimes I have to admit to the reader that a passage remains obscure to me. In the interests of accurate translation, I have stayed with Gerson's use of masculine nouns and pronouns, assuming, however, that the reader will realize that Gerson often used the masculine while intending to include both men and women.

I have tried to convert all Gerson's terms into English, and this process has brought a loss of the subtlety of some of his Latin expressions. As far as his French letters and treatises are concerned, it is much easier than with the Latin texts to render them into modern English, but this ease can at times be treacherous. The great Gerson philological expert Gilbert Ouy has warned me against the seemingly smooth surface of the text. Gerson can be just as precise and acute in his French as in his Latin. What looks easy can contain many layers of meaning.

I have added explanatory and background notes where I think it is helpful for the reader who might lack knowledge or be interested in checking the sources of Gerson's assertions. My translations from the Bible are made directly from the texts that Gerson provides. These are usually, but not always, consistent with the Vulgate text.

Since Gerson was so careful about taking into account a thousand years of writings on mystical theology, his mode of expression is extremely compact. But his language is basically straightforward.

INTRODUCTION

I rarely find Gerson using academic jargon, and I sense a strong desire to make himself clear to his students.

It is my hope that this English translation will make Gerson available for a new generation of students who will be able to see him as a theologian who took risks in trying to reach out for new audiences. In all his loneliness, Gerson spoke eloquently of his loves. I think he did so with power and conviction. These translations are intended to convey some of the spiritual depth to be found in the original texts that came from Gerson's tireless hand and restless mind.

Notes to the Introduction

1. See Henri Jadart, *Jean de Gerson. Recherches sur son origine, son village natal et sa famille* (Reims, 1881), p. 204, n. 1, quoting from the Larousse *Dictionnaire du XIXe siècle* 8, p. 1229: "People still in our day have the innocent attitude of admiring Gerson but like so many others he lives on his reputation!" Further references to Jadart's important study of Gerson's family and local background will refer to the work as "Jadart."

2. For the case of Bernard of Clairvaux, see Adriaan H. Bredero, "Conflicting Interpretations on Bernard of Clairvaux," *Citeaux Commentarii Cistercienses* 31 (1980), pp. 53–81, esp. 68–72.

3. There was, however, a very fine and precocious study of Gerson by a German historian, Johann Baptist Schwab, *Johannes Gerson. Professor der Theologie und Kanzler der Universität Paris,* originally published in two volumes in Würzburg in 1858. It was recently republished in its original form by Burt Franklin, New York (no date).

4. See the article on Gerson by L. Salembier, bringing together the various views expressed on Gerson, but distancing itself from his teaching on council and papacy, in the *Dictionnaire de théologie catholique* 6 (Paris, 1915), pp. 1313–30, esp. 1320–22. For a more recent bibliography on Gerson, see *Dictionnaire d'histoire et de géographie ecclésiastiques* 20 (1984), pp. 1056–57.

5. As in the work of Jadart (note 1 above) or in that by M. J. Pinet, *La vie ardente de Gerson* (Paris: Librairie Bloud & Gay, 1929).

6. My debt to Gilbert Ouy is enormous, as will be apparent in specific references to his articles. See, for example, his book, together with Danièle Calvot, *L'oeuvre de Gerson à Saint-Victor de Paris. Catalogue des manuscrits* (Paris: Éditions du Centre National de la Recherche Scientifique, 1990). See also his article "Humanism and Nationalism in France at the Beginning of the Fifteenth Century" in *The Birth of Identities: Denmark and Europe in the Middle Ages,* ed. Brian Patrick McGuire,

The Centre for Medieval Studies, Copenhagen University (Copenhagen: C. A. Reitzel, 1996), pp. 107–25.

7. Gerson pops up regularly in Francis Oakley's excellent *The Western Church in the Later Middle Ages* (Ithaca, N.Y., and London: Cornell University Press, 1979). For an excellent brief account of Gerson's actual involvement in the schism, see John B. Morrall, *Gerson and the Great Schism* (Manchester: University Press, 1960). A new awareness of Gerson in terms of popular piety can be seen in the pages of R. N. Swanson, *Religion and Devotion in Europe, c. 1215–c. 1515* (Cambridge, England: University Press, 1995).

8. Heiko Augustinus Oberman, *The Harvest of Medieval Theology: Gabriel Biel and Late Medieval Nominalism,* originally published by Harvard University Press, 1963; third edition, the Labyrinth Press, Durham, North Carolina, 1983. Also Oberman's *Forerunners of the Reformation* (New York, 1966); Steven Ozment, *Homo Spiritualis: A Comparative Study of the Anthropology of Johannes Tauler, Jean Gerson and Martin Luther* (1509–16) in the Context of Their Theological Thought, Studies in Medieval and Reformation Thought 6 (Leiden: E. J. Brill, 1969). More recently, Sven Grosse, *Heilsungewissheit und Scrupulositas im späten Mittelalter. Studien zu Johannes Gerson und Gattungen der Frömmigkeitstheologie seiner Zeit.* Beiträge zur Historischen Theologie 85 (Tübingen: J.C.B. Mohr, 1994).

9. See, for example, Louis B. Pascoe, *Jean Gerson: Principles of Church Reform,* Studies in Medieval and Reformation Thought 7 (Leiden: E. J. Brill, 1973). The Dutch church historian Guillaume Henri Marie Posthumus Meyjes has also done important work on Gerson's ecclesiology, but this is in Dutch. See his *Jean Gerson: zijn Kerkpolitiek en ecclesiologie.* Kerkhist. Studien 10 (s'Gravenhaage, 1963). Also important is Christoph Burger, *Aedificatio, Fructus, Utilitas. Johannes Gerson als Professor der Theologie und Kanzler der Universität Paris,* Beiträge zur historischen Theologie 70 (Tübingen: J.C.B. Mohr, 1986).

10. Published by Cambridge University Press in 1987.

11. For example, my "Loving the Holy Order: Jean Gerson and the Carthusians," in James Hogg, ed., *Die Kartäuser und ihre Welt–Kontakte und gegensitige Einflüsse, Analecta Cartusiana* 62 (Institut für Anglistik und Amerikanistik, Universität Salzburg, and Edwin Mellen Press, Lewiston, New York, 1993), pp. 100–139. Also, "Jean Gerson, the Carthusians, and the Experience of Mysticism," *The Mystical Tradition and the Carthusians* 3, ed. James Hogg, in Analecta Cartusiana 130 (Salzburg, 1995), pp. 61–86.

NOTES TO THE INTRODUCTION

12. James L. Connolly, *John Gerson: Reformer and Mystic* (Louvain: Librairie Universitaire, 1928).

13. For the chronology of Gerson's life, the most thorough treatment is by Palemon Glorieux, "La vie et les oeuvres de Gerson. Essai chronologique," in *Archives d'histoire doctrinale et littéraire du moyen âge* 25–26 (Paris, 1950–51), pp. 149–92. Glorieux summarized this study in the first volume of his *Jean Gerson. Oeuvres Complètes* (Paris: Desclée & Cie., 1960), pp. 105–39 (hereafter Glorieux's volumes of Gerson will be referred to as Gl, with the volume and page number (e.g., Gl 2.223), except for volume 7, which is divided into two parts (e.g., Gl 7.1.223 or Gl 7.2.223). The historian Max Liebermann wrote a number of fine and extremely detailed studies about aspects of Gerson's life in the Paris journal *Romania*, from no. 78 in 1957.

14. For the history of the University of Paris, the first volume of Hastings Rashdall, *The Universities of Europe in the Middle Ages*, ed. F. M. Powicke and A. B. Emden (Oxford: Oxford University Press, 1936 and later) remains an excellent introduction. More recent studies include Gordon Leff, *Paris and Oxford Universities in the Thirteenth and Fourteenth Centuries* (New York: John Wiley and Sons, 1968) and Stephen C. Ferruolo, *The Origins of the University* (Stanford, Calif.: Stanford University Press, 1985).

15. See P. Glorieux, "L'enseignement universitaire de Gerson," RTAM 23 (1956), pp. 88–113, esp. 88–89.

16. See Jadart (note 1 above), pp. 110–11. In a helpful letter to me (August 1996), Gilbert Ouy has expressed his skepticism about Jadart's evaluation concerning the social position of Gerson's parents. Dependent on what Gerson himself says in his letter to his patron about the poverty of his parents (see Letter 1, translated below), Gilbert Ouy concludes that it is likely Arnoul le Charlier merely rented land from the Benedictine abbey of St. Rémy. For me, the unanswered question remains whether the father's name, "le Charlier" (wheelwright), means that the father actually had this as a trade or merely had inherited the name.

17. See Glorieux, in *Archives* (note 13 above), p. 150.

18. The Celestine Order was an eremetical congregation that took its name from Pope Celestine V (1294), the controversial hermit who first was practically dragged from his hermitage to the papacy and then resigned a few months later. The Order grew out of the "brothers of the Holy Spirit" inside the Benedictine Order in the second half of the thirteenth century, and its main inspiration came from Peter of Morrone, the later Celestine V, who gave it its constitutions: *Instituta beati Petri*

(1274–94). The Order spread in France from the end of the thirteenth century and by Gerson's time had fifteen houses, known for the strictness of their lives. See Pierre-Roger Gaussin, *L'Europe des ordres et des congrégations,* Centre Européen de Recherches sur les Congrégations et Ordres Monastiques (Saint-Etienne, France, 1984). See also the articles "Célestin V" and "Célestins" in *Dictionnaire d'histoire et de géographie ecclésiastiques* 12 (Paris, 1953), pp. 79–104.

19. Letter b, Gl 2.8, "par la main de poncete vostre seur."

20. See Jadart (note 1 above), p. 8.

21. See Rashdall (note 14 above), pp. 510–11. Even though the hamlet of Gerson was within the geographical boundaries of Champagne, it was politically within the county of Rethel, which in 1384 came under the dominion of the duke of Burgundy, who later was to be Gerson's patron. The young Jean was thus singularly fortunate to be born where he was.

22. Another, perhaps better-known case is that of Robert Grosseteste, the learned bishop of Lincoln in the thirteenth century. See R. W. Southern, *Robert Grosseteste. The Growth of an English Mind in Medieval Europe* (Oxford: Clarendon Press, 1992), esp. chap. 4, "Outlines of a Provincial Career," pp. 63–70.

23. Letter 5 (Gl 2.35). Translated below.

24. Letter 9, to Nicolas (Gl 2.47). Translated below. See my comment in the article "Loving the Holy Order" (note 11 above), pp. 129–30.

25. Gl 8.369, no. 418: *Collectorium super Magnificat.* Gerson does not specifically say that the father who did so to his child was his own father, but the indication is very strong.

26. For Gerson's career at Paris, see Glorieux's chronology (note 13 above), pp. 151–55.

27. For a description of the procedures, volume 1 of Rashdall is still invaluable (note 14 above), pp. 474–89. Rashdall is quite pragmatic about the expenses involved for the candidate who was taking his degree and was expected to hold lavish dinners (still a collegial "must" in many European universities at the doctoral level). One wonders how Gerson was able to pay and who might have subsidized him.

28. There is an excellent treatment of this important development by Alan E. Bernstein, *Pierre d'Ailly and the Blanchard Affair: University and Chancellor of Paris at the Beginning of the Great Schism* (Leiden: E. J. Brill, 1978). For the College of Navarre and Gerson's colleagues, see p. 65, esp. note 35, with references to Gilbert Ouy's work.

NOTES TO THE INTRODUCTION

29. For a general treatment of the period, Barbara W. Tuchman's *A Distant Mirror: The Calamitous Fourteenth Century* (New York: Alfred A. Knopf, 1978) is good on military history but very weak when it comes to the history of the church and spirituality. Tuchman has a tendency to sensationalize and overdramatize. Much better is Johan Huizinga's classic *The Waning of the Middle Ages*, originally in Dutch, but whose 1924 English edition the author supervised (Penguin Books, 1955 and later). A complete translation of the 1921 Dutch version, with all the footnotes, is now available: *The Autumn of the Middle Ages*, trans. Rodney J. Payton and Ulrich Mammitzsch (University of Chicago Press, 1996).

30. A good outline for the period can be found in Daniel Waley, *Later Medieval Europe: Saint Louis to Luther* (London and New York: Longman, 1985), esp. chap. 7, "French Defeats and Chivalrous Ideals: The Hundred Years' War."

31. See Glorieux, *Archives* (note 13 above), p. 152.

32. For details, see Richard C. Famiglietti, *Royal Intrigue: Crisis at the Court of Charles VI, 1392–1420* (New York: AMS Press, 1986). For a broader treatment, see P. S. Lewis, *Later Medieval France: The Polity* (London and New York: Macmillan and St. Martin's Press, 1968).

33. As he himself indicated in his Letter 2, Gl 2.18, dated to 1400, in which he nevertheless complained that as chancellor he still had to deal with the fluidity of court life.

34. See Glorieux, *Archives* (note 13 above), p. 155. For the dukes of Burgundy, see the work of Richard Vaughan, such as *Philip the Bold: The Formation of the Burgundian State* (London: Longman, 1962). The period is especially rich in contemporary chronicles, such as the *Chronique du Religieux de Saint-Denys, contenant le règne de Charles VI, de 1380 à 1422*, 1–5 (Paris, 1840–44).

35. See Gerson's Letter 2, Gl 2.19, translated below.

36. See the careful study by E. Vansteenberghe, "Gerson à Bruges," RHE 31 (1935), pp. 5–52.

37. See N. Valois, "Gerson. Curé de Saint-Jean-en-Grève," *Bulletin de la Société de l'Histoire de Paris et de l'Ile de France* 28 (1901), pp. 49–57. The church has long since disappeared. It was approximately on the site of the present Hôtel de Ville.

38. For Gerson as a preacher, the work of Louis Mourin remains central. See his *Jean Gerson. Prédicateur Français* (Brugge: De Tempel, 1952).

39. This is from early 1397, a memorandum to the king, *Requête pour les condamnés à mort*, Gl 7.1.341–43.

NOTES TO THE INTRODUCTION

40. This is Letter 2, already referred to, and translated below.

41. Well translated by Betty Radice, in *The Letters of Abelard and Heloise* (Harmondsworth: Penguin Books, 1974), pp. 57–106. Michael Clanchy of the University of London has completed an important new study of Abelard.

42. As in his "Gerson. Émule de Pétrarque: Le 'Pastorium Carmen,' poème de jeunesse de Gerson, et la renaissance de l'églogue en France à la fin du XIVe siècle," *Romania* 88 (1967), pp. 175–231.

43. Letter 1 (Gl 2.1–4), translated below. See Gilbert Ouy's important article, "Une lettre de jeunesse de Jean Gerson," *Romania* 80 (1959), pp. 461–72.

44. As in the naming of Anselm as archbishop of Canterbury in 1095 (when he really may have not wanted office) or in the appointment of Absalon, bishop of Roskilde, as archbishop of Lund in 1177 (when he probably did desire the position).

45. Letter 2 (Gl 2.19).

46. See some of the statements in Letter 5, below, "Every form of puffed-up arrogance in unfamiliar matters is to be banished, so that we do not increase talk glorying in our loftiness."

47. *La Montaigne de Contemplation* is in Gl 7.1, pp. 16–55, and is the first work translated below.

48. See Boccaccio's preface to the *Decameron,* trans. G. H. McWilliam (Harmondsworth: Penguin Books, 1975), pp. 46–47.

49. I have dealt at length with these treatises in "Late Medieval Care and Control of Women: Jean Gerson and His Sisters," RHE 92 (1997), pp. 5–37.

50. Glorieux, *Archives* (note 13 above), p. 160.

51. Several of the works named here are translated below among Gerson's letters and treatises.

52. Contained in Gl 3.224–49 and partly translated in Steven E. Ozment, *Jean Gerson: Selections,* Textus Minores 38 (Leiden: E. J. Brill, 1969), pp. 26–45.

53. See Letter 7, from Bruges in the summer of 1400, translated below.

54. Gl 3.26–36. See P. Glorieux, "L'enseignement universitaire de Gerson," RTAM 23 (1956), pp. 88–113.

55. *De theologia mystica lectiones sex,* in Gl 3.250–92; the critical edition, however, is that of André Combes, *Ioannis Carlerii de Gerson de Mystica Theologia* (Lugano, Switzerland: Thesaurus Mundi, 1958).

56. Gl 8.18–47. Critical edition in Combes (note 55 above), pp. 125–217.

57. Glorieux, *Archives* (note 13 above), p. 167. The letter that accompanied the *Opus Tripartitum* is translated below (Letter 18, dated to about 1404). For the importance of Gerson's works, see the evaluation in Thomas Tentler, *Sin and Confession on the Eve of the Reformation* (Princeton, N.J.: Princeton University Press, 1977), as p. 46, where he is called "the greatest voice in the cure of souls."

58. See Gl 8.10–17, translated below.

59. Gl 9.669–86. See my treatment of Gerson on the education of the young in "Education, Confession, and Pious Fraud: Jean Gerson and a Late Medieval Change," ABR 47 (1996), pp. 310–38.

60. For the text of the epitaph, see Jadart (note 1 above), p. 108.

61. Glorieux, *Archives* (note 13 above), p. 162.

62. Letter 9 (Gl 2.45–49).

63. Letter 23 (Gl 2.86–90).

64. See my article on Gerson and his sisters, note 49 above. In note 23 in this article I point out that Gerson's treatise on the advantages of virginity over marriage as found in the Glorieux edition (7.416–21) has been much truncated, without any clear indication of the abbreviation, so one must go back to the earlier edition made by Ellies du Pin, vol. 3, col. 829–41, first published in Antwerp, 1706, and reissued by Georg Olms Verlag, Hildesheim, Zürich and New York, 1987.

65. Glorieux, *Archives* (note 13 above), p. 185.

66. See Gilbert Ouy, "Enquête sur les manuscrits autographes du chancelier Gerson et sur les copies faites par son frère le Célestin Jean Gerson," *Scriptorium* 16 (1962), pp. 275–301.

67. Gl 8.639.

68. See especially the treatises collected by Glorieux in his volume 10, *L'oeuvre polémique.*

69. See Glorieux, *Archives* (note 13 above), p. 168.

70. Again Glorieux has done the archival work; here on Gerson as an administrator, see his "Gerson au chapitre de Notre-Dame de Paris," RHE 56 (1961), pp. 424–48 and 827–54, esp. 445–48.

71. *Contre Charles de Savoisy,* in Gl 7.1.326–40. See Rashdall (note 14 above), 3:430–31.

72. Gl 7.1.329. This fantasy should not be ascribed only to medieval lack of historical sense. In the nineteenth century, University College, Oxford, celebrated its thousandth anniversary in 1872, on the claim

that it had been founded by Alfred the Great! See Rashdall (note 14 above), 3:177, n. 2.

73. Gl 7.1.331.

74. Gl 7.1.331: "Ce meffait a esté fait pres de l'ostel du roy, pres de la fontaine de justice royalle, de Parlement et de Chastelet, et en la principalle cité de toute France."

75. Gl 7.1.333: "...quan clergie y fauldra, bonne chevalerie n'y durera pas grandement." Gerson's account, however dramatized, can be confirmed in its essentials by contemporary chronicles, such as that by Jean Juvenal des Ursins. See M. J. Pinet, *La vie ardente de Gerson* (note 5 above), p. 111.

76. Glorieux, *Archives* (note 13 above), p. 168.

77. See the chapter "The Fall of Louis of Orléans," in Richard C. Famiglietti (note 32 above), pp. 39–64.

78. For a summary of Gerson's writings on the subject, see the dossier in Gl 10.164–70.

79. For this complicated story, see Van Steenberghe's article (note 36 above), pp. 34–37.

80. See N. Valois, "Gerson, Curé de Saint-Jean-en-Grève" (note 37 above), pp. 5–11.

81. Glorieux, *Archives* (note 13 above), p. 175.

82. See Richard C. Famiglietti (note 32 above), chap. 7, "The Cabochien Uprising (1413)," pp. 111–32.

83. The chronicler is Jean Jouvenel des Ursins. See Pinet, *La vie ardente de Gerson* (note 5 above), p. 154.

84. The best summary in English remains John B. Morrall, *Gerson and the Great Schism* (note 7 above), esp. pp. 94–111.

85. Contained in his *De probatione spirituum* (Gl 9.179, trans. Paschal Boland, *The Concept of Discretio Spirituum* [Washington, D.C.: Catholic University of America Press, 1959], p. 28): "Of special interest is the case of Bridget (of Sweden), who claims to have enjoyed visions not only of angels, but also of Jesus Christ, Mary, Agnes, and other saints, who talk to her with the familiarity of friends, or as a bridegroom to his bride. Truly there is danger here, either in approving or in disapproving of such writings. For what would be more disgraceful or incongruous for this Sacred Council than to declare that false, imaginary, or foolish visions are true and genuine revelations? On the other hand, to denounce those revelations which are declared authentic in many places and by different peoples, after various and numerous

examinations, would pose a threat, perhaps great, of spiritual harm to the Christian religion and the devotion of the faithful."

Gerson concluded that the council could not remain in silence on the matter but had to find some middle way between the two extreme positions.

86. The sermon is known as *Ambulate dum lucem habetis (Walk While You Have Light)* or *Sermo post recessum Joannis XXIII,* preached on 23 March 1415 (Gl 5.39–50).

87. See Francis Oakley (note 7 above), esp. pp. 55–70.

88. Glorieux, *Archives* (note 13 above), p. 178.

89. As in a letter to his brother Jean the Celestine, from Constance, on 1 January 1417 (Gl 3.199): "Since I am a pilgrim and a stranger, for in this way 'Gerson' is to be interpreted, and I remember in regular meditation the words of the heavenly pilgrim Paul: 'Our way of life is in heaven'" (Ph 3:20). This phrase, *nostra conversatio in coelis est,* became Gerson's motto.

90. Mark Stephen Burrows, *Jean Gerson and De Consolatione Theologiae (1418): The Consolation of a Biblical and Reforming Theology for a Disordered Age,* Beiträge zur historischen Theologie 78 (Tübingen: J.C.B. Mohr, 1991).

91. See M. J. Pinet, *La vie ardente de Gerson* (note 5 above), pp. 206–7. Connolly (note 12 above), p. 196, mistakenly thought that Gerson lived for his entire time in Lyon at Saint Paul's.

92. See the illustration in A. L. Masson, *Jean Gerson. Sa vie, son temps, ses oeuvres* (Lyon: Emmanuel Vitte, 1894), p. 406.

93. See the letters in Gl 3 and my articles on Gerson and the Carthusians (note 11 above).

94. *Tractatus super Cantica Canticorum* (Gl 8.565–639).

95. André Combes, *La théologie mystique de Gerson: Profile de son évolution* 1–2 (Rome, Paris, etc.: Desclée et socii, 1963–64).

96. See my article "Jean Gerson, the Carthusians, and the Experience of Mysticism" (note 11 above), esp. pp. 77–78.

97. *De Puella Aurelianensi* (Gl 9.661–65). See the fascinating article by Dorothy G. Wayman, "The Chancellor and Jeanne d'Arc, February-July, A.D. 1429," *Franciscan Studies* 17 (1957), pp. 272–305.

98. See the conclusion of my article "Late Medieval Care and Control of Women" (note 49 above). My colleague Gábor Klaniczay at the Department of Medieval History, Central European University in Budapest, Hungary, is preparing a monograph on the fifteenth-century

growth of the concept of witchcraft. Here Gerson's work will be a point of departure.

99. For an overview of these publications, see Christoph Burger (note 9 above), pp. 10–12.

100. As his three sermons, *Poenitemini. Contre la luxure* (Gl 7.2. 810–41).

101. See Gl 3.52, *De distinctione verarum revelationum a falsis*, translated below as *On Distinguishing True from False Revelations*. I have dealt at length with this important passage in "Jean Gerson and the End of Spiritual Friendship: Dilemmas of Conscience," *Friendship in Medieval Europe*, ed. Julian Haseldine (London: Sutton Publishing, 1998).

102. As quoted by Huizinga, *The Waning of the Middle Ages* (note 29 above), p. 189, who was keenly aware of Gerson's experience and teaching. About a third of Huizinga's great work is directly or indirectly dependent on his reading and interpretation of Gerson's writings, as can be seen from his bibliography, p. 323.

103. See the *Mystica Theologia Speculativa*, fortieth consideration (Gl 3.285): "de corporalibus unionibus nihil hic dicendum est."

104. *De confessione mollitiei (On the Confession of Masturbation)* (Gl 1.71–75). See my "Sexual Control and Spiritual Growth in the Late Middle Ages: The Case of Jean Gerson," *Tradition and Ecstasy: The Agony of the Fourteenth Century*, ed. Nancy van Deusen (Ottawa, Canada: Institute of Mediaeval Music, 1997), pp. 123–52.

105. See the seventeenth consideration in *The Art of Hearing Confessions* (Gl 8.14), translated below.

106. See his *De cognitione castitatis* (Gl 9.426), which I have dealt with in more detail in "Sexual Control and Spiritual Growth" (note 104 above).

107. See the opening of Letter 1*, to his sisters, translated below, in which Gerson tells them how busy he is and how he has stayed up that night in order to write them (Gl 2.14).

108. Gl 7.1.16: "La cause d'escripre en francois et aux simples gens de la matiere de contemplation." According to Glorieux, *Archives* (note 13 above), p. 160, the work was written at Bruges in 1400, during an illness that prevented Gerson from carrying out his intention of returning to Paris.

109. See my "Late Medieval Care and Control of Women" (note 49 above).

110. *Mountain* §17–18 (Gl 7.1.27–28).

111. *Mountain* §13 (Gl 7.1.23–24).

NOTES TO THE INTRODUCTION

112. *Mountain* §16 (Gl 7.1.26).

113. Here I am more positive about what Gerson offered women than is Jo Ann McNamara. See pp. 24–27 in "John Gerson and the Primacy of Clerical Authority," part of her provocative and exciting article "The Rhetoric of Orthodoxy: Clerical Authority and Female Innovation in the Struggle with Heresy," *Maps of Flesh and Light: The Religious Experience of Medieval Women Mystics,* ed. Ulrike Wiethaus (Syracuse, New York: Syracuse University Press, 1993), pp. 9–27.

114. *In festo S. Bernardi* (Gl 5.325–39).

115. See the chapter "The Challenge of Scholasticism" in Louis Lekai, *The Cistercians: Ideals and Reality* (Ohio: Kent State University Press, 1977), pp. 77–90.

116. Brian Patrick McGuire, "Gerson and Bernard: Languishing with Love," *Cîteaux Commentarii Cistercienses* 46 (1995), pp. 127–56.

117. "Une lettre de jeunesse de Jean Gerson," *Romania* 80 (1959), pp. 461–72, characterized so aptly as "l'oeuvre d'un très jeune homme, encore tout imprégné de l'enseignement reçu à la Faculté des Arts" (p. 465).

118. See M. J. Pinet, *La vie ardente de Gerson* (note 5 above), pp. 8–9. For the larger question of lay literacy, Gerson's works have been combed by Geneviève Hasenohr, "Religious Reading Amongst the Laity in France in the Fifteenth Century," in *Heresy and Literacy 1000–1530,* ed. Peter Biller and Anne Hudson (Cambridge, England: University Press, 1994), pp. 205–21.

119. Joinville, *The Life of Saint Louis,* part 2, chap. 1, trans. M. R. B. Shaw, in *Chronicles of the Crusades* (Harmondsworth: Penguin Books, 1963), p. 182.

120. Gl 3.9, inserted by Gerson himself in his *Discours de l'excellence de la virginité* (Gl 7.418).

121. The Dominicans had been barred from the University because of their teaching on the Immaculate Conception.

122. Gl 2.44. For Gerson's *De non esu carnium apud Carthusienses (On the Non-Eating of Meat Among the Carthusians),* see Gl 3.77–95, about which I have written in "Loving the Holy Order: Jean Gerson and the Carthusians" (note 11 above).

123. Letter 9, to Nicolas (Gl 2.47) (see note 24 above).

124. Gl 2.54–55. See Gilbert's seventh sermon on the Song of Songs, PL 184:43. From the later Middle Ages until the end of the nineteenth century Cistercian writers such as William of Saint Thierry and Gilbert of Hoyland were forgotten and their works ascribed to Bernard. As I

once wrote, "Bernard grew in the last medieval centuries" (*The Difficult Saint: Bernard of Clairvaux and His Tradition* [CP, 1991], p. 227).

125. Gl 2.55–64. Ruusbroec's work is translated by James A. Wiseman, *John Ruusbroec: The Spiritual Espousals and Other Writings*, CWS (1985).

126. Letter 14, Gl 2.63–64; *De vita spirituali animae*, Gl 3.113–202.

127. Gl 7.1.301–16, translated below.

128. Gl 2.72. The treatise is the first part of what became known as *Le miroir de l'âme* (Gl 7.1.193–203).

129. Gl 2.76–77. It used to be thought that the letter was intended for Gerson's father, who died on 14 September 1404, but an excellent article by Max Lieberman eliminated this possibility: "Jean Gerson et Philippe de Mézières," *Romania* 81 (1960), pp. 338–79.

130. The *Vitae Patrum* are brief accounts of the deeds and sayings of the desert fathers of the fourth and fifth centuries, first collected in Greek and later translated into Latin. The thirteenth-century James of Voragine's *Golden Legend* is the great medieval collection of the lives of the saints. See the references in my translation of the letter below.

131. *Rule of Life for a Recluse*, trans. Mary Paul Macpherson, in *Aelred of Rievaulx: Treatises and the Pastoral Prayer* (CP, 1982).

132. Gerson's attitude is very much that of the early Cistercians, such as Saint Bernard, who also felt that entrance into monastic life required the company of his kin and friends. See my *Friendship and Community: The Monastic Experience 350–1250* (CP, 1988), p. 253.

133. Gl 2.90–93, known as *Super moderatione casuum reservandorum in foro*. See Tentler (note 57 above), pp. 304–13.

134. The first use of this term I can find is that by Gerson's editor Jakob Wimpheling in the 1502 edition of his works: "Joannis Gerson consolatorii christianissimique doctoris...." See Ellies du Pin (note 64 above), 1:clxxix.

135. For the controversy, see the helpful review by Paul Verdeyen, *La théologie mystique de Guillaume de Saint-Thierry* (Paris: FAC-éditions, 1990), pp. 81–84.

136. For the origins of the legend, see Raymond J. Loenertz, "La légende parisienne de S. Denys l'Aréopagite, sa genèse et son premier témoin," *Analecta Bollandiana* 69 (1951), pp. 217–37.

137. See *Contre la fête des fous* (Gl 7.1.409–11); *Adversus superstitionem in audiendo missam* (Gl 10.141–43).

138. Known as *Beati qui persecutionem patiuntur* (Gl 5.107), a text that is lost to us.

139. For an excellent introduction to the modern debate about mysticism, see Bernard McGinn's appendix to his *The Foundations of Mysticism* (New York: Crossroad, 1991), esp. pp. 265–91.

140. The best English-language presentation that I know concerning the two complementary sides of Gerson's theology is David Schmiel, *Via Propria and Via Mystica in the Theology of Jean le Charlier de Gerson*, Graduate Study no. 10 (St. Louis, Mo.: School for Graduate Studies, Concordia Seminary, 1969). A good study of the terms found in Gerson is Johann Stelzenberger, *Die Mystik des Johannes Gerson*. Breslauer Studien zur historischen Theologie (Breslau: Verlag Müller & Seiffert, 1928). In French, André Combes is the undisputed master, but his books are immensely long and important discussions are lost in a morass of secondary considerations. See *La théologie mystique de Gerson. Profil de son évolution* 1–2 (Rome, Paris, Tournai, New York: Desclée et Socii, 1963–64). The best summary of André Combes's work on the mystical theology of Gerson is the long conclusion to his much earlier study, *Jean Gerson. Commentateur Dionysien* (Paris: Librairie philosophique J. Vrin, 1940), pp. 421–72.

141. Taken from *De mystica theologia. Tractatus Primus Speculativus*, to which I refer hereafter as SMT (*Speculative Mystical Theology*), as opposed to *Tractatus Secundus Practicus*, PMT (*Practical Mystical Theology*). The Latin text I use is that of André Combes, *Ioannis Carlerii de Gerson de Mystica Theologia* (Lugano, Switzerland: Thesaurus Mundi, 1958), referred to hereafer as Combes.

142. See PMT 12:10 (referring to the *Consideratio* and section number, as given in Combes, p. 213).

143. See PMT at the end, Combes, p. 217, translated below.

144. Gerson uses the term *concathenatio* (Combes 10:4, p. 27), which for us recalls the great study of Arthur O. Lovejoy, *The Great Chain of Being*, from his 1933 William James Lectures at Harvard (New York: Harper & Row, 1960). See esp. pp. 67–68 for Pseudo-Dionysius.

145. See Combes, *La théologie mystique de Gerson* (note 140 above), 2:25–27.

146. For an excellent presentation of this concept, see Robert A. Greene, "Synderesis, the Spark of Conscience, in the English Renaissance," *Journal of the History of Ideas* 52 (1991), pp. 195–219, esp. 195–201. I am grateful to my friend William Combes, emeritus professor of English, Western Michigan University, for this reference.

147. For Avicenna, see Etienne Gilson, *History of Christian Philosophy in the Middle Ages* (London: Sheed and Ward, 1955), esp. pp. 214–15.

148. The strongest criticism came from the Carthusian Vincent of Aggsbach. See Connolly (note 12 above), pp. 309–15.

149. See Bernard McGinn, *The Growth of Mysticism* (New York: Crossroad, 1994), pp. 375–95.

150. Guileli Alverni Opera Omnia 1–2 (Paris, 1674; reprinted Minerva, Frankfurt am Main, 1963). The *Rhetorica divina* is in 1:336–406.

151. *The Imitation of Christ* is available in English in a Penguin Classics edition, with remarks on the dispute over authorship. See also Masson (note 92 above), pp. 352–64.

152. See John Van Engen's fine introduction to *Devotio Moderna: Basic Writings*, CWS (1988).

153. PMT 11:8, Combes, p. 201. The *Viae Sion lugent* is included in the works of Bonaventure and called *Mystica Theologia* (*Opera Omnia* 8, ed. A. C. Peltier, Paris, 1866). A new edition is available in the series Sources chrétiennes. See Dennis D. Martin's translation in *Carthusian Spirituality*, CWS (1997).

154. *De distinctione verarum revelationum a falsis,* Gl 3.36–56. For the dating, see the same volume, p. x.

155. Gl 3.43. For this phenomenon see Caroline Walker Bynum, *Holy Feast and Holy Fast: The Religious Significance of Food to Medieval Women* (Berkeley: University of California Press, 1987), where Gerson is mentioned several times.

156. Gl 3.45. See chapter 73 of the *Rule of Saint Benedict.*

157. Gl 3.48. Cf. *Confessions* 6.13.

158. Gl 3.50.

159. Gl 3.52: "Omnis quippe vehementia est ad virtutem periculosissima comes...."

160. Known as *De probatione spirituum,* Gl 9.177–85.

161. The *De confessione mollitiei* is in Gl 8.71–75. See my article on Gerson and confession (note 59 above).

162. A complete English translation exists by Harry W. Robbins, ed. Charles W. Dunn, *The Romance of the Rose* (New York: E. P. Dutton & Co., 1962).

163. For an overview of the relevant sources, see the dossier in Gl 10.25–26. Most of these central texts are included in the collection edited by Eric Hicks, *Le débat sur le Roman de la Rose,* Bibliothèque du XVe siècle 43 (Paris: Éditions Honoré Champion, 1977).

164. Gl 7.1.301–16, written in French.

165. See Earl Jeffrey Richards, "*Seulette a part:* The 'Little Woman on the Sidelines' Takes Up Her Pen: The Letters of Christine de Pizan," in

Dear Sister: Medieval Women and the Epistolary Genre, ed. Karen Chere-watuk and Ulrike Wiethaus (Philadelphia: University of Pennsylvania Press, 1993), pp. 139–70.

166. Steven E. Ozment, ed., *Selections from A Deo exivit, Contra curiosi-tatem studentium and De mystica theologia speculativa* (Leiden: E. J. Brill, 1969).

167. Diana Elizabeth Adams-Smith, *Some French Works of Jean Gerson: An Introduction and Translation,* Ph.D. diss., University of South Car-olina, 1976 (available through University Microfilms, 1977).

168. See note 163 above.

169. *Ioannis Carlerii de Gerson De Mystica Theologia* (note 55 above).

The Mountain of Contemplation[1]

[1] *The reason for writing in French and to ordinary people[2]*
concerning the matter of contemplation.

Some persons will wonder and ask why, in a matter so lofty as
that of the contemplative life, I choose to write in French rather
than in Latin, and more to women than to men. They will say
that such a subject is not appropriate for ordinary people who
have no Latin.[3] To this challenge I respond that the matter has
been dealt with in Latin. Holy doctors have treated the subject
in an outstanding manner in various books and treatises, as
Saint Gregory in his *Moralia in Job*, Saint Bernard in *Sermons on
the Song of Songs*, Richard of Saint Victor, and several others.[4]
Clerics who know Latin can make use of such texts. But it is different for ordinary people, and especially for my sisters.[5] For
them I want to write about this way of life, for as the Apostle
says, the woman who is a virgin and does not marry will be anxious to please God alone, and not the world, as the married
woman compels herself to please her husband and to administer
her household (1 Cor 7:34).[6]

Therefore, nothing is more fitting, in writing to my sisters,
who by God's gift set out some time ago to live without marriage,
than to teach them how they will please God by always serving
him in constantly loving and honoring him. The lack of learning[7]
of my sisters cannot keep me from going ahead, for I intend to
speak only about what they can fully grasp according to the
understanding that I have seen in them.[8]

[2] Scholarship is not at all necessary for contemplative persons.[9]

However much advanced scholarship and great learning in God's law may be quite suitable for the person who wishes to come to the height of contemplation, nevertheless sometimes such knowledge blocks this pursuit. Learning is not in itself a problem. Rather, it is the arrogance and the self-inflation that the learned person derives from his knowledge. For it is clearly impossible to reach true contemplation except through humility, as the Apostle teaches (1 Cor 3:18). For if anyone, he says, seems wise in this world, he must become a fool in order to be wise. In other words, he should take on humble understanding and consider himself a fool with regard to God's wisdom. He must realize that he cannot understand God's works and judgments. The result is that a number of clerics are hindered in pursuing such a life, for they will not allow themselves to be humbled, nor to hand over their understanding to the mysteries of the incarnation of our Lord and the humility of his actions. But whoever does not enter by this gate, which is quite humble and low, he is a thief and his efforts are in vain, as Jesus says (Jn 10:1).

And so it is that if a man walks with his head erect, that is, with a great conviction of his understanding and knowledge, and does not wish to lower himself in the manner of a small child or a simple woman, he will never be able to enter a gate so humble. Instead, he will harm himself and regress, as did some of the disciples of our Lord Jesus Christ when they heard him preaching of the Sacrament of the Altar (cf. Jn 6:60–66). That is why many great scholars have wished at times that they had remained in a state of simplicity, like their mothers, without knowing Latin.[10]

I do not mean, however, that knowledge must not be not profitable in itself, providing one has the grace to use it well and humbly. The danger, however, is that arrogance comes with it. As the Apostle says, "Knowledge puffs up" (1 Cor 8:1). This process also takes place in accord with different temperaments in people. You see how a very good wine harms a person who has fever,[11] or how the sword is dangerous for someone who is in a rage, or how light will harm the eyes when they are enlarged and swollen. Similarly, knowledge will have a harmful effect on people who are already ill-disposed to it.

[3] Of two types of people and those who are more suited for contemplation.

Saint Gregory says in the sixth book of his *Moralia* that some people are by their nature or complexion or custom inclined to concentrate on externals and to busy themselves with worldly matters.[12] They cannot give themselves over or lift themselves up to the contemplative life, and they are much more effective in the active life. If, however, they force themselves into contemplation, they often will run into great errors and blasphemy. They should instead keep to the active life.

The other group consists of persons who are so calm, peaceful, and relaxed in their thoughts that there is no external activity that they can tolerate. They live and find their delight in looking at and admiring the works of God and the life of heaven and in thinking, in all humility, of their salvation. Such persons ought to keep themselves as much as possible from worldly concerns. They will work in vain, and they will make a greater loss than profit.

But there are some people who because of practice, ability, temperament, or the great love of God and their neighbor come to understand how to have the ability and knowledge to dedicate themselves now to one pursuit, now to another. Prelates of the church especially ought to live this way.

Some clerics are of the first state or condition. Therefore they often fall into error if they deal too much with profound thinking and leave behind external activities or occupations. Some ordinary people are of the other condition, so that they with no difficulty can live in solitude and think almost always of their salvation without any other worldly activity. So you see that ordinary people must not be excluded from being told about this life.

We have seen and see in many cases that holy hermits and some women have gained more in the love of God through this contemplative life than many great scholars manage to do. For such a way of life is better acquired through good and humble simplicity than through academic learning, just as Solomon says of God's wisdom, that it walks with the simple and talks with them.[13] There is also this commandment, that we seek God in simplicity of heart (cf. Wis 1:1), for he is quite simple and is found through simplicity.[14]

[4] Of the two manners of contemplation, the one in knowledge, the other in affectivity.

But in order to make this subject more clear, I will consider how the contemplative life has in itself degrees and parts. Of these parts the one is more subtle: it is that which seeks through reasons based on the true faith the nature of God and his being and also his works. This form of contemplation is able to find new truths or to make them known and teach them, or to defend them against the errors and lies of heretics and unbelievers. It is not my intention here to speak of this manner of contemplation, for it belongs to good theologians who are well instructed in Holy Scripture. This function is not for ordinary people, except through divine inspiration or a unique miracle, as happened to the apostles, who were quite ordinary and without learning, and as has been the case with many others.

Another manner of contemplation is that which concentrates principally on loving God and enjoying his goodness without trying to acquire clearer knowledge than that which faith has inspired and given. To this type of contemplation ordinary people can come, in leaving behind the cares of the world and in keeping their hearts pure and spotless. Such contemplation I will now speak of. I believe that it was for the most part this type of wisdom and contemplation that Saint Denis of France taught in his books of mystical theology.[15] This is the highest wisdom we can possess on earth. It was revealed and explained to him by Saint Paul.

[5] Of the difference between knowledge and wisdom.

The holy doctors see a great difference between knowledge and wisdom, especially Saint Bernard.[16] For knowledge belongs chiefly and almost solely to the understanding, while wisdom to affectivity.[17] Wisdom or sapience brings, in accord with its name, a form of savory knowledge. And this taste concerns the emotions, the desire, the appetite, and the will of a person. There can be in a person great knowledge or awareness, and at the same time only a little wisdom or none at all, for he or she will have no taste or feeling for what is known. I will demonstrate this point by some plain examples.

One can know about the nature of honey by hearing about it or by studying books, without ever having savored the sweet taste of honey. Doctors know about the nature of illnesses and have more knowledge than those who are ill. But in terms of feeling pain or experiencing it, it is obvious that sick persons feel it more and know more about it, not at all through reason but by experience. One could also have very great knowledge of the condition of a person without having any strong feeling of love or hate, pleasure or repulsion toward this person. On the contrary, one could have great attachment and enjoyment in a person without knowing him or her well. And so you see how we can consider wisdom as being great without great knowledge, and pure knowledge or learning existing without much wisdom.

[6] No one should be called wise if he is not good.
According to common usage in the language, it is usually said that those great scholars, whether theologians or philosophers, who have been introduced to the first type of contemplation I have mentioned, have wisdom or knowledge. This form of contemplation seems to have been, according to the philosophers, the essence of human bliss or beatitude. But it is wrong and misleading to speak in such a way if such scholars do not with their knowledge possess ardent affectivity through love for God and for his lovable creation. Without such a love and charity no joy in contemplation can by any means be attained. In my mind, Aristotle did not intend to indicate anything else.[18] And those who have acted differently are reproached by the Apostle, who asserts that those who claim to be wise, meaning to have wisdom, have been made fools (Rom 1:21). He gives the reason: because they have known God but have not glorified him nor

loved him as God, nor have they given him thanks. Thus we can see which scholars we in speaking the truth ought to call wise, or in possession of wisdom, and which are not, however learned they might be.

[7] How ordinary people can have wisdom, as is shown by plain examples.

Awareness or knowledge that one has of God by true faith alone is sufficient for coming to this wisdom, as said above, by loving God, serving, and honoring him. And it seems to me that Aristotle asserted this idea, that ordinary people can have happiness by believing in that to which philosophers give evidence concerning God and the angels, and by putting their thought and heart into it.[19] From which I conclude that simple Christians who have firm faith in the goodness of God and love him ardently have more true wisdom and a greater claim to be called wise than any scholars who have no love or affection for God and his saints. And the former also are more pleasing to God. But what is more: such scholars displease God and are like salt that has no taste (cf. Mt 5:13); such wise men are fools. A plain example can provide us with a demonstration.

A father has two children, of whom one knows nothing about the secrets of his father, except for the fact that this is his father, that he owes him his very existence, and that he ought to do everything to love, serve, and honor him, which he does with all his affection. The other son knows a great deal about the secrets of his father, who has revealed them to him. He knows how to read and to speak in a grand style about them, but he has little or no gentle or loving attachment to his father, or to his service. I ask which of the sons will be more loved by the father, more appreciated, and better rewarded? There is no doubt that it will be the first son. Moreover, he will be given access to the secrets of his father and to all his inheritance, while the second son will be condemned for his ingratitude, lack of devotion, and maliciousness.

[8] What are the works by which one comes to know God more perfectly?

I have clearly shown, I think, that it is neither wasteful nor inappropriate to speak to simple people about the contemplative life in order to bring them to love God and to savor him, in having the taste of holy and sweet affections, as through hope, good fear, ardent desire, as well as a sense of sorrow and sadness if one has angered him by sin, and similarly with other affections. I have shown that learning or knowledge is not necessary. What is required is a deep-rooted faith or belief in God, his power, wisdom, or goodness, and in his commandments, in the fundamental mysteries of our redemption, and in paradise and hell.

It is by no means a small matter to be able to acquire this wisdom of which I speak. For the excellent doctor, William, who was bishop of Auxerre, says that among all the works of God there is none that shows and brings us to know God and his goodness more than does this operation, through which one receives a sense of delight or spiritual enjoyment, felt in the soul when God visits it secretly, after one has humbled oneself before his majesty.[20] And if this happens, then an ordinary person, when he or she receives some of the benefits mentioned here in his soul, will know God better than any scholar or philosopher will be able to do through reasoning based on God's external actions. To this observation one can add the words of Jesus Christ, who thanked his Father for having revealed the great mysteries to infants and hidden them from the worldly wise (Mt 11:25). The examples I gave before, concerning honey and illness, show the truth of this matter.

[9] A brief continuation of what has been said and of what is to be said.

By now I have responded and given reasons why I am writing in French and for simple people, and especially for you, my own sisters, beloved in the carnal bond of family and even more beloved, if it should please God, through spiritual closeness. I want here to go on with my endeavor to show you sketchily something of the path of the contemplative life that applies to you and that will lead you to true wisdom and to your salvation. As Saint Augustine says,[21] many ordinary people without learning have reached salvation by having faith, hope, and charity, while others have been pushed into hell with their learning. Let these, then, be cleverly damned, as Saint Bernard says.[22] We, however, in our simplicity and naïveté will seek salvation.

[10] The love of God is the beginning and the end of the contemplative life.

The root and beginning of contemplative life should be the love of God. This means that for his love one leaves the life of the world and all cares and occupations, and one gives him the whole of one's being. Whoever acts differently is deceiving himself and often does not come to a good end, unless he corrects himself. This is a danger for those who join a religious order or who devote themselves to studies withdrawn from worldly life, not for the love of God, but out of lazy hypocrisy and to avoid working in the world, or in order to make a living, or because of vanity and pride in being considered great scholars or devout persons, or only out of curiosity to know, like most philosophers.

The end, also, of contemplative life must be the love of God. This means that in order to attain his love more and more and always in a better way, one will want to give up every other pursuit or occupation. Understand, when I here or elsewhere say "give up every other occupation," I mean the type of occupation that would significantly hinder contemplation on God. For I know quite well that a less demanding and more moderate involvement is sometimes necessary or very profitable for the contemplative life, in order to avoid idleness and harmful melancholy.[23] What I have said here is confirmed by the Apostle, that the end of the law of God is love and charity (1 Tm 1:5). The greatest master in the law of God, which is called wisdom or theology, is the one who loves best. He also has a more perfect life and a more noble estate, closer to God and worthy of praise, when he loves more. And since the contemplative life in itself is more suitable for loving well, as the school where one best can learn this art of loving, for this reason the contemplative life is so much praised and approved by Holy Scripture and the holy doctors, and first of all by the true God of holy love, Jesus Christ, who declared that Mary had taken the better part (Lk 10:42). And which part? She sat at his feet and listened to his words, and through listening she was inflamed with love for him.

It is true that one can sometimes love God more in the active life than another does in the contemplative life. The former is more perfect, although in a less perfect state. Moreover, they obviously err who believe that the aim of the contemplative life is only to know or to investigate new truths. Its main end is to love God and to enjoy his goodness and sweetness, although this spiritual taste or sensation can be considered a mode of knowledge. As Saint Augustine says, love is knowledge.[24] And this knowledge is of such a kind and so secret that one cannot understand it if one does not perceive it, for through doctrine or teaching, no one can be shown this knowledge. As people say when they are in great pain: no one knows what he does not feel.

[11] That worldly love is the first to be removed.

Whoever wants to begin knowing the art of loving well through the contemplative life should strive first of all to remove the foolish and contrary love that I can call by the general term of worldly love. For this love is like a snare that hinders the spiritual wings of the soul from reaching to the heights. It is like a thick mortar that clings to the feet of the soul so that it cannot freely move. Or it is like a chain that keeps the soul tied up and connected to the body so that it cannot get any distance from it, like a bear or a monkey that goes about on a stage and is tied so that it cannot go anywhere else. This love is the leash of the monkey by which the enemy always keeps hold of the soul. It cannot get far without the leash becoming tight on it. This love is also like the cage of a bird, or similarly with other images. This love is the evil queen who founds the city of confusion for our enemy from hell in the human creature, for she makes us love ourselves so much that we despise God. This love is the bad earth, sterile and cursed by God, from which no good fruit can come. It is the carrion that keeps the raven from coming back to Noah's ark (cf. Gn 8:6), meaning the soul to its lodging in paradise. Or this love is the madwoman who makes so much noise and cries out and clatters about so terribly when she raves ceaselessly in the house that the soul has to leave its lodging. The Holy Spirit, who should be the very owner of the place, cannot remain there and departs.

[12] The suffering involved in removing this worldly love.
Since worldly love is such as I have told, and good love cannot dwell with it, it is necessary to part from it. One must break with it, destroy its city, and throw it out of its house. But, unfortunately, this love is much stronger than many believe, and how hard it is to get rid of is much better understood by those who try than by those who do not care and make no effort. So it is with the bird who does not realize that it is trapped until it tries to get away.

This comparison helps explain the complaint of those who have recently found the desire to love God, for they feel more pain and suffering than they did before. This is also because the Enemy tries harder to keep them, as does the cat with a mouse when the latter wants to get too far away,[25] or the judge when prisoners break prison, for then he sends police to get them back, while before there was no need for police to pursue them.

Thus it is necessary that the true God of love, our Savior Jesus Christ, attracts to himself the soul who is to be his sweetheart, and to whom he wants to teach the art of good love. And he draws us in various ways, sometimes by inspiration and secret inner movements without any intermediary, sometimes through angels, often by way of other people who provide good teaching and instruction. Sometimes this process takes place through great gifts and blessings, or by adversity and tribulation, whether in illness, poverty, or war.

[13] Plain example about how one can leave behind worldly love.
The holy soul of the Song of Songs, feeling within herself the pain and harsh impediment of this worldly love, and wishing to hasten to God, her friend, pleads with him: "Draw me to you and we

will hasten to your anointing oils" (cf. Sg 1:3–4), meaning your sweetness. And thus God often acts toward his servants, for he sends them a sweetness, an odor, a taste, a sober joy, a brilliance, a peace, an opening of their mind, a sense of bliss, a soundless sound.[26] Briefly, there is an attraction, a process, and a movement that one is unable to describe, but which one does experience. Then the soul is freed from this bond of worldly love, and there is nothing that holds it back, not riches, nor carnal delights, nor enjoyment in drinking, in eating, in playing. Such a process is a source of amazement for worldly people, who are filled with foolish love. They mock and ridicule whatever this holy soul does, which is so drawn by God, for they see it leaving behind everything that they love and consider to be very good. But, in God's name, they do not know the condition of this soul and what it feels within itself.

We can take an example from nature. We see that among a hundred dogs there are four hunting dogs. These four smell a stag, which none of the dogs can see. Immediately these four dogs who have the scent of the stag will follow its track. Nothing at all will be able to keep them back, neither hedges, nor bushes, streams, rocks, nor food that they might see on their path. The other dogs who have not gotten the scent, or are mongrels without instincts, and perhaps busy devouring carrion, will not run after the stag. Or they might do so only for a moment, because they see the other four dogs running, but they will quickly give up the chase, as if they wonder why those four are tiring themselves out for nothing. The rest will not even leave their carrion.[27] Compare with these four dogs the people who have the good scent of God and of the goodness and the glory of the heavens, while worldly people who sense nothing at all are like the other dogs.

[14] How reading and listening to the lives of the saints is profitable.

Also the Holy Scriptures and examples that we read, hear, or think about concerning good persons often chase away worldly love. There is no need here to provide examples, for these are without number. Each day a person who dedicates himself to the good and thinks of salvation can have such an experience. It often happens that a person comes to hear a sermon or to read a book; he will be sad or indifferent or subject to temptation. Suddenly, in an instant, among the words that the person hears or reads or considers, he or she will find relief and a holy warmth and will feel liberated from temptation.

I know someone who, because he considers himself impervious to feeling devotion, starts reading some good teaching or the life of some saint.[28] Then this person quite easily will feel a sweetness,[29] more quickly than if he tried to think directly of God's goodness. This is not surprising, as Saint Gregory shows in his example,[30] for, while we cannot look at the sun in its round shape and in its perfect brightness, we can see it on the mountains on which it shines. Similarly, we see the light of God and his greatness in the saints on whom he shines. And also the merits of the saints of both sexes, when one reads of their words and when one speaks with them and receives their words, contribute to this devotion.

Thus you see what profit there is in giving oneself over to reading or listening to the words of the saints, even though one might gain nothing from them except for a short time. It is for a good reason that God calls his word the soul's nourishment. Thus it is not surprising that those who distance themselves from his word will perish with spiritual hunger and are thin and dried out in their devotion.[31]

[15] Of the help of angels and of adversity.

Without the help of angels, who could overcome or avoid the deceits and enticements of the enemy? Certainly nobody could. We should therefore show great honor and reverence to our good angel; however hidden the place where we are, we must do nothing impure that could displease the angel. Some people are so good natured, so full of recognition and gratitude toward God, that they serve him in prosperity just as well, or even better, than in adversity. Such people God often nurtures in prosperity; they have paradise in this world and in the next, for they praise and thank God with a good and full heart for all his gifts. It seems to them, and this is true, that whatever good they receive, even a little, is to be considered quite valuable, not because of the gift but because of him from whom it comes, meaning God.

One can think of the good son who in a strange land feels great joy when he receives from his father a gift, which he values highly. And if it happens that God takes away the goods from the people of whom I speak and sends them adversity, they accept it as something that comes from God just as prosperity does. In this way they praise God with a gentle heart at all times. Such was Job, according to his story, and so have been many others.

Others are of a harsher temperament, like the ass that needs goading. Such persons will better come to God through tribulation. God brings them to himself as the mother does the child who leaves her: she arranges that someone beats the child, and when it comes back crying to its mother, she receives it in her arms and warns the child that it is not to go away, for elsewhere it will come to harm.[32]

Truly, too few people turn so deeply and so humbly to God unless they are in need or feel deserted, or expect no help apart from God. This is especially the case when the pain they feel for the time being is not bad enough to prevent their minds from turning to the thought of God and of themselves. Thus a holy man responded well to a wealthy sick person who asked him to pray for him. The holy man asked when the rich man had more devotion and acted better, whether in illness or in health. The rich man answered that he was more devout when ill. So the holy man said, "I pray God that he will keep you in the state in which you are better."[33] And although one desires that tribulations should cease, the pain that one now feels, as the Apostle says (2 Cor 4:17), nevertheless brings forth an undeniable good. We see it in children at school, how they profit from being beaten, even though this treatment for the time being is harsh on them. There is nothing, in brief, that radically uproots worldly love from the soil of the soul as does tribulation that is well received and kept within limits. And what is more, unless through a miracle or a special gift, one cannot get rid of one's carnality without tribulation, whether exterior or through voluntary penitence and mortification.

[16] Here one begins to speak of the stairway of contemplation and of its three parts, which are humble penitence, secrecy of place in silence, and strong perseverance, as Bernard in his Sermons on the Song of Songs *presents them.*[34]

To come to the fruit of the contemplative life and to its height, one should have a stairway with three main parts. These can be called humble penitence, secrecy of place and silence, and strong perseverance. Within these sections there are several steps by which one climbs from one position to the other, from one virtue to the other, until one has reached the top of the tree or of the mountain of contemplation. Humble penitence begins, secrecy of place and silence provide the middle area, and strong perseverance comes at the end.

And before I begin to consider these three stages, in order better to understand my conception, I would like to make use of some common and easily understood images in order to show what is best to do, before we gain the perfect love of God. For it is fitting for us to climb from the imperfect to the perfect through a middle stage. One does not perfectly attain virtues all of a sudden; one acquires them as in nature, in which the perfect emerges from the imperfect. Fire begins with smoke, and then becomes flame together with smoke, and finally becomes pure flame, clear and bright in the coals. A seed sown onto the earth at first is dissolved and germinates, then lifts itself out of the earth and grows until it reaches maturity. A plant that is in bad soil is first uprooted and then replanted. It seems to be dead, but then comes to life again and will take on its full size. Thus one can see almost everything in such images.

Similarly, the person who wants to live in the contemplative life does not have perfection at the start. She must first get rid of the smoke, which is frustration with one's life, a smoke that makes her weep and troubles her, providing hardly any consolation. Then the flame of love will appear together with the smoke, and finally the fire will be pure and devoid of smoke. In the first stage the person will mortify her past carnal life. In the second she will germinate and grow out of the earth. In the third she will bear a perfect fruit. And so I say that like a plant this person will be transplanted from the bad earth of a worldly life, which will cause great pain and travail. In being replanted the person will still to some extent suffer grief, but when she finally has put down her roots, then she will become perfect and bear fruit.

These three states are well described by him who says that in the first, one languishes with love; in the second, one dies of love; and in the third one lives of love, as I will show at a later point.[35]

[17] How one should begin by working in the active life.

Humble penance is the first part, which belongs to the condition of beginners and the imperfect. Through it one mortifies worldly love in oneself, with its evil desires, movements, and habits. Humble penance chastises the flesh so that it is subject to the soul and should not rebel. It achieves its goal by fasting, lack of sleep, abstinence, afflictions, tears and sighs, and through manual labor according to its estate. If someone wants to reach perfect contemplative life before performing such penance and hard work, he is fooling himself and will be like the person who wants to get up onto a high mountain in a single leap. Gregory and the other saints say in this matter that the active life, which resides in affliction and corporal exertion, should be grasped before the contemplative one, for the active life provides a path and a disposition toward the contemplative.[36] Here we have the image of Jacob, who served [Laban] for Rachel, representing the contemplative life. First, however, he was given her sister, Leah, who stands for the active life (Gn 29:16–30).

Thus you can see that young people who are still full of carnal and other temptations, as well as great sinners who for a long time have lived a bad life, cannot suddenly give themselves over to the perfection of contemplation in its entirety. Why? Because when they would believe they are thinking of God and are pouring forth pure prayer in secret and in leisure, they would instead soon be thinking a lot more about their own bad inclinations and would become worse. And this is what Seneca means when he says that a person does not remain alone for a long time.[37] All the saints and philosophers for this reason reproach idleness. Nevertheless,

Seneca himself, and the saints also, often praise solitude and leisure[38] in the service of God, as holy hermits and other religious have shown. But this apparent contradiction needs to be understood according to diversity of persons and habits, as I show in dealing with the second stage.

[18] How the singular grace given to some cannot be followed by all.
   Through special grace some persons in youth have been sent into solitude or have remained alone, as Saint Benedict.[39] But in his *Rule* he advises, as do other hermits and doctors, against those who are so bold as to undertake such a practice.[40] The special grace given to one person does not apply for everyone. Those who have ventured to seek solitude and leisure without working and without having gotten well accustomed to community life have made a terrible mistake. They have tried to fly before their wings had grown and to fight against the Enemy before they had overcome other and lesser adversaries: the world and the flesh. So I do not expect those in our days who behave like hermits will benefit from so doing, nor will some of the women who retire into reclusion.[41]
   You see then, my beloved sisters, how much you needed up to now to dedicate yourself to hard work. Perhaps some of you still have this need, before you can isolate yourselves in secret and give yourselves wholly to the thought of God in the manner of hermits or recluses. For the way of hermitage or reclusion is found not only in the woods and deserted places, but anywhere that one can pursue it in escaping from the confusion of the world and all its cares and occupations. This is the reason why we see that in well-organized religious orders, the novices and newcomers are weighed down with a great burden of service in learning and laboring, getting little sleep, fasting, and singing, in order to keep them from thinking on their own about anything else. But those who are senior, are well tried in their penances, and have overcome evil temptations of the flesh, have more room in themselves for being alone and at leisure.
   In this respect it can happen that some persons are of such a dis-

position and have such difficulty in overcoming or taming themselves that they will never be fit to reach the perfection of contemplation. They will need always to be occupied and at work in the active life. I know many of this kind, whether clerics or not, while, on the contrary, some others have already reached the stage when active life becomes a great burden and an overwhelming impediment to contemplation. It happens that a person is so well disposed by temperament or through a special grace, that he will profit more from spending one day in giving himself wholly to contemplation than another will gain from offering a whole year.

I do not mean, nevertheless, that a person should give herself so much to one way of life that she should not occupy herself with the other, more or less according to the circumstances and the profit that one gains. There is no person so given over to the active life that she ought never to think about God and conscience or confession and repentance, just as there is no contemplative person who has no need for any labor. Thus in one person it is always necessary that Martha be with Mary, and Mary with Martha (cf. Lk 10:39–42), and to a greater or a lesser degree, as we have shown. But one attaches a person's name to a way of life according to the one to which someone most often dedicates herself.

[19] In what consists the perfection of the contemplative life, in comparison to worldly love.

It is appropriate, before I go on to other matters, to explain in what lies the perfection of the contemplative life. We have already said that the love of God is the end of contemplative life, but one might say that this love is the universal end of all activity. In the last resort, it is for the love of God that one should regulate all one's actions. For this reason I shall give some of the requirements for a perfect contemplative life, but not fully, as if I were describing what I know well. I shall speak of it as a blind person does of colors, in repeating what the saints describe in their writings. Also I will talk of what little I may have sensed for a long time and have sought with God's help. The rest I shall leave to those who have greater strength or expertise in this matter.

In order to make it easier to understand how perfect contemplative life comes through the love of God, I will show the process through its opposite, which is worldly love. For we know all too well this love; it is more familiar to us than divine love.

Let us consider what worldly love does in the person who is deeply caught up in it, as with the love of money, the love of rank or honors, or the love of base carnality. It is clear that a person languishes from it first out of a desire to have that which she foolishly loves. Then a person invests in this pursuit all her thought, her desire, and understanding, so that there is no other thing about which she can think, insofar as she forgets and loses all sense of shame. There is nothing that can hold her back, no task, no form of travail or danger, not even death, nor the counsel of friends, nor the fear of God or of his judgments. Whether she sleeps or dreams or is awake, this person cares to talk or hear of nothing else, to the point that she loses her grasp on reason and becomes like someone who is mad or drunk or out of her senses. There is nothing she will hesitate or refuse to do in order to get that object with which worldly love inflames and wounds her. She forgets all about virtues and the future life, so much so that if she happens to hear talk of hell, paradise, or death, all this seems to her a dream or fable. She will not dwell on such spiritual thoughts, for worldly love will soon lead her astray.

[20] What love of God the contemplative person possesses.

Let us now take the example of a person who would have such love of God that it makes her despise the world, just as worldly love causes God to be forgotten. This love would be so powerful, so intense, and so deeply rooted in this person's heart that she would be unable and unwilling to think of anything else and would take no notice of criticism, of abuse, of persecution, or even of death itself, because of this love. Everything that this person sees or hears of this world would look like a dream, a fable, a nonentity when compared with God and his glory. In brief, such a person would be considered crazy or intoxicated, because she would care as little, or even less, for this world, as others for God and paradise. I declare that this would be the perfect love toward which we must strive through contemplative life.

In this state the person is said to be dead to the world, for she feels no attachment to any part of the world and is united to God. She is asleep to the vanities of this world and awake to everlasting goods. All the senses of her body are, as it were, closed off and slumbering and darkened from all that is done by worldly persons. She is open only to the joys of the saints. This is why the holy doctors say in figurative language that when Moses wanted to speak to God, he entered into a dark cloud (cf. Ex 19:9), signifying that whoever wants to have in his or her contemplation this love of which I speak must enter into this dark cloud, in order to forget and not see or perceive other worldly things.

I intend in what follows to demonstrate how one can reach this state, for it is the end of the perfection of the contemplative life.[42] He who comes there has climbed onto the mountain where God transfigured himself in front of the three apostles (Mt 17:2). He speaks to God, as did Moses when he received the Law; he is ravished in his spirit or above his spirit; he dwells in heaven; he lives from love; he burns happily and peacefully without the darkness of smoke. But, alas, how very few people receive this grace and how little it lasts while one lives in this present exile!

[21] The second part of contemplation and the harsh assault that is involved.

We come now to the second and third parts, which bring us to the height of contemplation of which we have spoken. We assume that the devout person has become accustomed to the active life and through humble penance will have subjected her body, at least to a large degree, and worldly love no longer pleases her, however strongly it still tries to torment her. This person then will be in a state of listlessness,[43] for while she will no longer desire to take the pleasures she could have in the world, nevertheless, she will have none of the spiritual enjoyment for which she yearns. Then this person will suffer harsh assaults, often very painful, which she will have the utmost difficulty in overcoming, and will receive little or no comfort. This stage is represented by the dark and harmful smoke with no fire. It is also like the digging up of a plant that is to be transplanted elsewhere, in which great violence is done to it. Or it is like the death and decay of a seed when it is sown, for so dies the first and carnal life in order to give way to a spiritual one.

Alas, how hard it is to break through! How many will try and will soon give up and resume their previous habits! Some will often fall and rise again. Frequently they flee and come back, often despairing of reaching their goal and then finding hope again. They will often declare that it is enough for them to live as others do without trying to reach higher; then they will take heart again and blame their laziness and lack of courage.

There takes place in such persons a harsh battle and a great division. Who are the adversaries? The carnal will against the spiritual one, worldly love against divine love. But the love of God is still quite small and weak, and the love of the world remains strong and powerful. It refuses to abandon the lodging that it has had in a person since infancy. And what makes matters worse, one sees such love and senses how sweet it is to keep and bitter to lose, while divine love, which is not visible at all, is felt as hard to gain and sweet to lose.

You can see how harsh this prison is. But in God's name, there is nothing that free and good will cannot conquer and overcome through hard work and the hope of possessing something better in the time to come.[44] This hope is in accord with the promises and assertions given by Holy Scripture, and also by persons who have gotten past this point, having experienced first evil and then good, and who are therefore quite trustworthy.

[22] In what estate is the contemplative person in the second part?

After this battle and this state of listlessness, a person begins to feel better, for it is no longer so hard or so difficult as it previously was to sustain the absence of worldly love. Nevertheless, the person does not yet receive great pleasure in the divine love she seeks; one is now, as it were, between two states, neither wholly dead to the world, nor wholly alive in God. And here one can be said to be dying with love, for the person does not feel, as before, the pains of the interior illness she experienced in putting to death her carnal life. But at the same time she is not yet aroused or sufficiently revived for receiving the comfort of spiritual love.

In this state the person can climb to the second part of the stairway of contemplation, which I call the secret place or silence. For even though a person previously could sometimes seek out a secret and solitary place in order to pray to God and think of her salvation, still she was by no means certain of being able to dedicate herself wholly and often to this pursuit, because of the reasons I gave above. But now she can more boldly commit herself to being alone and strain to reach the perfection of contemplative life through dedicating herself so much to divine love that she will forget herself and others. Then the inner face of her soul will turn to spiritual matters and will turn away from material ones, except when these lead to loving and understanding spiritual matters.

In this stage she must see and vividly sense what the wise man said, "All is vanity" (Eccl 1:2), and find no rest, no comfort outside of the ultimate good of her rightful end and bliss, which is God. In him she must constantly and ceaselessly be moved by the attraction and the weight of love, until she reaches it, just as the rock that is outside its natural resting place tries to reach the earth, or fire reaches for the heights, until it gets there.

[23] Of two manners of silence and solitude.

According to different estates or conditions one can find the secret place, in order to be in peace and silence. It is true that the main hiding place and silence should be within the soul rather than outside of it. This means that the soul casts out of itself and its dwelling place every worldly care, every vain or harmful thought, which would keep it from getting to where she strains to reach. And it happens that although a person is often physically alone and apart from others, yet she will have to endure a very harmful and damnable companion in the guise of herself, with her fantasies, thoughts, and bouts of melancholy. Such phantasms will make terrific noise and chatter on at length. At one moment they will put one image and then another before a person; now they bring her to the kitchen, now to the market; then they will tell her about filthy carnal pleasures and show her various attractions, songs, and such vanities that draw one to evil and to sin. Saint Jerome humbly confesses that when he was in the desert without any companions except for wild beasts and scorpions, he imagined he was at dances accompanied by the women of Rome.[45]

Sometimes such fantasies will cause the soul of the lonely person to get furious with someone and scold him as if he were present and vilify him. Then the soul will count money and do business and make great profit. Sometimes, through wishful thinking, it will cross the sea and the land, fly, and reach the highest estate. Thus I have briefly touched on follies that are without number. In this case, the soul is neither in secret nor in solitude, even though it is superficially alone.

Certainly also the devout soul is not alone when it is in contemplation, for it is never less alone than when it is alone. But the difference is that this one has very good, profitable, and pleasant company, namely, with God and his saints, through its holy desire and devout prayer, while the other soul has very bad and harmful company, or at least is associated with those who do not benefit it at all.

[24] Of the exterior hiding place.

It is true that to gain within oneself the secrecy and the silence of the soul, it is profitable to seek secrecy and silence outside of oneself,[46] at least for beginners and for those who are not used to knowing how to retreat into themselves in the presence of others. This form of withdrawal, which is very difficult and requires great perfection, can only be acquired through a long and patient process of habituation.

Some prefer the secret places of the woods or forests or deserts. For others, such places in the fields are sufficient. For yet others, the hidden parts of churches or of their own dwelling places are best, when they arrange themselves so that they do not see anyone and no one sees them, or so that there is no one else present and they can live like hermits.[47] Arsenius, when he went to the church, put himself behind a pillar so that no one could see him and he could not see anyone.[48]

For some people, any sound whatsoever is harmful, whether of a person or of a bird, of song or of speech. But for others, hearing church chant often helps them to concentrate on what they want to think about. Saint Augustine confesses about himself that, soon after his conversion, when he heard the psalms or hymns being sung in church, he would weep, and the truth would penetrate into his heart, and he would experience a great good.[49]

Amid such differences, one cannot give a general rule as to which place is the best for seeking one's hidden life: each person should act according to the grace God has given her and also according to her estate, so that she can live and function among those with whom she must live without being seen as eccentric, vain, or hypocritical. For the person may be of such an estate or way of life that spending a long time in church will make her late for other duties. In brief, the easiest thing to do is to make a habit of being in one's lodgings, in one's room if one has one's own, or somewhere else within.[50] There one will learn to take pleasure, as I learned from a woman[51] who because of illness was forced for a long time to keep to one room. Once in speaking to me, she said, "I don't know what I will do when I lose this little room, for there is no other place where I can concentrate on my thoughts about God and myself."[52]

One must not always wait for the secrecy of solitude or for a definite place; wherever one is, in the fields, in town, even in the bath, as Saint John Chrysostom said, one can try to return to oneself and to withdraw from the world.[53] Often diversity and change of place or places are profitable for the enjoyment and self-renewal that one gains from them. Also the time of night is more fitting, for it has more silence, is more peaceful and reclusive, and lacks the temptations of the empty glory of the world.

[25] How one can prepare one's body when one wishes to contemplate, and the hindrances that some people experience.

The devout doctor William of Auvergne, formerly bishop of Paris, teaches us that the manner of bodily posture contributes to our having clarity of thought.[54] A person should prepare herself in the manner that will serve her best, whether kneeling, standing, sitting, bowing, or leaning up against something, or perhaps lying down. I refer to the situation when a person is alone and can act in such a way without eccentricity, for in church one should follow the others.[55]

This doctor also says that standing up and bending over on the left arm is a position that is useful and valuable. I think that he himself tried it out in such a way. I know someone else for whom there is no better posture of the body than to sit and to bend over on one's back, almost as if one were lying down, and with one's face toward heaven or toward the ground. For some other people, it is best to walk back and forth, which may sometimes prove relaxing. But doing so often and continually is, in my opinion, harmful for the soul's quietness, which it is essential to find in order to attain the condition of which we speak. It is not for nothing that Aristotle says that in sitting and resting the soul is made wise.[56]

Some people have a spirit that is so frivolous and fickle, so inclined to the deeds of the world, that it would be a minor form of hell for them to be without company or to be in a fixed place for even a short while. Such people will derive little or no profit from contemplative life; it is better for them to leave it and to give themselves over to the active life, unless by force of habit they can overcome their situation. There is nothing that hard work and diligent effort cannot overcome.[57]

There are some who will be so terribly tempted by blasphemy and other vices that it will be very hard for them to behave. They sometimes will be driven out of their minds or leave the faith; or else they become melancholy, depressive, angry, and displeased with everything. They learn through experience that it is much better for them to be in company and to do physical work, for then they will not brood. Such people too are no good in the contemplative life, unless by special grace, or at least such a life is for them too hard and very dangerous.

There are yet others who by nature or by grace, or through both together, love solitude, are concerned with their salvation, and have the desire to get to know God and spiritual things and to love them. Their carnal impulses are not strong enough not to be overcome. Such persons are suited for giving themselves to contemplative life, especially when they are gentle of heart and tender in devotion. It is difficult for a hard heart ever to come to the good.

It can happen that a person will come gradually from the active life all the way to the excellence of the contemplative life, but then will return to the active life. This reversion can take place in two ways, either through neglect and hypocrisy or else through an abundance of virtues. In the latter case the person will make use of one way of life without impeding the other, either at her own pleasure or in accord with her station in life. This is the estate prelates should have: they must live in a contemplative life that is so complete and deep-rooted that they can descend to the active life without wholly leaving the contemplative one. Such is the way of the angels, who guard us below without leaving the vision of God above (cf. Mt 18:10).

[26] Here begins a disputation on how the contemplative life is profitable, and first of all to one's self.

There are some people (and would to God that they acted without arrogance or stupidity) who are amazed that a person can dedicate herself to the contemplative life. They provide three reasons, among others, for their objection. The first is that such a person does good only to herself; the second that, in their opinion, such a person wants to know too much and to reach too high; the third, that one sees many such persons who get disappointed and become mad or melancholy. To these three reasons, if they deserve the name, I will reply briefly and simply, for the holy doctors have dealt with this subject in a comprehensive and subtle manner.

These doctors reply to the first objection that a person in the contemplative life benefits more fully and divinely and pleases

God more than in the active life. This is sufficient, for there is nothing after God that I should love so much as myself, not even all the rest of the world. Thus I should prefer to please God and keep to the life where I most please him rather than gain less merit or perhaps damn myself by wanting to save someone else. I mean this with other things being equal and a person being free to choose one way of life or the other. This is not true of those who have public offices, whether positions in the church or else-where, which compel them to concern themselves with active life; no more than of married women who have children and a household to supervise or the duty to serve their parents. For if such persons wanted to devote themselves entirely to contempla-tive life, they would incur damnation because they have the duty of attending to others. To such people, as we have already seen, it would be a bad temptation always to revert to contemplation and thereby to abandon their responsibilities. Thus they would be of no use or even harmful to their dependents and to the common good. One can rightly complain and even make fun of such people and their contemplative activity. But it is different for those who are not obliged by any office to serve others, or who do not neglect their other duties.

[27] Of the benefit that the contemplative person provides for others.
I shall show in what follows that the contemplative person greatly benefits others. First of all, she provides good example in her way of life and preaches by acts and deeds that God is to be loved above all, and that everything else is vanity and does not matter. This is by no means an unimportant lesson. It is all the more convincing as deeds are more genuine than words.

Second, contemplatives benefit all others because of their devout prayers. It often happens that because of their merit God will act through the agency of worldly persons, even evil ones, and provide a great good, such as peace between kingdoms. For it is true that we can do nothing without the special grace of God. This grace is obtained more by good contemplatives than by active persons. Contemplatives are like the body's eyes, which enlighten and direct all the deeds done by the other members of the body. And if the eyes do not work as the feet or the hands, then must one say that they serve nothing besides themselves? By no means. Such contemplatives are chosen to relay to God and, as it were, to inspire all the activities of those who are not elevated enough in spiritual matters that they know how or are able always to arrange everything in their lives for God.

I am not saying, however, that in case of necessity the person should not leave her contemplation in order to serve the need of another. The best would be if one could maintain both ways of life completely, as I think Saint Gregory, Saint Bernard, and others have done. Whoever has seen what excellence there is in the soul and spiritual goods in comparison with the body and corporal goods, such a person understands that the devout prayer of a contemplative profits the whole church more than do the thousands who live an active life in order to secure bodily needs.

Such a contemplative provides greater benefit than those who are busy in the world, not in doing good for others, but for themselves, and often at other people's expense. So I declare that if a person feels himself moved by the Holy Spirit to take on this contemplative life and sees himself so inclined, he can renounce the active life without any reproach and even deserve great credit and praise. This is the case, unless one fails to fulfill one's obligations to obey a superior because of holding public office or failing to help others in case of urgent necessity, when people would probably perish for want of assistance.

[28] A simple example shows that aiming at contemplative life is not being presumptuous.

As for the second objection mentioned above [see §26], which is that the person who aims at the end of contemplation in loving God totally with all her heart tries to reach too high and is presumptuous: one should not say such a thing, for if such a person is capable of doing so and has the grace for it, then she would be failing herself, I think, in not making use of God's gift. This is especially true of clerics and religious, whose lives are completely ordered for this end. They must give themselves over to contemplation more than to anything else. Scholars also, especially theologians, should do so. Otherwise their knowledge will not help but puff them up (cf. 1 Cor 8:1) and make them vain, empty, and arrogant.

An example can prove it. At the king's court there is a servant in his kitchen whom the king will grace by wanting to make him his chamberlain. The king judges that the servant is fit for this office and that is his pleasure. There is no doubt that if the said servant refuses this post and, because of his laziness or cowardice or gluttony says that he wants always to remain in the kitchen in a position of low station, then he is to blame. Similarly, the person who could serve God in an exalted estate is culpable if she always wants to busy herself with something lower. Her decision does not indicate humility but weakness of heart and cowardice. I am not saying, however, that those who seek through contemplation to find out too much are devoid of fault, for they are in great need of humility, the guardian and nurse of charity.

[29] On the excellence of contemplatives over others.

As for the third reason for being suspicious of the contemplative person, which is that one sees some of them being disappointed and becoming disturbed and depressed, I say that in the active life there are also many who are unhappy, for they lack the judgment necessary to bring their activities to a good end. Also, everyone does not have the gift of grace to live in contemplation, for the reasons that I previously gave [§3]. As the Apostle says, each has his own gift from God. If in a body all its members were eyes, then where would the hands be? (cf. 1 Cor 12:17–21). Actually, worldly persons easily judge contemplatives to be deranged and depressed because they do not act as the worldly do, for contemplatives look down on the world and remove from themselves all avarice, all display, all anger, envy, and vanity. These concerns ceaselessly occupy worldly persons, while contemplatives live in great repose and peace of mind, a blessing that is beyond comparison to anything else. And instead of the occupations that worldly persons have on the earth, in their narrow and petty concerns, contemplatives concern themselves with something much larger and greater than the whole world, that is, with God. Those who have experience know what I mean.

It is certain that the life of the rational creature concentrates more on the work of understanding and reason than on anything else. It is concerned with rational thought and voluntary love. Therefore they who are truly alive are only those who nourish themselves in contemplation with such food and drink, and not the people who hardly elevate their soul and their lives more than animals do. These drink and eat, laugh, play, exercise their bodies. So do animals. They can say that they serve others through their labor, but so do donkeys and horses, and sometimes even more! Yet it is well done when one cannot do better and when one acts honestly and for a good end in serving God and helping others.

I confess also that people given to contemplation are not as wise and prudent in terms of worldly activities as active people are. This is because contemplatives do not invest their intelligence or concentration in such matters; therefore they are judged to be stupid and ignorant, but they do not care, for their vocation, as the Apostle says, and their aim is to be fools in order to become wise (cf. 1 Cor 3:19; 2 Cor 11:19).

[30] On the necessity of grace.

I return to where I was, to the second segment of the stairway leading to the height of contemplation, which I have called the secret place and silence. I have explained something about the duality of secret place and silence, one within the soul, the other outside of it. The place within the soul is the aim of contemplation, and it benefits from seeking silence and solitude outside in the manner spoken of above.

My lord,[58] Saint Bernard, says that the soul's groom, Jesus Christ, is a shy friend who does not willingly come to his friend in the midst of a great multitude but seeks to be alone with her.[59] So it is necessary that the soul should reject all occupations, within and without, to recognize him so that it can receive him alone. Also, since God is simple and one, one ought to seek him in simplicity and unity of heart. The heart that is split into many parts with worldly cares that are bad and empty cannot be simple and unified.

But alas, to what misery the nobility of the soul has come through sin! In its primal state of innocence, the soul was wholly disposed to think of God, to love him, and to consider spiritual matters, without difficulty or hindrance, but now it is an unbelievably painful and heavy task because of the weight of its corruption. Those who exert themselves know what I mean. And what is it, O true God, that can replace the soul on its height, return it to unity, reduce it to simplicity, deliver it from this stormy sea that now overwhelms it with the thundering breakers of innumerable cares and all sorts of fantasies and imaginations surging ceaselessly and endlessly?

Surely, true God, it is mainly the strength of your grace that appeases the movement of this great sea within us. Your grace lifts up those who lie on the earth in the dust of worldly thoughts, in the filth of disordered pleasures, and allows them to sit above with the princes, meaning with the angels and the saints, and to dwell in heaven.[60] It is true that this gift of grace is offered to those who seek it diligently and fervently and who ready themselves for it.

[31] What is the elevation of the soul, and unity, and simplicity.

It is not to be understood that the soul leaves the body substantially, however much it is caught up in contemplation, at least in most cases. The soul is said to be where its whole heart is, and all its love. As a doctor of the church says: the soul is more real when it loves than when it animates, meaning when it gives life to the body.[61] Concerning this elevation of the soul outside of this world and beyond corporal matters and this delivery of the soul to itself or to the angels or God, where it cannot reach higher, I say that this process takes place by means of powerful and holy meditation, as well as through burning love. This combination of thought and love has so much power that it makes the soul forget or give up all other operations and fantasies. It is as if the soul is in a complete state of rest, or, if such operations do not wholly cease, at least they are unable to weaken, extinguish, or over-come the thinking and the loving of which I have spoken, because of its virtuous power. The soul must wholly concentrate upon and occupy itself with this thought and love and not take anything else into account, nor even look elsewhere, unless by chance, in passing, without stopping there.

Daily experience in lesser matters shows us that such a concentration of the soul's powers can take place. Aristotle says that sometimes a person will be so strongly focused on something that she will not at all see, even though her eyes are open, what is happening in front of her.[62] Often people will speak or act in the person's presence without her noticing anything, and she will continue in her train of thought as if she were asleep. So it sometimes happens that a common saying is applied to such a person: he is thinking of his loves.[63] Students often attain this manner of self-absorption when they want to deal with some subtle matter. Painters do the same, I think, as well as others who deal with intellectual skills that require a powerful imagination.

It is said of a philosopher named Archimedes that he was a great geometrician and made complex machines for warfare and for defending or assaulting cities, until one day the city where he resided was captured.[64] The prince had ordered that no one should ever kill him. Someone by chance found him drawing his models on the ground and asked him who he was. He was so caught up in making his drawings that he did not know what to say except that no one should bother him. Therefore he was killed. You see how powerful was his train of thought, which did not allow him to notice that the city was taken or recognize his enemies.

Another philosopher, called Carneades, often forgot to eat when he was at table. His maidservant had to direct his hand to the food in order to keep him from dying of hunger. Of him Valerius, who tells this story, says that he lived solely in his soul and was covered by a body that he considered to be alien and useless.[65] I have provided these examples in order to show how the soul can rid itself of pointless fantasies and cares in order to rise to something more holy and fitting, to come to unity and simplicity and think and live only in God, who is its place, its end, and its love. This process, however, is much more difficult to accomplish than it is in the case of the simple people of whom I talked before, the more that one must cultivate more spiritual, unfamiliar, and lofty thoughts.

[32] Mention of the book that Master Richard so excellently made on contemplation.

Master Richard of Saint Victor made a book in five parts, in which he treated with great subtlety and profound learning this matter of contemplation.[66] Here he points out six manners or types. Two of them are in the imagination, two in the reason, and two in the intelligence. In accord he places three types of heaven in the soul, so that the soul directs itself in thinking in diverse ways about corporal objects perceived through corporal senses, either through themselves, or through the angels in their estate, or through divinity. He points out especially in the fifth part of this book how contemplation develops and diversifies in three ways: the soul will sometimes enlarge its understanding, sometimes heighten it, sometimes cut it off somehow and forget it.[67]

Richard shows by authorities and examples from Holy Scripture and from nature how these developments take place and how they sometimes come about either through a great sense of wonder or deep devotion or in a rich sense of spiritual enjoyment and comfort. But my intention is to speak in a less subtle way and briefly, so I will give up explaining this doctor's teaching, unless by chance I do so later with some individual points, and also in a way that is easier for you to grasp and more familiar to you.

[33] The third part of contemplation, by a common example.

It is time for me to speak of the third part of the stairway of contemplation, which I have called strong perseverance. For with the grace of God, strong perseverance is that which elevates and places the person in the height of contemplation. It prepares her for a perfect state in which she can be said to be living from love, for then she receives the comfort of divine love without feeling the trials of the world and the flesh. Nothing remains for this person but to serve and love God, to think and to speak of him.

Through this love she flees the foolish pleasures of the world and derives joy from its troubles.

Thus there is nothing here that can harm the person: not prosperity, for the person either flees it or bears it with great humility and much gratitude; nor adversity, for the person desires it as that which leads to God and which cleanses and teaches the soul and makes it like Jesus Christ her friend, who was subject to so much tribulation. She receives it as a sure sign that her friend God loves her when he visits her and deigns to chastise her. In this estate the devout soul burns gently, sweetly, and purely with spiritual fire, like a pure coal that has been set on fire and burns without smoke or noise. Here the soul has taken root again in the good earth and bears fruit. Here the city of worldly love has been destroyed; the city of divine love reigns.

I do not mean, however, that in this mortal life a person will forever remain and never change, without any gift or special privilege, in this state of perfection. On the contrary, I declare that often, until the time of her death, a person will change and pass from one state of being to another. But once the person has reached the perfect state, she will remain there for a longer period and more often than the others, returning there sooner after descending into one of the first two estates.

The first estate is to be compared to the winter, when it is cold and dark; the second to the spring, when there are great variations in the weather, which is now warm, now cold and dark, now temperate. Now the sun will come forth; now it will be covered with clouds. Then it will rain, and then it will become fine again.

The third estate is similar to the warm summer, when there is almost continual light and heat, although sometimes there is rain and dark, and even at times a much more powerful storm and a more drastic change of weather than at any other time of year. Thus sometimes perfect contemplatives suffer more grievous temptations than other people, either to test them, to cleanse them, to keep them humble, or to destroy them, according to the secret judgment of God, for their pride and iniquity. There is the example of Lucifer, who was so attractive, wise, and lofty in contemplation.

One can also compare the first state to the day, as it is in the morning when light is wrapped in shadows and only barely begins to seep through. The second estate is like the day at terce; the third the day at noon. One could continue with such images or examples.

[34] *Explanation by common examples of how strong perseverance is necessary.*[68]

Whoever thinks that without strong perseverance he can get to the summit and height of the mountain of contemplation or have the total warmth of God's ardent love, he is like the person who tries to climb a great mountain but always stops and descends before he gets to its heights, as soon as he meets some difficulty or hindrance. Or he resembles the person wanting to start a fire with green or rotten wood who, when it does not catch quickly, or there is only smoke and then a small flame, or the fire easily goes out, will give up, knock everything over, and throw the logs all over the house. Or he can be compared to the one who cannot wait for the seed to die and the plant to take root, because of the delay or of the difficulties and dangers he perceives. Or this person is like the monkey who wants to eat a green nut, but, tasting how bitter the shell is, throws out the whole thing. Or one can think of lazy knights, who before they take a city to which they have laid siege, get bored and leave. And you see that by being so neglectful, one cannot reach the summit of the mountain, or have a fire, or wheat, or a plant, or the kernel of the nut, nor can one take a city. Thus one cannot attain the perfection of the contemplative life without strong perseverance.

[35] *Further hindrances in reaching the mountain of contemplation.*

Let us pause again for a little at one of the above examples and consider what one does who wishes to come to the summit of a high and steep mountain. He will climb continually without going back to the bottom or, if he stops, he will not resume at the base of the mountain but will start from the place he has reached. Similarly, I say that he who wishes to come to perfect contemplation should not cease or rest, for to rest is to descend or to retreat. Also, one must not always begin over again from the base but from the point already reached.

It is because of this lack of perseverance that so few people come to perfect contemplation. As soon as they have reached a certain height and experience drudgery and pain, they think they can rest and then fall back. There are others who do not know the art of climbing, for they want to leap at once right to the top of the mountain without beginning with the base and the middle. The base of this mountain is the consideration of one's sins and faults.

There are others who bear on their shoulders a great burden, and they know it well but do not get rid of it, thinking they can climb with it. This burden is worldly occupation and the great amount of thought one puts into it. Such a concern greatly weighs down the soul and makes it constantly return to it. There are others who, because of the little flies that bother them, will abandon their purpose, stop, and go down the mountain. These flies are flighty thoughts on which the soul must not dwell but which should be bypassed and, so to speak, driven away with the hand of holy indignation. But some will run after these flies like children do after butterflies.

There are yet others who are frightened as soon as they hear the bark of the dogs of hell. In other words, as soon as they have any ugly temptation, they stop doing anything and give themselves to chasing away such thoughts, while the best way to get rid of them would be to pay no attention to them. There is the example of the pilgrim who will not stop whenever dogs bark on his path but will pass by, and they will fall quiet. The more he would stop in order to defend himself or make them cease, the more they would bark, and the more he would be held up on his way.

There are others who do not always hold their right hand out to the one who must pull them up from above, that is, God. They keep it back; they want to support themselves and trust in their own strength. It is no wonder that they soon tumble down. Therefore, one should continually stretch out his hand for divine grace's help, without trusting in his own powers and without believing that he can come on his own to the place he tries to reach.

There are other people who believe that they already are at the summit while they are still far below, for they stop climbing and let themselves slip down. Others go all the way to the top, but they are too fast in rejoicing and boasting about this achievement, and they show no diligence in remaining where they are. Therefore, they soon tumble down and do not climb back as quickly as they would like; perhaps God will never help them to climb back there because of their pride, their foolishness, and their ingratitude. It is a horrible thought, and a reason for always humbling ourselves, that a person who has been so close to God, who has spoken with him familiarly and has made her nest in heaven like a bird does, should then come down into hell without the hope of returning.

Others, when they see themselves a bit higher on this mountain, make fun of those who are still lower down. Then it is right that God should abandon them and that in falling they should sense how little they can do by themselves. Some others want to climb this mountain mainly out of curiosity and so that they can say, "I was there," or because they want to know too much about the secrets of the heights, or only for their own pleasure, or because of the beautiful view on top, and not in order to please God and serve him more loyally and devoutly, completely and meritoriously. Such people will soon lose the help of God and his grace, and they will be terribly disappointed, for when they think they are on the mountain of God, they are on the mountain of the devil.

Other people want to go faster than it is right to do and want to get ahead of their guide, at a greater speed than the guide wants. You can see how foolish this is. Our guide is God's grace, as has been said, and if anyone cannot or does not bother to wait for a while for the movement of this grace and its help, this will be a reason for his losing it and not recovering it at another time when he might want it. The same is true for those who do not stop to follow the grace of God when it calls them and urges them to climb. They refuse or go elsewhere or indicate by word or deed that God's grace has to wait a bit longer. In God's name grace then departs.

One should therefore always be on guard in order to follow the visitation of God's grace and to proceed according to his movement and his will, neither too soon nor too late. Always in deep humility we should judge ourselves unworthy of remaining

110

at the foot of the mountain, all the more of reaching its summit. In this way, one will be taken up higher, as with a king who wishes to honor his knight. The more the knight humbles himself and says he does not deserve it, the more the king wants to make him sit in a high position and forces him to accept.

Above all, presumption displeases God. He is not pleased with the ways of those who by a direct route and with a spirit of impudence want to come to him as to their equal. One ought always to maintain a healthy sense of shame, trembling, fear, and doubt, with confidence in his goodness. For without this confidence the fear would be too great and would keep us from climbing our mountain, through trembling too much and being more troubled than we should be.

[36] Other hindrances.

We will speak now of yet more hindrances. Some people mortify their bodies too much, so that the soul cannot make use of it. Others are too burdened and heavy, weak and slumbering because of having stayed too long in the hospital or lazaret of carnality, through too much drinking or eating or making vain speech. They are cramped, sluggish, and paralyzed, and they have first to heal themselves at the bottom of the mountain through humble penitence.

There are others who in climbing sometimes feel great spiritual hunger to hear the word of God. Then they want to hear it or read it. Spending too much time on reading, they take more rest than is required at the time, so that they forget to continue the climb they have begun. But, on the other hand, it is true that such rest is often profitable and even is necessary, especially at the start or when one limits oneself but continues still to climb; that is, when one through reading seeks religious devotion more than knowledge.

There are others who resist or fight against the goad that prods them to climb higher; in other words, they are too prone to flee tribulation. There are others who have not yet found the right way, for they have failed to ask it from the wise and to seek good advice. Such people trust in their own capacities and want to be taught by nobody but themselves. Thus they take the wrong path and sometimes make shameful failures of themselves.

Others constantly ask the way and inquire about it through fervent study, so that they can talk and preach about it without having ever trodden on it. They talk about it from hearsay and make no attempt to climb. So it is not surprising if such persons now remain below, for one gets nowhere by speech alone; one must set out on foot in this endeavor. Such persons are like the heralds who exhort and instruct men to combat but not get near the fight. Or they resemble guides who point out the way in order to get alms from pilgrims but do not themselves take the path, not being even able to walk because they are ill and weak.

There are others who, after they have started out on the road by one path, soon jump over to another one, either out of lack of consistency or because they think they can find a route that is easier or more pleasant. Thus they do no climbing and make no progress, like dogs who never get the deer because they now run after one, now another, while they should follow the track of the first one without turning elsewhere. This is what well-trained dogs in fact do.

Other people do not watch out for themselves or for the perils of the road. They boldly go ahead without looking where they step. And so they fall from the heights to the depths. There are others who in climbing look behind themselves or down below, and, as soon as someone from below calls them, they leave everything. The more they remain there, the more they become unable to climb, for the contact with the world,[69] whether through talk or otherwise, hinders and retards them.

The person who gives himself too much over to such concerns or attaches his heart to them without quickly returning to the climb will often fail for a very long time to make progress. One should only delay out of necessity and for a brief moment, or at least see that when the body is down below, one's thoughts should be elsewhere, in the heights. This is difficult, however, for anyone who has not learned to do so and who has not attached to the mountain the spike and ropes of good custom.

There are other people who, as soon as they have climbed up, believe that they will never leave and that they can remain there as if this place were their inheritance. But in returning below, they sense their own weakness and confusion, and they come to see that the grace of God put them there and held them for as long or as short a time as pleased him. Then, being at the top, they learn to think with good humility of those at the bottom. Also, when they are at the base, they have hope of climbing up again and good patience in doing so, for this attitude is even more necessary in spiritual than in corporal adversity. The former brings temptations and harsh afflictions of the mind, which does not feel the comfort to which it is accustomed and which it desires.

There are yet others who in climbing will put themselves out too much with tears and afflictions and will neglect their duties. God treats them graciously by leaving them below for a certain time.

These are the hindrances on the mountain of contemplation. There are still many others that one can reduce to those already mentioned. They are to be met with humble penitence and in a secret place and silence.

[37] Some modes of thinking that can be maintained in contemplation.

In reading or hearing what has been said, one can ask what way of thinking one will find in contemplation, for one does not go there on corporal feet but on spiritual ones, which are the cogitative and affective functions of the soul. Here I answer that one does not always stick to one manner of thought but will react differently according to person, place, time, the grace of God, and the learning or knowledge that one possesses. One person will go in one direction, another in a different one, or the same person will today follow one manner, tomorrow another. I have, however, concluded that it would not be unprofitable to provide some examples about how some persons on various occasions have proceeded. This approach might make it easier to perceive or find the entrance to this path.

I well remember, my beloved sisters, that I once wrote to you on this subject in some of the letters I have sent you.[70] I have there also mentioned several other matters connected with what I write here or have written above and which I do not repeat here.

Master Richard of Saint Victor, in his book that I mentioned before [cf. §32], provides a method that seems to me more relevant and appropriate for well-educated clerics than for ordinary people. It is so general and would require such long explanations that I will pass by it and leave it to scholars.

Saint Augustine in his book *Confessions* provides an instance of contemplative experience when he was with his mother at a window looking out over a garden, a little before her death.[71] I think I will later briefly touch on this episode.[72] Saint Gregory speaks at length of contemplation in his *Moralia* [Book 6], in showing the perils and benefits found there, but I have not found any particular method for entering contemplation and enjoying it, which I seek. Saint Jerome provides one possible approach in what he wrote to the virgin called Eustochium[73]: that she should think about the hour of her death and the reward she then will receive, when our Lady and Jesus Christ with the angels and the virgins will come to meet her, to welcome her, and to sing the song that Mary, the sister of Moses, sang after the sons of Israel had crossed the Red Sea on dry feet: "Let us sing to the Lord, for he has triumphed gloriously" (Ex 15:1).[74]

Saint Jerome also says of himself that after sustaining powerful temptations of the flesh, he kept thumping his breast and shedding tears and asking God's help. Then it seemed to him that he was in the company of angels, for he felt great peace of conscience and joy, which God sent him after his penance and tribulation.[75] All the writers say in agreement that one must think of hell, of paradise, of one's sins, and of the vanity of the world. But I am looking for a more specific method of contemplative thought.

Saint Bernard, in all the sermons he made on the Song of Songs, treats some kind of spiritual marriage between God and the soul. Such a method is pursued in a more recent treatise dealing with the marriage of the soul with divine wisdom. This book is called *The Clock of Wisdom*.[76] It is true that this topic is perhaps too lofty and rather dangerous to deal with at the beginning of one's conversion to the mystical life, for when one believes one is thinking about spiritual marriage, one easily can slide into thoughts about carnal marriage.[77] But I know well that in this book other manners of contemplation are touched upon, as in thinking about a young man who dies and is unwilling or unable to repent,[78] or as in thinking of God and his judgment, or in considering our Lady at the hour of the passion of our Lord.[79] These are good and suitable ways of meditating, and here one can find them.

[38] Of the method Saint Bernard followed at the beginning.

Saint Bernard tells of himself that at the start of his conversion he saw that he needed more good works and merits than he could find in himself. And so he decided that he would do his best to acquire some of the merits of Jesus Christ. Ever since then, he kept thinking diligently about the life of Jesus Christ from his conception until the ascension, and of all the sufferings of Christ. Bernard made, so to speak, a bunch of myrrh, which he constantly placed on his breast in holy memory and in compassion with Christ.[80] By this I conclude that Saint Bernard began his contemplative life and found his way of ascent by thinking about the life of our Lord Jesus Christ. Similarly, we also read of Saint Cecilia, who always bore with her the gospel of our Lord, that is, the memory of his life, and did not cease speaking to him and praying to him.[81] And a more recent doctor, in a book called *The Prick of Love*, deals with this matter and especially with the passion of Jesus Christ.[82] He shows how everything is there to be found, and that it is the gate and the path, and whoever thinks that he can enter into contemplation by another way is deceiving himself, as is confirmed by Jesus Christ, who calls himself the way, the truth, and the life (Jn 14:6). He is the way by which one ought to take the path; the truth that must provide light for the one on the path; the life that ought to nourish, support, and reward him. I would like very much that this book be translated into French, for I consider it most profitable.[83]

There are some who will use no other method than to start reading some book of devotion or of the life of a saint, in order to acquire compunction according to the contents of the work. Such people will always need books. But this method is not sufficient in itself if one does not get used to meditating without a book.

Other people find the way of contemplation through religious services, but because of the effort required in church song, I consider this very difficult, especially at the beginning and if they wish to reach perfect contemplation, unless they already have a strong habit of spiritual isolation.[84]

[39] Another method through the example of mendicity or begging.

I know a person who profited greatly in reducing himself and his thoughts to unity and simplicity by considering that he was a poor, miserable creature who had nothing and who through his own effort could acquire nothing.[85] And so he thought that he would become a beggar and seek alms of spiritual goods from those of the court of paradise, who were rich in them and wonderfully generous and charitable. So he sat under a tree in a garden in a secret place and disposed himself so that he could first concentrate on his thoughts at his own ease and for the greatest length of time. Then he turned to calling without speech on one saint after the other, accordingly as his sense of devotion moved him, in asking for alms from each of them, in showing his need and poverty, in remembering their great grace and generosity, and in asking that they pray to God for his sake, since he was not worthy to present himself before God. It is true that this person met with many hindrances, especially because of other thoughts and fantasies, but he forced himself through strong perseverance to keep in this place and not to go away or move until he sensed in himself what he was seeking and that he was fixed on this prayer and on nothing else.

This state continued for several days, and sometimes it took two or three or four hours before this person had what he was seeking, the union and recollection of his thoughts and affections in a wholeness, as I have said to you. And now it is rare that he does not reach his aim, sooner or later. This person clearly perceived the truth of what Jesus Christ promised, that he opens to the person who perseveres in asking (Mt 7:7).

You can well imagine how great were this man's complaints, sighs, and groans to the saints, first to one, then to another, and especially to those whose day it was, when they let him spend two or three hours before them, at their feet, in continual battle against his thoughts. These would assault him noisily and keep him from ascending or speaking in terms of holy desires to the saints, whose help he did not feel. But in the end the saints did grant his prayers, and this person found that the difficulty he had previously experienced turned to his profit, for he thereby learned to make his request in a manner that was more genuine, wise, and ardent.

The result was that since then, as soon as he started praying, this man was very quickly, almost immediately, brought to unity and simplicity of thought through this behavior, and later through other means that he learned much more easily thanks to the good habit described above. I think this approach began with a very excellent doctor, William, once bishop of Paris, about whom I have read. This bishop declared that the poor, tramps, and prisoners had taught him how to pray to God. And I have seen in one of his books that he compares prayer to a messenger who goes to paradise to ask for help.[86] In this book also, as elsewhere, he provides arguments for Jesus Christ and his saints, and especially for our Lady, why they ought to help their creature who prays to them in pointing out his poverty.[87] He refers to those who come before judges, how devout they are in their prayers because of fear of the peril in which they see themselves.[88] William says that we should do the same before God, and even more so.

[40] *Further on this subject.*

To one who would choose this way of entering into contemplation, it would prove quite safe, easy, and in accord with what was said above, that the first degree of contemplation is humble penance. For here a person asks only for pardon and the grace of doing well in the time to come, and a remedy against the wounds and maladies of various sins. Here the prayers that Anselm made to different saints are profitable, and some of them can be found in French.[89] Also the book of which I just now spoke, called the *Divine Rhetoric*, by William of Paris, is very excellent and useful for that purpose, but I doubt if it exists in French.[90]

I have for a long time wanted to make on this subject a prayer presenting a pauper who goes from house to house asking for bread, or a pilgrim, or a prisoner, or somebody collecting alms not for himself but for charitable institutions.[91] For often a person can better attain a sense of devotion in praying for someone else, rather than for herself, and this act will profit her greatly. Many are obliged to carry out such practices because of their office, as with church persons and mendicants. But I say that everyone ought to pray in this manner both because of God's commandment and because of the goods they have received from others, whether these are nature's benefits from their parents or the fruits of fortune inherited from those who have acquired these for them, whether living or dead.

I once made a prayer to Jesus Christ that begins, "Jesus, true groom of virginity,"[92] and I intend, God willing, to write more on this matter very soon. It is true that all the writings of the world will never serve so much as strong perseverance with God's grace does in bringing one to come to the goal that the contemplative ought to reach. He can follow the example of the person of whom I spoke without naming him,[93] and set out on the task. For one cannot describe or engender affectivity through writing or talking.

[41] Further on this matter.

Whoever is pleased by this image of mendicity, he has a great amount of material of which he can make use. He can make it his practice to recollect himself and turn to God and his saints, for we suffer innumerable griefs, illnesses, and distresses, both in body and in soul, and there are a great many virtues we need to ask for. Also, there are many saints whom we can supplicate, sometimes all together, sometimes individually. And amid all our other needs, the hour of death is the final one, which we must fear most. At this hour we must seek help and, while we live, find friends and defenders who, please God, will come to our rescue at this dreadful time. This hour we must above all place before our eyes in order to keep it fresh in our memory wherever we go and whatever we do. We ought often in our secrecy of contemplation to ask ourselves: now tell me, poor and suffering soul, tell me if right now or in one hour you had to leave your body and appear before the most feared judgment of God, what would you do, what would you say, to whom would you have recourse? If you say to me that you would do such and such a thing, and you would then cry out for forgiveness with all your heart to God and to all the saints, then do so right now, for you do not know how ill you will be and how much time will remain for you to do so.

Here we must concentrate at length and fervently, until we get the feeling that death is approaching. We must also consider that our friends for whom we want to pray are in as great a need as if they lay on the bed of death. We should think how much they require our help, and we should pray as well for them and have as much compassion on them, as if were already happening what will happen and will happen soon. Let us also take pity and have mercy on our own soul, as if we already saw it amid the flames of purgatory; in doing so it helps to consider the pain and grief that one suffers in illness or otherwise, and how it will be if the soul must suffer as much in the next world.

[42] Further on this matter, and of God's three judgments.

In this act of contemplation we can place before our eyes the three judgments of God, which he passes for us: One as a father, in which sweet and pitiful mercy reigns and judges, and this happens in this life. The second judgment he passes as a lord over his servant, and in it a harsh justice reigns, for everything must be paid, and this is in purgatory. The third judgment he passes in hell, where a terrible and very cruel justice reigns for convicted sinners, for God punishes as a judge who cannot be moved to mercy toward evildoers worthy of eternal death.

So this is how we can escape the two final judgments, through appealing and submitting ourselves to the first court of mercy, which only exists in this life. It is good to choose it while it is still possible, and so that in this court we can have so great a number of intercessors for ourselves. We especially have our Lady there, who is queen of the court of mercy and is both our mother and advocate. Similarly, Jesus Christ is our father, brother, advocate, counsellor, mediator, and savior. He is very much a fool who does not submit himself with the prophet who said: "Lord, do not in your wrath accuse me nor in your anger excoriate me; have mercy on me Lord, for I am weak" (Ps 6:2–3).[94]

Here the prophet touches on the three judgments and says: Lord, do not judge me in your wrath: this is in hell. Do not in your anger punish me: this is in purgatory. But according to your mercy have pity on me, for I am frail and ill: this is in this life. What is more, we can require and obtain mitigation of the retribution that we have deserved in this life through the intercession already mentioned, and often even be completely forgiven. Whoever would keep in mind the way out of this prison where we are, which will be at the hour of death, and would think of these three judgments, he would have great joy in being punished in this world by illness, abuse, or poverty. He would easily lose interest in everything that belongs to this world. Whoever would keep thinking that he must die and does not know when, he would often ask himself whether he would dare to die in the state in which he is. If he would not, then he would quickly remove whatever hinders him from doing so.

[43] Further consideration of this topic, and against those who have no perseverance.

There are some people who are very careless or tardy as regards acquiring strong perseverance or the fruit of contemplation, for they will not pray or meditate unless they feel a sense of devotion and have the will and desire to do so. Such people think that otherwise they do not gain anything from the effort. They are like a person freezing with cold, who would refuse to come near the fire unless he was already warm, or like someone dying with hunger but would not want to look for food before he was full. For why does one enter into prayer or contemplation if not in order to be warmed by the fire of divine love or to be filled up with the gifts of God? These people are mistaken in believing that if they give themselves over to prayer and continue in it without being granted a sense of devotion, they will waste their time.

Here I answer that if such people strain to do their duty and fight against their bad thoughts, in great anguish because these thoughts will not depart and leave them in peace, then they gain greater merit than if devotion suddenly came to them, for serving God costs them more and causes them worse suffering. It is true that for anyone who wishes to follow the example of the anonymous person mentioned above [§39], it is necessary to have a great amount of time, without being burdened by other occupations for one's self or anyone else, and to compel one's self to remain a long time in one place, regardless of whether devotion may or may not appear, and to endeavor to attain and maintain this devotion. If she feels exhausted, she will tell herself to wait for another half hour in doing penance and in waiting for the alms of grace. Then when this half hour has passed, she can still bring herself to be there for another. Often in the last half hour she will profit more in terms of contemplation than she did in all the preceding time, and more than someone else will do in ten days or even in a month.

If ever, when leaving, she should find that she has been rejected without receiving the fruit of devotion, then she should humbly return to God in confessing that she is not worthy and that she has deserved harsh punishments rather than such comforts. And she should say: "Lord, your consolations belong to you, and I only deserve confusion, since it is only right that these comforts do not come from your mercy." Thus she will win God and will abandon her hard feelings for his sake. God will not forget her when the time and place come.

Certainly the person should not be too keen on obtaining such consolations in tears and devotion for her own sake, but only so that she thereby better can love God, and more ardently, diligently, and joyfully return to him. If, then, it pleases God that one should serve him for the time being without having such consolations, we must accept it and say, "All-powerful Lord, it is enough for me that you keep for me my lodging and reward in paradise without giving me anything for the time being. I ask only that you not be angry with me, but that I be in your grace and that in everything, your will be done." And whoever does have devotion should be careful to thank God with all one's heart in asking him that he make grow and strengthen what he has planted in the soul, without his giving anything in return.

[44] Image of a mountain containing three stages or dwelling places of faith, of hope, and of charity.

According to the idea of the mountain previously shown, we can form an appropriate image in order to lift ourselves into contemplation, as I know from the person who once did so.[95] I shall touch on the matter only very briefly.

Let us imagine a very dangerous ocean where all kinds of people are sailing hither and thither on various ships in order to reach a certain harbor. While the greater part of the ships perishes in different manners, because of the dangers and storms that are there, there rises up at the edge of the sea a very high rock, on top of which one is in safety. From the rock one can see without danger what is happening on this great sea. On this rock are three levels or dwelling places, the one at the bottom, the other in the middle, the third on top. In the first let us imagine that faith is lodged; in the second hope; and in the third charity.

When the person is at the first level, at the bottom, faith shows to him the awful dangers of the sea for the soul; thereby a great fear is aroused in the person. She sees the terrible judgments of God against sinners, whom he hurls down into the abyss of this sea in eternal damnation beyond hope. And here the devout person in firm faith concentrates on everything that can create in herself a holy fear and terror of the secret judgments of God, such as the fragility, mutability, and shortness of mortal life, the uncertainty of the hour of death, the horror of damnation, the great number of those who damn themselves, her own sins and faults in the past and each day. As also Jesus Christ and all the saints went through affliction and tribulation, so we should be certain that the evil and those who are damned will have still more pain. Therefore each person, no matter who, whether good or evil, ought to expect sooner or later to experience tribulation.

At the second stage or dwelling place, we find hope, which

gives confidence to the devout person, so that she not despair and be lost through too great fear. And here she must consider everything that is liable to give rise to hope in the goodness of God, for this is what he commands us to do. Here we should set before our minds the mercy of all the saints and the good things God has done for us and does without our merits, and especially the great gesture of charitable mercy shown in the passion of Jesus Christ, and the grace that God freely provided for sinners. There the devout soul will recover some courage and will project itself from one dwelling to the other in mingling fear and humility with good hope, for the one without the other is never sufficient.

At the third stage, where charity dwells, the devout soul will consider the greatness of its Lord, and how he makes us love, prize, and praise him, how he governs everything and sustains by his pure goodness all that he has created from nothingness. The soul will think of his many other great gifts, and of the glory that he gives his friends. Saint Augustine taught how to come to know God by lifting oneself in thought above the earth, the heaven, one's soul, and everything created.[96] And then, in a brief and sudden breakthrough, it seems as though the clouds part and the soul attains that which is God, but soon falls back.

But it is not right for you to be too curious here, nor to dwell here for too long. It will be enough for you to know God in paradise. In this world it is enough that you should believe in him and know that he is your creator, maker, and redeemer, and has all those other splendors that our faith teaches you, without your wanting to acquire a clear understanding of his nature. In this I offer you the teaching that Saint Dionysius provides.[97]

Every time that, in your contemplation, you think of God and you know what you are looking at, and it looks somewhat similar to the things here below, then know for sure that you are not seeing God through clear vision. The same is true of the angels, for God is not great in size, nor is he white, nor red, nor clear, nor colored, and neither are angels. It is true that people can recognize and sense something in a manner that cannot be written about or spoken of. Yet, they who know God in this way sense and know what it is they perceive, as in grasping a sweetness, a fullness, a taste, a melody, and such sensations that we cannot adequately describe by anything similar.[98]

We are well aware that love and joy are not objects which are corporal, great or small, white or black, and one could not make someone who has never felt them understand what they are. I do not say that one cannot conceive what God is in his human nature, for he has body and is formed like any other man, but I speak of God in his divine essence.

When the devout soul would have become accustomed to remaining in this crag or mountain through deep meditation and thinking, it would become ever easier for it to return there and to have faith, hope, and charity and to reach no end of beautiful acts of contemplation that it will find there. Here will be its harbor and its safe haven against all the mishaps of the great sea of the present world.

[45] Concerning the three manners of having grace.

There are countless ways, as I previously said, according to which one can adapt oneself and experience contemplation. I pass over them for the time being and leave it to each person according to her understanding and the grace that God gives her. I do not want to limit something that is so vast and abundant, as it were infinite, in keeping it to a brief list of petty images.

But in the end we again say that the grace of God can be especially present to the soul in three manners. The one is by justification, which cannot be felt but which makes the soul pleasing to God. The other manner is by feeling and comfort, as for those who in their contemplation receive and perceive various kinds of consolation and spiritual joys. Sometimes they will feel as if they were melting in some kind of sweetness, and all that they see, consider, or think about seem full of this sweetness. Sometimes they will receive a wondrous certitude, full of humility, according to which they are greatly displeased with themselves and take their sole pleasure in God. For whenever a person is pleased with herself and takes joy in herself and for herself, she can be certain that she does not have true humility. The comfort she enjoys does not come from God, for the true humility that always accompanies good and divine visitations points precisely at the faults by which a person becomes displeasing and is vile and repulsive to herself, even though she will derive much joy from the grace, mercy, and goodness of God.

Another time the soul will sense an expansion of the heart or of the intelligence and will contain in itself more than all the world. The soul will find God to be so excellent and of such infinite majesty that practically all that remains below will seem to be absolutely nothing except insofar as it reveals God's presence.

Sometimes the soul will feel something like a spiritual intoxication, which will move it into making, in a sober manner, spiritual praises, with holy and devout sighs. The soul will not be able to keep its joy to itself and will need to show its feelings outside. And it will sometimes seem that everything is full of God's glory and praise (cf. Ps 150:6).

The third manner of having grace is through union, as Saint Paul, the outstanding contemplative, experienced (cf. 2 Cor 12). But concerning this manner I am not worthy to open my mouth. I will leave it to the great.

ELEVEN RULES[99]

There follows here some advice that I have provided for my five sisters who are living with their father and in accord with his will. And let this matter be understood properly, so that nothing dangerous be detected in this arrangement, in terms of vows or promises.[100]

In the name of God, in order to provide instruction in living together in a more orderly and regular manner, you, good sisters in Jesus Christ, are to respect the rules written below:

First of all, each of you should be dedicated primarily to loving God and to keeping his commandments. Let no regulation or rule be deemed necessary for the salvation of your soul except the true law of Jesus Christ. Accept no other rule, except to the extent that it aids and profits you to this purpose.

Again, none of you is to make any change of estate or promise or vow, nor are you to change your place of abode or alter the goods that you now share in common without any division or appropriation, unless you first are given advice, especially by myself, if I am alive and you are able to ask me. If this is not the case, then I will provide someone available to you.

Again, go to confession each week at least once and receive the body of our Lord each month.

Again, if one of you says a harsh or unpleasant word to the other, then she is to be obliged to ask for forgiveness, or else you will not eat or drink with her until she has done so.[101]

Again, each day read aloud a part of a good book among you in order to strengthen you more and more in your holy endeavor. Consider especially carefully the books that deal with God's commandments, as the *Summa of Vices and Virtues*,[102] and other such treatises.

Again, if anyone by chance speaks to one of you of marriage, tell the others immediately, and let me be informed, so that everything be done in all matters with good counsel.

Again, when you are at work, you can at times say prayers together, especially after eating, in order to remove any evil melancholy and temptation.

Again, do not sleep in the nude without having any article of clothing. What you wear should be sufficiently roomy so that it does not irritate you, or at least you should wear your slip.

Again, you will dress and maintain yourselves without pomp and pride. Without any excess, you are always to maintain sufficient modesty and be as equal as possible in these matters.

Again, you are to say your hours and other prayers at certain regulated times, as at matins, terce, vespers, bedtime, and at midnight, if you can get up for a while.[103] You are to go to mass as often as this can be done, and especially on the feast days that are ordered, for these are days of obligation.[104] The rest of the time you are to work diligently, not so much in order to gain riches as to rid yourselves of idleness, laziness, and indolence, which are the mothers and causes of all evils.[105]

Again you are to obey humbly the one who will be chosen as prioress by the order of your supervisor, and she will keep herself humbly as the least and most servile of you. You will help her in all her actions, and similarly you are to act toward anyone else who has administrative duties.

You are to begin little by little in this way of life, from one virtue to another. Our Lord will give you the grace to persevere in becoming better and better, and thus to reach greater perfection, which the true spouse of virginity and loyal friend of chastity will grant you. Amen.

Sermon on the Feast of
Saint Bernard[1]

"Sustain me with flowers, refresh me with apples, because I am languishing with love" (Sg 2:5). This passage is written in the nuptial song of the groom and bride, which has been composed for the purpose of strengthening divine love. The words were commented on by the person on whom we now will preach. The church now reads them in praise of the singular bride of Christ, the glorious Virgin.[2]

A frozen heart cannot absorb the words of love, as the writings of the loving Bernard say.[3] You have testified that someone lacking love does not understand the language of love any more than the Latin-speaker understands the language of the barbarian. If this is the case, then how can there be hope that from my cold, and in fact frozen, heart any flame of love ever will produce words on fire? How can that eloquence of his be ignited, as when his word burned the offering of Elias like a torch? (1 Kgs 18:38) Thus we need that fire of love that the Lord sent on to earth when he wanted the offering to be consumed. I would say the fire is necessary both so that you can take hold of the words of love, and especially so that I can do the same and speak these words.

You, most blessed Bernard, are truly the person who shares the company of those fiery spirits whom scripture calls Seraphim (cf. Is 6:2 and 7). In grasping a humble faith I ask and now beseech through your love that the burning coal be taken from the altar of the one whose fire is in Zion and whose furnace is in Jerusalem. That furnace is not false in its desire but is the true God of love and is also an all-consuming fire (Dt 4:24; Heb 12:29). May you, Bernard, touch and purge my lips.[4]

For from above you kindle all our hearts in that love with which you once languished and burned and which now under your guidance we will learn for our happiness. We will at the same time ask that woman of love, the goddess of a love not impure but divine,[5] who sings in exultation, "I am the mother of the most beautiful love" (Sir 24:24). To her we as supplicants present the words of the angel, "Greetings, you who are full of grace, the Lord is with you" (Lk 1:28).

"Sustain me, etc." That voice, my fathers and brothers, is the voice of the lover. He is not any kind of lover but the one who is commonly said to love through love, who has been taken captive in love. Among the passions of the soul, none is more powerful than love, as Cicero learned from experience.[6] No passion that comes from above is more violent, more consuming, and less willing to let the soul be its own lawgiver. As Dionysius says in the fourth book of *On the Divine Names*, as no crime exceeds perverted and improper love in vice, so no virtue equals chaste and good love in its value.[7] Otherwise, how could the good doctor of the church, Augustine, have established that there are two loves in opposition, a good and a bad, just as there are two founders and rulers of the two cities, one divine, the other diabolical?[8] The good love rules over the virtues; the evil reigns among the vices. Good and evil love, Augustine says, make for good and evil ways of life.[9] Thus each love by its own fervid action impels those whom it possesses to languish. But they do so in different ways, as sexual love can show itself in evil and the words of the theme of this sermon manifest the good when the holy soul speaks as God's bride, saying "sustain me with flowers."

Wrongful love we will treat in the second part of our sermon, if time and your patience allow. We will deal here with the complaint of a mournful Christendom that laments a dreadful lethargy in its members, which results from such love. The first part of my treatment, however, will be dominated by the voice of Bernard, most loving and beloved by God, both to praise the saint and to edify ourselves.

Now let his person, so good and trustworthy, be introduced as if we were listening to him speaking about his love in this world. For I have thought I would weave together his doctrine of love in such a way that it will be more pleasing to listen to, easier to believe, more worthy in its majesty, and less prone to being imitated for the wrong reasons.[10] For who could more appropriately take upon himself the mastery of love than the one whose deeds and writings are fiery sparks of love? For a little while, then, turn your attention from me and imagine that it is Bernard himself who speaks and not I.[11]

BERNARD SPEAKS OF HIS SEARCH FOR LOVE

Sustain me with flowers of chaste desires, all you blessed and loving spirits. Sustain me with the fragrant apples of beautiful and ordered activities, for I am languishing with love. Here is my soul. I am a stranger in the land of my pilgrimage. I wandered about and sought the one whom I loved, nor could I love for long without that love with which I was pierced from I know not what early age. By its fire I was so consumed that love sighed in its lament, "Sustain me...." To my soul I offered the prospect of the gates of the senses, heaven and earth, the sea and all in them, which are both beautiful and most attractive.

The beauty of bodily forms came from the right ordering of their parts, along with a certain gentleness of color and light.[12] There was beauty in the proportion and melody of numbers, beauty in what can be touched and tasted. There was also beauty in smells, for they attract in a wondrous manner by perfect proportion.

I said to my soul, "Look, these objects are what you love. Sustain yourself with these flowers, be refreshed with these apples, and you will no longer complain about languishing with love. What are you fleeing? Why are you wrinkling your brow?" For my soul was running away. I certainly felt it was. It rejected all my admonitions with everything that I absorbed into myself through the senses of my body. But the same soul still accepted the teaching of another love almost from the cradle, dear God, from your handmaid, my mother, in the embrace of your holy church and your Holy Spirit. What kind of teacher was she? It was our catholic faith, which as soon as I began to grow, once I could walk, brought my soul to the utterly pure and serene font of your Holy Scripture. In it, just as soon as my soul saw itself and your face in what seemed to be the purest mirror, my soul was suddenly penetrated by burning javelins of divine sweetness and beauty, of worthiness, goodness, and love. It was like the Narcissus of whom the poets tell tales.[13]

From that point onward my soul decided to rid itself of the beauty of all other objects. It began to scorn any love save yours. It tired of the triviality of everyday objects. The soul presumed to have faith only in your own dignity, beauty, and nobility. It became so arrogant in love, as the common saying goes, that it could allow itself to love no one except the most powerful, richest, and most beautiful Being who is above all things. This was a great but good act of pride.

"What do these material objects have to do with you and me, O man," says the soul, "in seeking such beauties? How can we love them when the brute animals according to their abilities do the same as we do? I concede that all things are beautiful; they are attractive and delightful and worthy of love. How much more beauty and attractiveness are there in him who made all things. In an imprint, a shadow, a nod, or a scent, we find such passion that these things compel us by their great importunity and rapacity to love them. The stings of these impressions are overwhelming. They contain more the bitterness of aloe than the sweetness of honey.[14] Do not be surprised if the source from which all these things flow so compels me by its power and so attracts me by its beauty that its love gives delight and its experience holds no bitterness, only rejoicing and happiness. This is my God, by whose love I have been wounded. He chose me for himself. I have given myself to him. He has all of me."

"But when, alas, did he finally go away? And for how long? How long shall I cry out, bearing my burden, and he will not hear me (Hb 1:2)? I, a wretch, seek and do not find him. He wounded me and went away. 'I adjure you, daughters of Jerusalem, if you find my beloved, tell him that I am languishing with love' (Sg 5:8)."

In this way the soul truly languishes when it aspires constantly to its God.[15] I experienced so great a weariness that I became wholly feeble and faint.[16] I was not content with anything I did, or anything I saw in the world. And I said to my soul: Surely you are still untrained in love and not very learned, my soul. Can this not be the reason why your beloved has not come to you? If you choose, we can enter a school that will teach us the manner in which your friend, our God, must be loved. For without some kind of method, how can one please him? And if in other minor skills there is a method that provides results, how much the less can we do without this most divine learning by which alone one can live in the best way?

The soul consented. I came therefore to different schools, not only by bringing my body there but also by the intellectual energy of inquiry.[17] I asked in each of them whether they taught the art of love. In each school I got a reply that was confused and abrasive: "We teach love." But, in fact, when I tried to inquire further, I learned that this was not the same as the love of our God, the chaste love which my soul was seeking. In one of the schools men were taught to love money and to love taking pleasure in it. In another school they learned the enjoyment of worldly vanity.

The school that seemed to have been instituted on a firmer basis, the school of humanities and of various sciences, was concerned in all things with knowledge and not at all with love.[18] There youths were being carefully taught. The old were learning with the younger to inquire about causes, to dispute, to analyze books, and to distinguish with acumen truth from falsity. In all these activities the intellect was absorbed, but the emotions were completely absent.[19] They were kept at a distance, exiled in a desert land, pathless and waterless, a brackish place by the evil of the passions dwelling in it, a horrible wilderness and vast solitude (Dt 32:10).[20] Affectivity was kept outside the bounds of contact with him of whose way of life it is said, "Our way of life is in heaven" (Phil 3:20).[21] Immediately I, Bernard, withdrew from these schools, and my soul was gravely weighed down in pursuing those matters that starve one's affectivity or which leave one totally dried up from their intolerable pettiness.[22] And from that time onward, from the bottom of my heart I drew a deep sigh: You sons of men, so heavy in your hearts, says the Psalmist (Ps 4:3), how can you pass judgment without any feeling of affection? How can you speak diligently of love but not in the language of love, for you lack that love? Even though a person would have given his whole self for that love, he can despise it as if it were nothing (Sg 8:7). In that case, where is that love taught?

It is taught, I say, not by its own tongue but by the tongue of the affections. Where is it then found? Who will show me its school? Sustain me, I ask, with the flowers of chaste speech, whoever can do it. You who love alone can do so; refresh me with the apples of an ordered charity, for I languish with love.

THE NOVITIATE: SCHOOL OF CONTRITION AND PENANCE

In this way my soul was lamenting. It was languishing, heavy with love, and seeking a school where my soul could better be trained in the art of loving well and the ability to keep, sustain, and increase the love that has been instilled in it. Then from heaven the Lord spoke out in a loud voice inwardly to our ears: we were to seek the school of the religious life.[23] I believe that the religious life was instituted more to kindle the affectivity than to instruct the intellect alone. This is at least the case if the institutes of the religious life are maintained. Here from the outset the fervor of the novice's love is protected, better than in solitude, so that the still-tender soul does not stumble over that curse, "Woe to the one who is alone, for when this person falls, no one will be there to lift them up" (Eccl 4:10).[24]

Immediately I prepared my spirit. I was approximately in my twenty-second year of age in the year of the Lord 1112, fifteen years after the foundation of the house of Cîteaux, when I submitted myself with more than thirty of my comrades to the school of religion.[25]

But what kind of religious life and to what end? For I look for a religious life that is sparse, bound by rule, and austere. Alas, I see many that are more corrupt than the world. They are more decadent in what they eat, in the baseness of their morals, and in the unbridled rejection of every regular discipline. Here there is almost nothing of the religious life except for its fictive name or the religious habit and perhaps the singing, which does not reflect devotion but instead expresses boredom and irritation.

My sole end, however, was the love of God. Having been instilled in me by the grace of God, this love would be safely conceived and once born be made vigorous, strong, and fervent, overcoming all things in its power and being sweet and wise. It does not profit the religious life if anything else is sought, such as leisure or food, glory or riches, which the world denies them. Whatever base success can people have in such things when they are initiated in them from the start? But now I return to myself.

As soon as I entered the school of religion, it received me at first, as is the custom, in the place of the novices, where I lived for a while and then rose to the level of the more advanced. No one reaches the top all of a sudden. Finally, through God's assistance I was taken from one virtue to another to a more perfect state. First I am like an animal; second rational; and third spiritual, in accord with the three states of the person who desires the love of God, as I described in my *Epistle to the Brothers of Mont Dieu*.[26] This division is also in agreement with the three steps of the love of God my little book described.[27]

The first place is the school of discipline and contrition; the second, the school of sanctity and meditation; the third is the school of intimate solitude and contemplation.[28] In the first school the person seeking love languishes in love. Then he dies in love; and finally in the third he lives in love, for love is born in languid pain resulting from dissension among the passions. After its birth, once the passions have been mortified, the old human being dies, as Rachel died in the birth of Benjamin (Gn 35:18). In the third place, the love that has been born grows and matures. In this development the soul lives in the way of which the Apostle says, "I live, now not I, but Christ lives within me"

(Gal 2:20). In the first state there is war; in the second, truce; in the third, peace.

So long as mortal life is spent in love, all these elements are often present in a confused way. There is war, truce, peace, again war, again truce, and peace in turn, for everything is mixed up. We find hope, fear, grief, and joy. For scarcely even a half-hour is there silence in heaven (Rv 8:1). In this way, to use another image, the fire of divine love catches fire and grows. At first it burns powerfully with a great deal of smoke that comes from carnal desires. Only rarely does a flame suddenly leap out of this conflagration. Then the flame emerges more eagerly and is covered by the smoke of phantasms. Finally it shines forth as it does in a gentle way in burning coal. Calmly it burns, purified from all smokiness of both passions and phantasms.

With what weariness have I been burdened, with what pains have I been harassed, until this serene and calm fire of love touched my soul and before this fire managed to climb up to the love there conceived. How often did I lodge my complaint with trembling voice with all the male and female saints, and how often did I say to all my fathers and brothers serving Christ together with me: Sustain me with the flowers of your holy prayers, sustain me with the apples of your examples, for I am languishing with love.

Clearly I was still an untrained lover languishing in the novitiate. A harsh and awful conflict was tearing me apart. I had to sustain that terrible ancient woman the Apostle calls the old self (Rom 6:6), the corrupted flesh, and, in the wise man's parlance, the troublesome woman (Prv 21:19). Well known is her way of life, or rather death. This unhappy veteran persuades us. But why do I say "persuade"? In fact, she forces me to prostitute the beauty of my maiden youth and the freshness of my soul. From all sides she draws the basest seducers and vilest robbers of careless souls. For was not the eye an evil robber when it plundered the soul of Jeremiah?[29] The sense of touch and taste, the tongue and the ears, alas, what powerful seducers they are. Each of them takes hold of the covering of my soul and tries to win it over in its trickery: "Come sleep with me," the tempter says.

My soul cries out against the tempter with the mouth of synderesis,[30] in which no deception is found or can be found. It struggles, using the hands of conscience. "Away with you," it cries out. "Go from here into your evil time, you false deceivers. Do you perhaps not know what I am, whose daughter I am, and with whom you are speaking? Am I not the daughter of the eternal king with whose image I am imprinted, the king to whom I am wholly devoted? Am I then someone who would basely hand herself over to be prostituted to your lechery? This is not my intention. Seek elsewhere if you want to find those who will believe in your seductive allurements. I reject you, despise you, spit on you. Shame on you."[31]

Thus my soul spoke to the allurements of the flesh. But I, Bernard, very often asked myself: Bernard, for what have you come (cf. Mt 26:50)? Why are you here, Bernard? Have you not come to the school of chaste love in which you are taught to love God with your whole heart, your whole soul, your whole strength (cf. Dt 6:5; Mt 22:37)? The flesh should mean nothing to you. Bear its scourges with virility. In the end it will become silent even if now it is a great burden to you. It will serve you in obedience. But what then? Do you fear not only inner conflicts but also external battles (cf. 2 Cor 7:5)?

It is known how unhappy women twice impudently attacked me when I was naked. When I felt the one, I cried out, "Robbers, robbers," and awoke my comrades.[32] The other time when the sight of a woman aroused more strongly than usual this little old woman of my flesh, I submerged myself to the neck in freezing water until I almost caused my own death.[33] By such pricks my love at its birth was given life and often burst into tears and sighs. I wept a great deal and, bathed in tears, spoke of my love in the words of the Apostle, "O unhappy man, who will free me from this body of death? The grace of God through our Lord Jesus Christ" (Rom 7:24–25).

For I know that I cannot be chaste unless God gives me this grace (Wis 8:21). But he gives it to those who discipline themselves and who seek him out. And so sustain me with the flowers of your prayers, all men and women who are saints; refresh me with the apples of spiritual gifts, for I languish with love.

136

This was my situation in the school of contrition and penance. In this state, even if I in no way experienced glory, at least I suffered for your sake, whoever you are, generous youth of good character, whoever you may be in your outstanding and chaste being, you are still a novice in learning the art of loving well.[34] Learn from these things that I have suffered the same affliction you do. Act bravely, I ask you. I implore you to put all your effort into removing this filthy old flesh. I offer myself to you in your hope for the crown and as an example of victory. You must follow me; you must believe someone with experience. This brief struggle will bring the most wonderful fruit, unless you are overwhelmed and basely succumb. In that case you will be tortured by perpetual misery and the harshest lust. Even in old age, when you would think you will be safe from temptation, you will be condemned to forms of titillation.[35]

But above all else I warn you, good youth, and I repeat the point again and again in warning you: beware of the company of evil youths or of men of ill repute.[36] You know how the worst conversations corrupt good habits, and so all the more do touching and actions. Oh, what habits! What crimes! No, I mean what deaths! Oh, most heinous of crimes, for that association is to be feared in the worst form of contagion. Instead of the natural bond and institution by which it was fitting for us in mutual contact to be chaste and secure, this beastly corruption works on those whom the almighty God of nature will condemn if they do not come to their senses. God does so justly, for such people in the basest manner ruin those whom they ought to have saved and instructed, since they have been entrusted to them as youths of angelical purity.[37]

But you, noble youth, flee these monstrous diseases by knowing that they are the surest enemies of your reputation, as of your chastity, and indeed of your very life. But if your attackers use force, resist, cry out, speak openly. Show openly the existence of this terrible monster that must be persecuted with fire. Cry out with me: Robbers, robbers!

Finally, in all your affliction while you are giving birth to a chaste and divine love, keep yourself away from all forms of inactivity, for leisure time gives way to vices. May your refuge be in reading, fasting, and prayer. For the devil is not conquered except by fasting and prayer (cf. Mt 17:20). Speak out in this your hour of birth. Tell God and all who are with him, in the very depth of your soul: Sustain me with flowers of chastity, support me with apples of holy purity, for I am languishing with love.

But let us return to the order of our description. I was plagued by such great weariness; I was torn apart by empty display in trying to obey the love of God that had now been conceived within me. And what if some death follow this fervid weakness? What kind of death? The death of one or the other of this double love, the death of either carnal or spiritual love. But we can say more precisely that spiritual love prostrated, stepped on, and wiped out carnal love. In this it has been truly said, "Love is as strong as death" (Sg 8:6).

See how this love was killed in me, as was every bodily delight, when I went to my food as to torture. When hardened grease was carelessly placed before me, I used it for a long time instead of butter, until finally I was struck with horror at the very memory of these temptations to luxury. I reviled this thought as if it were diseased or corrupted blood.[38]

THE SCHOOL OF MEDITATION

And so my old flesh had a happy death, one that did not deprive me of my life but changed it. My life was renewed, as happens with the eagle's youth.[39] My soul struggled to bring forth the love of God that had now been conceived within me, while penance with her companions acted as midwife. Therefore meditation succeeded in the second school as a faithful helper that took over the function of nursing and bearing the one born to love. This meditation is a strong, powerful, and persevering focusing of the mind in order to investigate something. Is it not a strong and powerful awareness that can suck honey from the rock and oil from the most solid boulder in order to nourish its love (Dt 32:13)?

To be more precise, meditation does so by creating rapture. For rapture is a powerful involvement in a superior power with the total cessation of the operation of inferior powers or at least with a noticeable weakening of them.[40] In this meditation, according to the other image, the fire of divine love is lit. In the words of the prophet: In my meditation a fire is kindled (Ps 38:4). This takes place through the profuse weeping of careful consideration, drawing together and uniting all the power of this fire, so that from the material now prepared and, as it were, dried up from the coarse fluid of carnality, a purer flame will burst out and flare up.

Was not this meditation somewhat familiar to me from my youth, when it frequently forced me either to ignore or completely to neglect those objects that surrounded my bodily senses? The vaulting and the windows of the novices' cell, as well as the Lake of Geneva, and the saddle of my donkey, and many other things show that I paid no attention to them at all.[41] Here was the solitude that pleased me. Among oaks and beeches as my masters and doctors, I had a way of life that was very pleasant and familiar.[42] There I brought everything that provided nourishment in divine love. I absorbed,[43] directed, or regurgitated what I had collected, so that I could ruminate on it.[44] The scent of these matters I later left in my writings, especially *On the Song of Songs*, and in my prayers and meditations.[45]

In my meditation I was speaking with myself and to God, now in this manner, now in that: Who am I, Lord, who am I, you king of all creatures, that you would let me love you? What can you let me do, when you issue the terrible order that I love you and you threaten eternal wretchedness if I do not love you? To love you is the greatest enjoyment, the highest nobility, an unfathomable gentleness and ever joyous sweetness.[46]

You order me to love you. I will then love you, Lord, my strength (Ps 17:2). I will love you, not because you need my love but because you wish for it and command it. May what you wish come to be. May what you command be done. Rise up, Lord, in the judgment you have given (Ps 7:7). Whatever there is within me, let it love you, all my strength, all my heart. Let my whole soul desire you who are totally desirable. Let me love all of you, to whom in everything I owe all of myself. I am in debt to you because I was nothing and you made me. I am in debt because I perished and you remade me. A thousand times I have deserved death for my sins, but I am in debt a thousand times and more because your great mercy has come over me and you have snatched my soul a thousand times from the depths of hell (Ps 85:3).[47]

My soul is lukewarm and therefore deserves to be vomited up (cf. Rv 3:16). My soul has dried up in the love of its God. It is ungrateful for his gifts. I call on you, my soul: answer me. If someone so burned with your love that he bestowed all things freely on you, would you not love him? But if, beyond everything else, he gives even his self to you, nor can he give more, but to redeem you from death even willingly suffered the most terrible death, then how can you be so hard that you cannot love in return someone who loves you in such a manner? Truly your God is one who has not given small benefits but this heaven, this earth, this sea, and all that are in them (Ps 145:6). He did not spare his only Son, as his Apostle says, but handed him over for all of us. With his Son, he has given us all things (Rom 8:32).

But perhaps your ingratitude or greed will reply: These things have not been given to me alone, and so they are not a unique proof of love for me. You are deceived, my soul. You should know that a much more generous gift has been handed over to you than to many others, as if it were given to you alone. Imagine that this heaven, this earth, and this sea have been given to you alone. Or that God took on flesh and died in order to redeem you alone. Would you prefer this great gift to be for you alone rather than for many? Do you not want to rejoice in the company of all people, family members, and kin, and even in the company of the angels? Would you really choose to have no one share your gifts with you?

You have no sense, my soul, if you think this way! Why do you then not love the one who loves you? He loves you so much who by his authority both orders that he be loved and asks for love out of charity. He forces us to love through adversity and attracts us to love by prosperity. To whom does that voice belong if we return to its true sense: Day and night you will love me, desire me, dream about me, wait for me, think of me, hope for me, delight in me, be with me, make my soul finally become yours.[48]

On such things I once meditated at length as did the dove (Sg 2:10). Now my sermon of exhortation is directed at you who are to be counted as among the advanced, to you for whom the flesh is now overcome and for whom it is right to put all your strength into meditation, with every fiber of your being, in order to nourish, increase, and complete the love of God. Let neither loss of courage nor folly take hold of you, I ask. Nor should love of illuminating intellect alone, to the neglect of affectivity, compel you. It is especially in terms of virtue and merit that you are to concentrate affectivity.

Perhaps you will say: We have been placed here in order to study, to understand the scriptures. This is our calling. I do not deny or disapprove of this activity, brothers. Nevertheless, I bear testimony to you, as I expressed it in my letter *To the Brothers of Mont Dieu*, that no one ever fully understands who cannot place himself in the affectivity of the writers.[49] And what kind of affectivity? That of virtues, whose queen and mother is love herself. Then according to the measure of love the greatness of the revelation of divine precepts is judged.

I would not want you to believe me if the God of love himself had not indicated this when he called the apostles friends. As he said, "All things I have heard from my Father, I have made known to you" (Jn 15:15). From nature we should know how to hide our secrets from enemies and reveal them to friends. Over your enemies you have made me prudent (Ps 118:98), he says, to whom God has made known the secret and hidden matters of his wisdom. He provides the reason for this revelation: meditation and the love of God's precepts (cf. Ps 118:97).

Who then can deny that to love is to feel something, since the spiritual love that comes from above also exists as a form of sensation? To feel is to know, no less than to see, and often such a sensation is all the fuller and more certain than when touch or taste are moved by their objects in terms of sensation or actualization. Are not the sweetness of honey, the heat of fire, and the attractiveness of odors better distinguished by taste, touch, and smell than by vision? It is no different with the soul, which has its taste, its touch, its smell that come from the love from above.

Again, blessedness is owed to the pure of heart so that they see God (Mt 5:8). This purity is realized in no better way, no more genuinely or effectively, than through the cleansing activity that comes with love. Fuller cognition necessarily results from a fuller love. Furthermore, where love is, there is the eye.[50] Where the eye truly is, there is intention. But where intention is, the mind is at work. This is why cognition burns more brightly as love becomes more powerful. A power that is unified is stronger than one dispersed. There will then be a cognitive virtue that will be all the stronger as it is more concentrated within itself. But nothing other than love creates this unity. This conclusion has further implications. For who does not know that from strong heat the brightness of fire emerges? So from love cognition is generated.

You will now perhaps say that you have the love of God insofar as it is sufficient according to his command. I want you also to have his love as it is sufficient in terms of progress and perfection. For whoever does not make progress on the way to God regresses. It is clearly a great imperfection and the indication of a lazy servant to refuse to try to be perfect.[51]

But beware, I ask you, while the mind remains deprived of the richness of the spirit and while it languishes without the divine sweetness of love. Beware that it does not finally return to those base and carnal consolations that are unworthy of it. For surely the mind cannot maintain itself for long without consolation. Once we have tasted spiritual consolation, which only the love of God can provide, the flesh seems unimportant. Who, once aware of this, will not easily realize how much we must fear that some carnal delight, by a minor and easy fall, will steal over us unaware? Who will not fear the Apostle's curse: what you have begun with the spirit, you have completed with the flesh (Gal 3:3)?

Without the fervent love of God, we will never be able to forget the cares and wretchedness of this life. Carnal delight is not conquered by spiritual delight. Instead, carnal delight can even be nourished by spiritual delight. The love of God alone is the nail that can blunt the nail of impure love. And, my brothers, if it only be given to us in a limited way in some rapture to taste and see how sweet the Lord is (Ps 33:9), then you can cry forth from an affectivity that has been tested and experienced in sensing as the prophet did, and as some of you can do, how great is the vastness of your goodness, Lord, which you have hidden from those who are afraid of you (Ps 30:20). You will grow tired, I am sure, of that aridity in affectivity resulting from whatever intellectual learning you had. You will regret that your soul spent so long a time being troubled by verbal battles, and you will be ashamed to have clung like a snake to the ground. This is a waterless earth devoid of God's wisdom, while in affectivity is a savory and saving science. Finally you will feel ashamed that you had not yet learned the first letter of this alphabet of affective knowledge. And so you will want to rejoice in crying out with one of the great seekers of truth, and not without affection, "Late have I loved you, beauty both old and new; late have I loved you."[52]

THE SCHOOL OF CONTEMPLATION

But if there is given to you a more generous gift and a more powerful experience in extending your love to that which in the third place we have called a step of love, the ecstatic love that brings one to rapture above the mind, then you, with the Queen of Sheba, will not have any more spirit beyond the greatness of your devotion, exultation, or wonder (cf. 1 Kgs 10:4-5)[53]

For love, when contemplation provides this service in the third school, receives such strength that it assumes, joins, and unites the soul as the bride to God its groom, so that they are now not two but one spirit (Mt 19:5). And now is the soul more truly in God whom it loves than in the body to which it gives life, for there, in God, it is more truly kept.

And so the soul was first called turtledove and dove because of its sighing and meditation. It was called friend and daughter because of closeness and adoption.[54] Now it is called bride because it is brought into the bedchamber of the king to enjoy, in an unceasing torrent of pleasure, the embraces it has desired. There the soul conceives and is born of the Word.[55] And so the word is brought forth from the overshadowing power of the Highest (Lk 1:35), and in the virginal womb is that superior segment of the mind that is called either the spark or the summit of reason, or synderesis itself.[56] Its integrity cannot be violated even by demons, so long as that virgin soul perseveres.

It might come about that someone asks what is this word brought forth by the soul. You must accept, as I [Bernard] once replied, that only experience teaches this matter, not doctrine. One needs anointing, not reading.[57] Do you wish to come to terms with the meaning of this great secret? Taste and see: first taste; afterward you will see (cf. Ps 33:9).

I wish then to exhort all of you in common to strive for this step, going from the school of contrition and penance to the school of meditation and sanctity, then finally into the school of intimate solitude. Frequently you must ask God and all the saints who have been wounded through the words of the soul in this love: "Sustain me with flowers, refresh me with apples, for I languish with love."

What I have said here, reverend fathers and most learned men, concerns the good love that creates the city of God in us. I have done so in the person of our loving and devout Bernard, both for our encouragement and to his praise.

LAMENT ON THE STATE OF CHRISTENDOM[58]

The second part then was supposed to introduce a Christianity that weeps in its melancholy. The madness of its sons who, instead of living in love live in lunacy or insanity, has created and increases this depression. I fear, nevertheless, that after the words and taste of the sweetest love, the harshness of such an ungentle subject will throw you into confusion. What is the use of complaining when so much infighting resounds, when there is such a clatter in all of Christianity, with everyone crying out that they are languishing with love? It is a harsh and perverse love in their members, a love that does not in any way at all resemble the previous love we described.

The first love unites those who are divided, while this love divides those who are intimately joined. The first love does not seek what is its own, while this love takes what belongs to others. Contrition and meditation follow each love, but contrition and misfortune, that is, a fruitless contrition, are in its paths, and a meditation on iniquity in its bed. This meditation does not make us stand on the right path and does not make us hate evil. It does not lead into contemplation but turns into total confusion, in the horrible schism that has torn Christianity apart.

This self-love leads to the result that people who love only themselves have no bonds with each other. The person who is limited to himself, how can he ever enlarge himself for others? In this way come anger, rivalries, quarrels, animosity, insults, and all the confusions of a Babylon. Seek no other cause for them than self-love, since it does not restrain but inflames the basest passions. If the passions take control, what hope can we have that evil will be absent and good present? Add that self-love, because it knows how to meditate not on the law of God but only on money, whether it is that of Ceres, Bacchus, or Venus,[59] has no way of repelling these evils. Almost all things are hidden in darkness.

Many people, since they do not understand their own voices or those of others in this confused and blinding business of the wretched schism, are reduced to pandemonium. They inflict harm. They do not distinguish their enemies from their allies, as usually happens with those who fight in darkness. An illustration of this development is a huge letter recently published that mixes up and makes sordid all matters by its accusations and insults and with the crudest form of argument.[60]

Now then, amid these heavy duties and the chains of this love you are to hope in God's love. Trust that there will be room for contemplation. Hope that the people who have acted in such a way will instead think in the way of the devout Bernard, so that they will consider old times and everlasting ages.[61] The whole land has been laid waste in its desolation because there has been no one to think with his heart (Jer 12:11).

But now I lament this accumulation of all kinds of evils, now that the seeds of error are sown, and so it is to be feared that a very unfortunate crop of heresies will flourish from these roots and so invisibly occupy the fields of the church. She now rightly entreats: "Sustain me with the flowers of holy eloquence, which has not lost its bloom; sustain me with the apples of stable and orderly assertions for which I am languishing in love." And do not ask what languishes. The head languishes, as do the breast and the stomach. Why should I name the bodily parts? From the base of the foot to the crown of the head there is hardly any part of the church that is healthy. And even though what it suffers is very bad, even worse things will come, I am afraid, unless its groom and lover has mercy from on high.

AN EXPLANATION FOR BERNARD'S SUCCESS

But let us not dwell on these matters. Perhaps it is the finger of God, and it is necessary that scandals come (cf. Mt 18:7). Therefore the advice is most salubrious that each save his own soul. And if we can return a moment to what was said before, the love of God is what can save us. It can provide us with consolation in all matters. Saint Bernard provides a clear proof of this point because, being strengthened by the company of this love, he walked secure in the midst of schisms. But such a bird is rarely found on earth nowadays. There are indeed few who have shown such vitality in God's love.

If we now consider what accidental or extrinsic factors helped our saint to obtain this love, I find there to be four elements among others: the dedication of his mother, his apt character, his good education, and his attachment to solitude.

According to the story, we know that Bernard's mother was dedicated to her children with great devotion.[62] If because of a mother's sin, good was restored to the son, how much the more will this happen because of merit (cf. Sir 3:16)? Here I employ a moral teaching: Those who preach to the people ought especially to encourage mothers to take care of their children from boyhood and train them in the love and practice of religion.[63]

In our times, alas, there is a terrible inadequacy in the upbringing of infants and children. For it is as if with their very milk, they drink in the filth of all kinds of sin, through word and example. Also those who run schools ought to act toward them as mothers, after the example of the Apostle (1 Thes 2:7): "We are made infants in your midst and like a nurse who nourishes her own children." Those in charge should show the greatest concern that their pupils be clothed in good habits. If they are negligent, or, the greatest of all crimes, if they are responsible for the depravation of those under their care, then such school-teachers are worthy of as many deaths as the number of youths and scholars whom they have made perish.[64]

A second external factor in helping Bernard was his apt character. For he was delicate and soft and pleasing in his gentleness. In the first place this quality made him prone to meditation, as is read in his hagiography. Thus he was inclined to rapture and ecstasies because his soul was less immersed in his body.[65] In the second place this tendency made it easier for him to experience devotion and compunction. In the opposite situation it is said of the person with a hard heart that he will come to a bad end, since he imitates the obstinacy of the demon. On this basis the feminine sex is said to be devout.[66]

The third support for Bernard was a good education, first from his mother, and then in the austerity of a religious order. It is clear that abstinence, fasting, and a sober way of life prepare the soul for more easily contemplating spiritual matters, as we have in the example of the three youths in the furnace (Dn 1:17). Here we might attack excessive eating and drinking.[67]

The fourth support for Bernard was his love of solitude. For it is unbelievable how much harm is done by conversations among people, even when they are not thought to be damaging. As someone said very truthfully, friends are the robbers of time.[68] The first indication of a mind that is composed is the ability to stay in one place and to be with oneself, as Bernard and before him Seneca taught.[69]

Finally, it can be said that these four qualities disposed Bernard, through their accidental quality, to be a prophet and a worker of miracles. Among the latter I especially consider those

Early Letters[1]

LETTER 1   Gerson to a Benefactor (probably Pierre d'Ailly)
            Paris, perhaps as early as 1382[2]
[Gerson asks that his benefactor help him with a source of income. In this way he will be able to concentrate better on his studies.]

My special lord and most beloved father by filial adoption, it pleases me to remember the gifts you have given me in your great generosity, so that I do not seem to have been lost in a terrible plague of ingratitude. For as often as I have come hurrying through the twisting paths of this vale of misery from boyhood to the boundary of my present age, I have been sustained by your willing support. I have sailed out almost to the middle of the sea in a poor little ship whose boards are quite rotten and corroded with worms. This little ship, I say, has not been made secure with pitch applied to the hull nor with iron nails but stays afloat because it is barely kept together by a layer of mud. It has been a wonder that the hostile fury of the winds has not been able to rip the ship apart, nor have heaps of leaping waves swamped it, nor the rock torn it to pieces. Scylla has not overwhelmed the little ship, nor Charybdis sunk her.[3] Nor has the deadly song of the Sirens broken her, so long as you have stretched out your hands to help.[4]

The times, alas, are so detestably evil that the Stygian prisons would seem to have opened up with the citizens of the lower world and the evils of all its inhabitants and to have poisoned all climes of the world with their cockles.[5] Now this little ship of mine cannot maintain its anchor and has lost its rudder, so that it is driven here and there amid the waves. It shudders with horrible sounds when it is hit by their blows. Almost overcome, it is ready to descend into the deep. The anger of the unbridled ocean boils up so that it now seems to oppose the ship with rugged hills and to strike it with clouds on their heights, and again in the manner of Acheron to descend like thunder on the ship in a rapid fall.[6]

Alas, alas, amid the height of all evils, if only I can reach the ship of the fisherman, the help of those in danger, I will survive.[7] If his ship leads me, I will be able to get to the port I want, safe from the cruel hands of decadent sons, the unhappy offspring of the cuckoo[8] and a viperous race, which has been torn asunder, broken into two and wholly divided.[9]

This prospect seems not to bring relief to me in my uncertainty, only fear. Now before the wreck the sight has struck me with great fear and made me weep. The dolphins in their formations are harbingers of the storm, messengers of melancholy, most certain prophets of sorrow. Giving their tidings in wedge-shaped formation, alas, they come, bringing threats of cruel fate.

For me, prostrated by these dangers, I am at a total loss. My mind fails. I cannot look back. I am unable to go forward. I have no idea what to do, except, when I begin to sink, I lift up my arms. Shouting at the top of my voice, I call out into the waves: "Lord, save me." Then you can stretch out your hand to the one who is perishing and repair the damaged ship and bring it with generous help to port.

In another situation I could have stood safely on the proper path and have made moderate progress. Nor would it perhaps be right to judge me, who at least on the edge of the sea could have led a quiet life. You have taken me, who was to perish in this shipwreck, with my hands stretched out in submission.[10]

I ask what honor, what praise, what clemency would there have been if Palinurus had driven Aeneas from safety into unknown waves and, with the north wind blowing and flashes of lightning threatening, had left him behind to drown with his sail cast down and his rudder broken?[11] Or what reward would Tiphys have been given if he out of choice or negligence had catapulted the captain of his ship, Jason, into voracious Scylla?[12] Truly neither these nor the most eloquent of the Greeks, Ulysses, who wandered on the seas for ten years, were tricked by a similar fate.[13] Come then, may your paternity favor my path and may a loving charity not deny help to one who is in danger of perishing.

But perhaps you ask how I am asking to be helped. I really do not know. Nor do I have enough understanding in this matter. For being sick I ask for a cure from the doctor, but I do not see the potions or medicinal and healing herbs I should ask for. I know that you do. I am ignorant how you do so, unless perhaps I perceive in a certain general and confused manner, but shining forth everywhere.[14] If I am in error in this matter, correct me.

I ask, I say, that through you or your people who have the power, I be helped so that I can obtain a benefice or some assistance of this kind, even the smallest, if there be any possibility. Or, until this most harmful and pernicious present schism be rooted out or made milder through the most blessed groom of the church hierarchy,[15] that you help me from your own resources. I do not say riches, for I am not yet so bold or confident in rash presumption that I would want to eat the lord's bread. I yearn not to be made full but to be sustained by the left-over crumbs and bits from your table (cf. Mt 15:27; Mk 7:28; Lk 16:21). I do not want to be dressed up in brilliant clothes but only to be covered by some moth-eaten garb. And humbly I accept it, if you have been disappointed and it has become apparent (something I hope is not the case) that the charity which so pleases God does not compel you, even though by itself this charity should provide sufficient reason. This is the love that does not seek what is its own, that weeps over poverty when it is found in another, that thinks of spending its riches to enrich others, that alone distinguishes between the sons of the kingdom and those of perdition (cf. Jn 17:12). If I can use bold words, this is the love that potentially transforms the human person into God by the miracle of deification.[16]

But if all these considerations do not persuade you, then still the fraternal bond of love and the firm knot of attachment with Nicolas, who I hope dwells in heaven, will convince you.[17] No differently was Theseus united and joined to Pirithous,[18] as Polynices was to Tydeus,[19] as Pylades to Orestes,[20] and as the writer of the psalms, David, was joined in life to Jonathan in a love greater than that of a mother (cf. 1 Sm 18:1–4).[21] When Jonathan was dead, David, who survived him, wept and lamented and burned the more fervently in remembering him. It is reasonable that he who loves someone of noble mind also loves what belongs to him and does not hate, despise, or leave behind those who are his own.

I also hope that the holy and manifest poverty of my parents will draw you.[22] They earn a meager existence in heat and sweat through their own manual labor. After God they have all their hope in you. Under the shadow of your wings they give me some basic help and nourishment. However modest it is, it is the greatest of burdens for them with regard to their social position, so that they now bear burdens beyond their abilities. I fear, may God forbid, that they will become a parable for the neighbors (cf. Ps 68:12), a source of ridicule for strangers, and a ribald refrain for base people. Perhaps the iniquitous will turn their contempt against you in murmuring their ridicule against my parents: "Ha! Look at those whom a shady faith has deceived; an empty confidence has disappointed. They were leaning on a staff and thought it would hold up, but it gave way to them and they have fallen to the ground."

But the good God will treat me better and not send such a contrary fate against me. For he favors those who hope in him and does not desert them. Nor does he ever allow that the seed of the just should beg (cf. Prv 11:21). For us in the branches, the root will be decorated with the praise it deserves (cf. Rom 11:16). Perhaps this will be more than is hoped or more than it is appropriate for me at the present time to say.[23] But now I am almost shipwrecked and am in terror of the straits I am passing.

In these matters I add that I, thanks be to God, have not led a life ensnared in vices, especially not of a public kind. I do not deal with hidden ones, of which the conscience is judge and to which God, not men, bears witness. Why is it then that, even though the reasons for benefaction that previously existed are present, only now in even greater measure, I perceive your generosity either stops or becomes lukewarm? I really do not understand. Please enlighten me.[24]

Unhappy me (cf. Rom 7:24) if you quickly pass me by without

noticing, with ears that do not want to listen, if you run through these matters superficially, and if you turn your face away with a stern look in your eyes and your forehead wrinkled in furrows, so that you reject out of hand what you consider beneath your dignity, in saying, "What is this? I who have given an ox, am I forced to give a cow? Why does he murmur here and make speeches? He has time for his leisure but does not deign to support himself by his own efforts as others do. Senselessly he spends his time in sluggish activity, like some bird of prey."

Stop, father, let the palpitations of your angered mind cease, for the sake of your peace. The truth is not that I am lying about in rigid inactivity or wasting myself in squalid lack of exertion, nor am I kept back by any base lack of energy. Surely it is love of study that compels me. Certainly it is this concern in me, more powerful than any other force. I have scarcely or infrequently been involved in practical tasks because I have dedicated my efforts to study. And so that I do not draw the matter out into a long sermon, I would dare to say that if I wish to spend time in intense study and if I devote to this end my utmost powers (would that they could be even greater), I would then be able to offer my services more fully than I do now with scholarships, meager as they are in size.[25] I would walk on a more even path if I could be helped even a little by friends.

I have not yet, outstanding lord, lost my way in a failure of self-confidence. I am not so senseless or thoughtless, nor am I so much lacking in ability of mind, nor am I so spoiled by fortuitous goods or freely given favors, that wherever you might be, whether in the neighborhood or far away, I ever could spend my life in a satisfactory and decent way if I stopped desiring to pursue my studies.

While I was writing the draft of this letter, an unforeseen situation arose, as if fortune had not been sufficiently harsh on me. For Master Walter, in my mind the best person to administer my benefice, to whom I was writing concerning an undecided misunderstanding, has informed my brother Jean concerning the incomes from the said benefice.[26] The abbot of Saint Rémy or a certain monk has denied my claim or otherwise taken it over. Nothing more was told me.

Help me, I beg you, and bring the matter to an end, since no further prayers or words are necessary if you deign to take up this cause into your ample hands, in showing maternal kindness and generosity.

Bear with me in my unattractive prolixity. Forgive my loving boldness, more the result of confidence in you, perhaps, than of my merits. Forgive the crude style, which indicates the lack of expertise of its maker. Give me also happiness in the honeyed speech of your letters, if it pleases you. I ask you that you recommend me to Lord Ar, who because of great love is your alter ego and my most outstanding master.[27] Fare you well.

Written at Paris. Jean de Gerson.

LETTER B. Elisabeth la Chardenière to her Sons Nicolas and Jean dated to c. 1396–97[28]
[With the help of her daughter Poncete, Gerson's mother writes to his brothers at Paris and encourages them always to keep her and her salvation in their thoughts and prayers, to live good lives, and to obey their brother.]

Sweet children of my heart, your mother greets you, the one who so gently brought you up, the one who after the pain of bearing you and the suffering of giving birth to you has always so tenderly until this time loved you. I am the mother who often makes herself give birth to you in God through weeping, tears, and continual prayers, so that you can have the sweet Jesus with you through grace in your hearts.

I, being your mother, call upon you now as my two dear children. Since I cannot do so in speech, I address you in this letter. I ask you to listen to me. Do not close your ears to the words of the one who often patiently listened to the crying and wailing of your infancy. Listen then, listen and follow the first instruction of your mother as she gives it.

This is that you fear and love God with all your heart and all your mind, so much so that you for nothing would consent to sin.

This means that you do nothing against any of these command-ments. Be pure and simple in body and soul, as is fitting for youths who want to belong to the church, and for children who have such examples of living well in their other brothers and sisters.[29] For I think you often can listen to good teachings where you are, both from your brother and from others. It is enough for me to say this, in that I assert I would rather see your bodily death than see you living and persisting in mortal sin's filth.[30]

My sweet children, think often that you are in my presence, that you see me and hear me speaking. Act also in the presence of God when you are alone, as if you were close to me and as if I were looking at you. But also give me as your mother the same as I give you. Pray for me attentively, devoutly, ardently, I who often weep and sigh to God for you.

You would be most unnatural children, may God not allow that, if you forgot me, who has remembered and thought of you, and who will continue to do so as long as it pleases God. Think of my old age and of the great and terrible need that I now have and will have at the last moment of death. Think of the terror and fear I have that my repentance will not be sufficient for my trespasses. Put before your mind's eye that you see me, your mother, on her deathbed holding out to you her hands joined together, praying and asking that you aid me before God through prayer and good works. If I were in this state, and I will be, when God wills, can you two children yourselves be so hard and thank-less that you will not help me according to your ability? Certainly I do not believe this will happen. On the contrary, you will exert yourselves in all ways to help my poor soul in this final and supreme need through all good prayers and devotions. Then think often in a vivid and profound way that you are looking at me in this state and are assisting me as much as there is time and you can do, for it is good to anticipate what is to come. Pray with care to God that he pardons my misdeeds and receives me in his glorious company, and that I can see you. Amen.

Dear children, remember also your good father, with whom alone I have lived for such a long time and in harmony in God's service. Take as an example your good sisters and pray devoutly for them, for they do not forget you. Pray also for your two other older brothers and make sure that the brother with whom you are living is always pleased with you, as he now is.[31] This makes me so happy that I cannot tell you. In the opposite case I would feel so much pain that it would almost kill me.

And when you will have the time and occasion, at least once each week, read this letter most attentively and carefully, and put yourself in a secret place with prayer and good thoughts toward God. Compel yourself to conquer and overcome all the evil temptations of the world, of the flesh, and of the enemy.

And may the blessed Creator and Savior, who has made you come to the world by means of me, give you according to your desire power, knowledge, grace, and will to serve him and to accomplish what your mother in tears and sighs now writes to you by the hand of Poncete your sister,[32] so that you may remember me, your old and weak mother, and so that foolish youth does not make you forget God and me and yourselves.

Written at Gerson, etc.[33]

LETTER E.   Arnoul le Charlier to Gerson
               Written at the hamlet of Gerson, c. 1395–96[34]
[Gerson's father praises the spiritual progress and daily routine of his daughters, who continue to live at home with their parents.]

Thanks be to God. First of all they love God and fear sin, and they fast one or two days a week and recite daily their hours to our Lady. Marion has learned the hours since the death of her husband. They are not more troubled than they were at the age of six years.[35] I do not think that they will even consider marrying until and insofar as it will be acceptable for us and you.

LETTER 1*   Gerson to his Sisters[36]
              Bruges, winter 1399–1400
[Gerson provides his sisters with recommendations for their daily life of prayer.]

156

My dear and much-beloved sisters, greetings in Jesus Christ, and perseverance in serving him well, amen.

It would be difficult to express the joy and consolation that I gain from the good news that I so often have of you. May it never be God's will that through temptation of the enemy or otherwise my joy be turned into sadness by hearing the contrary about you.

Most beloved sisters, even though you have sufficient letters and books so that you can always be learning how to serve God and have spiritual consolations, you can now profit from even more of these. Even though I at present have many occupations, nevertheless I have taken the opportunity to stay up this night in order briefly to write you about the procession and pilgrimage that I have taken up in recent time.[37] I describe also the special requests that I make according to the seven days of the week, according to the seven gifts of the Holy Spirit, the seven petitions of the Our Father, and in opposition to the seven mortal sins in correspondence with the seven beatitudes, and according to the seven states that are in paradise. For now I write only brief and concise advice about what one is to know in particular about each day and especially concerning the subjects of meditation. As for the good thoughts that will come in excess through the inspiration of the Holy Spirit and which will be found in study and holy meditation, I cannot and know not how to write about all of them. This is also not necessary.

First of all, when you send your prayer in great humility and reverence before the majesty of God or his saints, always call on your good angel with your prayer and also on the male or female saint[38] whose feast day it might be, so that your messenger, meaning your prayer, gains good safe-conduct and company.

Sundays I commend to God, the blessed Trinity, so that we pay homage to each of the persons, to the power of the Father, the wisdom of the Son, and the goodness of the Holy Spirit. I consider thereby the Trinity's greatness and its marvelous concern for humankind.

Mondays I commend to the holy angels and consider the benefits that they provide for us.

Tuesdays to the prophets, patriarchs, apostles, disciples, and evangelists.

Wednesdays to the holy martyrs and the strength and constancy they had.

Thursdays I commend to the holy confessors, hermits, and religious.

Fridays to the passion of Jesus Christ and to the words and other deeds he offered on this day.

Saturdays to our Lady and to the holy virgins.

Sundays I concentrate most on asking for the gift of holy fear and trembling before God and the beatitude of humility and spiritual poverty and to escape from the sin of pride and all its branches.[39] And say: that God may deliver me from evil, which is the first request of the Our Father if we begin at the end.

Mondays I concentrate most in asking for the second gift, which is holy compassion for myself and my neighbor and the beatitude of generosity against the sin of envy, and that God not let me be overcome by temptations, which is the second request of the Our Father.

Tuesdays I ask especially for the gift of knowledge, so that I can well know how to recognize my weakness, my goal, my situation, and the state of my friends. Thus I come to the third beatitude, which consists in holy sighs and devout tears against the sin of anger. I ask that God forgive my offenses as I forgive those who offend me, which is the third petition.

Wednesdays I ask for the gift of fortitude against all temptations. In the face of every form of laziness I ask for the strength to do well, and the fourth beatitude, which is to desire good works of justice and to have great thirst and hunger for them, and ask that God give me my bread, both the daily material bread, and the spiritual one to have strength.

Thursdays I ask for the gift of counsel, so that I can know in all cases what path or state I should maintain for serving God better and so that the sin of avarice does not hold me back. I ask for the fifth beatitude, which is called mercy, and that the will of God be done on earth as it is in heaven.

Fridays I ask for the gift of understanding, so that I can understand in all the scriptures whatever I will see and in the affairs of the world the mysteries hidden there, and so in what I will see, I will know how to turn it to my spiritual profit. Just as when I will see the heavens, I will know how to consider that there is my country, where there is a very fine dwelling place. When I will see that a dog loves its master, I will know how to make use of this fact for my instruction; and so in general with everything that I will see or hear or feel. I ask for the beatitude that is called purity of heart, which is opposed to lust, and ask that God and not sin come to me.

Saturdays I will ask for the gift of wisdom, so that I can taste and savor in a spiritual manner that immense sweetness of grace both of the virtues and of God's goodness and not pay attention to the sweetness of the world. This grace is opposed to the sin of gluttony. I will ask for the beatitude of peace of heart and good conscience and that the name of God be sanctified in us, so that we be freed from all corruption.

Beloved sisters, if each day you will learn something through your books or otherwise according to the matters described above, you will be able to gain profit in knowledge, virtue, and devotion.

But I do not wish that you for this reason abandon your good meditations and your own ways of making your visits or pilgrimages to male and female saints both for yourselves and for your friends, dead and alive. For I well know how often that which moves one person to devotion does not so easily move someone else. Therefore each of you should do what God will teach her. As for me, I find that the method described above is good for me.

Furthermore, every time that you wish to enter into prayer, think first of all of your sins and your great lack of worth, and say to God and his saints: "Lord, I wish to pray to you, not because I have confidence in my own goodness or virtue or worth, but in your immense grace and mercy." For certainly otherwise pride would soon hinder your prayer and would make it displeasing to God. And be careful that you remain in this meditation and prayer until you feel that your heart has no trust whatsoever in itself but only in the mercy of God. And then you will be able at this point to begin to think more about other matters.

Moreover, every time you feel that no form of devotion will come to you, consider it is certain that this can happen through the good prayers of a male or female saint or some friend of yours, man or woman, and not by your own good works. And so you will return to yourselves every time you will be tempted by vainglory and you will not fear, for you will recognize the faults and will rightly say: "You have committed this sin or that. How would you then dare to think that for your good deeds God would give you a sense of devotion?"

When you turn to a saint, say to him or her without hesitation that God has sent you in order to ask for alms of grace. And you will speak the truth, for without God's inspiration you would not have the will to pray to any saint. Thus you can say that since God wishes that you make your request, then he or she ought not to refuse it. Also, since the saints are so full of charity and mercy, they ought not to refuse to pray for those who ask them, as it would be a great rudeness to refuse to pray to God for another person if this one asked for it. Say also to the saints that they converted many who did not pray to them but who persecuted them. Thus they ought to treat better those who pray to them.

And afterward, consider on each saint's feast the acts of mercy which he or she performed in life in order to ask that the saint will do something similar for you to bring some good to your soul. See what a great number there are of saints and angels, and ask each of them that he or she will ask for one day of pardon from God in order to lessen the suffering you have deserved, and you will have more than a billion if they will listen to you and if you ask them devoutly.

Above all else let us pray that God judges and punishes us in his court of mercy in this world and not in his court of strict justice in hell. And this is what you pray when you say: *Domine, ne in furore tuo arguas me* (Lord, do not accuse me in your anger, Ps 6:1).[40] Complete, then, your procession into hell in order to avoid and fear it, and in purgatory and in paradise also for your people and for the holy church and especially for your parents. Amen.

LETTER 2   Gerson to an Unknown Person[41]
Perhaps to Pierre d'Ailly or the chapter of Paris
Bruges, February(?) 1400

[In this remarkable letter Gerson reviews the reasons why he has left his post at Paris and lost confidence in the academic life. He wants to resign the post of chancellor of the university and remain at Bruges as dean of the chapter.]

The following contains some of the difficulties and calamities I have experienced in the office of chancellor of the University of Paris. This list I have drawn up in a direct and free way in order to consider the counsels of most holy persons who fear God.

I am forced [in my position as chancellor] to please or serve many very great lords who are most hostile. I do not want to provide their names for those who know them anyway. I think it is mad not to flee this dilemma when it is inflicted on me, for displeasure of the ruler is death (cf. Prv 16:14) and no one can serve two lords (Mt 6:24).

I am forced to favor "friends" who are not satisfied with trying to destroy me but who also go to troublesome and very powerful men to slander all that I do and use every one of my words against me. This type of persecution is of a very personal type. In such a situation it is right and necessary to give way and to overcome evil with good (Rom 12:21), so that I do not get dragged into total ruin with these friends by making vain efforts. The events that newly took place can teach this lesson. The example of Christ and of Paul and further evidence indicate that in this case for the shepherd to flee is not flight.[42]

I am forced to struggle with the most importune and even most oppressive people to the point of sinning. But it is better to fall into the hands of God than of men when these can be avoided. Otherwise one who loves danger will perish in it.

I am forced because of the consideration of others or because of the custom of the age to promote those who lack knowledge and are morally corrupt, and sometimes to prefer them to those who are more capable, even though the wise man says: "Do not seek to be made a judge unless you have the power to uproot injustices (Sir 7:6).[43]

I am forced to deal with and to accommodate men who are most uncouth and whose ways are completely different from my own. I

161

have to be associated with them in familiarity or I am considered to be impolite. I thus skirt danger, for one must rejoice with those who rejoice (Rom 12:15).

I am constantly forced to hear the rumors that infect the place. They take away peace of mind. In such a heap of gossipy talk, sin is present, for it is self-evident how spiritual matters quickly are dispersed in such concerns.

I am forced to work on inane sermons, which eat up the greatest part of my time without any fruit of edification. I am appropriately described in the words, "With foolish labor you will wear yourself out" (Ex 18:18).

I am forced again to be submerged in the vicissitudes of court life, even though this is not always the case. Otherwise I am considered to be ungrateful. The sole reason I sought the office of chancellor was to get away from this duty.[44] God provided here something different from what I hoped for. Why is it then that when the end is achieved, the motion does not cease?[45]

I am forced amid these and similar concerns to miss masses and prayers or to say them without being recollected. In such devotions there is more benefit if they are performed well than if they are divided up in a random manner. I leave it to others to consider more profoundly how small a benefit there is, and indeed how dangerous such behavior often is, when it is a question of moral standards within the church. There we find the saying of the Apostle: "Do not hastily ordain anyone and do not get involved in the sins of others" (1 Tm 5:22).

I am forced in material life almost to beg and to live in a downtrodden way, for the golden mean is not safe with bitter poverty, according to the requirements of one's position.[46] Elsewhere I would be abundantly provided for and be able to provide for a household, but now it is necessary with great detriment to go without one and to live with grammar students and school boys.[47]

I am forced in order to live to hold the office of dean, where I am bound to benefit others through words and examples.[48] And yet if I am not resident as chancellor, according to the oath that everyone knows, then what murmuring and damage are caused.

I am rightly called a two-headed monster and am also considered to be an example of ambition, indeed of perjury.

I am forced to be envied for the benefice that is joined to the office or to give it up amid derision and with loss, having to fight forever even with the strongest and unconquerable enemy.[49] This is utterly abhorrent to my ways and brings to my ears the sound of that saying, "Why have you not better endured injury" (1 Cor 6:7)?

I am forced to pursue a new prebend.[50] Past habits can easily teach me and my friends to subject ourselves to this new care where there is so much hope of provision. And indeed I am not obliged to seek it, nor can I be forced to labor at my own expense, without any stipend. Nor can I be required to desert this place where without any burden, at least of a dangerous type, I could take my rest, and to avoid all the scandals that have preceded and will follow the matter.[51] But if scandals should arise after I resign the chancellorship, as my friends warn, let them take place immediately, for the same or even greater scandals will take place if I do not give up any of my positions. I prefer that this preferment to office take place in another person, under another, and for another, rather than in me and under me. And notice what Sallust says: It is the height of idiocy to strive in vain and to tire oneself out in seeking nothing but hatred.[52]

I am forced to follow the crowd in doing what I do not want or what is not permitted, just as one who is an enemy or is suspected of having ambition. It is not enough to hide this fact or to flee it or to be silent, or even to cry out openly. As it has been written, "You are not to follow the crowd in doing evil" (Ex 23:2).

I am forced in the face of pernicious dogmas that some people already have sown either to go against my conscience and remain silent, or with the greatest danger to myself and, even more important, to truth, to correct them by revoking them. But I can only correct them if those who have favored them allow me to do so, instead of confirming them. Plato persuades us that where evil prevails, one is not to dwell, and here the advice given by Ezekiel and Jeremiah is valid concerning when one is to sigh over something (cf. Ez 21:7; Jer 45:3).[53]

I am forced to suffer from every evil tongue as if I were a

target for the arrow. These tongues rage against me in an intolerable and irrational way, and they are expert in knowing how to reach their target. They realize how much danger there is not only in words but also to life itself because of a certain conspiracy here unnamed.[54] Therefore they in this way see that time must at last be redeemed because the times are evil (Eph 5:16). Indeed, they are much worse: the times are full of danger and everywhere replete with the seeds of sedition. The citadel of Zion has been taken as a trap for Jerusalem itself (cf. Is 8:14). In such a shipwreck he is truly happy and not without benefit if he even naked can swim away.[55]

On the contrary, for the time being no good can be attributed to me, except a certain hope of profiting others, as some imagine. I hope that they are not blind in their judgment, being overwhelmed by my insignificance. For I sense myself to be useless for this purpose and have for a long time felt this way. I have truly known how it is to be more for others than for oneself.

Here it must be considered by keen judgment, both from past events and from the facts of the matter, if one does more harm than good when a person is persecuted for his own ways and when justice is endangered through him. And so we have the scriptural passage: "[Blessed are you] if people persecute you" (Mt 5:11; cf. Jn 15:20).

It should be considered how small is the hope of doing any good among those who are wise in their own eyes and who take time out for nothing except with the Athenians to speak or hear anything that is new (Acts 17:21).[56] In Athens, however, it was a question of a crowd of people among whom some were concerned about their own salvation and generously sought advice. But among these people [of Paris] who do not seek their own salvation, preaching becomes not only wasteful but also destructive and worthy of contempt if it is anything more than a curiosity. Where no one will listen, do not utter any word (Sir 32:6). Think of the example of Christ, who was silent before Herod, who wanted to hear something entertaining (Lk 23:9).

It should be considered what good can be done at Bruges solely by the example of life, without any words. Such a noteworthy benefit compels one to persist in so distinguished an office.[57]

It should be considered by the experienced what might be the use of subordinates' words in dealing with magnates. Indeed, such people get most angry with those who say something to them that does not agree with their desires or when someone refuses to stick to the saying: "Tell us what pleases us" (Is 30:10). It should also be considered what happened to Micaiah, if they do not remember.[58] Therefore many doctors of theology and preachers in what they reply to magnates amaze them by speaking as jesters and entertainers. These learned men are willing to dance about, altering and varying their songs, that is their doctrines, according to the whims of such magnates.

It should be considered that nature or custom is repelled by what belong to another nature, and in such a case nothing ever can be done with a good result. But it is my nature and custom in terms of action to be wholly inept and inert, full of scruples and fear, most easily upset, so that I continually mull over something more than a thousand times. Why then should I attempt to go against the current? Why should I use force on nature, which, even though I should remove it with a two-pronged fork, as Horace says, nevertheless will return to where it was before?[59]

What if someone should object about the provision [of offices] for my brothers and the honor of my friends? I concede that this carnal consideration could in the end overcome me, especially when my parents in the flesh who live in the country cannot take care of such matters. Indeed, toward my brothers and sisters themselves I by no means act without masculine courage nor do I lack concern for the younger ones who would climb to the heights.[60] But in the face of imminent and total shipwreck one can only stay afloat if even the dearest, the most necessary goods are willingly cast overboard. Similarly one must flee a fire without taking one's own possessions, as I violently ripped myself away from what was surely a profitable way of life at court. I do not regret doing so, even though my friends tried to resist. But if I am said to have fled these dangers out of fear, then I can use that statement of Terence: If heaven falls in, without a doubt the vague threats of friends will be understood.[61] Many things in the past will be seen as presaging the future in terms of particular events. Nevertheless, I do not speak of them nor do I reveal them while they lie hidden within.

Let it be considered what a great number there is of theological masters who are much less suitable for contemplation and who deserve instead [of me] to carry out all their office's duties more vigilantly, freely, and happily. It is not necessary here to seek a man in whom there be no blemish, because such a bird on earth is rare, nor am I such a one at all. I ask you to see how unbearable such an error would be and how vain I would be even in having others to think such things of me and thus wanting to be preferred, in the way that an ugly ape prefers its own offspring to ponies. For it is no counsel against the Lord (Prv 21:30) if I am removed from their eyes so that another person can be in charge. I think from what I have heard and what has happened that [Pope] Benedict was tricked by his friends not to yield office because of the deception of pride, as if the church would lose anything by his resignation and as if no one else could be found for the necessary direction of the church.[62] This truly was the temptation of the noonday demon (Ps 90:6).

It should be considered how much love for God there is in the quiet of contemplation of those who live in the way of former saints. And so, if someone is found to be even slightly suitable for this activity, I think it must be conceded that his talent is such, and he is not to do other things, or at least not to take on too great a task. For the function of the eye is to see, not to labor. Each has his own gift from God (1 Cor 7:7). For this reason Gregory Nazianzen resigned, and Pope Celestine V and many others did the same.[63]

It should be considered whether, if I were called to the episcopacy or to some great temporal good, my friends would advise me to spurn it all and to keep the office of chancellor. I by no means think they would. I am, however, in no doubt that it is more secure for me to want to step down from this position rather than to want to go up higher. But if in cases of resignation of office for something greater or because of death there is a procedure for conferring the chancellorship on someone else, then let it be done now as it would be then. The process can take place with even greater consideration, as there can be more time for deliberation than would be possible in the former cases.

Let it be considered that many of my friends and those who say that they envision dangers would be able, without provoking hatred arising from envy or causing adversity, freely to take on that burden with which I am so heavily weighed down. This would not at all be unreasonable, since I am plagued by those who hate me. Perhaps it is the fault of my ambition or impunity that our hope, as you know, has been withdrawn and taken away.[64] But if they refuse [to take over the office], let them be sure to deal with me fairly. They should realize that they do not wish to lift a finger to remove the burdens that they want to remain on my shoulders. In the end I think that no one is in doubt that it is permitted in accord with all laws to resign such an office, to hand it over to the hand of the superior and either to enter a religious order or to live differently, especially for one who has been provided with another benefice.[65] But if it is permitted, I know myself and my own ways. I am sure, with every certitude, that in such a matter I will find what is necessary and what is best for me.[66]

But if those who imagine, in loving me so much,[67] that it would not be best for the state or the progress of others, let them hear the divine thunder: What does it profit a person if he should gain the whole world (Mt 16:28)? Let them be on their guard so that they not be among those of whom elsewhere it is said: "The enemies of a man are the members of his own household" (Mt 10:36).[68] They should also think of what is sung by young people: "What you think will harm you, even if it is dear to you, leave it behind."[69]

And so that they do not accuse me of changeableness if now I so passionately flee that which I once so diligently pursued, let them know that my knowledge has grown with age and experience, and my hopes have been greatly frustrated. One thing, indeed, is certain: the wise man changes his ways with the times.

But if a charge of ill repute be made against me, I know that through bad and good reputation one goes to heaven (cf. 2 Cor 6:8). I know how little it ought to matter that I be judged by a human court, for he who judges me is the Lord (1 Cor 4:3–4). But the life of a Christian is measured out not by popular rumor but in simplicity of conscience. It is wiser and better to do that freely which in the end death itself will extort from a person, however unwilling.

LETTER 3   Gerson to Pierre d'Ailly[70]
Bruges, 1 April 1400
[Gerson has recovered his hope and provides his analysis of the situation of the church plus recommendations for reform at the faculty of theology of Paris.]

Reverend father and special lord, I turn the powers of my mind to our condition and order, if there is any order at all in this our time of tempest. I can consider the general disaster of the church, which is so much to be pitied because its size and merits have been diminished in a reduction of religious feeling. One can only weep, and according to the advice of Ezekiel (9:4), sigh over all the abominations that take place, rather than think of help or hope for some remedy. So from the base of the foot all the way to the crown of the head, a raging corruption of sins has filled the entire body of Christianity. It has such deep roots in the hearts of men, this now old and hapless iniquity, that it seems as if one can only despair of providing human counsel or aid. For it is as if the advice of elders has disappeared (Ez 7:26), as well as speech from the prophet and law from the priest.

Let us now then go in this savage storm or whirlpool, so that we not only desire to aid those who steer the ship of the church, its prelates, but also take hold of them by force when they are perversely difficult to correct and the number of fools is infinite (Eccl 1:15). This is the time when a person scarcely is able to save himself in the midst of a depraved nation (Phil 2:15), unless some madness might impose itself on men, a heavy burden and fearful on the shoulders even of the greatest.[71]

Such things perhaps had to be said for those who are not yet caught in this noose in order that they beware and dedicate themselves to a more modest commitment. But what about those who already have put their feet in the net and are walking in their imperfections? I weep for myself more than for others, and for my unhappy fate, since in obligating myself by taking up the office of chancellor of Paris, I have until now been cast about by unbelievable difficulties, for I am neither allowed to exercise authority nor is any means given me to remove this burden from my shoulders. But I do not include myself. I have already wasted innumerable writings and words [on myself].[72]

What you then think and judge, good father, concerning your own episcopal burden, I think I clearly can see.[73] For if I well know your modest and most composed way of being, you regularly deplore the height of your position and, sighing, wish for a lower one. Why is this not so? Why does the pastoral burden in your condition not make you anxious and full of sorrows, and in the end subject you to dangers of soul and body? It does so, I assert, with everyone. But they alone experience this awareness for whom the fear of God is before their eyes. Before God's fearful judgments, such people do not close their eyes, as they do who seeing cannot see and understanding do not understand (cf. Mt 13:13). They who glory when they do evil and exult in the worst things will certainly perish all the more unhappily and dangerously because they have been oblivious to the truth. According to the prophet's curse, they are said to live according to their hearts' whims and to walk in its inventions (Ps 80:13).

Someone might ask what it is about the present situation that makes it worse than before. There are many factors, which cannot be explained. There is no doubt that conditions get daily worse when each person adds something to the heap of iniquity and no one reduces it. If you are in doubt, then take a look at the hateful schism. Here, in the most evident passivity of former pastors, the worst customs have been slowly allowed to take root, so that according to Seneca's saying,[74] the possibility of any remedy is absent because what formerly were vices have now become habits. I speak as someone with experience.

This one example, even though others are without number, I assert to underline my assertion, that in major churches and in cathedrals false remnants from sacrilegious rites of pagans and idolaters almost everywhere are carried out. Neither the place of prayer nor the presence of the holy Body of Christ, nor the celebration of the divine office, keep churchmen from acting in the most vile dissoluteness and performing such acts about which it is a horror either to write or even to think.[75] But if one of the prelates of these churches tried to stop such practices, he would immediately be ridiculed, hissed at, and attacked. "Behold," they say, "a third Cato has fallen from the heavens.[76] How much wiser and more useful to the church were your predecessors who not only tolerated these practices but also flattered those who performed them." Thus the negligence of former prelates in providing authority for vile and heinous crime is to be condemned and already has been condemned, unless they should repent.

Some people excuse themselves, I know, by saying that they by no means lack the will to get rid of such practices but have not the power to do so. And they perhaps could be heard, if they concerned themselves with as much devotion as they show in the maintenance of the most insignificant secular laws. They ought to restrain such people from sacrilege not in a gentle way, as Eli did with his sons (1 Sm 2:22–26), but through the hands even of lay princes. And what if, to what already has been named, you add an abominable evil, something most like a monster? Those whom the bishop ought to have as helpers and defenders of his flock have become the most shameful wolves against him. They have turned into lions or the most rapacious swine, atrocious in their fury, in word, example, and deed. I speak of the clergy and, above all else, of cathedral chapters.[77] But whether it is the unworthiness, the arrogance, or the iniquity of the bishops that is the origin of such abuses, they themselves will see.

For the preaching of the word of God, which is the greatest medicine for spiritual illnesses and the specific duty of prelates, has been deserted by these men as if it were a superfluous task, hateful and beneath their magnitude. In this way the preaching of God's word is handed over to I not know whom. Such people, by lack of knowledge or by their way of life, have contaminated what should be treated with utter discretion, and they have turned the divine word, as it were, into song, fable, and laughter for those who listen (cf. 2 Tm 4:4).[78]

All this irreparable damage reverts immediately onto the heads of prelates. For they with wondrous care channel great expense into protecting their temporal goods with lawyers, defenders, prosecutors, and other officials of this kind. They maintain them with lavish salaries, doing so by what prelates take as plunder from their sheep.

Where, I ask, have you seen a theologian who has been appointed in order to minister to spiritual needs, to sow good seed and to preserve it, and for whom, in accord with papal decree, temporal goods even sparingly have been given?[79] And since temporal benefits for the clergy cannot long exist without spiritual services, because the former were given by the devotion of lay people, it is to be feared that both of them very soon will be taken out of our hands.[80] The road already is wide and clear, ready for this development. Has it come to the point that strictness within every discipline has been so erased from the church that those who profess even the most ascetic religious professions can sin more freely than deacons or secular clerics once could do?[81]

These matters I have in faithfulness brought up with you, dearly beloved father, not to teach you, for I am too weak to provide counsel even for myself, nor to criticize you, but to look at matters as a whole and in sadness to deal with the situation. These affairs are, I am sure, all the more known to you, the more experienced you are in them, and so all the more burdensome, for whoever increases knowledge also increases sorrow (Eccl 1:18). Such concerns are all the more present in you as zeal for God's house burns the more ardently in your holy breast.

But what I have begun, I will in pious boldness complete, for I have great trust in your devotion, since I love you greatly. In order to record some of what seems necessary to be done, I have written with my own hand, as I lay prone in the bed of my illness,[82] on this one evening and out of a pious impulse, a list[83] noting these matters. This I send to you. Accept it happily, and be well in the Lord, most loved father.

Written at Bruges on the first of April, 1400.

[Gerson's Proposals for Teaching Theology, Added to the Letter]
Reverend father, under your correction and that of our masters in the faculty of theology, a reformation of the following matters, among others, seems to be necessary[84]:

First of all, pointless teachings that are fruitless or superficial are not to be dealt with by the theological community, since thereby useful teachings that are necessary for salvation are abandoned. People do not know what is necessary because they have learned what is superfluous, as Seneca says.[85]

Second, through these useless teachings, they who do not study are seduced because they think that the theologians in principle are they who dedicate themselves to such concerns, spurning the Bible and the other doctors of the church.

Third, through such teachings the terms used by the holy fathers are changed, in opposition to Augustine's saying that it is necessary for us to use language in accord with a fixed rule.[86] Corruption of any type of knowledge can hardly come about more quickly than through this new method.

Fourth, through these teachings theologians are ridiculed by the other faculties. For they then are called dreamers and are said to know nothing about solid truth and morals and the Bible.

Fifth, through these teachings numberless paths to error are opened. For theologians speak and make up for themselves at will terms that other doctors and masters neither understand nor have any interest in understanding. They say the most unbelievable and absurd things, which are said to follow from their senseless fictions.[87]

Sixth, through these useless teachings the church and faith are strengthened neither on the inside nor on the outside. Such teachings apparently instead give opportunities for believing that God is not at all simple and one, as Bradwardine says.[88]

Seventh, through these teachings many theologians are both actively and passively scandalized. For some are called uncouth by others, and some on the contrary are called meddlesome or dreamers. Such theologians rush ahead with propositions from these doctrines. There are infinite durations of time in the godhead,[89] according to what is prior and posterior, although it is eternal. And the same for what can be measured. The Holy Spirit is produced freely, in opposition, and contingently on the part of the "principle by which it is." In the godhead the Holy Spirit is absolute potentiality for nonbeing. To produce the Son in godhead, as it is, is nothing. The Holy Spirit is produced before it becomes the highest perfection. Father and Holy Spirit are not knowledge, and Father and Son are not love. The Son in the godhead could produce another son, because it has the same potency with the Father. And so on, in innumerable other matters.

Likewise, for many years there has been the greatest controversy over the subject of the terms that an earlier generation[90] so limited in order to say that no predicate can be expressed of God which speaks of imperfection. Others go in the opposite direction and say that every predicate can be universally expressed, to the extent of it being possible to say that God is damned.

Likewise, it seems necessary to make sure that the faculty [of theology] can never determine matters of faith in allowing the other faculties to have equal voices with it in this area, as is now done in the University, since danger to faith and shame to the theological faculty can follow, with no remedy.[91]

Likewise, it is said that the life and morals of some persons scandalize the faculty. If this is true, something must be done about it.

Likewise, nothing has been done to deal with or repair errors that at other times have emerged and have been imported to the faculty. The result is that from elsewhere some of the bachelors of theology bring wrong teachings in which the public school of theology has been scandalized. In this matter the chancellor excuses himself, because he could not find other masters who were willing to provide sufficient time to supervise [these bachelors].[92] Also, he has been afraid of a more dangerous split coming from what he has noticed, and because he has been advised to use discretion.

Likewise, our masters of theology are to be admonished, especially those who have provided the opportunity, that they encourage their bachelors and scholars to flee or abandon these most empty teachings, which are useless and sterile. They are not to approve of them by showing any interest or attention but instead to condemn them. In God's goodness such teachings have already been looked upon as sophisms banned from theology. The subjects dealt with in the second, third, and fourth books of *Sentences* are to be given more attention, for this textbook is hardly read any longer except for its first book. They are to spend time on useful doctrines and similarly on the Bible.[93] Also, books containing the doctrines mentioned above are not to be read independently without the permission of the faculty.

For the honor of God it should be considered carefully how great is the need for the education of the people and the solution of moral questions in our times. And so one must believe that in such a critical situation and amid so many dangers to souls, one can hardly be satisfied with playing about, not to speak of engaging in fantasies, with matters that are wholly superfluous. It also seems that it requires a great and trained intelligence to clarify such questions and investigate them in depth, even though perfection and true depth are to be found elsewhere. But they who refuse to spend their time and teaching in matters of substance do not realize this fact.

Likewise, it might be useful, as once in the time of plagues the faculty of medicine composed a little treatise in order to inform people, similarly it might be done through the faculty of theology or at the order of someone that a little treatise be made on the main points of our religion, and especially on its precepts, for the instruction of uneducated people.[94] For such people, sermons in our time are either not made, or hardly ever given, or else they are badly given.

Likewise, it might be necessary to provide for an inquisitor or someone who would be able to function as an inquisitor in dealing with matters that are publicized with too much freedom and great rashness, at places of entertainment and elsewhere.[95]

Likewise, it might be better to establish the practice that instead of an expert in canon law, each cathedral and metropolitan church have someone to teach theology, etc.[96]

Likewise, in view of scandals arising from past teachings on dogma, it would be right to provide for the future by having all such teachings written down in a single list, and this list be made public in the schools. It would be said that the masters will not accept such wrong teachings, and from that time everyone should abandon these and similar doctrines. Unless the faculty of theology does this or something similar, it might be necessary for the chancellor to make some similar provision, by not admitting to the licentiate in theology those who are guilty of such teachings, even when the faculty wants to accept them. Nevertheless, it would be more wholesome that in such a matter the chancellor proceed in agreement with the faculty.[97]

LETTER 4   Gerson to His Friends at the College of Navarre[98]
                Bruges, 27 April 1400

[Gerson thanks them for their support and indicates that he has given way to their request, and to that of the duke of Burgundy, that he return to the post of chancellor of the University. His illness, however, forces him to remain in Bruges for the time being.]

Your letters and their great love brought to me no small consolation in my misfortune, which, as I hope, has a happy side. For it is the scourge of the Father of mercies that until now has truly directed me, beyond all hope and any merit of mine. He acted in this way to provide a way in temptation so that I could bear it (1 Cor 10:13). Therefore I give thanks to your kindest goodness, which provided compassion for someone who has been scourged in such a way. Your concern has sent documents filled with consolation, which have weighed down messengers. Such help I cannot claim for myself nor do I consider myself worthy to accept it.

Thus it truly was fitting for those who professed wisdom to console one of their company, however much a failure he might be, because he still was subjected to tribulation. I once tried, without any pretense, with great effort and expense and conscious of my fragility, to remove from my fragile shoulders the great burden of the chancellorship of Paris and to hand it over to someone else. Nevertheless, I have been caught in a labyrinth from which there is no exit. It is as if I have put my feet in a trap and walk in my faults (Jb 18:8). I have been disappointed in my hope and feel that which Terence said, that it is not often permitted for a man to be as he wishes.[99]

I have been ordered by him to whom, after God, I owe my self and all my works (I speak of my lord, the lord of Burgundy), whose advice I hope will be nothing but modest, humble, and salubrious. May God forgive me. For those who gave the same counsel, I set forth in obedience, but my journey was stopped by the one who once blocked Balaam's donkey (Nm 22:22–30).[100] For the time being the Lord has delayed my carrying out the office of chancellor, I who was ready voluntarily to give it up completely. Now I am willing to exercise it in accord with obedience. In this matter I do what you command, nor do I see any other way for the time being, except for me to send you an authorization that someone take my place in carrying out all functions with which I would now have dealt.

Be well, and remember me in your prayers.

Written at Bruges on 27 April.

LETTER 5   Gerson to His Colleagues at the College of
             Navarre[101]
             Bruges, 29 April 1400

[Gerson describes his attachment to his colleagues but also indicates the distance he kept from them while he was a student at the college. He wanted to return to Paris but had been prevented by illness. Now he thinks over his own situation. He mistrusts the intellectual life when it is a question of showing one's brilliance with novelties. Finally, he warns against empty talk and companionship for its own sake.]

It is a joy, beloved colleagues and brothers in Christ, it is a great joy, since I cannot address you, to speak to you in writing. For conversations among friends are always pleasant. But if according to the old man in Terence, the closest bond for friends comes from nearness,[102] then there should be much friendship for me in this venerable college where you dwell. I was not only close to it but quite familiar with it from early adolescence, for I was always resident there and was formed in my ways from my social contacts there.

I shall therefore console myself in the period of quiet that has been imposed on me by speaking with you. The divine scourge has forced me into a bed of illness, where it has compelled me to lie flat and motionless. I hope this will be useful and, through God's great mercy, not only something I can endure but something I want to experience. Why so? Because this kind of rest has made it impossible for me to read or pray or to have any extended period of healthy thought. But then it has also made you closer to me, if I do not resist. How can this be so? For divine grace until now either has taken away bodily pain and anxiousness of spirit or grace has tempered them almost beyond hope and truly beyond all my merit.

Thanks be to him who now has judged that he would correct me, his servant, in my resistance to him. He acts not in anger or wrath, but with a filial rod. And Lord, if life is such and in these matters you correct me in the life of my spirit and give me life, then in peace there is a most harsh bitterness (cf. Is 38:16–17).

But I return to you, to whom I have desired to reveal some of my thoughts in friendship, and even if I do not gain anything else but a certain pleasure in communicating with you.

My thinking, which perhaps is not so solid, has stimulated me a great deal. Also the kind persuasion of friends has helped me, so that from what I have heard, read, and understood I might offer to write down some concerns chosen for the learning or edification of others. "Your unencumbered intelligence will be sharpened," my friends say, "the industry of your predecessors will be imitated, and your name will be consecrated for the memory of those to come; finally, perhaps not a few who otherwise would have read nothing will come upon your writings and either because of attachment to them or their novelty, as happens, gain profit from them."[103]

But a more modest consideration than these concerns takes hold of me when I realize that there is no end to making more books (Eccl 12:12). I see so many and such great tomes written by outstanding men of the greatest genius and wisdom and yet neglected by most people, so that they are barely known by name alone. I see, I say, and in sighing detest either our laziness or arrogance. At the same time I think of what worth my ever-so-unimportant writings might have if those that are so excellent are stepped upon.

I am afraid, moreover, that I will enter into the same vice of which I vehemently accuse others. And what is this, you ask? There are those who by all kinds of trifles and clumsy novelties clutter up parchment and the minds of listeners, especially of those who are experts. They fill them with the sterile cockles (if only they were not also diseased) of their doctrines and burden the stomach of memory not with food but with husks. They sow the field of the heart with thorns rather than with grain and end up with what Seneca said: "They do not know what is necessary because they have learned what is superfluous."[104]

If only those who read or listen to such things would come to themselves again and start out anew in a better way after such failures by turning their eyes to writings that are better for them! They will weep, I assert, at their own fates and over the time wasted in covering over the tablet of their soul, which should be painted with what is useful. Instead, they are content with what is petty, writing letters that will do no good for the soul, unless it has to be said that these have deformed their souls.

But they say we have the same possibility that was given to earlier masters in their writings. They also complain that it is wretched to use what already has been discovered and never to be able to discover anything. Here we find what Horace said of the poets, that both the ignorant and the learned can write poems.[105]

We do write, but our sentences have no weight, our words no number or measure. For all that we write is flabby, mean, slack.[106] We do not write what is new. Instead we repeat what is old but treat and transmit it in a new way. Trying to make these materials our own, we devalue them and make them absurd, as in the vernacular proverb according to which the canals dug by the ancients are solid enough not for those who improve them but for those who try to destroy them.[107] Terence noted something similar concerning those who from good Greek comedies could not make good Latin ones.[108] And so they take excerpts, or more properly make lacerations, from outstanding books and proven expressions, and tend to darken great tomes. Through lack of care in writing and reading they render their originals either superfluous or dead in their core. You can see in those who lecture on the *Sentences* [of Peter Lombard], how it shames each of them to follow even the great theologians, and so the variety of sterility grows immensely.[109]

How much wiser it would be to make use of what already has been well invented, rather than to invent what is sought for. Why should one try to produce such things in undermining what already has been well made? Why do we allow loquacious youngsters to express themselves with ease and, since they look only at a few aspects of the question, to demonstrate their facility? The most solid and reliable tradition comes not from those who go into argumentative dialectics or those who live base, sordid, and lost lives but from most pious and well-trained men who practice what they preach. Therefore we should remember the saying of the man who saw, read, and wrote many things (I speak of Jean Buridan), who in the preface to his outstanding tract on ethics frankly admits that he will not attach himself to new reasonings, however much they seem apparent, since he has often been tricked by them.[110] This never happened in the writings of the ancients, especially in moral questions. Therefore Aristotle says in the sixth book of his *Ethics* that it is necessary to be attentive to the demonstrations or statements of those with experience, who are older or prudent, no less than to the demonstration itself.[111] And so he sees many uses for the one who has experience.

Responding, therefore, I will reply to my own thoughts and the exhortations of my friends concerning writing down new matters. The use of what has been well constructed, in sober humility, is sufficient for the time being for me and those like me. Every form of puffed-up arrogance in unfamiliar matters is to be banished, so that we do not increase talk glorying in our loftiness. We must be content with a common, as I might call it, Minerva. We are to follow the well-trodden path that has more space and is further from the danger of errors and scandals. We have so many living fountains of salvific wisdom. We are not, I ask, to tire ourselves out with vain and, indeed, foolish labor in digging out empty reservoirs. I exhort and repeating myself I will again and again advise that we embrace the writings of those who are more tried and tested in this pursuit. And so our abilities are not only limited but minimal, and we do not have the capacity of interpreting so many books, even the useful ones, when they come our way.

With some writers we can in passing quickly consider them, as if it were not right for us completely to ignore them, and then we can part from them forever. With others we at times make use of them in accord with our need for them or as we enjoy or find them appropriate. But some writers we should regularly call to our side in familiarity and place them like the most faithful servants within the chambers of our minds, amid its secrets and everyday conversations.

If someone out of curiosity comes to ask which writers or what books there are that I think are to be preferred to others, I will answer that I cannot provide a single and definitive response. The variety of students according to age, intelligence, character, and the times requires different types of advice. But this one saying of the Apostle should remain set deep in the minds of theologians: the fullness of the law and the end of its precept are charity or love (cf. Rom 13:10).

When, therefore, in accord with the requirement of an end, other things have to be moderated, whatever more greatly and more directly contributes to building charity should be preferred in reading, remembering, and meditating. This is the case insofar as the intellect is refreshed by affectivity, where indeed there is more merit. From wisdom comes this savory knowledge, as one is filled in a rich feast (Ps 62:6).

In order to discern these matters, the new listener of theology should be skilled in consulting one of the many whose teaching, way of life, and reputation please him, who can easily teach because of long and varied exercise in living, reading, and living well, rather than embrace the teaching of one who questions the course of studies. They should desire instruction either in that part of theology that schoolmen discuss, or in that which edifies, regulates, and forms the way of life of those who read the subject. Or they should seek instruction in that which is appropriate for them when they preach.

These three elements are not completely disparate. With them the true disciple of theology should involve himself, daily and, if not in equal measure, at least in turn and to a certain degree. For the first scholastic concern puffs up and disturbs a person when it lacks the second element of edification, while the second ingredient without the first does not provide sufficient keenness of intellect, and, finally, the third element of preaching without the two others often does not so much instruct others as repel and ruin them.

For the first element we are helped, for example, by questions on the *Sentences*, especially by those doctors of theology who wrote with great purity and substance. Among these, in my judgment, Lord Bonaventure and Saint Thomas [Aquinas] and Durand [of Saint Pourçain] are to be numbered.[112] Henry of Ghent excels in his *Quotlibeta*.[113] More recent theologians are outstanding in many areas. Among them, however, this one practice is less acceptable, that purely physical or metaphysical matters, or even more shamefully, questions of logic, are mixed in with theological terms.

Moreover, in the second and third elements of edification and preaching, once the first [that of scholastic theology] is assumed, uplifting stories belong, in which living persons are justly remembered, such as Gregory's *Dialogues*,[114] the *Ecclesiastical or Three-Part Histories*,[115] the *Collations*[116] and the *Lives of the Fathers*,[117] the *Confessions* of Augustine,[118] and the holy meditations of him and others, the *Divine Rhetoric* of William of Paris,[119] the legends of the saints and similar writings. Here one finds devout reading and receives much encouragement to follow the impulses of virtue. Only if one has not previously been carried off or inflated by one's understanding is it possible for the subtle eye of the attentive person in its simplicity to reach the most lofty speculation. This is something that is both desirable and salubrious. It is error to say that these matters, being more banal and

181

facile, block out our recognition of more subtle concerns, provided they are dealt with in the appropriate time and measure.

Mystical expositions of the divine scriptures also consider this subject. There are many of them from celebrated and most holy doctors, as with Gregory the Great in his *Moralia* and *Pastoral Care*,[120] with Bernard in his *Sermons on the Song of Songs*,[121] with Richard of Saint Victor in his work on contemplation and other works that can never be admired to a sufficient degree, as well as with the work of William of Paris, who by pleasing artifice combined in a clear manner speculative matters with moralizing comparisons.[122]

But with the writings of the pagans I would by no means try to keep them from being transmitted. I commend them and, as it were, as a pilgrim I run through them, both for their abundance of moral statements, for the style and elaboration in the words, and for the special expertise of poems and stories, and finally for a certain pleasure in the variety of what one can read, even though in holy doctors, as in Augustine *The City of God*, in Orosius, in Jerome and Lactantius and in similar writers many of these elements I believe are to be found in abundance and no less usefully.[123]

Again, one has to deal with each of the aforesaid matters in different ways. In the first [scholastic theology], the exercise of disputation strengthens one's colleagues. I am thinking not in terms of impudent, stiff-necked, bitter forms of disputation, raising a tumult in stubborn animosity. I refer to modest behavior, as befits the search for truth, which sharpens and stimulates the mind, renews and kindles study, and also stabilizes the position of truth once falsity in the opposition is revealed. This will mean that the person devoted to study will not be afraid even in public to defend what he knows he in private has learned well.[124]

Truly in the second area [of edification] one needs, if it is to be made complete, a discreet silence, so that one is separated for a time from the company not only of people but also of cares and worldly affairs. It is even necessary at one point to take time off from prior study, since it cannot wholly provide the peace of mind of which we speak. Then, once the door is closed on oneself, the mind can learn to be drawn to those matters of which it has read, and it will consider for itself how terrible God is in his counsels over the sons of men (Ps 65:5), and how hard he is on the evil and how merciful to his elect. A person will ascend the watchtower of eternity, from which he will see with the wise man that vanity of vanities and all things are vanity (Eccl 1:2). I will not review these many matters, since the savory reading of those books that have been named will teach us everything.

But on the basis of experience I would add that nothing is more harmful to mental peace and contemplation, nothing is more wasteful of that most precious thing, time, and nothing more of a hindrance to the perfection of those who study, as conversations.[125] I mean not only the base ones, which wholly corrupt good habits, but also those that are extended at length and to no purpose and which fly on the wings of common rumors, or deal with childish jokes and clumsy tales or people's conflicts in opposing each other and similar matters. Here, from morning until night, the day is slowly eaten up and even much of the deepest night. Through such conversations people entertain themselves by indulging themselves in laziness, anger, or disgust, and so they become more depressed, more upset, and more scatterbrained.

I am deceived if anyone ever ascends onto the Lord's mountain and into the ark of contemplation unless he has come to terms with this empty talk. He has to become a person who refuses to listen and a mute who does not open his mouth. And I glory in this one thing in the Lord, that the college made it possible that there were few opportunities for such confabulations. I rarely had a chance to talk and to experience leisure, since it was so rare that there was someone else with whom I could enjoy engaging in the exchange of words, for so great among us was the difference of background and studies.[126]

I do not deny, however, that talks with proven men can be profitable when these have experienced the ascent of contemplation and the dangers of its steepness through their own efforts and trials.

Finally, as for the third and final concern [preaching], which is born from and nourished by the first two, it can be made use of sometimes among a few companions and sometimes in public. But when it leads only to curiosity or scandal and, to be brief, does not contain anything to instill charity in the listeners, this activity is to be fled and rejected. Gregory's *Pastoral Care*[127] will teach you how much caution is to be shown in discretion.

Be well then, colleagues and brothers joined through a special charity. Pursue your studies well and commend me in your prayers.

Written at Bruges, the twenty-ninth of April, in the year 1400.

LETTER 6   Gerson to His Colleagues at the College of Navarre[128]

Bruges, written between May and September 1400

[Another meditation on the state of the University of Paris. Gerson is concerned both about arrogant teachers and undisciplined students. But his major worry is the fact that the University public does not have access to good sermons, after the expulsion of the Dominicans in the early 1390s. Now it looks as if they might be able to return.]

Behold I obey your desires, colleagues and beloved brothers. Lately I expressed to you in a letter some of my thoughts, and I especially advised this one thing, that you concentrate your study on the most important teachings. Then it will not be necessary for you, like Vergil, to seek gold in the mud,[129] or from the rock of sterile doctrine to draw forth honey or oil from the hardest rock (Dt 32:13). I added that the intellect is to be developed so that a crude and arid emotional life is not to be deserted but must be transferred into affectivity of heart. You wrote back in a kindly way that you had accepted these recommendations and asked that I again provide something similar. And so let it be done.

Receive again something that will alleviate through familiar talk with you my sense of revulsion. My gift will remove a burden from a mind full of indignant grief and pour out the bile of bitterness, in which, nevertheless, until now there has been a certain amount of usefulness.[130]

Once often, but recently even more frequently and profoundly, in the leisure of my bad health, I considered in pious meditation the state of the good University of Paris, my mother, so that I, one of the least of her sons, might make up for my absence from her by being mentally present. Inevitably I think about many facets of the University that deserve praise. The University appears as a bright spiritual sun that shines upon the structure of the church, scattering dark shadows of error with its gleaming, pure brilliance. The University also seems to be that river of paradise divided into four parts, watering the entire face of the earth (cf. Gn 2:10).[131]

Alas, nothing here with us is blessed in all its parts. Rushing in upon my thoughts come many sorrowful matters that call for a strict hand of correction and improvement. This is the case with rivalries among opposing opinions and the excessively obstinate statements that here resound. These interrupt very much the study of truth and overstrain the whole body of the University, upsetting it, driving away modesty, and making it more prone to upheaval than its calling requires.

I want to separate you from the midst of these waves of inquietude and contention, as much as I can do, and not to try in vain to overcome all the base efforts of evil men, especially when they draw the origins of their faction or impiety from a higher source.[132] Take hold of what I say. Otherwise peace will never be given to you. There will never be any sense of security in your studies or an adequate feeling of tranquility. Blocking your way are also some affected partialities and a stubborn insistence on winning, as well as prejudice or outright contempt of persons and of nations.[133] For they do not allow us to walk in the house of the Lord with consent (cf. Ps 54:15), through the path of truth and of charity, which ought to be available for everyone, as something peaceful and not obstructed in any way by such things. For in Christ there is neither foreigner nor Scythian nor barbarian, etc. (cf. Col 3:11).[134]

I see another problem in the studies of the University, and indeed a very great one. For there is a great defect and error in terms of the discipline of its youths in morals, even in their basic learning in the most basic matters. This is caused by the very great numbers of teachers in whose multitude there are some who are harmful to their pupils, saving the praise of the good and those of whom I speak without reproach. But others show blind ignorance or lazy negligence, or they wrongly pursue adulation. Sometimes they act out of an inappropriate fickleness, or, something intolerable in its pestilence, by the contagious example of the most base way of life. Such teachers do not pull up the evil roots of such proclivities but nourish and increase them. Either they are afraid to correct their pupils, who might leave them, or religion and piety are uncouth for them. They think it beneath their position to teach such things to their pupils, or they are afraid that if they teach that which they neglect, they will fall into that impropriety which is most noticeable for youths: it is shameful for the teacher when his guilt refutes him. Thus restraints on the young are removed, and they indulge in their inventions, freed according to the desire of their hearts. Headlong they rush off the path into vices. Youth thus become contentious, unsettled, impudent, prone to inflicting injuries, and most short-tempered when offenses are committed against them. Moreover, they are devoid of religion, for they know nothing more about the Christian religion than pagans. Finally, as Jude the Apostle said of some, they are blemishes (Jude 12), or as the common folk say, sacks of coal, the one defiling the other in the worst ways. But just as they behave at home, so too they act abroad in public speech.

Instead of the modesty of behavior that should be observed there, they confound all things with the most insolent and hostile hissing, gestures, and murmuring. They basely spurn the word of God in the one who is spreading it. They hinder him, disturb him, and cut him off. This injury is not to be considered something minor, as we know from Aristotle's statement: It is no small matter for a youth to be trained in one way or the other.[135] There is no doubt that from youths who are not obedient or are badly instructed, young men and later adults are made who are not only useless for the community of the University but who also pollute its entire body and lacerate it. These creatures arm themselves in cruelty for the destruction of the good.

Why should one wonder if out of unschooled disciples pernicious doctors are made? The conferring of an academic degree does not root out evil. Rather, it can increase it out of pride or bring forth what has been latent. In the end the foundation of doctrine falters in a person when it has been established too quickly, imperfectly, or ineptly. Whatever you build on top of it in terms of more learning necessarily will be insecure and will have less than solid strength.

In this my meditation I see these dangers and am confounded by them. I am shaken at the same time by lamentation and weeping. I really can find no sufficient answer to what I should do or how I should take care and by what means I can rightly win people over. I would write of such matters to the teachers themselves and with the seal [of the chancellorship]. But this would be a huge task, and with most of them I have no contact based on mutual recognition or closeness. I could write to all collectively. But I must watch out not to consume myself in foolish exertions, since many of the teachers either would ridicule the zeal of my humble self and assert their own rights, or they would become enraged, or accuse me of presumption. Believe me, the truth is most bitter. But I do not know how it can be that no one more than the learned, being wise in their own eyes, takes every tender piece of advice or fraternal correction as an insult and an injury that has to be avenged.

As a last resort I would preach of these matters to the youths themselves, but you know that I am absent, and they are harsh to those who direct them, as Horace says.[136] Because of the most strident din from their passions they become deaf to the truth. Nor can the ignorant be taught by words. Folly has been lodged in the heart of the youth, says the wise man, and the rod of discipline will drive it away (Prv 22:15). The rod speaks, not words.

A third defect harshly presses against my soul, something which newly has come about and has placed a mark of not small shame on the glory of the University. Very often I have been told by worthy persons who have come to me from near and far that often sermons are lacking at the University, even Sunday sermons to the clergy. This development lately has come about like some monster and is hardly bearable. It forces me, as other matters do, to weep over the wretched division and mournful mutilation of a considerable part of the University of Paris, especially in the holy faculty of theology. This split was caused by the errors of Jean de Monzon, assertions that were rash and impious.[137]

I do not want anyone to think that here I will justify or defend the part I played in the rejection or removal of the Friars Preachers. It only needs to be considered what they themselves did. For in faith and constancy I affirm that the condemnation of the errors of the forenamed Jean de Monzon was done according to reason and catholic faith. When he was defended at the papal court, I myself was present, then being a bachelor of theology lecturing on the Bible, together with other excellent and most wise men sent as legates from the University.[138]

But why is it that they who fell do not make an effort to rise again? Why does not the good mother University, which once was angered at its sons, not finally remember mercy, or will it confine its mercy in its wrath (Ps 76:10)? Will it forever cast aside so many sheep of its flock because they lost their way and wandered off? But if these refuse to return, the example of Christ the good shepherd should be imitated, so that they be sought out and by a certain gentle force be returned, in spite of their resistance to their own flock (cf. Jn 10:11). And how much more this effort ought to be made now, when the friars ask for and pray with all their hearts and desires, as we are told, for this result.[139]

But I seem to see some people before me, if only they were zealous in accord with knowledge, who now object; we are prepared, they say, to receive them, and to restore peace, but the integrity of the faith, the honor of the University, and its security from loss by no means can allow it to ignore its travails and expenses. I am not speaking in such a way that I think such matters are to be neglected. I deny, however, that such great animosity is necessary, or that the wounded but live limb is to be amputated, as is said, according to what was said about Sulla's victory: the medicine exceeded the measure.[140] We are Christians and are daily engaged in the school of charity under him who says, "Learn from me because I am gentle and humble of heart" (Mt 11:20), and, "Unless you forgive sins," etc. (Mt 18:35). Therefore what we need is not so much what can be required from the rigor of the law but what provides benefit.

I do remember why and how the said friars were separated by indirect means from the company of the University. For it was decided and concluded that whoever refused to take an oath of condemnation against the said errors would be deprived of every degree and honor in the University. These errors had first been condemned by the University and then by the bishop. The bachelors who were then to be accepted from the said friars delayed doing so. They explained that they had not yet asked for or received permission from their superiors to swear such an oath. For this reason they subsequently neither obtained degrees nor teaching chairs nor gave sermons. I heard afterward, however, that either all or most of them were ready to fulfill the said condition.[141] But even if they now wished to do so, they would seem to be forbidden entrance to the faculty.

I wish that everyone would pay attention and direct gentle thoughts to considering how great a spiritual loss it is and has been. From that time and until now a great number of sermons, lessons, and fruitful instructions have ceased both in the University and elsewhere. Even a natural form of piety requires that a mother go out to her errant son or that a body be moved in sympathy for a sick member. Now consider the damage to ourselves in terms of sermons, intellectual arguments, and the like. Then listen to the warning summarized in the verse: If you do not wish to spare others, spare yourself.[142]

I will not speak of the scandals, shame, and imprisonment suffered by those of whom we speak. Such things should nevertheless have made those who want to be considered as kind and good more quickly to have shown mercy on those who had been expelled. I admit, in opposition, that the University has suffered great losses in terms of labor and expenses. But these matters are in my judgment easily to be forgotten or disregarded for the sake of the commerce of peace, for fraternal reconciliation, and for the reintegration of so important a segment that was cut off. Unless I am deceived and the present situation is acceptable, only in this way can integrity and honor be restored to the University.

Perhaps many will cry out here that they are in agreement because they are zealous for peace or wish to seem to be. But I am afraid that when the time comes for excusing the friars, nothing which can be offered for reconciliation will be enough for these people, for the friars are accused of having not kept the faith or the honor of the University. And so in the end there will be neither reconciliation nor peace.

I am not so bold that I would claim to define how those matters of which we have spoken, the faith and honor of the University, can remain unharmed. But I am firmly convinced of this one thing, that this reconciliation can easily take place if not all, or even many, but just a few members of the University wish with a few of the friars to make an effort on the basis of an upright and sound will. If they refuse to do so in their hearts, however, then whatever smooth-tongued mouths claim can in no way be obtained, whether by prayers or by gifts. Why is this so? Because such people always will contend that this is a matter of faith and they can not concede anything here.

What then remains except that each person withdraws into himself? He can set before the eyes of his heart this mournful schism with its past misfortunes. Let each see to it that he repairs this damage with diligence and keenness, insofar as he receives from above the ability or grace to do so. Once all desire for rivalry has been put aside, let him then look for peace and pursue it. This is what I am trying to do now. This is what I on my behalf offer in these writings. But to what degree I will make progress or will fail, that remains wholly uncertain in my mind. I know the way men behave in public. I know how different they are in their judgments and opinions. I know what implacable and untamed feelings reign in the hearts of some and how much an enjoyment of contradicting others flourishes in their unrestrained tongues. I also know how much ferocious license rages in their efforts to persecute the good. Finally, I know how few of them seek, through a good, concerned faith, what belongs to Jesus Christ and not what is their own.

I have desired that these writings not be made public but be given to a few who I think will profit by them and not be opposed to them. Others will object if these writings are brought to the few. They will react angrily and even consider it to be a crime or a sign of instability that I seem to have preferred peace with the Jacobites[143] or to have written for this purpose. But I will freely admit and not consider it to be a source of shame that both now and previously I have always in modesty wished for or sought reconciliation with the friars, and even in the midst of disputes this has been my desire.

Let them perish who glory in the base mutilation of the mother or the mystical body, who do not desire healing but show cruel anger to those who seek a remedy and who by demoniacal impiety let themselves be compelled more to schism than to a most attractive union. This mode of persecution is to be rejected if such people act in rage against those who in peace love unity. The generous foot of living virtue is to stamp out such persecution, but provided that a harmful scandal does not thereby arise in the University or the state. This result, I think, is to be feared more than real persecution.

Now and elsewhere I have avoided openly saying or doing some of the things that my zeal suggested were to be said or done. Unless I am lying to myself, I have been truthful and devout to these people. It will then be up to you either to reveal these little letters or to conceal them, to deal with the matter for those who are outside,[144] or entirely to set it aside. But who knows what the good Lord will desire and if he will give the voice of power to this voice when we bring up the matter. Who knows if those hearing this voice will listen. Or if they in understanding it will grasp it, and in securing the good of peace will work in a more generous spirit. This is what I ask, what I beg, what I implore through him who is our peace. In him be well, and remember me in your prayers. Written at Bruges.

LETTER 7   Gerson to His Colleagues at the College of
Navarre[145]
Bruges, between July and September 1400

*[Gerson regrets the fact that intellectuals, especially students, prefer new
and incomplete writings to old and tried ones. His own notes have been
plundered and copied, something he regrets. He hopes that the taste of
such muddied waters will make students yearn for the purer springs that
are their sources.]*

It is good when human nature, being eager for understanding,
sets aside its curiosity for always hearing or conveying something
new, and instead with sober humility first makes use of what
already has been well composed. On this subject I remember
having written to you a certain letter that was not brief.[146] But this
point of view cannot or barely can persuade scholastics, especially younger ones. It delights them to transcribe, the faster the
better, or to study more recent compilations rather than old
ones. They are like boys who even though the most unripe fruits
are more sour, eat them more avidly than ripe ones, which are
healthy for the digestion. Let them believe this who will.

If I may say something about myself, since the matter now
touches me, I would prefer that no one be in doubt that I would
prefer that studious men give themselves entirely to understanding the books of the most proven doctors of the past rather than
wasting their time with the sterile ignorance of my little works.
For I ought not thus to boast of my fame in the mouth of men, a
place full of noise, nor to love my writings as if they were my own
sons, as Aristotle speaks of the poets.[147] Instead, I should with a
calm mind insist on rejecting anything that contributes to my
glory when thereby the true and solid glory of God is less
increased. It is increased less if more salubrious teachings are put
aside and my more useless ones occupy the minds of others. And
where, I ask, is the humility that is the root of wisdom? Where is
that canticle—To God alone be honor and glory[148]—if magnanimity is not magnanimity but great and evil animosity, causing the
increase of one's own glory in the loss of divine glory? This is the

magnanimity that does great things in nonetheless saying with Christ: If I seek my glory, it is nothing (cf. Jn 8:54).

In this way when someone achieves fame, then infamy arrives. But the one who is magnanimous cannot be hindered from performing a task in which God is honored and one's neighbor is edified. But its opposite necessarily happens in those who seek vain glory. Rejoicing in fame they are puffed up, and being disgraced they waste away and give up. They are cast about in the wind like weathercocks or reeds blown this way and that by the wind of popular favor.

But I feel that a zeal that can be either brotherly or malicious might oppose me when I say such things. Why then do I write something or not tear up what I have written? Or if my own need requires that I write in such a way and maintain what is my own, why do I then not make sure that these writings do not reach the public and instead keep them private? Indeed, I hardly had strong enough protection against thieves in my household to keep such writings from almost all being secretly plundered, in spite of my forbidding it. This has happened with works that were not corrected and which were scattered about in notes, so that when I myself reread them I could scarcely understand them, nor could I bring them together into any wholeness. All the more I ask to be forgiven and beseech that if others have such writings in this primitive and corrupt form, then if there is no copy with the author or any chance of improving them, may a consuming flame absorb them or may they be torn into shreds and go into the burial place of eternal forgetfulness.

Added to this problem is the insistence both of friends and sometimes of rivals who ask, by themselves and through others, until one gets tired of hearing, that those writings which one would prefer to have put aside and kept separate from the rest of one's work instead either be published in corrected form or be condemned as something that should be renounced. Again, the situation is such that the curiosity of some people desires novelties, although these are quite unequal in worth to older compositions. They either take pleasure in consumption, as happens with bodily food, or lack the energy to consider what is old. And so the reading of what is new can do good for them. Certainly some profit, even a small one, is more desirable in these newer writings than none at all in the older ones.

Finally, who does not know that as in faces, so in souls, there are numberless differences? The spiritual taste varies, just as we perceive with the bodily sense of taste, so that for one person something is repulsive, while for someone else, it provides healthy sustenance. Who knows in the end if, once small rivulets have been tasted, students will be drawn by their sweetness to imagine more savory things from their sources. Or else they will grow tired of the rivulets' more muddy content and seek out the purer sources.

LETTER 8   Gerson to the Carthusian Jean de Gonnant[149]
             Paris, 1401
[Gerson is sending the former knight a treatise defending the Carthusian practice of not eating meat. If Jean de Gonnant has trouble with the Latin, he can get help from other Carthusians.]

To the outstanding person Jean de Gonnant, who once in the world was a remarkable knight and now in the service of Christ fights in a more illustrious way with the excellent company of Carthusians, his Jean, unworthy chancellor of the church of Paris, asks that he may obtain the triumph of eternal joy.

You remember in your sagacity, as I believe, how you once asked from my celebrated teacher, now the bishop of Cambrai, that he through a treatise based on divine law and effective disputation might restrain and refute the carnal men who with blind eyes and foaming mouths bark out against the way of life of the Carthusians.[150] They claim that they live contrary to reason and piety because of their perpetual observance of abstinence from meat. This same teacher of mine attempted to do so before I, however unworthy, succeeded him in the office and seat of chancellor. He nevertheless did not get to tackle the problem, as I see it, for there were a great number of obstacles that regularly impeded him. Therefore, not forgetting you and your petition, I have finally gotten an opportunity in one of my lessons to make an attempt, although I am unequal in ability, to satisfy the good and fervent zeal of your religious order. If I complete what I want to do, then give thanks to him from whom every good and perfect gift comes (Jas 1:17). If I am less successful in my attempt, then let your brothers, my fathers, and others whose wisdom goes deeper, add to or correct my imperfect work.

Be well and remember me in your prayers. And if you perhaps are not capable of listening to Latin eloquence, do not complain, for you have a sufficient number of interpreters.[151] I speak of the said fathers. I prostrate myself before their knees and in seeking the help of their prayers I, a beggar, make my request.

LETTER 9   Gerson to his Brother Nicolas[152]
            Paris, 5 December 1401

[Gerson shares with his brother the sense of isolation and separation he felt after Nicolas left to live as a Celestine monk. Rightfully he should have rejoiced in his brother's choice to leave the temptations and dangers of the academic life and to follow a better way. He himself never had the opportunity to do the same. He reminds Nicolas of his mother's concern for him.]

True brother according to the flesh, but more true in the love of Christ, greetings and blessings to you.

My little letter comes to you later than I was hoping, but not because I have forgotten you. The truth knows that a crowd of other tasks rushed in and hindered me. Drawing me to them they kept me from you. Now that I have been given a very little space of time for a pause, I have said goodbye to other cares and give my hand and my pen to you, who truly occupy my mind.

I will admit in the first place that the laxness of my mind has shown me how I still am not wholly capable of loving heavenly things. Moreover, I realize how much the tempter is not absent from me, as I know he is not from you, nor hardly from any mortals whose life is temptation on the earth. And so, brother, after you had left and you were happily joined to that angelic society

195

that exists in human bodies,[153] and we were separated from the sight of each other, I indeed felt both on the road and at Paris a certain tenderness toward you in my heart, more than I had felt at other times. Your absence then seemed to me more of a burden and my fate harsher than usual. I sighed for you as an ox that is separated from its mate. The trauma of separation from you was devouring me. It caused great pain and mangled my soul. Amid my thoughts and my words about you, tears that were not asked for came to my eyes, and I was in pain.

In the depths of my soul I was accusing myself of doing wrong. I also reproached myself for a foolish lack of nerve, which grieved at your happy state, for I knew it would have been more correct to rejoice. I knew, I would say, as I knew myself, and whenever I returned to myself and spoke in the light of faith and experience, that the present life is nothing. Whatever is in the least related to us and all flesh is like grass, and all glory is like the flower of the field (Is 40:6).

I considered many similar thoughts. Getting up I entered God's sanctuary and I thought vividly about the last things for the just, about ancient days and eternal years (Ps 76:5). Then it was that you seemed to me to be happy in the hope that brings such happiness, for you have sailed into a port protected from the waves and storms of the world. My soul magnified the Lord and my spirit rejoiced in God my savior (Lk 1:46). In this way he was a brother to me, so long as he was well and reason prevailed.[154]

But on the contrary there suddenly rose up in turn a great crowd of carnal affections that objected within me to your bodily weakness and cried out at the unbearable hardships in the austerity of your religious order.[155] From within myself came the complaint of a proud sensuality, which chided me for being harsh and whispered that I at one time was guilty of treating you in a way that was hardly brotherly or kind. It told me that I then had cast you far away from me as one who was a stranger and an outsider. His company, the voice said, was necessary and pleasant for you. If he had stayed with you in a less harsh way of life, he would also have saved his soul.

Thus in my ears resounded a base sensuality, which is blind, only barely seeing what is present and caring only for the comfort of the body. And this sensuality persuaded me that the happiness of another condition was wretched. It did not take into account how wretched and miserable and poor, blind and naked its own fate is.

I have said, nevertheless, and I repeat, that I was badly shaken by these voices, and I almost was made to agree with them. But I struggled as reason illuminated by faith regularly struggles in the good Lord. This sense of reason strongly congratulated you on your status and sighed deeply at mine, nor was it fooled. For right reason does not consider the vexation of the body, nor the abdication of sordid sensuality, the extension of fasts and vigils, nor the cold nor heat in order that it can deplore such things in you. Reason rather would weep if, being freely separated and liberated from such pain in the world, you had inwardly incurred the most pernicious illnesses of vices and the cruelest wounds by fleeing the religion that is adverse to such diseases. Reason would lament if, in leaving the manna of the desert and the path of promise, you had aspired to the fleshpots of Egypt (cf. Ex 16:3) and in looking back had sunk into the side road of damnation (cf. Gn 1:26). Prudently you have distanced yourself, fleeing so that you can be saved from weakness of spirit and from the storm (Ps 54:9). Is this storm not in the world where the worst and most contagious society everywhere pollutes, where there are iniquity and travail in its midst and injustice too, where in its streets oppression and fraud (Ps 54:12) and similar monstrous crimes are part of everyday life?

And so, most beloved brother of my heart, do not waste away in your spirit if you by chance sense creeping into your soul that treacherous softness I now described concerning myself.[156] For I suspect that this will easily happen since he who tempts you does not sleep, but also he who guards you does not sleep (Ps 120:3). Arise then quickly with his help and say with the glorious Martin, on whose feast day you were professed: "Lord my helper, I will not be afraid of what man might do to me" (Ps 117:6).[157] Do not wish that security from temptations be promised to you in an empty manner, but rather listen to the wise man: "Son, in entering into the service of God, remain in fear and justice and prepare your soul for temptation" (Sir 2:1). Whether one temptation or another, diverse in form, rises up against you, act in a manly way and let your heart be comforted and wait for the Lord (Ps 26:14).

Finally, beloved brother, do not in vain receive the grace that has been conferred on you. Do not complain; do not be ungrateful, but say with the prophet: "I will speak of the mercies of the Lord forever" (Ps 88:2). Say to your soul: Bless, my soul, the Lord and all that is within me, blessed be his holy name (Ps 102:1), and repeat all that follows. For it is he who separated you from your mother's womb and now has separated you from the world and given you a pledge of your future inheritance (cf. Eph 1:14). It is he who from your boyhood has shown mercy on you, giving you a good and God-fearing heart that is compassionate on those in affliction. He has added from above his mercy, to drive you away from the evil world in which you would irrevocably have been plunged if you had obtained your licentiate or master's degree in arts.[158] Since you were close to this result, accept from others such a conjecture.

God showed great mercy to you, since you had no relatives or friends who wanted you to become something great in the world and so would have been opposed to your intention. It is, and always has been, quite different for me, as well as for countless other people who read in the book of experience that one's enemies are the members of one's own household (Mt 10:36).[159] In order that we can take care of their children, they want us never to be children.[160] Even though this type of love was much less harmful to me, I did suffer from it.[161]

Finally, do not forget the mercy of God in your parents and your sisters in the flesh, especially in the mother who unceasingly with prayers, also before you were conceived, beseeched the Lord that you would be such a person, as another Hannah did for Samuel (1 Sm 1:21–28).[162] Then, when you were born and grew to an adult, she shed almost perpetual tears that you would be in this state, as I fondly recall. You remember, I think, the letter that offered an indication of this concern and that shows her as another mother of Augustine toward you.[163] Give to her in return your prayers. In you alone all of us will have an intercessor with God. Do so brother, and live happily in the Lord.

I ask to be recommended to our father, the venerable lord prior of your house, and to each of the brothers living there.

I do not yet have the writings that I decided to send to you. But meanwhile study Augustine *On the Psalms* in one of the volumes that I know you have with you.[164] For this is a Christian teaching for you and those like you who daily sing the psalms. It is exceedingly useful and fitting, insofar as from the dry honeycomb of the letter of the psalms, you know how to draw forth the most delicious honey of its interior meaning through your chant.

Meanwhile, live with your fathers and brothers. Let us pray for each other. Written on the fifth of December.

LETTER 10   Gerson to the Superior of his Brother Nicolas[165]
            Paris, 7 December 1401
[Gerson is concerned about whether his brother Nicolas will be able to endure the ascetic demands of life in a Celestine house, and he asks the superior to look after his brother.]

Venerable father and most beloved lord in Christ.

Let not your charity become angry, I beseech, if I presume to give advice about what you are doing and until now have done concerning and for your son, my brother Nicolas. I am very concerned because I love a great deal, since, if we believe Ovid, or even more so, experience, love is something full of concerned fear.[166]

In fear I therefore ask and in the love of Christ (cf. Phil 1:8)[167] beseech that you not give up your efforts with my same brother but steadfastly support his weakness in soul and body with gentle compassion. Show yourself, I ask, to be attentive to him in such a way that he makes known to you all his needs, even his bodily ones, in all faithfulness. Otherwise he will easily perish in his simplicity and fearfulness, or because of indiscreet fervor he will be dissolved in tears and other exercises of a religious observance that in itself is harsh.

You know that it is necessary to exceed one's own powers in

being professed, something which I admire and greatly fear when I consider the matter within myself. I would give up hope if I did not place it in God and after him in you, beloved father, and in the other brothers of your religious order, in which I think it can reasonably be hoped that they not be cruel and not so indiscreet as to let themselves lose a soul for which the Lord has died and that they decided in such concord to take to themselves after long testing.

Let him then in all things entrust himself and his affairs to your counsel, as I trust he will do. I seek confidence that he will not perish. I beg and implore you not to let him perish, but let me have in him an eternal man of prayer with God.[168] In whom be well, and remember me a sinner.

Written at Paris on the night of the feast of the conception of the glorious Virgin.

LETTER 11   Gerson to his Brother Nicolas in Sending the Treatise *On the Distinction of True from False Revelations*
Paris, early in 1402
[See the opening of this treatise, translated below.]

LETTER 12   Gerson to his Brother Nicolas (or to his Superior)[169]
Paris, 13 April 1402
[Gerson sets forth a program for spiritual development, which he found confirmed in the teaching of Saint Bernard: contrition, solitude, and perseverance.]

When lately I reread the *Sermons on the Song of Songs* of Bernard, beloved father and brother, I came to that place which teaches the ways by which one comes to the spiritual generation of the Word, that is, to the contemplation of the ark. I rejoiced not a little because it was so much in harmony with the subject of which I had written recently at Bruges, in the bed of my illness, the little treatise of which you have a copy.[170] I had not known until then that anyone else had dealt in such a way and in such an order on the ark in which contemplation is obtained. The result was that the same writings of mine please me as being more dependable.

These then are the words of Saint Bernard, in the hundredth homily:

> This vision is not a result of our effort but of grace, of revelation rather than of investigation. But if anyone still can come to it by effort, first be aware of that which is said: Wash yourself and be made clean (Is 1:16); secondly, as you would write of wisdom in time of leisure, only the one who has few obligations will grasp it (Sir 38:25). Third, that you be forceful, and you will take hold of the joy of the kingdom, which for a long time has been removed from you, so that you may have a heart that is cleansed, made ready, and proven. In the first place you will be made anxious; in the second devout; in the third passionate. This is what is suitable, available, and urgent.

Thus far he wrote.[171]

You see, father and brother, in what manner these three elements agree in those three steps of the ladder of mystical contemplation that I have called bitter contrition, leisure or solitude, and strong perseverance. Thanks be to him from whom all truth comes and in whom every truth agrees.

But if now or at another time someone might accuse me of rashness for overstepping my territory in treating this material, which is most profound and hidden, I would in fact admit it, but I would answer that which very recently I recall having said when I was with you. For I know from many writings and the words of some that there is a knowledge and elevation of mind that we can have beyond the common and usual norm of cognition.[172] In this way, even if in no other, I can know that we lack something of the perfection that the holy fathers possessed and taught. For in such a way even a blind person can recognize colors by some unclear conception and realize that he is blind. I once asked a certain blind man who showed intelligence in his speech how he knew he was blind. I know, he answered, because I sense that a certain wholeness of perfection that I sense is present in other things is absent for me.

Finally, father and brother, I am afraid that none of the three forenamed steps is so much lacking as necessary dedication in your religious exercise. This devotion is in no way, and for no other reason, to be abandoned. Thus you have been called. Do not resist with force, for he will not grant this to you easily. Your enemies, indeed, will show contempt for your sabbaths, meaning your vocation (Lam 1:7). You do not know, moreover, what is more useful for you and more pleasing to God. When he wishes it and when it will be his pleasure, he will reveal what he has hidden from the wise of this world and shows to children (Mt 11:25; Lk 10:21). Only children attain this knowledge, because it comes not from our merit but from God's predilection. The main reason for desiring this gift from above is so that we become children who with our own eyes contemplate his great and immense majesty. God will perhaps call you, giving you an opportunity for leisure through sickness or by some other means. So in the meantime, perform your task and give yourself over, not as much as you might like but only as much as is allowed, to seeing and tasting how sweet is the Lord (Ps 33:9). Be well in him, remembering me in your prayers, and I commend to you my brother in the flesh who is my ward.[173]

Written at Paris, 13 April.

LETTER 13   First Letter of Gerson to Barthélemy Clantier[174]
              Paris, March 1402
[He has reread Ruusbroec's The Spiritual Espousals *and expresses serious reservations about its third book.]*

To the venerable father and dearest brother of good simplicity in the love of Christ, the Carthusian brother Barthélemy, his Jean, unworthy chancellor of the church of Paris, [wishes] that he may share in the nuptials of the lamb (Rv 19:7, 9).

A while ago I read in a cursory manner a certain book obtained through you, whose title is *The Spiritual Espousals*.[175] Very recently I reread it more carefully and found that it contains much material that is beneficial and profound. For the first part provides instruction about the active life. The second deals with the spiritual life, which can be called affective, and uses varied and attractive teachings conveyed in similes and figures of speech, whose understanding only those with experience fully grasp. They are people who are more likely to be influenced through affectivity than in the intellect. What they perceive comes more from an intimate flavor of a certain taste than through a process of reasoning or discourse. The third part of the work tries to express the excellence of the contemplative life, which sometimes approaches the beatific vision.

Some people say, as I have learned, that an ignorant person who cannot read or write composed the said book.[176] And so they assert that it could not have been made without a miracle and divine inspiration. Consequently, all of its contents are most true and holy. But I have decided that my conclusion on this matter is not to be hidden from you. Otherwise it might happen that uncertain or false statements will be embraced as certain and divine truth. You know what the Apostle orders: "Do not be carried off by all kinds of alien teachings" (Heb 13:9).

As I would judge for the time being, the first two parts are sufficiently useful. In them nothing can be found that cannot be maintained according to good faith and purity of morals, although the contents put many demands on a modest reader, especially one not wholly expert in the matters of affectivity spoken about in the second part. But the style of the book is not base or mean.

Nevertheless, I cannot be made to believe that this book was composed from the mouth of an illiterate as if by a miracle. For his style has more the taste and fragrance of human than divine eloquence. For the words of the poets, as of Terence and Boethius, and sentences of philosophers, and the flow of the exposition clearly show there that attentive effort and diligent labor went into the writing of the work. Obviously, the style of divine scripture, of the prophets and evangelists, is quite different from this manner of speaking.

Someone who stubbornly insists on the opposite might here say that God is the lord of knowledge (1 Sm 2:3) and has the power now in one way and now in another to write through the mouths of his scribes. We acknowledge that it is possible for this to happen.

But my opponent does not sufficiently explain how this took place according to his proposition, especially since the author asserts that in interpreting with Latin words he had expended considerable effort.[177] Why should this have been necessary if he only functioned as the pen for a writer composing at great speed (cf. Ps 44:2)? I speak of the Holy Spirit, who does not know tardiness in his efforts,[178] and whose speech runs quickly (Ps 147:15).

But there is another more important reason that forces me to think in this way. For the third part of the same book is to be wholly rejected and removed. It is either badly expressed or plainly objectionable, deviating from the healthy teaching of the holy doctors who have spoken of our beatitude. It does not agree with the clear decision expressed in the decree that sets forth how our beatitude consists in two actions, vision and enjoyment, with the light of glory.[179] And if this process is completed in beatitude, so that God is not our vision and splendor in essence but only its object, then how much more distant will this experience be from any incomplete grasp of beatitude that we might be able to taste here, on the way to heaven?

The third part of the said book asserts that the soul which perfectly contemplates God not only sees him through the splendor that is the divine essence but also is the divine splendor itself. For the author imagines, as his writings make it sound, that the soul then ceases to be in the existence it formerly had in its own genus, and it is converted or transformed and absorbed into the divine being. In that divinity it is lost in the ideal existence it had from eternity in the divine essence. Of its being John says in his gospel, "That what was made is life in it" (Jn 1:3). And the author asserts that this is the cause of our temporal existence and is one with it according to its essential existence. He adds that the soul of the one who contemplates is lost in such an abyss of divine being that it cannot be recovered by any creature. A comparison can be adduced, which, however, he does not use: If a little drop of wine be cast into the sea, it is clear that it is soon absorbed and converted into the sea.[180]

This point of view is defective in many ways. Still, I was not easily convinced that some falsity is to be suspected in this third part, since in the other earlier sections I saw so many truths and deep matters. I was also encouraged when I read the protests of the author against his quickly being condemned by those who did not understand and would spoil the work completely. Moreover, every doctor of theology should be quite open to interpreting in a positive way what others say, if it can be done without danger to the faith or for the uneducated, rather than harshly to issue condemnations. Nevertheless, a diligent and repeated inspection of what he said showed more and more error in his writings.

There follow a few of his sayings, which I have taken word for word. In the second chapter of the third book he says the spirit loses itself in that emptiness through a fruitful love. With nothing intermediary, it takes on the splendor of God and without letup is made into that splendor which it receives.[181] In the third chapter: Our created being depends on the eternal being and according to essential existence is one with it.[182] There follows: All who are lifted above their creation into the height of contemplative life are made one with this deifying splendor. In fact, they are the splendor itself. They then see, perceive, and find through this deifying light that they exist according to its being and uncreated life and that they are the same simple abyss of divinity. There follows: And with that light by which they see and which they see they become one.[183]

In the first chapter he said: All devout spirits are made one with God in the profound flow of love. This takes place not through any unity whatsoever but through that which is the divine being in itself, in the way that deifying blessedness requires.[184] In the fourth chapter he says expressly: There the spirit is translated above itself and unified with God, tasting and seeing in the unity of the living abyss in which it possesses in itself according to its own uncreated being immense riches that he has according to the manner by which God tastes and sees them.[185]

From these and similar sayings we judge the intention of the author to be what we have described. For certitude about his intention cannot be taken from what he implies but from the writings themselves. But if the author fails in explaining himself, with the result that he openly either errs or fails to express his meaning, then he is responsible for speaking in such a manner not only to the learned and educated but also to the untaught and the ignorant.

But we ought not to wonder or be angered. Nor are we to accuse those of rash judgment who read him, especially when these are trained in biblical scholarship. Such people gather his intention from his words, examine what they have brought together, and then say they understand it. Once understood, if it is erroneous, they do not fail to refute it. For the author does not have greater or more sanctified authority than the best and holiest doctors of sacred theology, who nevertheless left their works to the free examination of others, as Augustine did.[186]

In a word, the material of the third part deals not with those matters that are known and written down through affectivity and experience but through the inspired intellect in holy persons. But the knowledge of such things and their discernment are especially to be sought among trained theologians[187] and not among devout persons alone.

Furthermore, I am not unaware that there were and are certain theologians who like to discuss out of curiosity if on the basis of God's absolute power a rational soul can know and reach beatitude formally through the divine essence without any medium, so that God would be knowledge and enjoyment for that soul, not as its object but as its form.[188] In this way God would not only be the cognition, which is known by the soul, but that through which the soul would know. And similarly concerning enjoyment. Whatever might be possible here, no one should be so presumptuous as to make assertions as if they were facts, for the decision of the church is opposed.

I have never seen a theologian who, I do not say could have put forth, but who actually has ever formulated a question concerning what our author explains in his own way.[189] For he shows how the soul can see God and find beatitude in him, not as a fact or as a possibility, but as if the soul ceases to exist in its own being and is transformed into that divine ideal being it had from eternity in God. (For the time being I would like to omit discussing the plurality of ideas in God, something that is dealt with by many in ignorance.) But if the body of Christ or another beatified body in this way through contemplation or beatification should come to discard its soul, then it would have the essence of God to provide its formal principle of life. Otherwise, this body would be without life. But neither would the soul then be of the same species as before, since it would have no other life and existence than what it had from eternity in God's making.[190] In this being, as it was from eternity, any soul, even a damned one, was divine life and its beatitude. Then the human body would not be able to find its soul in glory as a formal principle giving it life. Or if the soul did function in this way, then it would not now be lost in the manner of which our author speaks.[191] Other absurdities without number would follow. These are too time-consuming to pursue.

But the writer might seem perhaps to make use of Paul's passage on behalf of the assertion: "He who clings to God is of one spirit with him" (1 Cor 6:17). Many sayings of Christ are found in this sentence, as when he asks the Father that the faithful be one as the Father and Son themselves are one (cf. Jn 17:22). There is a long and well-trodden interpretation of the holy fathers on these passages. They said that this unity is not essential, nor does it exist through a precise likeness, but only assimilation and participation are there meant, just as Luke says that the assembly of believers was of one heart and one mind (Acts 4:32). Likewise concerning two friends, it is common usage to say the same. Similarly, a coal on fire and the air that has been given light are called one in their fire and light. Through this image Boethius proves that every good is God, according to what the Psalmist says, "I said you are gods" (Ps 81:6). This is not so in terms of the truth and unity of the divine essence and in proper speech, but in terms of participation and assimilation, in imitation and appellation.[192] But if this author then replies that he has understood his own writings in a similar way concerning unification of the spirit with God, I do not challenge or contradict him concerning his intention. But I do not hesitate to assert that his explanation sounds different, because he should say nothing more concerning those who contemplate except that all in general are sons of God through the grace of adoption.

Perhaps you will be surprised, beloved father and brother in Christ, and you will wonder in hearing how a man so devout and educated could fall into such error or ignorance. Do not only be amazed but also afraid. Humbly desire to have wisdom, when you hear that not only he but innumerable others of not insignificant sanctity left the path of truth. These the author himself justly criticized in the end of the second part, people who arrogated to themselves the sublimity of contemplation.[193] You can read how he shows that they have been seduced by the noonday devil (cf. Ps 90:6). They were from the sect of Beghards, which was once condemned by the church's decree.[194]

The author was, as I think, close to them in time. It could be that in opposition to his fantasy about beatific or contemplative vision, which by chance he then held in common with many, the decree was expressly drawn up establishing that beatitude comes from two acts.[195] Therefore, it is not necessary that he be judged to have been a stubborn heretic before this matter was decided, if at that point or afterward he was always prepared to hear the church. Now, however, it would be different for others.

Finally, let us consider, I ask, how all who are not sufficiently formed or trained in theology through constant and dedicated occupation must be careful not to become too attached to such unusual treatises. They contain many truths, for the devil does not try to persuade us of falsity without mixing in truths. There is a danger that such persons will presume that these are difficult matters of theology, which are being treated with new words and can be looked upon with admiration and devotion. We need to speak according to a certain rule, as Augustine says.[196] Otherwise, those who act differently will make ready an easy road to the precipice.

In order to decide such questions or to understand or explain them fully, it is not enough that a person be devout or have acquired this type of contemplation, however holy and good it may be. It is not enough to live in affectivity and fervor of charity, when a person in heartfelt devotion moves toward virtue (cf. Ps 72:7). For even uneducated women and ignorant people who cannot read or write have the capacity of ascending to and obtaining this type of contemplation, assuming a simple faith. It is much easier for them than for men of great intelligence who are learned in theology.[197] Such theologians, however, greatly excel in another form of contemplation, concerned with the investigation of the divine truths by which saving faith, as Augustine says, is conceived, nourished, defended, and strengthened.[198] These types of contemplation can be distinguished from each other. Experience is the master, as Hugh [of Saint Victor] says: "Often love enters where understanding remains outside."[199] No one, however, should with his own word be called a contemplative or a wise and excellent theologian who lacks the first type of contemplation.

Does anyone then wish to be and to be called truly wise? Let that person have both types of contemplation, both that of affectivity, which gives taste, and that of intellect, which provides the brightness of knowledge, so that wisdom, meaning wise science, is formed. But if one must be lacking, then I think it would be better to share in the first rather than in the second type, as it is more desirable to have good and humble affectivity, devout toward God, rather than a cold intellect that is enlightened by study alone. For knowledge puffs up, if it exists on its own, while charity builds up (1 Cor 8:1).

Nevertheless, when we seek to find the truth of faith as handed over in the Holy Scriptures, we are rather to ask and consult theologians who concentrate on the second type of contemplation, instead of going to the unlearned who are brilliant in the first type, saving the possibility that a miracle of revelation has taken place in them. We should follow this procedure, unless by chance it is obvious that such theologians have depraved wills and are intolerably corrupt in morals. This condition sometimes makes people lie not only about the faith but also concerning moral principles, something to which the Apostle and Aristotle in their experience bear witness (cf. 1 Cor 6:12–13).[200]

To these considerations I would add that from lack of pious affectivity and even more from its corruption through vice, the most learned theologians sometimes err, for their wickedness has blinded them (Wis 2:21) and they have given themselves over to a debased mind (Rom 1:28). Similarly, from the limited light of the intellect and an insufficient instruction in the study also of secular learning, and sometimes especially in logic, others sometimes fall into the most dangerous errors. Claiming to have great devotion toward the virtues, these are the people whom the Apostle said have zeal but not according to knowledge (Rom 10:2). If they do not have knowledge in humility and do not restrict themselves within the boundaries of their knowledge, there will be no one more stubborn or more ridiculous in fabricating errors.

Those with insufficient learning ought not to write or teach with a light heart. They are not to be followed without great caution and without previous discussion and examination by the learned. In such persons we often find much that is either false or badly explained. It provides abundant material for error in the uneducated, although these writings can be most profound.

Among such writings are included some narratives or rules or particular doctrines in some ancient fathers, which are said to be more admired than imitated, such as in John, called Climacus.[201] He says that the virtues exclude affectivity and adds some very austere points on penance and sin. Also to be noted is John Cassian on free will.[202] Others convey teachings that have been little examined or are too rigid, which the common school of theological truth rightly does not admit or rejects out of hand.[203]

Therefore, honey with the honeycomb is good (cf. Sg 5:1), the taste of devotion with the light of learning. Or if anyone would attain one of them, then he should make use of his gift and walk in his calling (Eph 4:1), being filled with his own mind (Rom 14:5), eating the honey sufficient for him (cf. Prv 25:16) and not tasting more than is necessary. Horace uttered a just proverb, afterward taken over by Jerome and not far from our subject: What belongs to medicine, doctors promise; what belongs to building, builders deal with.[204] This agrees with that maxim of logicians: We are to have faith in each who is an expert in his art.

Farewell, beloved father and brother in Christ, and let me share in your prayers.

Here ends the letter of the chancellor of Paris Jean Gerson.

LETTER 14　　Gerson to Pierre d'Ailly[205]
　　　　　　　Paris, 1402

[Letter accompanying Gerson's sending the treatise On the Spiritual
Life of the Soul. *Gerson here shows his devotion to Pierre for the attention his former teacher has shown him.]*

To the reverend father in Christ and professor of sacred theology, the outstanding Lord Pierre bishop of Cambrai, his disciple
Jean, unworthy chancellor of the church of Paris, in humble obedience and the desire that he knows what is right for the salvation of all.

Your benevolence, my illustrious teacher, deigned to require
from me to provide for you in writing one of my lessons, which
you were not ashamed to attend. You did not avoid such an
unusual act, you, the brightest star of the school of theology. I
admit that I felt embarrassed, and the entire school in union was
amazed at this lowering of your dignity and your wisdom, as if
you asked for the light of the sun to come from a single star, the
water of the sea from a river, or the wool of a sheep from a goat.

In this way it is true that where there is wisdom, there is humility. As the wise man bears witness to the converse, that there is
wisdom where humility is found (Prv 11:2). You then, the greater
you are, the more, according to the wise man's counsel, you humble yourself in all things. But this humility should be less surprising for me, because you love and embrace my learning, limited as
it is, of which you have been the nurturer, source, and author
until now. Each should protect the work that he has done, as
Ovid says.[206] So in this place the word of Christ is not ineptly
joined: My teaching is not mine but is of the Father who sent me
(Jn 7:16). And certainly, father, you have sent me, because
through you I have been given the license for teaching in the faculty of theology. Through you and under you I have been decorated with the insignia of master. You also promoted me in the
office of chancellor where I succeeded you, even though I was
not of equal merit.[207]

I have added more to this treatise than you requested.[208] And so the lessons that follow I decided to draw from the same material, not in order to teach you, for this would be completely presumptuous, but to comply with obedience. Either I could give you, amid your heavy cares, a taste of your old intellectual leisure, or, something more modest, so that you would correct or complete what is imperfect in what your eyes have seen.

I want, nevertheless, that another reader more easily shows indulgence to this, our little work, if he by chance should cast a glance on it and if its uncultivated language seems not sufficiently complete or attractive as it should be for such a treatise. Then let the kind interpreter consider that there is one style for school lessons, and another for treatises.[209] He should know that the parts do not hold so well together when they have been produced at various times and occasions, as much as when they have been composed together as a whole for one purpose. Nevertheless, I gave these lessons the form of a treatise, as much as was possible, dividing them into three parts according to the triple subject matter and in conformity with the three words of the Apostle, which within are recalled. These provide, as it were, a certain theme: In him we live and move and have our being (Acts 17:28). For we live in God in the life that grace gives. We move in him and to him by the weight of meritorious activity, and finally through a kind of circle based on the intelligible, we are in him as in our center through the quiet of stable and serene contemplation.

The first state is for all who are in grace, as beginners. The second for the more advanced, the third for the perfect. The first state is in the baptism of water or fire; the second in the temptations we experience on the pilgrimage of this life; the third in the consolation of angelic care. In this manner Christ first was baptized, afterward was tempted, and finally was consoled. Similarly, there is a life that animates, a path of movement, and a truth that remains stable, alpha and omega, the beginning, middle, and end. In it we live through the faith formed in us, for the just person lives by faith (Hb 2:4; Rom 1:17) and does so through the power of reason. We are moved through hope, desiring what is above, in the power of emotion. We have our being through the charity rooted in the power of desire.[210]

The first part of the work, which is broader and is divided up into lessons, concerns the life of the soul and its death, as well as spiritual illnesses. It considers the content of sins in terms of their origin[211] and in drawing forth the moral instances that then follow. The second part deals with the second life of the soul, which is its motion or instinct, looking into the distinction between good inspirations and influences from evil angels in various areas, and on the manner of overcoming temptation. The third part speaks of the life of the soul, which finds stability and consolation through contemplation.

Farewell, father in Christ. Let us pray for each other's salvation.

LETTER 15   Gerson to Pierre Col[212]
             Paris, around October 1402 (or perhaps a few
             months later)

[Further considerations on The Romance of the Rose *and Gerson's concern that the reading of the poem will corrupt the morals of young people.]*

You write such things of me, learned man and beloved brother in the charity of Christ, that I would never claim for myself. Nor am I worthy of such honor; I rather shrink from this praise since it has been mingled with trifling matters, or rather, if you will forgive one who says the truth, brother, with falsity and madness. And so it has happened that even in the midst of my occupations, I do not delay to write back to you. For my devotion ought to love you in return and reciprocate to you, who I do not say pretend to love me, for such pretense is wholly absent from you, who truly show this love.

There is, moreover, the hope by which I trust you will not deny the faith you so much placed in me. Finally, you must consider my profession, which is supposed to oppose error and vice as much as it can and which has led to my lately writing something in the French language. Here, based on the course of a day, I made a plea not against the Fool of Love but against writings, words, and pictures that encourage, stimulate, and excite forbidden loves, which are more bitter than death.

I do not intend to repeat or to convert into Latin the arguments of the text you can read there. Having brought my speech to an end, I think it sufficient to say that writings, words, and pictures that are provocative, lustful, and prurient are to be cursed and banned from the commonwealth of Christian religion. This is to be done by every person who is illuminated by catholic faith and not at all corrupted by base passion.

But how can I hope to persuade those who do not want to be persuaded, who are pleased by such errors, and who have been blinded by the evil of those who have given themselves over to a debased mind (cf. Rom 1:28)? Such people turn away their eyes so that they do not see what the result will be. In the end they will incur that most harsh type of curse for delighting in an evil habit, into which their iniquity seduced and tricked them. Among such persons I ought not to include you, dearest brother, and I ask heaven in supplication that I never have to do so.

But I intended to deal with some of the subjects contained in your work, which was shown to me yesterday evening. These aspects must be corrected and removed. What else can I say? I speak with you as a brother; almost all its contents are to be faulted in one area or another. Moreover, that treatise as you have received it, if I am allowed to give any advice, should be consumed by greedy flame and be torn up into tiny pieces so it might perish in eternal forgetfulness.[213]

First of all, I want to admonish you and those like you that a so-exaggerated admiration of this author, who is scarcely to be numbered among the mediocre, keeps you in ignorance of wiser writers. Many surpass him, as the whale of Brittany exceeds the dolphins and as cypresses are outstanding among bushes. But consider now the precipice onto which you have ventured in dealing with theological matters.

You say that a child of two or three years is in the state of innocence. This is the heresy of Pelagius, for which one is to be judged heretical if he asserts it with obstinacy.[214] You have asserted many more statements that corrupt what belongs to

214

incorruptible reason. Such arguments more and more bind you in the knots of the same heresy, like birds snared in traps or in lime that try to fly away. So enervating and harmful it is to work against truth. Let not my work be read but that of Augustine in his *On Marriage and Concupiscence*, especially in the second book.[215] You have thought, nevertheless, as I believe, what you should not have thought, that a child is very much in the state of innocence either because he is ignorant or because he has not yet actively committed sin. But your mind should have warned you about the original corruption of diseased concupiscence, for from it all are brought to evil.

You say—and I am amazed that you have written such a thing without being ashamed or repentant—you say that the foolish lover alone judges well concerning such a harmful and even insane passion. As for the one who has not experienced it, in which category you put me (and it is you who says this, not I), such a person recognizes this passion only in a mirror and an enigma (1 Cor 13:12).[216] It is as if it is necessary that all who are to judge rightly and incorruptedly first must be corrupted by the same vices. It is quite different; no one bears a more distorted judgment about evil deeds than those who are corrupted by this feverish sickness and lethal illness. They are made abominable in their deeds (cf. Ps 13:1). Many examples could be supplied from sensuality. Every corrupt judge is a bad one to investigate the truth, as Horace says.[217]

But what you add about the private parts of women being once sanctified by custom,[218] I do not know what kind of Bible has taught you, unless you perhaps have another one than we do. Or perhaps the words of Luke have inspired you and led you astray, that every male that first opens the womb will be called holy to the Lord (Lk 2:23). What, I ask you, will be called holy to the Lord? If you are silent, I will answer: the firstborn son.

But your author, who is almost your god, has written of several good things, you say, many of which are completely beyond the common understanding of all the learned and which are only known if one reads through the treatise ten times. What if he also has mixed in many more evil things, which are all the more contrary to these goods? What remains to say except that he, in the manner of the Fool of Love, has been out of his mind, has changed his mind, has contradicted himself, and, according to the saying of Terence, has tried to go mad in a reasonable way?[219] Therefore this work is rightly called a formless chaos, also the confusion of Babel (Gn 11:9), a kind of German gruel, and a Proteus that changes himself into all shapes. This work could be described in the phrase that schoolboys recite: He is in agreement with no one when he is in disagreement with himself.[220]

You bring up the question of theologians whom you say sometimes fall into a mad love, of a kind with which you threaten me (from this evil may it not be a false Cupid who will protect me but the true God of love).[221] This position seems more intended to slander theologians than to deal with the question in a pertinent way. Through the excuse of a greater fault in these theologians, you apparently want these crimes either to be diminished or removed or made acceptable. For if Cicero in describing the eloquent man said that the good man is an expert at speaking, all the more when I speak of the theologian, I must understand a good man who is learned in the Bible.[222]

But again, if your author spoke improperly not out of attachment to such language, then explain how anyone could have made him bring up those matters by which Reason speaks with so obscene and filthy a voice. Your author is more to be blamed not because he introduced Nature speaking of God, but because it speaks in such a way of these mysteries that only the supernatural revelation, freely given, provides.

Also, because in your little work attacking me you have placed me together with an outstanding woman,[223] I ask about that manly woman to whom your piece is directed, although it is so confused in its progression that at one point you leave her to go to Theological Eloquence, and now on the contrary you quickly return. But, I say, can that amazon have argued for the erroneous position in this proverb: It is better to deceive than to be deceived? Did she not, more correctly, refute this point of view? Your anxious and false maneuver to avoid the matter shows that the woman was prodding you with a great spur when you tried to escape by saying that in this section a false interpolation corrupted the text.[224] But you cannot explain how you know, and I do not see it.

The woman prudently added there that in reading your author queens have blushed.[225] Those whose minds are well trained and endowed with natural modesty would also feel shame. You are a member of this company, as your writings show, whether you like it or not. Your good character was such as to speak of nothing obscene there. It is not then a consequence that those persons who blush in such a way reveal that they are to be suspected of these crimes. Rather, if they blush, the case is in their favor, as Terence says.[226]

I do not intend to deal with everything in your treatise. Otherwise almost every line would have to be removed, as when you say that it is not the natural appetite of the human being that in matrimony one man be joined with one woman and one woman with one man.[227] For this is false and disagrees with one of your own sayings when you defend Genius as the god of nature, since you say that he speaks of union in matrimony alone.[228]

Similarly, how is it that you have thought to hide the baseness of the author by the argument that he taught evil so that it can be known and thus avoided?[229] Further, you allege that someone known to you, being taken captive by love, made a remedy for himself from this honeyed poison, as if he could draw an antidote from the poison.[230] All such assertions are ridiculous.

It is just as much opposed to catholic faith to make such a claim as when some people say that the Song of Songs was made to the praise of the daughter of Pharaoh. Whoever made such a blasphemous statement lied. But it seems even more devious when you try to assert that one must return to the text of the book. The book does not contain, you say, all that its attackers impute to it.[231] I do not want to contradict you, for I prefer surrender and accept defeat rather than let such base and contagious material again be reviewed.

In the end of your treatise you write that they by whom this book was spurned and vilified went down on their knees before Baal (cf. 1 Kgs 19:18). Let me say freely what I feel: This description either distorts the meaning and is vicious or, if you are serious in what you say, then you are spreading scandalous, injurious, and false teachings that smack of heresy against faith and morals and which are to be eradicated.

You could never with all your praises so much exalt my limited ability as much as you disparage me, perhaps because of the freedom you have of speaking with me, in claiming that I wrote what I did so that people, whom we know seek what is forbidden,[232] would be provoked by a great flame and encouraged to reread this poem. As if I would change my calling into a lie and as if it were my function to act falsely against moral doctrine and against myself, like your author, and even more so, against the Christian religion, to speak with my heart what is not in my heart! I would rather die than ever be found covered by such falsehood! Take care, rather, that this deception has not infected your author. For while he condemns carnal love, whose praises he often has sung, does he not desire, in accord with your knowledge, to make people more easily attracted to it?

What can I say of that protest by your author other than that he has tried to hide his immorality with a veil? He says that nothing of what he wrote was his own. He was thus a narrator rather than an author. In that case those of you who admire him should not give him praise for speaking well! Similarly, you should not want these evil sayings to be spread to his shame when he conveys his arguments. Do not rage against us with such hatred or speak such bombastic words in swollen arrogance against us, if it is the text itself that is to be blamed. We are not accusing persons but the writings themselves, whoever composed them. Perhaps, nevertheless, you should consider that the person who administers toxic potion, even if it was made by someone else, is not to be judged as without responsibility. What is happening here, good Lord, when he makes one excuse and on the same pretense blocks this excuse? This procedure surely provides no excuse but puts one in the category described in the saying: "By your own words I will judge you, evil slave" (Lk 19:22).

Finally, O Christian court,[233] I have never harmed you in intent or word. You cannot correct all crimes, I admit. Otherwise there would be nothing reserved for divine justice in the future. It is sufficient with many offenses that laws and public ordinances oppose them, as with simony, theft, homicide, adultery, and so too against this most contagious laxity in speaking or writing what is evil, especially when there is no public prosecutor to be found. I do not, however, intend to excuse the many churchmen who have done nothing against the several books of Ovid, or the lies of magicians, or specifically against this book and others that have contributed to the downfall of many. I excuse only those whom no official function required to condemn such matters or who for their part, in spoken or written word, in general or specifically, as I now do and many before me, have condemned such things.

Nor do I think we should leave out what is written in the Acts of the Apostles, that all newly converted to the faith, who previously had practiced magic, burned their books, which were valued at fifty thousand silver coins (Acts 19:19). Behold, before God I assert, and if you find anything in me worthy of trust, I affirm that if I owned the sole copy of that author's book, and it were worth a thousand pounds and more, I would rather give it over to be burned by hungry flames than sell it so that it would be made available in such a way. See how much I am willing, or rather how I am not at all willing, to reread it.

This attitude does not result, as you think, from ignorance, even though I am very ignorant, but comes from my own conscience and that of others. Thus I remember that I once tasted, already from youth, all those sources or almost all of those from which the sayings of your author like small streams being drawn forth came to him: Boethius, Ovid, Terence, Juvenal, Alan of Lille, William of Saint Amour, Abelard with his Heloise, Martianus Capella, and perhaps others.[234] A little manuscript, moreover, whose title is *The Soul's Journey into God*,[235] written by Lord Bonaventure, which I read through in one day, I would not hesitate because of the depth of its knowledge to oppose to the whole of your book, or even to ten books like it. And yet you judge us to be too brutish and stupid to understand this *Romance of the Rose*!

But as for your admonition that I reread the book so that I can understand it, I have something in return. Read, brother, and read again the fourth book of *On Christian Doctrine*.[236] This book is somewhat more difficult than your book in the vernacular. You will see, believe me, that we do not do injury to eloquence in joining it to theology. You will perhaps be ashamed for boldly claiming things that you have not fully considered. Augustine clearly contradicts you in the most precise words there, in the fourth book of *On Christian Doctrine*, at the opening of the work, and also in the very functioning of his writings, which are expressed with such power of eloquence.[237] Nevertheless, I have spoken with restrained modesty, if you have noticed, when I brought in someone representing Theological Eloquence in using everyday language.[238] I carefully restrained every form of idle curiosity for which I might have been accused.

Now it is time to stop joking, good brother who is most worthy to foster a better cause. This lust for conquest or chatter should be shut up. We must deal with a matter that is serious and venerable. I tell you, if I knew that my own brother had composed such a book and made it public, and that he in the end had refused to repent this act even though he had been sufficiently warned and admonished, then I would no more offer prayers in our Lord Jesus Christ for him who had died impenitent than I would pray for someone who was damned.

Farewell in Christ. Commit yourself from now on to more fruitful and chaste studies and do not give an opportunity for scandal to the uneducated. If anything said in harshness by chance has offended you, then forgive my faith, which has presumed much of you because it loves you greatly. Finally, consider it all to have been done in zeal for catholic truth and in desire of our salvation. Let us pray for each other that we be saved.

LETTER 16   Gerson to the Duke of Orléans[239]
Tarascon, 5 January 1404
[Gerson sends him the sermon that he a few days earlier had given at Tarascon,[240] and he summarizes his principles in dealing with papal resignation of office.]

To the most serene prince and outstanding descendant of kings, the lord of Orléans,[241] his Jean, unworthy chancellor of the church of Paris, offers humble obedience and hopes he may happily obtain the gift of peace in this life and also of eternal peace.

I have written a great deal before now, great lord, and said much that was intended to be useful for the peace of the church. I pursue the peace that lives in exile by barking as much as I can. I am like a puppy, who according to the power he has gotten from above for the work of God's tabernacle, gives together with men those gifts that I seem to have received from his hand.

I am not unaware that these matters, dealt with under so many headings, can easily be understood in various ways, and perhaps adversely. But if the various elements in the situation are distinguished according to time and circumstance, as these ought to be considered in terms of their variety, I think a knot of truth will be found that is joined to these questions. For we know that good intentions revolve around the same center and hinge on the same place.

And so I thought that I had preached in a satisfactory manner that the way of cession was the quickest and best.[242] I judged that it could be accepted in preparing the agreement of both of those who were rivals for the papacy and bound by divine law, and that this would not lead to the compulsion that they alleged. And so no one was forcing them to remove themselves from office. I did not conclude the necessity of withdrawal of obedience, even though I did not presume to attack this conclusion with stubborn animosity. But after our Lord Benedict is said to have accepted the way of resignation and other actions that were asked for as being appropriate for the peace and reformation of the church, I in all humility spoke to the contrary, in the face of no small expression of hatred and amid dangers, that Benedict was to be defended as not having irreversibly lost the papacy. He was not to be judged a heretic or schismatic. His restoration was also acceptable, something I preached before a distinguished assembly of the people.[243] In this way our obedience, being united with him, hoped more easily to reach the gate of universal peace.

In brief, I was not so much sent as forced to go as legate to our lord[244] in this matter on behalf of the most excellent University of studies. Being its son, I could not refuse to do so. First at Marseilles, then at Tarascon, I preached this sermon, which the brilliance of your most noble presence illuminated.

This sermon, as well as a previous statement, your highness deigned to require from my mean person. What am I that I would presume to refuse either this request or anything at all? Behold, receive the sermon, such as it is, where some few parts of what I had written down are marked in the margin, since the brevity of time made it impossible for me to include them.

May you fare well, outstanding lordship, so you may acquire general peace and your own salvation.

Written at Tarascon, in the year of the Lord 1403 [1404] on the vigil of the Epiphany.[245]

LETTER 17   Gerson to a Bishop[246]
                Paris, prior to March 1404
[Letter accompanying a treatise in French, The Mirror of the Soul, dealing with the ten commandments of the law.]

Reverend father in Christ and respected lord. The Lord complains through the prophet Isaiah: Therefore, he says, my people have been led into captivity because they have not had knowledge and its magnates have died of hunger and the multitude is dried out with thirst (Is 5:13). This knowledge is to be interpreted as nothing else than awareness of God's law and of his commands, which are necessary or profitable for obtaining salvation. Concerning this knowledge the saying of the Apostle is true: The ignorant one will be ignored (1 Cor 14:38), for with any other form of ignorance salvation can be obtained. And since there are many of the uneducated to whom the word of God is not being preached or is not preached in such a way that they come to the aforementioned knowledge, either because of this ignorance or the neglect of the preachers, I thought it would be useful if, as if I were composing a painting, I provided in a summary with key phrases the content of our law and the record of its precepts. In this way parish priests who are not so well educated will have something substantial and appropriate they can read out either in whole or part on Sundays and feast days to their parishioners, so that these will know and understand for what and on account of what and by whom these laws were made. Moreover, they will know what to believe and what they are obliged to do and what not to do according to divine law, and how to rise again from sin.

And perhaps a similar work has been attempted by those who are more expert, and it has been composed with more fruitful brevity. If it is so, I certainly am not jealous. Only, reverend father, your pastoral care should deign to attend to the matter, whatever way it is done, so that on each Sunday and feast day the content of divine law will be made known everywhere in your diocese, so that your people do not perish through ignorance and not be led into the captivity of sin. Otherwise blood might be required from a sentinel who has not announced coming destruction or the sword (cf. Ez 33:6).[247] Instead, let him be freed by such a declaration. May the rebels alone perish in their own blood.

My devotion sends you the forenamed little work. If you think it is good enough, then in your generous charity take advantage of the small burden in providing for copyists and the limited expense, which would be put to good use. Have the work duplicated and corrected and sent out with your decree of publication, as has been mentioned, in the absence of sermons and as much as the grace of God will help parish priests in presenting it.

Finally, if anything needs to be added or removed or corrected according to the dictate of your prudent lordship, then it will be right to do so. But I know that after detailed examination by myself and many others who are more expert, I found nothing that cannot be sustained by a reader of good will, in accord with the purity of faith and morals. And much more could have here been added, but the kind brevity of modern idleness has eliminated it. Be well. Written at Paris.

LETTER 18   Gerson to an Unknown Person[248]
               Paris, around 1404
[Letter sending the Threefold Work *and explaining how to use it.]*

To a Christian, from one who is eager to support him, offering prosperous growth in virtue, if vices are repelled.

I thought it would be beneficial to hand over the three-part work that follows, concerning the commandments, confession, and the science of dying, treating them in all possible brevity, in order to help in particular four types of Christians: First, priests and curates who are uneducated but have to hear confessions. Second, any untaught lay or religious persons who cannot be present in church for the usual sermons or preaching in order to come to know God's commands. Third, children and youths who from the beginning of childhood ought to be taught in a basic manner the general content and principal points of our faith. And fourth, persons who frequent the Maison-Dieu or other hospices and take care of the infirm.[249]

Therefore, in order to make this teaching known, persons dealing with these four conditions should be attentive. The content of the teaching concerns superiors and prelates in the church who direct lesser curates in their areas. The crass ignorance of such curates in terms of divine law and the insufficient learning of ordinary people will be made the responsibility of prelates as a matter involving sin. Parents also ought to be firm with those who run schools, for the sake of their offspring. Similarly, those who supervise and are in charge of hospices and hospitals should take care. And, in general, they who by word or deed or other means have brought other persons to sin, and who because of their function should have taught them but have neglected to do so, such persons ought by their own expense and efforts make this or similar teachings public, to secure the correction of others. By doing this as a penance, they provide some satisfaction for sin. Such a work of mercy is more acceptable to God than a corporal work of mercy.[250] Let then they who have been named make sure that this teaching is written in books and is made available in pictures, either in whole or in part, in public places, as in parish churches, in schools, in hospitals, and in religious institutions.[251]

In summary, it seems right that the secular power issues a decree concerning this matter or that indulgences be given by the prelates of the church. The author has unburdened himself in the presence of your most holy Christian life. Let each who glories in you and with you do what he knows to be good.[252]

LETTER 19   Gerson to an Old Man[253]
                Paris, probably 1403–4
[Advice on how to ready oneself for death. Gerson sends his correspondent his treatise The Science of Dying Well.*]*

Noble and religious lord and father in Jesus Christ. I thank God that this small treatise that I once made has come into your hands and that you have gained profit from it, in that he has given you the desire and the will to carry out its contents.[254] For it is necessary to work on that which you know and judge needs to be done, which is to think of the future, and more than previously, about yourself alone. For you are going to your end, and you must not fail in this concern, for the danger and the loss there would have no remedy. One would judge a man who is going to die to be a fool if he at such a time was talking all the while and asking about the needs of others.

You should often remember the story I told you yesterday of Saint Anthony, as the angel said to him, "Oh, Anthony, think of yourself and leave to God the disposition of other people."[255] God is wise enough in doing with them that which pleases him. The examples of such an attitude are numberless, as are the authorities. But I will tell you everything and give in good charity the counsel I find profitable and necessary for you and to bring you in a good way to the end of your life. This age is more burdened than any other by the enemy, and with greater deception.

So, you should take with you someone who knows how to read French and Latin, who will be near you constantly day and night whether you sleep or are awake, while you eat and drink, for two ends. First of all, he will read prayers or teachings in which you will find more meaning than you did in the past, for now is the time when you should make use of what you once collected. The other purpose is that he will encourage you at all times, whenever he sees that you want to do the opposite because you have company or in other situations. He will keep you from speaking more of worldly matters than you would do if you were dead to the world and the world to you.

In order to reach this perfection, you have left behind the world in solitude. However you used or misused it formerly, it is better to leave the world at a late point rather than never. The person of whom I speak will by your command and instruction always be ready to say to you, "Sire, think of yourself; think of your end, of your salvation, of your death," or in similar language, in following the example of the emperor and Saint John the Almsgiver. You know the type of story.[256]

And you have with you, thanks be to God, good and devout people to help you in this purpose and to look up the passages in the scriptures that will be profitable for you to read and to speak with you at the dinner table or elsewhere in a similar language as I mentioned with your cleric.

Furthermore, according to my modest advice you will rid yourself of every other occupation and every outside presence that might distract you from the concerns that have been mentioned. And suppose that some care [claims your attention],[257] I prefer that you go to sleep or do nothing at all rather than occupying yourself with such dangerous occupations, which do more harm to the soul than the enemy himself does.

I am sending to you a small treatise I once made to teach how one dies. You can have it read out to you and copied. And do not be displeased that I write to you in such a familiar manner and as if I am teaching you, for you have encouraged me. Love, moreover, makes me do so, as the God of good love knows. Also, I am writing to you in French so that Robert and others can read it for you and to you if this is necessary.[258] May God give you his grace and perseverance in this matter and to all your devout company.

Let us pray for each other that we be saved. It is good to wait in silence for the salvation of the Lord (Lam 3:26).

LETTER 20   Gerson to Pierre d'Ailly[259]
              Paris, 1405

[Gerson again defends the sermon he gave at Tarascon and says he had been misunderstood and misinterpreted. He sends the text to Pierre d'Ailly and asks his friend to defend him.]

I had decided, reverend father and outstanding teacher, that if I had any free time from my duties of writing, I would complain at greater length about the perversity shown in interpreting what I said, or rather what I did not say, in my sermon on the feast of the Circumcision given at Tarascon before our lord,[260] when I was legate on behalf of the good University of Paris, my mother. Now I truly experience the saying of the Comic, that there is nothing that cannot be made worse in the wrongful telling of it.[261]

I think that this is one of the greatest difficulties that make the office of preacher so burdensome. These problems and dangers Gregory the Great and John Chrysostom each wrote about at great length in their *Pastoral Care*.[262] Augustine did the same in the fourth book of his *On Christian Doctrine*.[263] For it often happens, and I speak as someone who a hundred times has had the experience, that those who are present at a sermon not only distort what has been well said but staunchly assert statements as having been made that in no way have been uttered. The number of fools is infinite (Eccl 1:15). It is, however, the assertion of the wise man that the fool does not seize the words of prudence unless you say what he is turning over in his heart (Prv 18:2). Also true is the saying of Apuleius that there are many who philosophize only with their corporal ears but have no understanding or make changes because of a variety of passions and affections.[264] This is the same as when we take our argument from the sound of bells, for they say, if I can speak in a common way, whatever we might wish.

But I am aware of having said nothing at the time except what agrees with the holy faith and good counsel and that has been confirmed in the investigation of the truth. Nevertheless, how many things, O good Jesus, have been told to me about the same sermon that I never said or even thought. How many statements have been extracted from it in a perverse way and even more perversely attacked! I would boldly assert that some of those who afterward preached should consider their eagerness either to contradict or vainly to please. In their zeal they have been ignorant of what was said. Such preachers tried to attack the truths I set forth and used lines of reasoning that clearly were in error. But, in the midst of my huge task of defending the truth, I do not wish to deal only with what men say. I have no desire that we fight, as it is said, in the shade.[265]

These people have taken the proper and limited content of my words in such a way that through frequent transposition of terms or omission of one word, they have changed the meaning. They claim to have grasped this content, while I, on the contrary, would have preferred to have found out exactly what they were saying. I never would have shrunk back from meeting them in order to defend the truth. But what am I to do? Nothing was objected, to my knowledge, while I was present and could have verbally responded. But a long time afterward, when I was not present and could not hear their voices, I heard by rumors alone that many and diverse things were spoken and preached in opposition to me. I have already explained why I was not ready to reply to them because of the great effort this would have required.

I learned, however, yesterday evening, that one of my most faithful friends wrote that he had heard from someone else who similarly had heard from other serious people, as he was saying, that I had claimed, among other things, that when a person is at the brink of death any priest has the same power as the pope to give forgiveness from punishment and guilt.[266] I am most certain that I never thought or said such a thing, although because of the power of the order of priesthood, in case of necessity, confession is properly made, as theologians agree.[267] But what could I have said, from which such an error could have been taken by people who perhaps were hostile to the form of my words? Should I explain the question in a fuller sermon written for those present?

You most wise teacher, before whose eyes I am totally open, you know me within and without. Deign to take the rod of my defense in this matter. In this way you can calm the opposing voices that have turned against me, if this seems right to you. Finally, the whole of the sermon, which until now I have without any addition kept from the hands of others, I am ready to send to you if you think it is a good idea.

May the Lord give you strength so that you may obtain happiness in the Lord and so that union more quickly be reestablished over the domain of God's holy church.

Your disciple Jean, chancellor of the church of Paris.

LETTER 21   Gerson to the Hermit Antoine, a Recluse of Mont-Valérien[268]
Paris, no date

[Gerson had at first been in doubt about Antoine and had opposed his decision to follow the eremitical life. He tells of his change of attitude, admonishes him to follow clerical authority, and sends a rule to which he should comply.]

Jean, unworthy chancellor of the church of Paris, to the hermit on Mont-Valérien, Antoine, that he obtain the benefit of eremitical solitude.

You have received several indications of my fervent zeal for your salvation, both mutual conversation and letters by which you could sense my anxious concern that in walking on the path that seemed right perhaps you would find that its novelties led you to death. For it was as if you walked with great and wondrous things above you, and followed your own point of view, the worst possible guide. You have depended on the shepherd's staff of your own prudence, with your eyes and ears closed to the opposing advice of anyone else. I was not in doubt that if you walked in such a way, the foot of pride would tread on you, the hand of the sinner would shake you, and you would fall there where all fall who act in iniquity (Ps 35:12–13).

Oh, the evil foot of pride that is wise in its own eyes and prudent for itself! God withdraws from anyone who is arrogant and gives his grace to the humble (Jas 4:6). But what arrogance is greater, what pride is more dangerous than to think that you alone know what is right in one's situation, when human frailty is completely deceived either through blind love or latent ambition or some other diabolical deception of this type? Such illusions lie in ambush in a thousand ways and place innumerable traps before the feet of the one who walks. They are conquered only by humility. But humility in the soul is twofold: there being one in the will, another in the intellect or reason. Each type is difficult to obtain, but according to my judgment there are more problems with humility in the intellect. Nothing lies in wait more deceitfully nor flatters more falsely nor enters by stealth more imperceptibly nor is put to flight with more difficulty than the conviction that one is able to pass judgment on one's own situation. People think that no one else is able to see the individual concerns that they think they alone can consider, also in terms of experience. Each says to himself: "No one knows what belongs to a person except the spirit of the person which is within" (1 Cor 2:11). Similarly, there are many things that human presumption is keen on inventing when it is driven by the machinations of the devil.

You know how I once feared for, and not in a small way, such attitudes in you. Now, with the help of the good God to whom thanks are truly to be given, I dare to breathe more freely in the hope of better things. Several times and from several persons, and in the very testimony of your letter, I lately found how you have been so humbled that you have completely cast aside your own sense of self and discretionary powers. These you have submitted to the judgment of your clerical superior or of those to whom he might have decided to hand you over.

This is good. Stand fast in this position. You have made a virtue of necessity.[269] On this foundation of humility consolidate your strength without ceasing. Dig in your foot. Then you cannot be moved so that you suddenly fall. Let your mind be this way, ever constant in the preparation of your spirit, so that you never in the least matter depart from the opinion, judgment, consideration, or counsel, if you know it, of the one to whom you entrusted yourself and ought to entrust yourself, the churchman of whom I speak. Be under him as soft as clay in the hands of the potter on his wheel or as pliable as molten iron under the hammer of the smith, while you say with the prophet: "My heart is ready, my heart is ready" (Ps 56:8).

Even if he should decide to remove you from your place, you are to make no judgment or reserve anything for yourself, nor are you to wander about at the beck and call of different and varied forms of advice. You are to ask this only from the Lord: that through his intermediary he will direct your ways and will not allow the same person or others appointed by him to be deceived in guiding you. For thus in humility you are to enter under the yoke of another and in no other way will you fulfill what the prophet says: "Place your thought in the Lord and he will take care of you" (Ps 54:23).[270]

Although your entrance to that place never seemed to me to have been made with sufficient discretion (you have read my reasons), many things are to be tolerated because they have been done, even though they were displeasing. May God turn everything to the good (cf. Gn 50:20), and so he will turn you, not from pride, but in the other foundation of the soul, its will or intellect. In this way you will be opposed to yourself.

Fare well, remembering me in your prayers, and make sure to carry out the contents of the rule I have included with the present letter. And whatever you think needs to be interpreted or explained, you must ask about in letters.

Contents of the Rule

Before all else, make a singular effort to observe the commands of God, which bind us all and whose transgression brings death.

Let no vow or form of observance be made that prejudices or hinders the maintenance of this law of Christ.

Your abstinence should be moderated so that it not hinder the pure elevation of your mind through excessive consumption of food or drink, nor should it destroy the body and impede the required use of reason through an excessive abstinence that weakens and empties the brain and sometimes leads to depressive states and insanity. This indiscreet form of abstinence is all the more dangerous insofar as it is less likely that sanity be restored once such an observance has upset the power of reason. We say the same thing about sleep, clothing, bedding, and other forms of care concerned with the body, as also with the act of writing and with tears themselves, in that these help tire out the body.

As for vows made in the past, you are to have no scruples. They cannot compel you to a harsher abstinence than you can bear in accord with the exercise of reason. For to divine authority is added the express authority of your superior, the bishop of Paris. He can either modify such vows or dispense from them, whenever the said practices are harmful to your health.[271] Thus, as soon as you sense that your fasting on bread and water or other practices noticeably disturb your powers of reason, either cease from them immediately or temper them. In this you will be able to follow not only your own judgment but also that of those who are looking after you. It does not much matter if you should eat something that might be brought to you, provided you maintain the general precept of the church and so long as you show the kind of moderate temperance here expressed.

At the same time do your best to gain solitude of mind from all earthly cares and from worldly men. Do not burden your mind with superfluous cares under the pretense of saving other people. This type of consideration will take away all your solitude and easily cast you into the abyss of pride and consequently into apostasy. Get rid of every such thought immediately, as if it were the worst possible source of your undoing, no matter in what garment of good appearance it might be dressed. Prepare yourself, as if you were alone in the world, to seek your salvation and as if by chance this duty were placed on you as a calling bestowed by someone else. Say meanwhile to yourself and your thoughts: He who judges others and governs them is the Lord; he is powerful, wise, and good and will save them without me. For me this one thing remains to do for other people: to pray, to weep, to feel pity.

Also, you are to write to no one, or to very few persons, and most rarely, unless you have need of instruction. Similarly, speak to few, and not at any hour.[272] And rather seek instruction from others whom you wish to teach, always in a spirit of humility, and do not in any way deal with profound questions or difficult cases, or with sermons and confessions. Considering yourself unworthy, refer these to more prudent persons. In these matters also you can more securely read some treatise rather than produce something of your own.

Also, to remove depression[273] and distraction of mind and for deliverance from self-contempt, consider for yourself in turn or in different ways the moral treatises of the saints. You are to study them frequently. In this way you will not be alone, since you will speak without danger with those who are dead or absent, by reading their writings, such as the *Moralia in Job* of Gregory the Great, the codex of regular institutes of Saint Benedict, Augustine, Cassian, and others; also the *Sermons on the Song of Songs* of Bernard and similar works of the saints.[274]

Be suspicious at all times of any unusual visions, whether in the day or at night, and explain them either by an injury to the head or else by your bad deeds and sins. We say the same about spiritual sensations of sweetness, unless they are clearly perceived as bringing about a sense of humility and contempt for your own base condition. It is impossible that a person who is pleased with himself in such experiences be completely pleasing to God. In such a situation you send God away as the soul's groom, and a man commits fornication with his own pleasures.

From this time onward, never bind yourself by any new vow without the special permission of your superior. Nor are you to alter your manner of living in this hermitage without the same permission given with the counsel of others. You will violate this permission especially by opening your cell to anyone unless there arises a case of necessity, for it has no law.[275]

Remember that you are the wild and untamed beast, which is in need of such reclusion. If you freely open your prison to someone, you provide a path to your own destruction and that of others. But there will be a key so placed that it can be obtained quickly enough if cases of necessity possibly arise for you.

LETTER 22   Gerson and Pierre d'Ailly to Gregory XII, the Roman Pope[276]
Genoa, 15 September 1407

[After initial hope that the new Roman pope would give up his office voluntarily (via cessionis), Gerson and Pierre d'Ailly express bitter disappointment. They repeat their reasons for the way of cession and add to their letter a memorandum.]

To the most reverend father and lord, the Lord Angelo, who at Rome has had himself called Gregory XII,[277] his devoted in Christian love Pierre, bishop of Cambrai, and Jean, chancellor of the church of Paris, ask that peace also follow him.

So humble, spiritual, and plain an offering of the most advantageous way of ending, or rather of wholly exterminating, the cursed present schism through the brief word of cession has brought great joy to all Christian people, orthodox father, now that inextricable labyrinths of debates are put behind us. This gift, moreover, provided further material for rejoicing to those who have studied and professed holy wisdom, since they expected their author to be an outstanding professor of theology. It is sad to think how rare such persons are in this turbulent period for the direction of the church. Everyone was holding forth on how someone finally was given by God who would provide an end to the pestilent schism and the beginnings of a salvific peace. They bore witness that he was an angel divinely sent who, as it were, being without flesh and blood, would spurn all things of flesh and blood because of the love of the spirit and for the glory of the house of God and its peace, which he loved. And so everyone was rejoicing in unison.

But the theologians to a certain degree seemed to have a special reason to express exultation, for they realized that one of their number and profession had learned, as was fitting in the school of theology, such sincere and spiritual ideas and expressed the most pious affections.[278] They thought that he would act in an adequate way to repel the base slander of those who say that theologians are useless for the direction of the church, since now someone could be found whose cession of power, being in accord with charity and true theology, would bring more good in the church than the desire for domination of innumerable others. This person's wisdom, which is from above (Jas 3:17), being peaceful and virtuous, has all truth, stretching from one end of the earth to the other, powerfully and gently governing all things (Wis 8:1). It is more effective in overcoming the schism than the worldly wisdom of others, which is beastly and diabolical.

And from where, I ask, most wise father, has this most holy and truthful opening in your letter come, that "he who humbles himself will be exalted" (Lk 14:11)? It could only be from the school of theology. The phrases that follow are almost universal in application. They are not to be disputed according to legal debate but reflect the judgment of Solomon, who linked natural and truly maternal affection with a voluntary offering in the way of cession (cf. 1 Kgs 3). We could deal with this subject at greater length, but let us come to the central question.

We make known, most honored father, that amid many general and particular occasions that keep us under obligation in the pursuit of peace, this opportunity has seemed to be sufficient for us so that on behalf of the said professors of theology we might grasp whatever souls we can reach in daring to speak through our writings.[279] We have been listened to with kindness by those before whom we have been placed. We do not wish to teach you, as the Greek proverb speaks of Minerva,[280] but we would in a certain way save you for yourself. I mean from the unaccustomed disturbances of the "apostles,"[281] and from the unsettled movements of secular affairs. You have been distracted from your accustomed spirit of serene contemplation and wrenched out of the familiar embraces of lovely Rachel.[282]

Thus there is no doubt that you, whatever you are, are capable both of hearing and of seeing what needs to be done according to the eternal rules of sacred wisdom in so important a matter, the restoration of union, a dilemma that preceding ages hardly have known. We have made clear through these few considerations, both theological and moral, what it has been our intention in a simple way and without stylistic adornment to set forth. We ask that we be received with the same sincerity of intention as we are aware of having shown before God in writing you. In this desire we send your reverend paternity our good wishes.

Written at Genoa, 15 September.

LETTER 23   Gerson to his Brother Nicolas the Celestine[283]
               Paris, around 1408

[Both brothers are concerned about their younger brother, Jean (3), who also has entered the Celestine Order. Nicolas had criticized Gerson for the advice he had given. Gerson defends himself, appealing to the authority of his mentor, Pierre d'Ailly, who had accompanied him in visiting the Celestine house.]

It has pleased the humble charity of the most reverend father, my excellent tutor, who no one denies is endowed with foresight and the most faithful discretion (I mean the bishop of Cambrai), it has pleased him, I say, to bring me to visit you and your house.[284] At length, amid many matters I agreed with you and your prior that we could write in return concerning the situation of our brother, the novice, in terms of what seemed necessary to ask and to get to know. For the law of love is such that in speech or in writing, friends enjoy visiting each other, instructing each other, and consoling each other.[285]

I, moreover, would consider myself to exercise a reasonable claim of guardianship in judging of his condition, both because of my own experience and because of the learning I have acquired, now that I have almost come to old age,[286] in the cases when I get to know the temptations that come from above or the traumas that might emerge amid his intention, assuming that he reveals them in a brotherly manner. For so the nature of human beings is made, as is said in Terence, that we see better what belongs to others than what is in ourselves.[287] This maxim especially applies to inexperienced youths, who in their ignorance quickly lie to themselves. Moreover, they frequently believe that spiritual illness is great health. This happens to the point that they get angry with those who want to take care of them and are harsh with those who want them to take care. They are hard on those who admonish them, unless these come to say what these youths are concerned with in their hearts (Prv 18:2).[288]

It is more likely to happen that such people often presume they should speak, instruct, counsel, and take over direction from those who are much more senior and experienced. This is no different than if a sick person taught a doctor how he should be cured by him and which medicine or what procedures, rules, and diet he was to follow. Understand, brother, what I say. This is my situation, which began long ago and now continues: I am cast aside; I am told what to do.[289] I do not wish to say any more. But now if it is so, brother, that I am unworthy, foolish, of evil life, not knowing anything about the circumstances involved in the intention of our brother, then let God see and judge me according to the judgment of those who love his name (Ps 68:37). But if you think otherwise, I ask that you not now be harsh in rejecting the love I have offered. Do not persist in this manner for your own sake or your own opinion in defending your way of life.[290] If you do so, you will willfully harm the one who loves you in truth.[291]

May your embrace be so ample that it will receive two brothers at the same time, the other and myself, for your heart has become too narrow if it is necessary to remove me from it. But this is not necessary, nor is it opportune or even what you wish; I know this even though it is I who speak in such a way. But I demand a word that shows the voluntary operation of love. Let us communicate with each other as those who love, if we really do love each other.

But you perhaps will object, no, you certainly do object. You say these letters disturb our brother. They upset him. They deprive him of sleep and give rise to a plague of fantasies in him.[292] So he should be left to himself and to God and given over to his own conscience. Why is it necessary to rummage through his secrets? Why is it necessary to speak through writings with someone who wants only peace and quiet?

You will see, brother, how I can respond. I wish as a friend and brother either to console or to rejoice with him who rejoices and to weep with him who weeps (Rom 12:15). Or I desire as the one who is more experienced and learned to teach by discussing the diverse paths and stumbling blocks of temptation. By teaching him I can discuss, especially while he is still at a crossroad, what is best for him and for his salvation. I can show him how to consider the circumstances that most easily deceive the person who does not expect them, for they have an appearance of what seems in general to be good but which in its individual manifestation is turned into the worst form of evil.[293]

Yes, I accept that he is tormented by the most awful nightmares. Indeed, the forenamed reverend father and I are very much afraid of this affliction of his. I nevertheless do not remember that it came over him while he was in the world.[294] O Christ who brings salvation, what is to happen to Jean when he is sick and old if such a torment comes over him while he is still young, vital, and vigorous? No affliction can make him more dull of mind, slack in memory, unstable in the judgment of reason, and generally unfit for all things. Such a disturbance differs only a little from mania or madness. So what good will your attention and your community's prayers be able to do if he is transformed from a sane and bright person into a fool and a madman?[295]

Let it not be, you will say, that we ever see this happen. I ask also that it not be. Nevertheless, I cannot stop being afraid of this outcome, especially when this very thing that I was afraid of happening in the future now has happened so quickly.

It did not come about, you will say, because of the strictness or condition of his religious life. It was the contents of letters that caused this overstimulation by their sting. Unwillingly he goes over them again and again, nor can any effort remove them from the house of memory. These letters obtrude upon him against his will and attach their beaks to his mind. And so his head gets disturbed. He lacks sleep. His brain twists about in dizziness.

I understand that you will say that in your judgment this situation should never have arisen, according to your own experience of the monastic life, if it had not been caused through what was expressed in writing. But pay attention, brother: would only two or three letters be enough for a modest and disciplined youth who was accustomed to hear much harsher things? What could lead him into such a bad state except harsh fasting, excessive vigils, a rigorous program of vocal prayer, a strict collection of readings, and similar practices? You cannot claim that others who do similar things by no means experience similar reactions.

You might remember that the forenamed reverend father and I spoke to you about this matter and remarked on it. For men are made in different ways, just as there are different callings by God. As in the physical body, so also in the mystical body, the members do not have the same function: the eye has one, the hand another, the nose a third. And so one person is called to understand scripture, another to prayer and vigils, a third and a fourth to other activities. I know from myself that if I were forced to keep vigils as others do, I would be hardly or not at all different from the mad person, despite any advantage I might have, as the popular saying goes.[296]

Finally, all the articles and similar things that I have written to you in truth are founded on the root of this consideration. They should be taken into account in a healthy manner in carrying out a religious life's profession. I preferred for the time being to write of these matters to you, most beloved brother, rather than to our other brother, so that as a most indulgent father and brother I could make satisfaction for our still delicate son and brother. And so he asked that I not write anything more. Or rather, he has implored me, how justly as all of you see, and in a discreet way. I do not want, however, to disappoint him. I do not want to ask anything harsher of him, even if I thought that I was within my jurisdiction to do so. If nothing hinders his peace and quiet nor will disturb it except my letters, then I freely, or even gladly, will stop them. But in my mind this explanation lacks any probability.

Finally, brother, I turn to you and your fellow brothers, through the common religion of the Christian faith, which we all have professed under the abbot Christ in baptism and in which the salvation of all flesh consists. I address you through the common mother of us all, charity, which is the end of all law, that the bond of brotherly love move you to a wise and praiseworthy compassion so that you show mercy on this our brother. You will act mercifully if you act according to discretion. You will not be able to do so if any sensual attachment of your own hinders you from accepting advice given by others. You must not spurn their warnings or convince yourself that they are to be rejected. Finally, in spite of difficulties or events in present or future, you must be willing to be deterred from the judgment you have made about the profession of our brother.

Be well, brother so close to my heart, remember me in your prayers. And do not be reluctant to write something true and worthwhile about your own condition and those of your brethren, especially of this novice brother. I promise that I will receive and interpret everything in the same way that I ask that what I send be received and interpreted.

LETTER 24   Gerson to a bishop[297]
Paris, prior to April 1408
[Letter-treatise concerning the moderation of the types of cases reserved for absolution from the bishop's court.]

To his episcopal dignity, from someone who is zealous that he uses the keys [of the kingdom of heaven] well.

Pastoral authority in reserved cases as a forum of conscience, just as any other power, has been given to church prelates in order to build up the church, not to destroy it, as the Apostle says (cf. 2 Cor 13:10), as well as for the benefit of the Christian people for their salvation. But it is most certainly apparent through several experts in hearing confessions at this time that the strict reservation of some cases, especially in graver and hidden types of carnal sin, keeps numberless persons from confessing such sins. We find boys and girls and very shy women and unlearned country people from whom the confession of such sins can hardly be extracted even if the confessor is attentive, gentle, careful, and discreet. But if such matters are left to the bishop or to confessors who come from far away and whose presence is publicly known, such penitents will take flight in terror.

We have seen how thousands of people fail to come. Two or three hundred or even a thousand confessors would never be enough even in one diocese in order to listen in full to all those cases and give absolution. And so what good does it do—certainly it does great harm—to add one source of shame to another, one more heavy burden upon the burden and difficulty of confessing such sins? The result is almost beyond belief. This especially is the case when the secret sin is such that its author will forever hide himself out of a desire that neither the bishop nor anyone else thereby will punish him and thus gain knowledge of his act.

But you will say: If such a person does not reveal himself, he will be damned. We quite agree. But one is obliged to stand in the way of damnation in all ways rather than to increase its chances. In our experience, this terror of reserved sin keeps no one or very few from sinning, but it holds untold persons back from confession, because of the causes already given or because of others. Women especially in this manner are kept away. First of all, they are afraid of being noticed by their husbands when such confessors come. When the husbands are jealous, they immediately turn the situation against their wives, and so there arise arguments, fights, discord, with the result that love is broken off. Other things happen that create even worse evils: would that such dissension did not often end in death![298]

Second, women are often made by such confessors to give money, wax,[299] or similar things, or public penances are imposed on them. Again they will be noticed by their husbands, and so dangers also arise here. Third, they feel shame they dare not confess to a great prelate or to a famous theologian as to others, in spite of the fact that he is good and suitable for this function. And each can recall from experience several such cases where penitents have held back.

Similarly, also in men similar reasons sometimes are to be considered, especially if someone has gotten involved in an episcopal case and is charged with having harmed the bishop or his church. How can such a person be convinced to confess to the bishop or to his vicar? Or perhaps someone is aware of the financial gain made by such confessors, as has become common, so that he, being scandalized, keeps himself from confession. There are a thousand such reasons that hold numberless persons back from confession.

And this must be understood concerning hidden sins: they are a different matter than is the case with some public sins. According to some professors established laws once reserved only the latter type. Why so? So that a heavy and public punishment, inflicted by the authorities, would weigh more harshly on such persons, to provide an example and create fear in other persons. But with hidden acts this rationale disappears, because in such matters no penance can be imposed when the penitent refuses to accept it. Otherwise we have the memorable saying of William of Paris: It is better for salvation to give the penitent a very small and light penance that he accepts, leaving him in God's hand to be punished in purgatory, rather than to give him a great penance that he cannot carry out and thus to cast him into hell.[300]

May your loving care thus provide for this concern, your episcopal dignity. Do not close the kingdom of God to the sheep of Christ's flock. Beware of imposing heavy burdens on their weak necks when they are about to fall. Therefore cease from the reservation of such hidden cases, for people scarcely come, alas, to these confessors, no matter how famous they may be.[301]

Finally, if you cannot accept that all hidden cases, since we are not speaking of public ones, be left indiscriminately to any confessor without concern for the age of the penitents, at least it seems right first of all that no case be judged under reservation when minors wish to confess, meaning those who have not reached their fourteenth year. They do not have the complete use of reason, nor can they easily resist their own temptations or the evils of others, nor do they easily have the boldness to appear before official persons whom they do not know. All the less do they dare to confess shameful matters.

We must take into account also the sense of modesty and concern for reputation in women or their relatives, if women frequently either publicly or from a great distance are sent to confessors.

Also, it is best that we in the end easily and quickly leave the power over hidden cases to curates and to bishops and generally to all who in good faith wish to profit souls and know how to do so and are not interested in economic gain or in exposing people.[302] Such persons are to be carefully sought out, brought forward, and consulted, for the praise of God and the salvation of the people, as confessors and preachers. They make God's goodness come over us in this worst of times when we, alas, greatly experience what is written in Genesis (6:12): "All flesh had corrupted its ways." Everywhere we witness the shipwreck of the evil. But from it the ark of penance saves those who confess. It is much better to make wider the entrance to the ark rather than to let a very narrow opening prevent those who should be drawn into entering. Indeed, according to the parable in the gospel, they should almost be forced to enter.[303]

It is moreover necessary, when the good Lord will bring back universal peace, that there be someone of each obedience[304] who has a general and express license for confession, so that each person can be absolved, not only legally but also sacramentally, by any discreet priest, for all matters in any situation where he sinned in connection with the question of the cession of the papacy.[305] May God, who is blessed forever, direct all things. Amen.

[A postscript is attached to the letter, listing cases normally reserved that Gerson thinks should be taken off the list and made available for absolution from any priest.]

Some of the special cases are solitary masturbation; sexual contact with the same sex; sexual activity with the opposite sex when the seed is ejaculated outside of the proper vessel, both in marriage and outside of it; sexual abuse in any degree of blood relationship and in every type of carnal sin without respect for family bond, religious vow, priestly rank, or decency of bodily parts. This especially when parents come into too close contact with daughters and sons. When they are at leisure or are partying, they are made into beasts, such as those of whom the Satirist spoke: For how can drunken Venus care about the genitals and the head when she knows no distance between them?[306]

Likewise sacrileges in lesser matters and the use of magic in a limited way. Blows given by youthful clerics to each other. Undetermined amounts of restitution in minor cases,[307] and similar affairs of this kind.

LETTER 25   Gerson to Jean Morel[308]
                   Paris, about 1408(?)
[Jean Morel has submitted to the judgment of Gerson an account of Ermine of Reims, whose life contained many wondrous events. Gerson explains why he accepts its authenticity.]

To the religious and good man, most beloved in fraternal charity in Christ, Lord Jean Morel, regular canon of the church of Saint Denis of Reims, Jean Gerson, unworthy chancellor of the church of Paris, wishes that he reaches the harbor of true religion.

Several times before now, sometimes by letter, sometimes in person, you have asked me to consider a book that has been edited in many manuscripts concerning the life, habits, and death of a certain plain and pious woman, called Ermine. This is especially because the book contains wondrous and unusual visions which that woman asserts were given her and shown while she was awake, recently from the vigil of the feast of All Souls of the year 1395 until the following feast of Saint Louis, on which day she left the world. Most recently you asked me with many pleas and supplications and begged so much that I could not delay any longer. In order to instruct the less learned and to close the mouths of those who want to undermine the faith of the simple and to harm the reputation of those who live well and piously, I decided to describe in brief what I judged should be thought about the contents of that little book.

I complied with your concern, which I have no doubt is from God. I reviewed that book and studied it as long and as much as I thought required. Without any rash attachment and in submitting the matter to the judgment of the Holy See and the resident Sovereign Pontiff, and to the discretion of all who know better, I can say as a triple conclusion what follows:

First conclusion: In the said book there is nothing that should be considered contrary to the catholic faith or any of its articles of belief. The basis for this finding is that everything there set forth is possible in itself or in similar cases for divine omnipotence. Divine law also permits such things, for events of the same type or from which the same judgment can be made are read about in authentic stories in the *Lives of the Fathers*.[309] We find how they were attacked or deluded many times by demons and how similar things were done to them.

Second conclusion: Although it is not necessary for salvation to believe that each individual event happened as a fact and in the way it is told in the book, I think, nevertheless, that it is rash and crude to insist on dissenting from such things or to attack them with stubborn ill will. The rationale of the first point is that very many such events are concerned with matters that are irrelevant for the faith; many occurrences are asserted to be miracles that can be naturally explained, even though similar events can take place miraculously. Still, not everything, as is asserted, can be excluded from the category of miracle.

The rationale of the second point is that a natural sense of equity insists that someone who wants to be believed in his assertions, especially when they are strengthened by an oath, at least should not be attacked in a stubborn manner for falsity or perjury. In this way all political discourse would perish if no faith were entrusted in anyone.[310] This is a principle of natural law confirmed by divine law, that what you hate to have done to you by someone else, you are careful not ever to do to another.[311] Thus no one who lives in a civilized manner should stubbornly refuse to believe what another person says when no falsity or clear breach of truth is apparent.

The contents of the book of which we speak have been put forward through serious and repeated attestation and in the face of death. It is especially important that they breech no truth of the faith. In fact, the faith is rather corroborated and honored. Also, a pious belief in the book's contents does not seem to give rise to any danger in morals. Thus what already has been said is clear. Add to this that the hand of God should not be shortened (Is 59:1), for it formerly could do similar and greater things than in our times.[312] Nor does it have to follow that if many such events can take place, that these can be denied to be miracles. For as the same death takes place for different reasons, so the same effect can happen in divers ways. When something unclear happens in connection with a miracle, it seems that divine omnipotence is more honored, as well as Christian religion, in attributing to a miracle that which happened, rather than in stubbornly denying the miraculous.

Here I always assume that true doctrine remains unharmed. For in the spreading of heresy even the raising of the dead would be wholly suspect for me and worthy of detestation. In this matter it is true what the wise man says: "He who believes too easily is shallow in his heart" (Sir 19:4). And certainly this one fact does not prevent one's admiration or the possibility of a miracle, that it was an uneducated countrywoman who knew how to express all that is described in the book.[313]

Third conclusion: Both because of the limited learning of many people in scripture and sacred history and because of the obstinate incredulity of some people, who are stiff-necked, it is not appropriate now to make this book available to the general public without restriction, but only to make it known to those who it is likely will be edified by it.

The reason for the first statement is so that what is holy not be cast to the dogs, as pearls are thrown before swine (Mt 7:6). All the thoughts of such people are of drinking and carousing. For such persons, all talk of God and religion, of angels and demons, is a fable. They reject and trample on these as if they were unworthy of their assent, for their minds are puffed up and gross.

The reason for the second assertion is that great profit can be gathered through the matters that there are narrated for those who are stable in their way of life and concerned with their own salvation. First, because that woman is a model for penance, austerity, and tears. It is the gospel truth that the kingdom of heaven is given to those who do penance (cf. Mt 3:2). Therefore this woman, being poor, old, uneducated, seems to be given us to provide a powerful example of the apostolic truth that God has chosen what is weak in the world to overcome what is powerful (1 Cor 1:27). Are not the demons strong, of whose prince the Bible says that there is no power on earth that can be compared to his?[314] But what greater confusion could be made for the strong, or what finer trick could be played on the dragon who was made for deception than that he be conquered so often and so basely by an insignificant woman, and such a woman? Clearly he seems to me to have seen her, to have been outraged, to have frothed and to have gnashed his teeth and to have been consumed with envy when she overcame the desire of sin.

In such a matter there is nothing surprising if similar things do not happen with even stronger persons. For graces are divided in such a way that one and the same spirit operates, giving out individual graces to individual persons as it desires (1 Cor 12:11). It has done so with the humble and the great.

But as for those who have conquered the world (here I refer to lesser enemies), the flesh, and the blood, God spares them so that he does not let them be overwhelmed by the weight of spiritual temptations and to be oppressed beyond what they can bear (cf. 1 Cor 10:13). God chose that woman, poor in spirit, rich in faith, so that no flesh might be glorified in her sight (1 Cor 1:29). But from deeds of this type one can consider how shrewd is the iniquity of demons, how base and extreme their desire to harm, how full of fury and cleverness they are in seducing people, at one time with terror, at another with allurements, and again with a thousand kinds of false miracles.

In the face of all these devices, it is necessary and sufficient to have the triple assistance of the virtue that we read abounded in this woman. The first is a profound and true humility by which she judged herself to be unworthy of all good and deserving all evil. This she expressed not only with her mouth, as many do, but interiorly, with all her heart. This conviction came from a most passionate and conscientious awareness of her own weakness and imperfection with respect to divine power and goodness. Such humility is that which avoids the snares that have been set out everywhere, according to the oracle given by God to Saint Anthony.[315]

The second source of assistance is a firm faith that is alive and trusts God, so that without his consent, will, and providence, no adverse power can harm a person. Thus when the madness of enemies is boldly provoked to harm us, we will have an unshakable faith that they can do nothing, except insofar as the Most High should allow it. In this manner I think is fulfilled the saying about hell's lion: Resist him, they say, you who are strong in faith (1 Pt 5:9).

The third source of help is prudent simplicity and, as I might say, an untaught wisdom, which does not depend on its own prudence but does all things with counsel (Prv 13:10). This is dove-like and at the same time serpent-like discretion (cf. Mt 10:16), the director and helmsman of the virtues, without which virtue lapses into vice. For as soon as someone is wise in his own eyes and spurns advice, virtue is driven from him and he is exposed to all the contempt of demons. Indeed, according to one of the sayings of a holy father, he now is made a demon unto himself.[316]

It appears at the end of the said book[317] how terrible will be the sufferings of hell and how great the joys of heaven. I am not unaware, most beloved brother in Christ, that many more things could be said in a useful manner about the admirable life of this devout and pious woman, but I think what I have said is enough to satisfy your request. The time will come perhaps when I will have more leisure, so that I can respond at great length. There is no doubt that objections can be made in almost all matters, even those that are most true.

I have signed this letter in my own hand in testimony of both my agreement and consent. This is the hand which you know, which cannot be imitated and has no desire to deceive, and which I think could not lie with impunity. Farewell.

LETTER 26   Gerson's Second Letter to Barthélemy Clantier[318]
              Paris, April-June 1408
[John of Schoonhoven has replied to Gerson's first letter to Barthélemy and has defended Ruusbroec. Gerson answers this letter and divides his reply into eight sections.][319]

Grace and peace be to you, a man who in the example of Job is blameless and upright and God-fearing (Jb 1:1).

There was brought to me lately, as you know, a letter of considerable size that tries to rescue the modes of expression found in the third section of a treatise by a certain person entitled *The Spiritual Espousals.* Elsewhere, in order to preserve the integrity of catholic truth with less educated minds, I showed through a letter sent to you that these forms of expression cannot be maintained.[320]

But what are we to do? Where do we turn, amid so many occupations? Thus there is no end of making more books or letters, in arguing and replying (cf. Eccl 12:12). Let us remain, then, within the limits of the first letter. Through considerations that reflect an accessible and plain style, the matter can be treated on the basis of the same letter.

The first consideration: we should speak in accord with a certain rule. We have the most memorable and true statement of Augustine, which removes the barbarous confusion of tongues from sacred doctrine.[321] For what other way is more effective in preventing the building of the tower of David for the good than that of allowing any variation one likes with names or terms? For then one person would not understand another, but we would fall into the confusion of Babel (cf. Gn 11:9).

Thus the author of that treatise is not sufficiently excused by his defender, who says: And if there is any error in what he says, that alone consists in what he names, for names are arbitrary, and so such an error is not of great weight. For if the holy doctors such as Augustine and Jerome had indiscriminately allowed the heretics' ways of speaking, then they could immediately have made peace with them. It would, however, have been an evil peace. There should be noted the response of Basil the Great in a similar case, when he did not wish even in a single word to deviate from anything that profited catholic faith.[322] The same was the case with Jerome with the word *homousion*.[323] So there are others without number.

There was in my time a certain teacher in the schools who in a response said that the Father is the cause of the Son. He said, "The Father produces the Son." He was forced immediately to revoke his statement, nor was his explanation in any way allowed, even though it was most true according to his understanding and mode of expression.

The second consideration: the manner of speaking of theologians, if it is found to be unsuitable and metaphorical, or unusual and figurative, ought not to be drawn out or become common usage but should be explained in its proper sense. Otherwise, it would have been fruitless to have doctors of theology, who have been appointed mainly for the function of explaining Holy Scripture rather than to add more and more confusion to the matter. So if someone wishes to assert according to the literal sense that God in order to free humankind did not disdain the womb of a virgin, he would [according to such theologians] certainly be accused of error.[324]

Men of inferior academic training and knowledge should thus be tolerant if their sayings are made to conform to proper usage and are not allowed to be expanded so that they undermine catholic faith. This consideration, I think, has influenced the most recent doctors, including Thomas Aquinas, Bonaventure, and the like, in leaving out all verbal decoration and in handing down a theology through questions, with fixed rules and a precise form of words. In this way we ought to find the greatest security in a theology that is both practical and speculative, when it brings all previous doctors of theology back to one proper and safe way of expression.[325]

Third consideration: one should have faith in the person who is an expert in his art. This is the reason why authority for interpreting Holy Scripture according to doctrine is given to doctors of sacred theology, and why this is especially done in the schools, in conveying this teaching to those who both in intellect and through continual exercise are capable of understanding it.[326]

The subject with which the third part of the forenamed treatise deals comes from the contents of Holy Scripture, or more correctly, from the highest theology, which is called mystical and which in a scholastic manner Albert the Great and certain others dealt with in their own clear language.[327] Who then will not be amazed to hear from the defender of this author that these matters are not to be treated in the schools? Thus are they to be made public, now in writings, now in talk in the vernacular language among servants, uneducated youths, slow-witted old people, the uneducated crowd, broken-down old women, at one time in the marketplace, at another in the back streets? Are men who are quite learned, both in ability and training, to be kept from speaking about such matters because they are schoolmen?

Fourth consideration: he who clings to God is one spirit (1 Cor 6:17).[328] This unity no one can understand or explain, however much he piles on words, in any other sense than through assimilation, as John says in his canonical epistle: "We know that when he appears we will be like him" (1 Jn 3:2). Any other manner of speaking in the holy doctors, as in Dionysius and others, is metaphorical or figurative, hyperbolic or emphatic, and if it is not related to this rule is to be rejected.

For assimilation does not take away our nature; it perfects it.[329] Nor does it remove the being that a creature has in its own genus, since a rational soul cannot lose this except through annihilation. It follows that the similitude adduced through some doctor that the adding of a drop of water into a large jar of the strongest wine is like the union of the contemplative soul with God: this image is to be totally rejected as having the error, or more properly, the madness of Amaury, who was condemned because he said that the creature is converted into God and into his own first ideal existence, as Hostiensis notes in his gloss on the first chapter, "We condemn, on the Holy Trinity and the catholic faith."[330] Finally, a similar fantasy elsewhere at Paris has been condemned as empty and unintelligible against an Augustinian.[331]

The fifth proposition: we should blame the devotion of those people who try to mix up their conclusions with statements that are unlearned, alien, and unusual, and those who are so involved in praising or defending these, and in defending themselves, that they become more confused than able to elucidate the matter.

I would bring forward in this place, so that I do not seem to depend on myself alone, a part of a certain sermon made in the chapter of the Carthusian brothers[332] in the year 1406. The theme is, "Let us see if the vines are budding" (Sg 7:12):

> They exercise the fourth false form of devotion, vanity, and curiosity, when, without mortifying their own will and serving the Lord in zeal, they believe the spiritual life to consist in rumination or rather in fantasizing about spiritual matters, thinking that this fantasy or at least the delight that comes from it makes up devotion. Thereby they come to this conclusion: not being content with the ways of speaking in Holy Scripture, they invent for themselves or imagine more abstract forms for spiritual concerns, so that they can gain greater delight from them. Also, because of this tendency, they cloak the most obvious matters in obscure and abstract forms, so that they can derive greater pleasure from them. Calling their abasement or perhaps some other form of contemplation a submersion in a profound abyss, they consider divine love to be annihilation or reduction into nothingness. The loving movement of the mind into God they consider to be a flowing into God; also an inclination to an act for God's sake they consider to be a flowing out from God, and similar matters. They do so in spite of the fact that Christ, the prophets, the apostles, and all the doctors who treat Holy Scripture have tried, as much as they could and insofar as it was helpful, to make it easy to express that which once was difficult to convey in modes of speech.
>
> This false devotion is most dangerous for religious because, as daily (alas) and woeful experience teaches and has taught many who appeared to be spiritual and religious it deceives, infatuates, and totally blinds. As a result, they have become lax in regular observances, on which they have looked down. They have been

rebellious against their superiors, whom they have thought to be crude. Some have taken flight and apostatized. Others even have become heretics or before their time have prophesied, saying, "This is what the Lord says, when the Lord has not spoken" (Ez 22:28). But their pride, or at least their heads so full of fantasies, has dreamed all this up. Some people also have shown their wondrous foolishness in public by celebrations, dancing, leaping about, and such practices.[333] The fourth form of devotion is a wine that is full of fumes, meaning one that generates lecherous behavior, concerning which the apostolic prohibition could be accepted in a mystical sense: "Do not get drunk in wine, for in it there is debauchery" (Eph 5:18). And truly in this very thing there is a spiritual lechery according to which they who are falsely devout do not seek to honor and worship God but their own delight. This is what is said here.

If you, the author of this sermon, whoever you may be, if you had seen the letter recently shown to me, what would you have said? How could you have stomached its contents?

The sixth consideration: Plato is a friend; Socrates is a friend; more a friend is the truth.

Excessive attachment to some doctor or a teaching perverts not only practical judgment, as happens most frequently, but also one's speculative powers, something that is less apparent. It is as if, in the manner of the Pythagoreans, it is not allowed to ask anything more than whether such a master did make a statement. We must rid ourselves of persistent and heated defense of this or that doctrine, for it creates hateful controversy and jealous insults.

My conscience is open with you, God, that I was in no way led by hatred of anyone to write what I wrote. I then expressed as truthfully as possible, in the way I come more and more to see, the excessive impropriety of those ways of speaking. And so I said, among other concerns, after I had considered the unity of the soul to God:

Through this image Boethius proves that every good is God according to the saying, "I said you are gods" (Ps 81:6). This is not so in terms of the truth and unity of divine essence and in proper speech, but in terms of participation and assimilation, in imitation and appellation. But if this author replies that he has understood his writings in a similar way concerning unification of the spirit with God, I do not challenge or contradict him about his intention. But I do not hesitate to assert that his explanation sounds different.[334]

I ask you, reader, if my speech could be gentler. I add that I tried afterward, both in speech and writing, to excuse the said author, after he showed me that he elsewhere had expressed better how a creature in no way loses the being that it has in its proper genus. But if he had inserted the same thing into the statements of the third part of his treatise, he would not in this way have given occasion for error and for incriminating himself not only among the uneducated but also with those who have a complete education and training.

Anyone who perhaps comes upon a little treatise that I attempted to prepare about mystical theology in speculative and practical terms will see that what I say is true.[335] It was my central concern to make familiar the knowledge of the scholastics in those matters that devout people have conveyed more through emotional statements and figurative speech than by direct presentation. Note the place where mystical theology is shown to differ from ordinary theology, among other points because it unites and transforms.

The seventh consideration: whether they who love are making up dreams for themselves, as Vergil says.[336] Concerning this saying the statement of my previous letter on this subject is based on experience and solid reason. It is expressed thus:

From lack of pious affectivity and even moreso from its corruption through vice, the most learned theologians sometimes err, for their wickedness has blinded them (Wis 2:21) and they have given themselves over to a debased mind (Rom 1:28). Similarly, from the limited light of the intellect and an insufficient instruction in the study also of secular learning, and sometimes especially in logic, others sometimes fall into the most dangerous errors. Claiming to have great devotion toward the virtues, these are the people whom the Apostle said have zeal but not according to knowledge (Rom 10:2). If they do not have their knowledge in humility and unless they restrict themselves within the boundaries of their knowledge, there will be no one who is more stubborn or more ridiculous in fabricating errors. Those with insufficient learning ought not to write or teach with a light heart. They are not to be followed without great caution, and without previous discussion and examination by the learned. In such persons we often find much that is either false or badly explained, and that thus provides abundant material for the uneducated for error, although these writings in many respects are most profound.[337]

I add now that it happened in our time with a certain woman who was considered by many to be a prophetess and a maker of miracles, whom I saw and to whom I spoke. She finally said and ordered to be written that her spirit in contemplating God was annihilated in true destruction and then recreated. And when she was asked how she could know this, she answered that she had experienced it.[338]

The day would not be long enough if I wanted to count such countless insanities of these people who are not so much in love as out of their minds.[339] They have not acted according to knowledge, as seems to have been the case with the Beghards. This I remember once pointing out in a certain little treatise, *On Distinguishing True from False Revelations*.[340]

The eighth consideration: he is not to be taught or even to be warned who prefers to defend his error rather than to correct it. This point Horace made at the end of his *Poetry*.[341] A more harsh correction is therefore required if someone acts aggressively to save, as it were, his own impropriety of phrasing. How can this be, or in what order? It seems that the judgment of the bishop and the inquisitor is to be asked for, since the small root of an erroneous statement creeps like a cancer. A tiny spark of error, as was clear with Arius, when it is not smothered at the right time or stopped, bursts forth into a great flame.[342]

This recently happened at Paris in the sacred faculty of theology against those who tried to introduce the erroneous teaching of Raymond Lull. Even though it in many aspects is very profound and true, since it nevertheless in other matters departed from the manner used by the holy doctors and from the rule of doctrinal tradition and what is used in the schools, that teaching was repudiated and prohibited by public decree.[343]

I will say here what I think. If I should notice that such modes of expression were being made public in the good University of Paris, either through sermons or in the schools, I would proceed immediately on the basis of the office in which I unworthily serve and seek the censure of the faculty of theology, so that these matters might be examined. Once examined, they will be judged according to their merits.[344]

Farewell, deserving father. Be always mindful of me in your prayers.

LETTER 27   Gerson to the Abbot of Saint Denis[345]
             Paris, 8 October 1408
[He asks him, for the sake of concord and peace, to remove discreetly a panel concerning the relics of Saint Denis. He would prefer multiple relics of the same body parts of saints in different places rather than skepticism about the cult of relics.]

To the reverend father and lord in Christ, sincerely loved, the lord abbot of Saint Denis in France, his Jean, chancellor of Paris, that he share in the path of Christian religion in piety, sobriety, and peace.

A hatred of strife, as well as a love of our mother the church and of truth, justice, and peace, have frequently led me, I confess, to come to you in a spirit of intimate faith, in my petition and supplication to your reverend paternity. I bear witness to this fact through charity, the common mother of all that lives. I ask that you order a certain panel that has been set up in your church of Saint Denis in France voluntarily be removed, rather than that the matter lead to harsh litigation. For this panel is said to have led Parisians into mendacious and intolerable error concerning the relics of the head of the same most saintly Denis.[346] For behold, before God I do not lie, that there was last year a careful investigation made by many nobles, up to the number of thirty, as far as I gather, or about that number, both of the Parlement of Paris and of the faculties of theology and canon law. They came to agreement without any hesitation or doubt that the forenamed panel was both harmful and notorious as a libel against the charity owed God and neighbor. This is what I have concluded after I considered the weight of the arguments brought forward.

I think, moreover, that if the panel remains, there will finally burst forth, which I abhor, a great and horrid conflagration of dissension between these two most celebrated churches, yours and ours, which the consideration alone of their pastor and patron Denis should have bound together. He ennobled our church by his pastoral seat and government, and yours by the precious relics of his body. I sense, believe me, that more seeds of this type of dissension have been made ready than I can conveniently say or write.

I know, moreover, that even if it were permitted to let the said panel remain displayed there, despite the assertion that in the opinion of so many this is not allowable, I would still have no doubt that such a practice was neither decent nor expedient. And so if this panel is freely and secretly moved in the way we have mentioned, what loss or shame or ill fame can it bring to you or your church? None at all, unless someone with stiff-necked animosity insists that it is a base act to remove from sight without scandal the source of scandals. If a kind of food scandalizes my brother, affirms the Apostle, I will forever not eat meat (1 Cor 8:13).

But if by chance you in your prudent and wise circumspection might answer that you are not pleased with such an addition of this kind to the church, as I clearly suspect displeases you, but that you do not have all the heads of your monastery with their opinions, as it were, in your hand, let it be.[347] But it will nevertheless be your duty to try, reverend father, insofar as this can be done now while the matter remains under control, rather than if new problems should arise and make the situation all the more difficult. It will be my task similarly to contribute my efforts, as I promise you, that either we reach a complete understanding or at least that the former dissension does not become even worse. For the time being the specific and general reasons for condemning this panel and for justifying the observance of the people of Paris have elsewhere been sufficiently brought forth in terms of what is probable.[348]

But the rite of veneration of relics would come to a bad end in many churches, as in yours, if any variation in such a cult were called intolerable error and falsehood. The veil from above of hearts in terms of divine interpretation would have to be removed (cf. 2 Cor 3:15–16), when the relics that one church or religious order says it has, another similarly claims to possess, as we see with the heads of Saint John the Baptist, Benedict, Mary Magdalene, Lazarus, and relics of this kind without number.[349] And so nothing prohibits that each contradictory object remains at the same time with the other part. Even if the object does not exist in absolute truth, still there is a sufficient probability of reasons for what is asserted. It thus becomes praiseworthy to defend the relic from lies and error, since error and falsehood in religious matters require the presence of guilt.[350]

Written at Paris on the eighth of October, at which time I was thinking about making a sermon for the birth of the same precious Areopagite Dionysius, who in his coming sought glory to God in the highest and peace in our land to men of good will (Lk 2:14). This peace I ask and beg that we again have. So that it can be done as we have said, let the poison of useless and even dangerous contention be more quickly removed, for the honor of God. In him be well, and be convinced that now fairness and gentleness are required. In the year 1408, in the month of October.

LETTER 28   Gerson to Pierre d'Ailly[351]
Paris, 16 October 1408 (or 1411)
[Gerson is getting ready to isolate himself in prayer and contemplation. He is writing his sermon for the feast of All Saints. He recommends to his former teacher Dionysius's work On the Divine Names.*]*

From the two letters of your worthiness, reverend father and outstanding teacher, the anxiousness of your mind was made apparent to me, because concern for the Lord's house and for the state has overwhelmed you. Truly I see something, you say, that is heavy for me and hardly bearable. Therefore your lordship has convinced me in my poverty to write something about the gentle yoke of Christ (Mt 11:30).

But where can I better begin, putting aside any initial excuses, than with the tyrannous yoke of the devil, the flesh, and the world, in all its harshness and cruelty, even though we in our madness sometimes consider it to be gentle, because our spiritual taste is disturbed by fever. But the beginning of salvation is the awareness that one is sick and suffering, for he who has lost feeling to evil does not feel such pain. It is therefore good that everything you see troubles you, in terms of what is temporal and mortal. Everywhere are emptiness, madness, and falsity.

Why is it so? Clearly in order that in sighing and longing you will say with the prophet: "Who will give me wings like a dove, so that I will fly and find rest" (Ps 54:7). Then, as if he were at peace in his vow, he would rejoice and add, "Behold I fled far away and remained in solitude" (Ps 54:8). In this solitude, if I am right, he has prepared a dwelling and a residence where the Apostle also was when he said, "Our way of life is in heaven" (Phil 3:20).[352]

Is there not great solitude in heaven? Is it not a deserted place?[353] Here the Lord promises through the prophet: Your ruins of old will be rebuilt (Is 58:12). In this desert the ninety-nine sheep have been left behind. But how can a dwelling place be set in this solitude, the church replies, singing of a confessor that he has been placed on this pilgrimage with his body alone, while his thoughts and dedication are active in another, eternal country.[354] But truly what fruit comes forth for the one who flees and distances himself in this way, as the prophet explains when he says: I was waiting for him who has saved me from weakness of spirit and the tempest (Ps 54:9). The Apostle says: Within are fear, behold weakness of spirit; outside are clashes, behold the tempest (cf. 2 Cor 7:5). You will openly admit that the two fight against your soul. But what remains to be added except to pour forth prayer with the prophet and say what follows: Cast them down, Lord, and confuse their speech (Ps 54:10)? Otherwise the pride that has been lifted up will make for itself a tower against the just faithful of the church. The cause is given: because I saw iniquity and strife in the city (Ps 54:9) and all the other troubles that follow.

Act then, outstanding teacher, and do what you heard through the prophet. Receive the wings as of the dove (Ps 54:7), dwelling on ancient days and being mindful of eternal years (cf. Ps 76:5). And so you will distance yourself, making the Most High your refuge so that evil cannot reach you (Ps 90:10). Leave behind in contempt whatever you freely can on earth. You must do so now. You must go away, for you cannot remain here. So you will be weaned from the breast of earthly consolation. You will seek another food that is more solid, the nourishment of interior devotion. Desist from wrath and forsake anger; do not fret (Ps 36:8). It is a sign of indiscreet zeal to be consumed with worry. Put your thoughts, your hope, your prayer, and your help in the Lord, and he will nourish you with solid food (cf. Ps 120:2; 54:23).

I would not say such things in being your teacher, but I speak with you in order to deal with my folly and to provoke my laziness. Let us take care that what often happens to weak children does not happen to us. When they fall down, they get angry with themselves, and they sometimes pound their heads on the ground and show other signs of impatience. They grieve that they have fallen. But they are not grieving in a good way when they are angered at their own weakness, as if they ought to be able by themselves to stand up.

We often act like big children in our adversities, so that we wax angry in public affairs. We are indignant with ourselves or our neighbors and do not seek help. Nor do we flee, in looking to him who ought to save us from weakness of spirit and the tempest (Ps 54:9), just as the child who has fallen should seek help not in himself but from the father or mother who looks after him.

I have heard that many were harshly and deservedly tormented and had in vain wasted away in themselves, for they had fallen by sinning. These God did not bring to rise up again so long as they were trapped in their anger in considering the filth of their sin and transgression, because this seems more to reflect proud presumption rather than a sense of being humbled. As soon as such persons are converted, however, they turn their eyes to the Lord and lift their hands in humility so that he will pick them up. Then they are heard, cleansed, and lifted up.

These matters, then, I have spoken of rapidly and in a certain rapture of mind. More precisely, I have set them forth without leaving space for correction and send them with my letter. I have done so in order that we not be devoured by considering present or imminent evils, but being all the more vigilant we can say to the Lord with Josaphat: When we do not know what we ought to do, this alone remains for us, that we direct our eyes to you (2 Chr 20:12). So we will be consoled in our weeping because we will be humbled, as we ought to be, under the powerful hand of God, and we will seek his help, for which we should ask and in which we can hope.

In this way the yoke of Christ will become gentle for us (Mt 11:30), and it will be sweet in the consideration and hope of salvation. In this manner the burden will be made light for us, since we will place the whole load on the shoulders of his providence and goodness. In this way we will also know how to experience what Christ promises in saying, "Blessed are they who mourn, for they will be comforted" (Mt 5:5).

On these words I composed a sermon elsewhere, in the distinguished University of Paris,[355] and I now have decided to make another about something with which I am concerned. It is based on that saying which well fits our wretched age and the subject about which we are speaking: "Blessed are they who suffer persecution for justice's sake" (Mt 5:10). I hope that I will deserve your presence, outstanding lord. Contact through the spoken word is a more complete experience than taking time off for writing letters. Meanwhile farewell.

Written at Paris on the morning of the octave of the feast of Saint Denis,[356] in whose writings I suggest you look at the eighth chapter *On the Divine Names*, where he defends the justice of God against those who insult him by saying that God always sends his calamities upon the just, more than on others.[357]

Your disciple Jean, unworthy chancellor of the church of Paris.

On Mystical Theology:
The First and Speculative
Treatise[1]

PROLOGUE
"Repent and believe in the gospel" (Mk 1:15)

(1) I bound myself recently by a promise to approach that subject which I now think you are expecting me to consider: to show, that is, "whether it is better to have the knowledge of God through a repentant affectivity rather than through an investigative intellect."[2] Therefore, I am obliged to work out whether by chance through pious efforts and with God's assistance it is possible to arrive at a common understanding of these matters, which the divine Dionysius treats, concerning a theology that is mystical and thus is hidden.[3] There is no doubt that he was taught by him who says, "We speak of wisdom among the perfect, wisdom that is hidden in mystery" (Prv 25:27).

(2) I am also considering if those matters concerning contemplation, meditation, rapture, ecstasy, extra-mental projection, division of spirit and soul, and the like, which outstanding doctors have described in their writings, can so openly take place and in a certain way be revealed that other people than they who experience them, rare as they are, can understand them.[4] Or at least they can strongly believe that these holy persons have had a knowledge far more elevated than our common knowledge. These persons have been lifted up through divine contemplation to an extra-mental projection.

(3) I would say that this is common for everyone when confronted by something that is either unusual or arduous. For the mind is usually drawn in various ways according to the variety of what it considers. I have often experienced this myself, namely in the present matter.[5]

(4) I have in mind the treatment of material of which nothing is more sublime or divine, but which cannot be more difficult in pursuing, just as none can be found more congenial to salvation. In considering something attached to the hinge of our happiness, I have trembled at the sight of the majesty of this wisdom. I am afraid that in trying to investigate the matter, I will be driven from the experience of glory.[6] Moreover, I have been afraid that some proud presumption will vex me, for who can attempt great things without being overcome by them? I have been afraid, finally, that I will be seen to possess an insatiable singularity, which I condemned as criminal in my two last lessons.[7]

(5) Truly, such considerations can disturb me and make me retrace my steps so that I do not advance, at least if I confide in my own powers alone and not in him who says, "Seek the Lord always" (Ps 104:4). If I am restricted by my double public office, will I not be frightened in seeing the damnation of the servant who hid the talent of her lord (Mt 25:25)?[8] I will also hear from the angel in Tobias that "it is honorable to reveal and confess God's works" (Tb 12:7).

(6) Finally, if the author of the book of Wisdom had feared what we have mentioned, he would have not said of wisdom: "I convey that which I have learned without falsehood and without reservation, and I do not hide its integrity" (Wis 7:13).

(7) But notice what is added concerning boasting or signs of boasting: would that "he who glories, glory in the Lord" (1 Cor 1:31). Who will provide assistance to someone living on the earth, even if he has placed his dwelling beyond heaven's stars, even if he has slept in the bed of contemplation, even if he has tasted the hidden manna of devotion (Is 14:13; Nm 24:21; Rv 2:17)?[9]

(8) What is the purpose of all this? Who would not shudder in utter horror since Lucifer was removed from the palace of heaven, from the midst of the stones of fire (Ez 28:16), and was driven into

the dung-pit of damnation? Who would not shudder since "on that day," when two are lying in one bed, one will be taken, the other left behind (Mt 24:40; Lk 17:34)?[10] Finally, who would not shudder since the sons of Israel were laid low in the desert, they who were eating the bread of heaven (Ps 105:26; Ex 16:15), and his enemies, they who lied to him, "the Lord fed with the best of wheat and from the rock filled them with honey" (Ps 80:17)?

(9) Woe to me if I should seek my glory. For that is nothing at all. Nevertheless, it will condemn me. Alas, if I should glory in my damnation and in nothingness.

(10) The apostolic trumpet will terrify me, saying: "If I have prophecy and know all mysteries and have all knowledge; if I have faith so I can move mountains, but do not have charity, I am nothing" (1 Cor 13:2). But who can be sure, unless by a miracle, that he has charity? What do you know, poor little man, if some light of understanding or some frail warmth of devotion seems to be given to you, wicked servant that you are (cf. Mt 18:32)? Can this be useful for others, so that they receive enlightenment and so gain warmth, if in truth you are like a taper that has been lit but is quickly reduced to ash?

(11) Let it not be, most merciful God, if we are to speak of you and rejoice in you. Let us rejoice with fear and teach in humility. We will seek the unique glory of your name through your servants, my lords and brothers. I seem to want to tell them the secrets of your wisdom. Thus, for the time being, I will put aside more sterile intellectual pursuits, which turn the mind in different directions. Instead, let the word of your spirit put them on fire to seek you in simplicity of heart (Wis 1:1) in order to understand what it means: "Rest and see how sweet is the Lord" (cf. Ps 33:9).[11]

(12) Finally, may they be roused so that they do not give themselves over to intellect alone in instructing in such a way that desiccated affectivity, horrible and vile, is abandoned even to the passions.[12] For by what other persons or in what other place can this doctrine of mystical theology be conveyed?[13]

(13) But if this understanding I want to attain is denied to me, may God forgive our sins. May the holy desire I seem to have either take away my sin, if my yearning is unholy and I am being

deceived, or, if I am acting rightly, then may he justify me "in his justifications" (Ps 118:80). It is he who "hears the desire of the poor" and "hears the readying of their heart in his ear to do justice to the orphan and the needy, so that man while on earth cannot come to magnify himself any longer" (Ps 10:17–18).[14]

(14) I have begun with these considerations especially in order to scoop out of the deep a place for humility, by which the whole structure of what is to be said can be strengthened from collapsing. I have also begun as the holy Dionysius does, with a prayer.[15] Now I will treat the material divided up into considerations or annotations in the manner of chapters, by which the listener will be refreshed by pauses and not tired out by continuous and confusing speech.

(15) And I am not about to bring forward anything new that cannot be found in other books of the saints. For what could they have left out? But I will explain their ideas in my own words and in my own order.

Here ends the Prologue

(16) This treatise on mystical theology contains forty-four considerations and eight main sections or subject matters. The first part, from the first consideration to the ninth, concerns certain preliminary questions or teachings pertaining to mystical theology. Further annotations are found in the headings of the individual sections.

The first part begins. Its first consideration deals with the definition of holy Dionysius and his division of mystical theology and explains the meaning of this name and of his book.

(1) Mystical theology is something beyond that which can be given a symbolic or a proper name.

(2) Thus the holy Dionysius treats it separately, after he was taught by Paul, who was aware of divine secrets.[16] He would have written a symbolic theology, which uses bodily likenesses transferred to God, such as lion, light, sheep, stone, and similar things, according to which God is said to be given every name.[17]

And since he had provided a theology proper from the effects found in creatures, especially the more perfect created beings,[18] we rise up in affirming some things concerning God, in that he is being, life, from which is derived the existence of all things. Dionysius finally comes to a more perfect way than the others for finding God. In abnegation and mental projection God is seen, as it were, in a divine darkness. This is "in a concealed place" where "he made the darkness his hiding place" (Ps 26:5 and 17:12). Seeing this, one of the prophets cried out, "Truly you are the hidden God" (Is 45:15).

(3) Therefore, this book of Dionysius is entitled *On Mystical Theology*, for "mystical" is interpreted as "hidden." The first book we do not have, while the second is called *On the Divine Names*.[19]

The second consideration treats the denial of likenesses and explains that no one, unless experienced, can in any way judge what is tasted within.

(1) Mystical theology begins in the doctrine gathered from the internalized experiences lived in the hearts of devout souls, just as the other half of theology proceeds from those matters that operate extrinsically.

(2) All the learned are in agreement that mystical doctrine proceeds through denial, so that God is not a lion, an ox, a stone, etc.[20] But who would claim that mystical theology only deals with denial and leaves nothing for what is positively known and experienced concerning God?

(3) And truly, since the soul is constituted in such a way that it both does something and undergoes something, then it necessarily experiences something.

(4) That experience, which is considered to be intrinsic, cannot lead to intimate or immediate knowledge for those who are unfamiliar with such matters, just as no one can claim that a perfect and intimate knowledge of love is attained by the one who has never loved. The same is the case with joy or sadness or any other interior passion of the soul, if one has never been affected

by such a passion. This is the way color is described for the blind and music for the deaf.

(5) The saints use various names to describe these interior forms of experimental knowledge of God, and these have been multiplied beyond number according to their variety. They speak of contemplation, ecstasy, rapture, liquefaction, transformation, union, exultation. They talk of a jubilation beyond the spirit, of being taken into a divine darkness,[21] of tasting God, of embracing the bridegroom, of kissing him (Sg 1:1), of being born from God, of obeying his word, of being brought into the divine cellars (Sg 1:3), of being drunk in a torrent of delight, of running into an odor of his perfumes (Sg 1:3), of hearing his voice, and entering into the bedroom (Sg 3:4), and of finding sleep and rest in peace in him (Ps 4:9).[22]

Third Consideration: The capacity of the rational soul and its judgment. It prefers the unlearned person who rightly perceives knowledge to the learned philosopher.

(1) Mystical theology, since it begins in experiences that are known with more complete certitude, thus ought to be judged as more perfect and more certain.[23]

(2) No one can be in doubt that the rational soul is preeminent, both in essence and in virtue and operation, above all other creatures, except the angels, in relation to which it is placed slightly lower.

(3) Therefore if God is known through what is made and his power and divinity are eternal, he truly is more fully known in or from these effects (Rom 1:20). It is clear that the more perfect these effects are, the more certainly they point to God, precisely because they are more certain. Indeed, how will a proof of a type that is extrinsically certain be judged, if that which is intrinsic is not most certain for the soul that experiences it?[24]

(4) From these considerations I draw a pleasing corollary: If philosophy is said to be all knowledge proceeding from what is experienced, then mystical theology will be a philosophy. Those who are learned in it, however much they otherwise are

unlearned, will rightly be called philosophers. Thus Christ rejoiced in saying, "I confess to you, Lord Father of heaven and earth, that you have hidden these things from the wise and clever and revealed them to children. Thus, Father, because it has pleased you," and not because we have deserved so (Mt 11:25–27). Therefore, Wisdom also spoke to children and the law of God "gives understanding to children" (Ps 118:130).

Fourth Consideration: No one can reach the interior realms of the spirit unless he is taught and filled with experience.

(1) Although no one perfectly attains mystical theology who ignores its principles, which are received through interior experience, nevertheless, there should be no refusal from presenting and receiving its teaching.

(2) A likeness to other physical sciences makes this first part clear. If one ignores the fact that fire is hot and water cold, or that the eclipse of the moon is made through the interposition of the earth diametrically between the sun and the moon, and so on with similar matters, then conclusions from such things that are deduced will not create certitude, even of a lesser kind, unless something is known of the principles.

(3) In our case, if knowledge of the principles is present, it is possessed through faith alone and through belief, by which we consent to those who tell us what they have experienced.

(4) Nevertheless, let us add as the second part of our consideration that there are few or no natural sciences that many approach to treat and learn where the principles of the sciences are gained from experience proper. In fact, many of the natural sciences are based on presuppositions from what others have asserted and proven. Thus Ptolemy in astrology, Hippocrates and Galen in medicine, and others in these same fields, as well as scientists in other areas, are known to have carefully made such proofs and continue to do so every day.

(5) This procedure was noted by Pythagoras, Plato, Aristotle, and our philosopher Paul.[25] The first of these asked his disciples to keep silent for five years and believe what he said.[26] The sec-

ond said that they would profit from belief.[27] The third said that a learner needs to believe.[28] The fourth expressed almost the same words in a different context: "Anyone who would approach God must believe" (Heb 11:6).

The fifth consideration attacks the unlearned and presumptuous, and prefers intimate experience to all others in joy, savor, and perspicacity.

(1) No one knows what spirits are "except the spirit that is in a person" (1 Cor 2:11). Therefore those who refuse to believe so that they finally may understand are ignorant and by no means suitable auditors of mystical theology.[29]

(2) This truth is both self-evident and confirmed by the authority of the prophet, who says, "Unless you believe, you will not understand" (cf. Is 7:9),[30] as the preceding considerations have shown. On the other side, it is possible for them to know many things that those who are trustworthy have passed on. Holy persons who have experienced such matters assert them in speech as well as in writing. I ask that you consider how rude, ignorant, and impious it is to refuse to believe in them.

(3) We can in no way let ourselves suspect that these saints wanted to deceive others. They have shown the most truthful honesty. They sought no material gain and no recognition, and they did not labor out of hatred or any other base passion. Who could think that such persons could be deceived in such sure experience, as we have described?

(4) Consider also that it is not one or two who speak of such matters, but a thousand, or rather, innumerable are the assertions of those in complete agreement that mystical theology is attained through intimate experience. Moreover, it is far more sublime, more joyful, more pleasing, and more penetrating than can be narrated. It is above other extrinsic forms of knowledge. It is as if the latter creep around among the dull and inert, while mystical theology takes off on generous wings and flies away, rising above everything else.

(5) But if there is no one who can accept it when his assertions about his own interior experiences are not believed, then how

rude and irrational it is, indeed how destructive for all social contacts among men, if faith is denied to the great number of such persons of the highest trustworthiness and quality. They who do not believe will themselves see that this is the case.

The sixth consideration shows how internal forms of affectivity cannot be fully expressed in words.

(1) Interior operations, especially in terms of affectivity, cannot be described with clarity or conveyed in writing in the manner in which they are felt.[31]

(2) This is the reason why the Apostle said that he heard "secret words, which it was not permitted a person to utter" (2 Cor 12:4). Paul was able to convey to the blessed Dionysius through the example of grace only a small part of what he had received. Again, blessed Dionysius conceived from the words of the Apostle more than he was permitted to leave behind in writing.

(3) An example of such a matter based on the senses can be found in mirrors placed across from each other and containing multiple images. The image is less clear in the first mirror than the object itself. Then the image of the first image is less clear in the second mirror, and so on in the third, the fourth, and others, to the degree that the mutual reflection begins to disappear.

The seventh consideration sets forth the cause of the judgments by which error is made concerning the teachings of doctors that can seem in opposition, even though they are in total conformity to those who understand.

(1) It is possible to find that a person who is less experienced in devout forms of affectivity can be more learned in discussing the same matters.

(2) Let us take our argument from comparisons. Medicine has many parts that are based on experience alone, but this aspect by no means keeps those who have not experienced such matters from being considered as better theorists than those who have such experience.[32] Moreover, those who have been blind from birth can have great power of cognitive reasoning in many areas,

the same power that many others have primarily only through vision. And so concerning the blind Saint Didymus, his hagiographer Saint Jerome tells that in those disciplines that are grasped through vision, such as mathematical sciences, he was most learned.[33] In such sciences it is evident that many of those who can see are wholly ignorant.

(3) Why then in our case should a similar result be denied, that a man who is little or not at all devout can study the writings of those who are devout, compare them with each other, conclude or deduce one thing from another, attacking or supporting it? But the word also has the implication of more banal accountants, who keep track of things. And so in this way the school of theology every day concerns itself with the articles of faith, even though their content has not been experienced.

(4) This consideration, together with the previous ones, shows agreement in the sayings of saints that seem to be in opposition to each other. Some say that only the good and devout receive the true knowledge of God. Others contradict this and say that many pagan philosophers, and even many very wicked theologians, know more about God. Certainly this is the case when "even the demons believe and shudder" (Jas 2:19). Thus, the first intend to speak of the experimental knowledge of mystical theology, while the second deal with knowledge obtained through the reason concerning symbolic, proper, and even mystical theology.[34]

The eighth consideration indicates the benefit of this book, and how those who convey it or have conveyed it err about this matter, and how or by whom they are to be examined.

(1) It is good that schoolmen, even those lacking devotion, carefully look in devout writings for mystical theology, provided they have belief in them.

(2) This is said, first, in order to point out that if a certain glowing love is generated from familiar contacts with such writings, it can happen that there grows up a desire to experience things that schoolmen for the time being believe by faith alone and that they can communicate to each other by learned reasoning. "Your speech

has powerfully caught on fire," says the Psalmist, "and your servant has loved it" (Ps 118:140). For who has approached the fire and his clothing has not burned or grown hot?

(3) Again, another benefit is for those for whom preaching taken from such doctrine can inflame to the love of God. This is a love the person already has imagined, but the speaker's heart has remained cold, as the voice of the magpie, which does not understand itself. The person comes to hear concepts that are as if they are nothing but words articulated and formulated by someone.

(4) At that point we understand that many have devotion "but not according to knowledge" (Rom 10:2). Such persons are clearly very susceptible to errors, even more so than those lacking devotion, if they do not regulate their affectivity to the norm of Christ's law. They are in danger if they cling to their own intellectual powers and thus to their own form of prudence, in spurning the advice of others. This has been made clear in the experience of Beghards and Turlupins.[35] They have followed their own desires without rule or order, putting aside the law of Christ. Their heinous form of presumption has prompted them to say that a person, after he has reached a state of peace in his spirit, is released from the laws of divine precepts. The angel of Satan brought this peace in them, "in transfiguring himself into an angel of light." In this manner he simulated a peace very much like that one which the Apostle said surpasses all understanding (2 Cor 11:14; Phil 4:7).

(5) Thus it is necessary, in order to correct or direct such people, that there be men who have studied their books and who have devotion in accord with knowledge. Still, I want to warn them against presuming to condemn more quickly than they ought devout and simple persons. Such people are to be admired for their affective lives when schoolmen clearly find nothing contrary either to faith or to good morals. They should treat unknown issues with silence, suspending judgment, or hand them over to the examination and guidance of experts.

(6) The greater experts are those whom both types of learning have distinguished, in intellect and in affectivity. Such were Augustine, Hugh of Saint Victor, Bonaventure, William of Paris,[36]

Saint Thomas, and a very few others. We will try below to explain the reason for their rarity.

(7) Finally, the consideration is to be added: "Provided they believe them," for otherwise they who investigate such things "will be deficient in their examination" (Ps 63:7). They will acquire for themselves nothing but the traps of infidelity and will be blinded by the thick clouds of darkness surrounding them.

The second section of the first part concerns the nature of the rational soul and its six powers, from the ninth to the seventeenth considerations. The ninth consideration shows the manner of procedure in this work, excluding those subjects that are less useful for our purpose and concentrating on the properties of the soul.

(1) In order to acquire a speculative knowledge of mystical theology, it is profitable to know the nature of the rational soul and its powers, both cognitive and affective.

(2) This consideration is self-evident, because, if nature is ignored, then so are its passions. We will set forth the elements which show that there is a mystical theology. We will provide a general statement concerning the degree to which the study of mystical theology does good, and for whom it does good. We will try to make it understandable, God willing, what this mystical theology is and in what power of the soul it is lodged. Also, by what form of reasoning it is obtained and what benefit or end it provides. These goals cannot be attained if we ignore the nature of the soul. The best way of teaching is through the resolution of initial statements through principles that are self-evident, or through simple essences of things.[37] We must separate these from a confusion of accidents and from the outer layer of external circumstances. So here we must in some way divide up the simple substance of the soul into different names, according to the multiplicity of effects that it can produce. In this way we can show how one quality exists, since it elicits given results, and another provides different ones.

(3) In this process it seems to be praiseworthy and astute to proceed in the manner of formalization,[38] so that such distinctions

can be made in the same way as mathematicians abstract from movement and matter. The point is abstracted from the third dimension, the line from the second dimension, and the surface from the single dimension.

(4) Mathematicians, however, assert that these things exist within objects, outside of any intellectual operation, just as the abstract intellect imagines them. They are present in a manner that is universal, distinct, eternal, and the like. I clearly disagree with them in this point of view, for I do not understand the basis for the argument, especially in view of divine simplicity.[39]

(5) There is nothing wrong, however, in seeking abstractions,[40] if objects in their natures are such that the intellect in dealing with them can use such abstractions in order more easily to reach understanding. Nevertheless, one ought to know that the object itself is not to be divided up in the same way as the intellect can separate it into distinct parts. Otherwise the object would be separated from itself in terms of a real distinction.[41] The intellect can conceive, for example, that the productive will of volition really differs from the will that elicits volition. In this way intellect and will exist within the same essence of the soul, even though they are distinguished from that essence in relation to its object.

(6) This subject, however, is not very useful and so does not merit our struggling with it and having to spend more time here. Such matters are more the province of arts masters, logicians, and metaphysicians than of theologians, especially since we are dealing with mystical theology.

(7) Let us speak, then, of the rational soul, concerning the different powers it has according to its diversity of functions and actions. These powers are distinct not in terms of the soul's essence but according to the names of these properties. Therefore, we say that the soul is virtuous; thus it is in itself fruitful, just as if it contained such powers in itself in a real manner or distinct in another way in relation to object. Actually, it is much more the case when virtue is not so much united as unitary, it is stronger than when it is divided up in itself.[42] In this way God's wisdom is more perfect according to deduction, as Augustine points out several places in his *On the Trinity*, for it is identical with fortitude,

justice, and goodness.[43] The same is the case with other forms of perfection, although they may be separated from these by some distinction.

(8) Let those who understand differently perceive what is right. I truly do not understand! But let us then assume in what we propose that the powers of the soul are wholly distinct in nature, dividing the rational soul first into simple intelligence, second into reason, third into sensuality or animality or cognitive sensual power, and thus for the cognitive powers. But to divide affectivity proportionately, first we deal with synderesis, the apex of the mind,[44] second with will or rational appetite, and third with animal appetite. We will presently set forth the proper rational foundations of these powers.

The tenth consideration deals with the simplicity of the intellect, insofar as the soul's light is both like an angel and open to God. We will also consider how this light is signified in the scriptures with various names.

(1) Simple intelligence is the cognitive power of the soul that absorbs directly from God a certain natural light. In and through this light first principles are known to be true and absolutely certain, once their terms are grasped.[45]

(2) The principles of this type are sometimes called dignities,[46] sometimes common conceptions of the mind,[47] sometimes prime rules, which are unchangeable and cannot be otherwise. The following statements provide examples: what is stated about something is affirmation or negation; the whole is greater than its part; the intellectual is more perfect than the nonintellectual; the spiritual is more perfect than the corporal, other things being equal; if a man understands, then he lives; and similar assertions.[48]

(3) For a definition of this natural light, the following can be said with some likelihood: It is a connatural disposition created together with the soul, which some seem to call the dwelling place of principles.[49] More likely, it is the soul itself, existing as a certain light of an intellectual nature derived from the infinite

light of primary intelligence, which is God. Of it John says, "It was the true light, which enlightens everyone who comes into this world" (Jn 1:9). As the Psalmist says, "The light of your countenance has been stamped upon us, Lord" (Ps 4:7).

(4) But as Dionysius says in the seventh chapter of *On the Divine Names*, in the progression of objects from God there arises a certain chain of being, so that what is lowest in the higher being is first in the lesser being.[50] The human being is a little less than the angel (Ps 8:6), for the intelligence of an angel is more simple than that of a human being. In its nature an angel has as a lesser power that which the human person possesses as something supreme in its nature. In accord with this power of intelligence are joined, with no other intermediary bond, two intellects, the angelic and the human.

(5) We think that it is not acceptable that there is some median between the rational soul and God. Augustine speaks against this point of view in asserting that there is nothing above our minds besides God.[51] But who would deny that an angel in this manner rightly can be called superior to our soul and closer to God, in that it is more perfect? No one indeed. Let us then say that each one receives directly and equally from God three things, which are nature, grace, and glory. But for the rest, as there is a hierarchy among the angels, so there is an arrangement of angels for men according to three hierarchical actions, which Dionysius frequently names. These are to purify, to illuminate, and to perfect.[52] They function according to grace and are secondary forms of perfection.

(6) Finally, there is this power of simple intelligence, sometimes called mind, or highest heaven, or spirit, or the light of intelligence, or the shadow of angelic intellect, or the divine light in which truth shines forth without change and is perceived.[53] Sometimes it is called the spark and apex of reason.

The eleventh consideration deals with the power of reason, how it at one time serves the intellect, at another the senses, and is called by a dual name.

(1) Reason is the cognitive power of the soul, able to deduce

conclusions from premises, able also to elicit what is not sensed from what is sensed, and abstractions from the essences of things.[54] The reason needs no bodily organ for its own operation.[55]

(2) This description in its final section is seen to distinguish reason from sensation, which uses an organ. At the same time reason is distinguished from simple intelligence, whose operation is noted more in the reception of simple thought from God's superior light, rather than attending to the deduction of conclusions from principles. This is proper to reason, whether the principles are taken from experiences through the senses, or from what simple intelligence has grasped on high.

(3) This dual use of reason manifests itself in superior principles known in themselves in the light of simple intelligence, and in inferior ones obtained through experience, such as the fact that fire is hot.[56] From this duality it is said that there is a superior part of reason and an inferior one.[57] Reason, moreover, is said to have two forms, one for higher matters, the other for lower ones. Because of this capacity, reason is said to be placed, as it were, on the boundary between two worlds, the spiritual and the corporal.[58] We call the superior form of reason the male one, and the inferior one the female. For reason has a natural vigor and power in dealing with higher matters and can contract when it deals with inferior ones, in the same way a man differs from a woman in terms of power.

(4) Finally, we sometimes give reason other names, so that it is heaven in the midst of the soul, or it is in the shadow of the simple intelligence, as the simple intelligence is in the shadow of the angel, and the angel in the shadow of God.

The twelfth consideration divides up the power of the senses. It shows how this power perceives and conveys itself clearly to the internal functions entrusted to it.

(1) The cognitive power of the senses is a power of the soul that uses in its operation a bodily organ, both exterior and interior, for those things that can be sensed in themselves or that can be known through their accidents.

(2) It should be clear from the start that this power is different from the two preceding ones.[59] This cognitive power has many functions and also many names. For when it registers directly the movement of objects that are exterior, then it is called the exterior sense, according to five types: vision, hearing, taste, smell, and touch. Or it receives directly sense impressions made in these five senses and distinguishes among these, and then it is the communal sense.[60] Or the cognitive sense deals with judgments or sensations received in the communal sense and divides them up, and this is called the imagination, fantasy, or formative power. And if from what is sensed something insensate is elicited, this we call the power of evaluation, which judges between what is profitable and what is harmful.

(3) These two powers are capable of retaining phenomena despite their absence, the one through imagination, sometimes called the communal sense, the other by way of evaluation, to which the name of memory has been given.

(4) A further discussion of these powers and their organs is left to medical doctors and natural scientists. For our purposes these considerations are sufficient.

(5) Furthermore, this cognitive power of the senses is sometimes called soul, sometimes animality, or sensuality. Other names given it are the terrestrial or lowest heaven, the imagination, or the shadow of reason, in which shadow, again, the various degrees are designated according to the variety of their functions. And so the exterior sense is the last light of cognitive power, which fails or dies only in vegetative or nutritive potency. Thereby the communal sense, having this light beneath itself, is placed as if in its shadow, in the shadow of fantasy, just as fantasy is placed in the shadow of evaluative power. This ability we put in the shadow of reason.

The thirteenth consideration concerns the affective powers in genus and subdivides their species.

(1) To each cognitive power there corresponds a proportional affective power.

(2) For when something is grasped by cognitive power, then it can be suitable or unsuitable for it. In accord with the reasoning set before it, we experience how the soul in a certain manner approves of this understanding, if it is suitable, as something appropriate, and how it rejects it if it is inappropriate.

(3) Expanding on this point, I would say that there is no being that does not have an appetite in proportion to its end. This appetite is what the being has by right of divine law, but the appetite is not properly said to be affective except in objects that function in terms of cognition.

(4) There are then three affective powers, proportional to the forms of cognition: synderesis, will, and the sensitive appetite.[61]

The fourteenth consideration defines the synderesis of the mind, explains its understanding according to its object, and provides appropriate names.

(1) Synderesis is an appetitive power of the soul that comes immediately from God. It takes on a certain natural inclination to the good.[62] Through this proclivity it is drawn to follow the movement of the good on the basis of the understanding presented to it in the simple intelligence.

(2) For just as intelligence is present in respect to truth when it is primary and certain, so synderesis is simply present with respect to the final good, without any admission of evil. Just as the simple intelligence cannot disagree with such first truths when it knows what the terms mean, so too synderesis cannot avoid seeking positively the first principles of morals, provided these be shown to it through the understanding. The question whether synderesis is able not to will these principles has to be left unresolved. The common opinion, however, affirms that synderesis does try to attain these principles.

(3) In this manner we can use the name synderesis in three ways. Synderesis can be an inclination of the sort from whose essential being there is a probability according to which we posit it to derive from the essence of simple intelligence.[63] Synderesis can be the act of this power consequent to its grasp of this understand-

ing.[64] Third, synderesis can be a habit derived from a frequency of actions.[65] This distinction is not different from that concerning intelligence according to power, or according to its action, or according to the habit derived from actions.

(4) We call synderesis by other names, such as a habit active in principles, or a spark of intelligence on whose basis there are movement and attraction toward the good.[66] It can also be called a virginal part of the soul, or a natural stimulus to the good, or the apex of the mind,[67] or an ineradicable instinct, or any such name, as what is the first heaven in affective potency, and so in relation to those names recorded concerning cognitive potency.

The fifteenth consideration considers the term appetite. According to this power the rational appetite is known.

(1) The rational appetite is an affective power of the soul capable of being immediately moved by the cognitive grasp of the reason.

(2) This appetite, if considered in respect to what is possible or impossible, is sometimes called will. If it is looked upon in terms of the acts derived from it, it is called liberty. But if it is seen in respect to objects and not according to goals or possibilities, then it is called choice or elective appetite. And if it is considered with regard to acts involving commands, this appetite is called the dominative or executive. If there is present a will to carry out those actions that now are chosen, it is called purpose. The inclination to carry out these things is called conscience, unless we are to say that conscience involves two things at the same time, judgment and an accompanying inclination.[68]

(3) If we are to consider the passions arising from rational appetite, then this appetite is to be given the comprehensive name of affective rational appetite or rational inclination. But if the appetite is considered in respect to good or evil as they are grasped through the reason, then it is to be called concupiscible. But if that good or evil is presented as something difficult, it is called irascible, although according to the Philosopher and his followers these two powers, the irascible

and the concupiscible, properly have their roots in the senses alone. But Augustine and the theologians deal differently with the matter.[69]

The sixteenth consideration places the animal appetite not only in man but also in beasts.

(1) Animal or sensual appetite is an affective power of the soul apt to be moved solely by the contact of the senses.

(2) This word *solely* has been added so that you will not be pulled in two directions by the controversy concerning whether the rational appetite can be moved immediately from sense cognition only on the basis of rational deliberation.[70]

(3) Also, we divide this appetite into the irascible and concupiscible through those elements that are to be called objective reasons.

(4) Besides this appetite, some seem to have posited a natural sense toward good and evil, taking from it many wondrous effects in creatures in respect to flight or pursuit.[71] These actions cannot be explained on the basis of sense cognition, as when an enemy is present but not seen, hair stands up on end, almost trembling, while we react differently in a friend's presence. Or we have the example of an ant, which, providing for the winter, gathers a heap of grain, and so in similar instances without number.[72]

(5) Why then should one be surprised if the bodies of animals are directed by secret instincts or impulses to their ends, when in other bodies that are less perfect and with a lesser degree of organization, we find just as many wondrous natural forms in order to reach their ends?[73] Indeed, there are very many such forms of attraction, of whose end we are ignorant, as with the attraction of iron to a magnet, of the sea to the moon, and of other objects to yet others.

(6) But we have now posited this natural sense in all things. In another way, it can be called the law of nature or natural inclination or the movement of inerrant intelligence. We are in complete agreement with this position.

*The seventh principal part, concerning love and its triple property,
and similarly on rapture and ecstasy, from the thirty-fifth consideration
until the fortieth. The thirty-fifth consideration posits how the rational
soul without the inspiration of God and his love cannot come to its
rightful end.*

(1) The rational spirit, like the spiritual sailor, is taught
through mystical theology. Unless the Lord calls and fills the
mind's sail with the wind of his secrets, then the spirit cannot
come from the sea of sensuality to the shore of eternity, that is,
from carnal to spiritual things. Without God's love he cannot
find rest by being brought to the deifying harbor, where he is
strengthened.

(2) This is clear enough from the preceding image, as we
showed in the last consideration. For there it became clear that
we do not obtain a secure harbor in God through knowledge
alone, and so we conclude that this happens differently, by
means of loving affection. In this way we are brought to our
deifying harbor and we cling to it, as the prophet says: "For me to
cling to God is good" (Ps 72:28). Again it is written, "He who
clings to God is one spirit" (1 Cor 6:17).

(3) This process is clarified by the properties of love, of which
it is enough at present to touch on three. For love ravishes,
unites, and fulfills. First of all, love ravishes the beloved and
thereby creates ecstasy. Second, love unites with the beloved and
makes the two like one.[74] Third, love is complete in itself and
seeks nothing else but to love. And so concerning these properties we will proceed below.

*The thirty-sixth consideration explains the power of love when it is
joined to rapture and ecstasy and distinguishes their properties, as
exemplified through Paul and a case from the world of nature.*

(1) Love ravishes the beloved and creates ecstasy, and this is
called rapture because of the manner in which the mind is lifted
up or the natural powers of the person reach beyond the lower
powers in the actualization of their operation. This happens in
such a way that inferior powers either cease or are weakened.

Rapture can also be a powerful and ardent actualization in a superior power, as a result of which the inferior powers cease or are weakened and tied up so that they cannot block the superior power in its operation.

(2) Thus we say that ecstasy is a kind of rapture, which takes place more appropriately in the superior part of the rational soul, which is called spirit, mind, or intelligence. The mind is so much suspended within in its own activity that the inferior powers cease from acting. Neither reason nor imagination nor the exterior senses function. In fact, sometimes the natural powers concerned with nutrition, growth, and movement cannot go ahead in their proper operations.

(3) Therefore rapture has to be distinguished and in some way contrasted with ecstasy.[75] Rapture has a lesser effect in suspending or blocking the action of the inferior powers. But rapture is nevertheless found in every superior power in respect to the inferior one. Ecstasy, however, takes place in the mind alone. It not only weakens the acts of inferior potencies but wholly removes them, so long as it lasts.

(4) And so Paul, for example, expresses in his rapture two elements that concur with the description of ecstasy (2 Cor 12:2–4). The power that is ravished is described as the third heaven of the soul, as explained above. Heaven in the cognitive power is the mind or intelligence, while in affectivity heaven is the mind's summit or its spark. Second, Paul's rapture expresses the cessation of all inferior powers in their acts. Otherwise how would Paul not have known whether he was in the body or outside of it? Ecstasy is then a rapture of the mind with the cessation of all operations in the inferior powers.

(5) This process can again be subdivided according to the dual power of the mind, one cognitive and the other affective. The first ecstasy is a rapture in spirit; the second a rapture beyond the spirit, unless by chance we wish to distinguish these raptures differently, according to their objects. Rapture in the spirit is spoken of in terms of intelligibles below God; rapture beyond the spirit, with respect to the divine.

(6) Perhaps we find both types intermingled in the scriptures.

For we find concerning the queen of Sheba that there was no more spirit in her, since an overwhelming admiration suspended the acts of all her powers in relation to what she had contemplated concerning the wisdom of Solomon (3 Kgs 10:4–5).[76] And this can be called a stupor or a spasm.

(7) Now that we have dealt with rapture and ecstasy according to their names, it remains to find out how these arise through love. Since love is the root of any other of the affections, if we show that affection rather than cognition creates rapture, then we will have sufficiently clarified what we seek.

(8) In the first place, love can be compared to a weight, just as a man of wisdom has said: "My love is my weight. I am drawn by it wherever I am taken."[77] It is necessary that love be able to attract and take hold.[78] Heavy objects are brought to a place of stability and rest by a certain attraction, rather than from any knowledge about this center or concerning how weight is attracted to the center of the world. It is apparent in heavy beings that do have cognition that even if all cognition ceases, nevertheless they are moved toward the center without any hindrance.

(9) Although love, especially the type of which we speak, perhaps has more similarity to the nature of lightness, which is to be lifted up, still that same lightness can be called a weight, in accord with the intent of the sage just mentioned.[79]

(10) Again, we experience in iron that its property of attraction to a magnet takes place without any element of cognition. Also, nutritive power draws up the heavy nutriment without the operation of any cognition. From here we can proceed to rapture in cognitive powers.

The thirty-seventh consideration covers rapture of the imagination in the passions by providing examples.

(1) Rapture of the imagination beyond the inferior sensitive powers takes place through the affection of love.

(2) It is clear that the affection of love or desire can attract or ravish the imaginative power with such great force that the inferior powers of the exterior senses do not notice the proper

objects being placed before them. This realization came to the philosopher through experience.[80]

(3) And this is the first rapture, in the first heaven of the soul. What in principle creates this rapture, other than a fervent interior desire for the object that has been made present through the imagination? For imaginative cognition alone does not suffice to create this deep attachment. We see this rapture in those who are seized by love, and in many others whom we call melancholics or hallucinators, or in those who suddenly become fearful and angry or who get violently caught up in some cause.

(4) As the imagination or other superior powers are lifted beyond the exterior senses and ravished, so on the contrary it is clear for the soul that whenever it is thus detained in the sensation of an exterior object through touch, taste, and sight, then the operations of the superior powers cease or are impeded. This process, however, is properly called not rapture but distraction or submergence, when a superior power is brought down by an inferior one, and the superior power is forced to abandon its action.[81] This takes place in us because of the corruption of sin and unfortunately happens all too easily and frequently.

The thirty-eighth consideration shows how it is to be explained that the power of rapture is present in the reason, as appears in those who dedicate themselves to study.

(1) Rapture of the reason in its activity beyond the inferior powers takes place through love in the will.

(2) This has been made clear by those devoted to the investigation of the general rules in various arts. Such persons distance themselves from motion and matter. Meditating on spiritual things, they seek to deduce and reason from what is known to what is unknown. Sometimes the appetite of the will that is concerned with such matters makes such persons abandon not only the operations of the exterior senses, so that they do not know what takes place outside of themselves, but also they abandon the activity of fantasy or imagination, so that no corporeal phantasm

can penetrate. And if the latter tries to interfere, it is suppressed by the superior power of the reason and the will.

(3) This is apparent in certain persons whose story is known in Valerius Maximus.[82]

The thirty-ninth consideration concerns mental rapture or its spark. This is experienced only by the more perfect.

(1) Rapture of mind beyond the inferior powers takes place through the spark of affectivity, which is connected or appropriated to the mind. It is called ecstatic love or mental projection.[83]

(2) From the previous forms of rapture, which are more frequent and more easily attainable, and thus easier to understand, we learn how the mind in its actions can be so elevated and fixed with the result that none of the inferior powers can disturb it. Through its own affective power the mind will so actualize itself that its intellective power will recognize neither itself nor anything else.

(3) If we concede that this process functions in a reasonable way, then we are very close to understanding everything that the most sublime doctors, especially Dionysius, taught concerning mystical theology. Moreover, we will see what such doctors claim takes place in the wise and the devout: ecstasy, mental projection, anagogical movement, rapture into the third heaven, division of the mind and spirit, introduction into God's darkness, as with Moses, or into the holy of holies with the protective cloud, as with Aaron (Ex 19:9 and 40:34–8). We will consider violent love, which is a love that takes hold of the mind, as well as the death of the soul while the spirit lives. We will reach the illuminative night of shadows, the death of Rachel in the birth of Benjamin (Gn 35:16–19), and the anagogical turning back of the Jordan (Ps 113:3).[84] The intelligences will show themselves, and similar manifestations will take place.

The eighth principle part concerns the power of love, which unites the lover with God and gives stability and rest, until the end of the first treatise. The fortieth consideration sets aside the various modes of union and, as it also shows, comes to that which is said to unite the soul to God.

(1) Love unites the lover with the beloved, and thus it creates stability and rest with him.

(2) This has been said in accord with the properties of love. In order to understand them, something must be said concerning the various and diverse modes of unions. But since this union of which we speak is not corporal but spiritual, nothing is to be said here concerning bodily unions.[85]

(3) We find many forms of spiritual union, as through processes of attachment, formation, or actualization. There can also be union assisted by a superior being, or a union through a being that has merged, or through a hypostatic bond where several natures combine in one person.[86] But of all these the highest union is in the divine essence or nature in which three persons exist in the greatest unity. But we must leave behind these forms of union, since they are less appropriate for our purposes here.

(4) This union of the lover with the beloved is mentioned by Aristotle in his *Ethics* when he says: "The friend is another self."[87] The basis of this union seems to be expressed by the same writer when he says: "Friends are of one mind in what they do or do not desire."[88] Therefore our spirit, when it clings to God through intimate love, is one spirit with him through the conformity of will.[89] Only a perfect love, which perfectly clings to God, can truly pray: "Your will be done on earth as in heaven" (Mt 6:10). And whoever prays thus also prays "in spirit and in truth," as Truth taught us to pray in the gospel (Jn 4:23). For he himself prayed to the Father in saying, "But not as I will, but as you wish" (Mt 26:39).

(5) And so, whoever is thus united to God and clings through a loving conformity of will, he is indeed given stability in him and with him. We can add what the Psalmist says: "Their judges are devoured, joined to the rock" (Ps 140:6), meaning that they attain complete stability in God.

On Mystical Theology: The Second and Practical Treatise

Here begins the prologue of Jean Gerson in the second part of mystical theology, concerning its practice, written by him in twelve considerations or forms of action.

(1) We have been treating in our lessons, in spite of many interruptions, the subject of mystical theology. We have followed the order that is observed in other sciences, where the speculative part is treated before the practical one. Nevertheless, this science more than many others has the property that it can neither be completely treated nor fully understood in speculative terms unless its practical employment comes first.[1] Therefore it will from this point be my task to show through certain considerations the manners and ways by which we have access to mystical theology.

(2) As for our inquiry into the definition and content of mystical theology, as well as into its difference from speculative theology and such matters as we considered in the preceding treatise, this background material is not sufficient for the Christian, and especially not for someone holding office in the church.[2] Action and practice are required. In order to make these possible, it can be of some benefit to show what is necessary or appropriate for attaining and fulfilling this goal. These results can upset the person who experiences them, so that they are avoided. Thus it is important for us to clarify all the questions we formerly took up in order to treat them in this work.

(3) We therefore say, in the first place, that Jesus Christ has kept the mastery of mystical theology and ecstatic or perfect prayer for himself alone and according to his own will.³ No human effort is sufficient to obtain it, although such effort should not be completely neglected. Consider how "everything given that is good and is a perfect gift comes from above, descending from the Father of lights" (Jas 1:17). The basis of this consideration is clear, that the gift of perfect prayer flows from the divine will that holds "a light in its hands," as the holy Job says (Jb 36:32).⁴ In explaining this passage Saint Gregory says that when he desires it, he illuminates; he blocks it out when he so wishes.⁵

(4) Later I will indicate how human effort does not suffice. But the Apostle shows that it is not to be wholly rejected when he calls us fellow helpers with God.⁶ Fellow helpers, he says, not those who force or who prevent (1 Cor 3:9), for we are not to say, "It is our exalted hand and not the Lord who did all these things" (Dt 32:17).

(5) Nevertheless, twelve forms of activity are to be noted in the practice of theology, in the same number of considerations. The first deals with waiting for God's call; the second, the awareness of one's own makeup; the third looks at one's duty or proper state of being; the fourth, the extension of self to perfection; the fifth, the flight from occupations; the sixth, the putting aside of curiosity. The seventh considers how one is to put on forbearance; the eighth faces the origins of the passions and affections; the ninth asks about the suitable time and place for making one's quest; the tenth, the moderation of indulgence in sleep and food; the eleventh, the silent dependence on holy meditations that bring forth forms of affectivity. The twelfth consideration deals with how to remove the spirit from phantasms.

The first consideration of mystical theology in practice shows three manners of calling, according to the triple conversion of the soul into God, and a triple status of those who seek this state.

(1) Each person should wait for God's call, in that he calls all people to salvation. For according to the Apostle, "He wants all to be saved" (1 Tm 2:4). This explains why there is a natural and

indestructible appetite in everyone for beatitude.[7] Nevertheless, on the road of the divine calling one person walks one way, another another, according to the types of their graces, functions, and activities, as the Apostle has reasoned:

> To one is given through the Spirit the utterance of wisdom, to another that of knowledge, to another faith, to another the grace of virtues, to another prophecy, to another the discernment of spirits, to another the gift of languages, to another the interpretation of languages. One and the same Spirit is behind all of these activities. He hands out to each as he wills (1 Cor 12:8–11).

"Just as the body is one and has many members," so it has diverse and various functions (1 Cor 12:12).

(2) Behold the utterance of wisdom, which is very much like the grace of contemplation or even is considered to be the same, is given through the Spirit to this person or that one, but not to all. The same is the case with the grace of healing, or faith, which I think is in the gift of peace in having faith. Likewise with the operation of virtues, prophecy, and the other gifts.[8] It is not appropriate that anyone who has been called should try indiscriminately to obtain the grace of administering or operating these various functions. Similarly, it is not necessary for everyone to give himself or herself over to the pursuit of wisdom or contemplation.

(3) The Philosopher taught this point in other sciences and skills, and after him Cicero, that we should take care to admit that "we all cannot do all things."[9] This fact is so apparent that it does not need to be explained on the basis of too great a curiosity. The assignment of causes in a particular situation can vary, and frequently it is difficult to judge concerning each one. You are chosen for this activity in the mystical body, you for that one, in trying to fulfill your call to salvation.

(4) It can be of great profit to receive counsel and to believe in it, when it is given by experienced and spiritual men, of whatever kind they are, for they judge all things (1 Cor 2:15). It also helps to pay attention to personal circumstances, such as the composition of the body in one way or another, as well as one's position in society, the place, the time, or the age. Finally one should consider

how the soul has been endowed with powers of intelligence, memory, or judgment, or what type it is in terms of the irascible, the concupiscible, or the rational.[10]

(5) The result is that not everyone through the will can rise higher to the grace of contemplation or reach its mode of being.

(6) We find those persons who, like servants, have learned to be brought to God in fear and trembling, as if they were before the most harsh judge and austere master, whose condemnation is irrevocable.[11] They are frequently emitting cries "from the sigh of the heart" (Ps 37:9), lamenting to God: "Who has known the power of your wrath and who can reckon your anger in the fear of you" (Ps 89:11)? "If you, Lord, mark our iniquities, then who can survive" (Ps 129:3)? And also this statement: "You will not enter into judgment with your servant, Lord, because no one alive is righteous in your sight" (Ps 142:2). And again: "Lord, do not in your wrath accuse me, nor in your anger chasten me" (Ps 6:2). Different people approach this matter in different ways. For some it is not so much a reward that is desired as an eternal punishment that is feared. They show caution in their fear, and this is permissible.

(7) You will find others whom we can call mercenaries, for they seek from God a heavenly reward for their service, as if from a most generous king or as from the Father "of mercies and the God of all consolation" (2 Cor 1:3). They say to him, "Father, I have sinned in heaven and before you. Now I am not worthy to be called your son. But make me like one of your hired hands" (Lk 15:18–19). And they act rightly as sons aware of wrongdoing, but they do not thereby reach perfection.

(8) There are those, moreover, who are moved neither by fear of punishment nor expectation of reward, but through awareness of divine dignity and paternal goodness. Their love is called filial.

(9) There are yet others, though they are quite rare, who with neither a servile nor a mercenary attitude, nor even a filial one, are taken into God. It is as if they forget his harshness, his rewards, his fatherly authority. They are joined to him as one friend to another (cf. Ex 33:11). But the bond is even stronger and more sweet, as in that of the bride to the groom. The one

who joins in such a union will perhaps say: "I am my beloved's, and his desire is for me" (Sg 7:10), as well as: "What is there for me in heaven?," meaning as a reward, "and from you what have I wished for on the earth," meaning in avoiding punishment. "My flesh and my heart may fail, but he is the God of my heart and my portion forever" (Ps 72:25–26).

(10) The first group [servants] we number among the beginners; the others [mercenaries] among the more proficient; while the perfect are the rest. But the latter, just like the first, often consider and criticize themselves. In total submission of mind such persons remember that they have the most severe judge and that he is their master or lord or saving father, who will revenge their acts of neglect. Otherwise why would it be said: "Unless you maintain yourself earnestly in the fear of God, your house will be quickly undermined" (Sir 27:4)? Nevertheless, they dare even after offenses and adulteries to return to the groom, for they know that he said through Jeremiah: "You truly have committed fornication with your many lovers. But come back to me and I will receive you; therefore at least now call on me and say that I am your father, the one who has guided you through your youth" (Jer 3:1,4).

(11) In the same manner let each person freely be judged. I for now think that the observation made by many is more appropriate. It sees God as our Father, who is in heaven (Mt 6:9), either in order to inculcate an initial fear or to infuse filial love. Thus we are to ask with reverent trust for whatever is necessary as we all expend great effort on our journey to him. And so we have these names, which strike in us more fear than love: God, master, the just judge who quickly takes revenge, and the like. But we again have these names: friend, spouse, the lovely one who provides enjoyment in beds of fragrance, the beloved one, the beauty, of ruddy complexion, placed between the breasts, whose left hand is under the beloved's head and whose right hand embraces her (cf. Sg 1:12,15; 5:19; 2:6). For some people such descriptions can seem to make God weaker than seems adequate or genuine for his love.

(12) This name of "our Father," however, in a wondrous way

maintains a balance between the two extremes, so that both fear and love are included, since love protects itself in fear.

(13) You have truly shown, our Father, the precious wisdom of your charity, when you taught us to begin our prayers in this way. It would be pleasing to dwell more fully on this idea, if it were not necessary for us to get on with the treatment we have begun.

The second consideration shows that we must be vigilant in getting to know ourselves, for a natural inclination disposes or hinders a person in many areas. This point is exemplified. Also an innate good from our parents or acquired in youth can be wondrously operative.

(1) According to philosophy, souls follow bodies. This fact is known through daily experience and so must be accepted not as a result of necessity or compulsion but as a result of natural inclination.[12] This quality assists in wondrous ways in directing us to one or the another operation. Similarly, the converse is true, that when there is no such inclination, then the mind's freedom, disciplined training, or regular efforts can hardly overcome this absence.

(2) Saint Gregory, who without doubt was often taken for long periods into the height of contemplation, says that some are to be found who are so restless and unsettled that they either cannot bear the leisure of contemplation or can do so only with great difficulty. There are others of a more tranquil nature who are more apt and prone to contemplation. Gregory says that the first type of person should be given over to action, the second to contemplation.[13]

(3) But who does not know that some people thrive more in irascible virtue, while some do best in the rational, and others in the concupiscible? In this area we see that others more quickly come to the grace of compunction and consequently to that of contemplation, for they become aware and come to hate the vileness of their shameful acts. Through the irascible power such persons strive toward what is upright. Others, however, on the basis of judgment in right reason are more drawn to the good itself. The love of truth easily persuades such people, who are

aware of the great splendor of living in accord with that same reason. They have adopted this reason in order to cultivate it.

(4) Again, in other people you will see a gentle and friendly heart. They can be inclined to those acts that belong to compassion or love. This type is well described by the holy soul in the Song of Songs (Sg 5:6). It becomes totally liquefied, so that its beloved is spoken of as being wholly lovable, sweet, and desirable. Very easily drawn to the tranquility of contemplation, such a soul now considers the passion of the Lord, now the dignity of God and his love for the soul, and now the good and sorrowful lives of male and female saints in the past. This process takes place according to the concupiscible power. The feminine sex is especially endowed in this capacity, and so it is often called pious and devout.[14]

(5) It is apparent how someone is easily brought in this or that way to contemplation, for the actions leading to such activities are latent in the persons who experience them.[15] For the senses are inclined to obey the spirit manifesting itself from above, provided it has its proper sign, meaning that it is appropriate for the person taken up in that spirit.

(6) Now if I try to conjecture from men's actions how they are, the irascible side was more apparent in Ambrose and Jerome; in Augustine and Saint Thomas the rational; in Gregory and Bernard the concupiscible. I do not doubt, nevertheless, that in each of them could be found a gentle and loving heart, which could be fashioned to what creates love. Otherwise, how will the hard heart not be badly off on the last day (Sir 3:27)? In each of these fathers there was also a passionate desire to investigate the truth and fervent zeal to root out every form of shameful behavior.

(7) Finally, I think of all who are well born or who have this grace by the miracle of God alone, such as John the Baptist, or from the inflowing of superior bodies, or from immediate heredity in their parents, or from a good education, which forms good behavior. They all should give thanks, from wherever this grace comes, and not receive it in a vacuum.

(8) For let each see to it, as Bernard says, "that the word, which goes forth from the mouth of God, does not return to him empty

but prospers and accomplishes all those things for which he sent it."[16] Bernard might also say: "The grace of God in me was not in vain" (1 Cor 15:10). One does injury to the donor when one neglects the gift and does not use it for the purpose for which it has been given. There is no doubt that such a reaction shows an intolerable pride, which is both displeasing and ungrateful.

The third consideration deals briefly with status and functions in the entire church and shows what belong to each of them.

(1) Who can enumerate the great variety of positions in society? For as has already been said, in the physical as in the mystical body the different members have different functions.[17] Contemplation requires leisure and release from outside cares. But many people are found who are bound by their status and functions so that they cannot live without a great din of cares and exercising of the body or of the senses. What then can be done except to keep such people from seeking the quiet of contemplation? Otherwise a man who is obliged to live amid noisy pursuits can make no one happy: "For his enemies will see him and they will ridicule his days of rest" (Lam 1:7).

(2) We can be silent here about the mechanical trades, or those of the merchant and agricultural worker, as well as concerning the bond of matrimony, which forces a woman to think about worldly matters in terms of how she is to please her husband, or compels the husband to provide for the children and wife (cf. 1 Cor 7:33–34). Let us concern ourselves with the prelates of the church. Gregory says of them that before all else, they must be exalted in the act of contemplation.[18] But if such churchmen primarily wish to devote themselves to acquiring contemplation when they should be taking care of the spiritual and bodily needs of the faithful, they deceive and mock themselves. They succumb to base temptation and idle curiosity if they abandon the care of the people and seek to enjoy the sweetness of contemplative leisure. In such a way they fail to keep God's precept, by concentrating on what is voluntary and not required.[19]

(3) But contemplation can become so familiar to someone

that a person can deal with both activities ambidextrously.[20] Undisturbed, such a person becomes like an angel of God, active in contemplating and in activity being contemplative. Or the person at least will be able without great difficulty to arrange it so that he can go from one to the other, accordingly as he needs. In such a case he has been placed in a state in which he exercises perfection.

(4) Furthermore it belongs to the state and office of churchmen, especially the religious, to grow in the acquisition of this perfection, since they have been placed for this purpose in the school of devotion and prayer. They are to be, as it were, the eyes that direct the other members of the mystical body, both toward themselves and toward God.[21]

(5) We are, nevertheless, aware that there is among ecclesiastics a great variety of ages and conditions. Some belong to the age of childhood, others of adolescence, others of youth, or of manhood, or of old age. Each of these has its own requirements. Still, whatever actions, teachings, or duties are found in these different ages and conditions, it is necessary that they direct themselves to reaching the end of contemplative peace.[22]

(6) Careful attention is to be given to infants and children, although their capacities are limited, so that they not be infected by perverse and obscene words, pictures, or examples.[23] They are instead to be filled with the opposite: words, pictures, and examples that are completely chaste and religiously pious. "Once the jar has been permeated, it will keep the odor for a long time."[24] Woe to those who scandalize such little ones, or to those who do not teach in the way they should (Mt 18:6–7).

(7) Youths should be kept in check through tasks, also bodily ones, which will repress the arousal of violent passions. When these have been moderated through habit and age, then in the remainder of their lives there will be left room for freely acquiring the leisure of contemplation.

The fourth consideration says that everyone is obliged to seek perfection, under penalty of present and future damnation. The life of contemplation is to be preferred to that of action.

(1) Many people say: "The average way of life is good enough for me. If I can be saved with the lowest, that is enough. I don't want the merits of apostles or martyrs. I have no desire to soar in the heights but am perfectly content to stay on the ground." But such people should realize that the lack of desire to be perfect is in itself an imperfection. When one does not make progress on God's road, then one regresses.[25] The lazy servant was damned when he was content with keeping the talent and did not lend it out for gain (Mt 25:26).

(2) We can illustrate this point through a familiar example. A certain noble magnate who is head of family has several sons. Each of them is very capable of increasing the family fortune through honest means and by his own efforts. One of them sits in the house, lazy and inactive, while the others work. He cares about nothing or lives in a base manner. He shows no interest in anything of quality or worth in relation to his talents or his father's nobility. He says that the goods he already has are enough for him and that he can use them for any life he wants. The father encourages him to more noble and arduous deeds. He admonishes and exhorts him. Is it not apparent that the son, if he hears and fails to obey, will become hateful to the father?

(3) In this way they are found guilty with the heavenly Father, when he draws them to "higher gifts" (1 Cor 12:31) and more holy deeds, if they grow slack in clinging to what is base. They will be damned if they do not work for perfection. We want it to be understood that those who have no status or a low office cannot contend that they are unable to rise to higher things without violating God's precept. In all things it is right to seek what is highest. Hereby we obey God's command.

(4) We are further warned that even if Mary together with Martha served Christ, their guest, still he in his divine wisdom praised the former, for she, intent on him alone, had chosen "the better part" (Lk 10:38–42). And so the person is cursed who chooses the inferior part when he could do otherwise.[26]

(5) From these considerations it becomes clear that since the contemplative life, as the theologians show, is more perfect than the active, then people who are suited for contemplation and are not obliged to engage in practical functions can rightly give themselves over to contemplation and put aside active pursuits. Here we put our faith in what Augustine says: If no one, by way of a superior's order and out of clear necessity, imposes on us the task of charity, which is action, then we can pursue the contemplation of truth.[27]

(6) At the same time, no one is to stand in the way of his own potential for advancing in the active life. He will bring condemnation on himself if he hides the talent by which he can be occupied in preaching or helping and ministering to the poor (Mt 25:18, 28). Just as the contemplative person who serves God with heart or eye abundantly benefits the church, so others serve with their hands, mouth, or feet.

(7) Furthermore, there are many who are to be judged liable to damnation for failing to seek contemplation, for they are placed in the school of religion, which is the school of devotion, prayer, and weeping. It is fitting for churchmen to act in such a way. They can put aside their work with people for the sake of rest, so that they may keep the Lord's statutes and fulfill his law (Ps 118:5, 8, 33). There are indeed found many men and women of this kind in the world. Such people have a store of holy leisure. They are receptive to instruction and have an innate talent, so that they turn themselves completely toward God and take hold of him. And so let faith, hope, and charity be present in them. No finer disposition could be sought for them than that they move wholly toward a good and pleasing affection of the heart (Ps 72:7).

The fifth consideration shows that we are to flee superficial concerns and to be drawn with love into God through delight in psalmody. This is especially to be encouraged for monks and nuns. Singing at too high a pitch hinders such an experience.

(1) Write wisdom, says the wise man, in time of holy leisure, for he who reduces his activities, he will receive wisdom (Sir

38:25). Therefore let your actions be limited to a few areas, if you wish to attain a good mental state. This is something that no one who is busy will find, if Seneca is to be believed.[28] Seneca does not say, "He was very busy," for this is known to be false in those who have reached perfection.

(2) A bird that has its wings tied or glued together cannot lift itself through the empty air.[29] Nor can a man whose feet are tied swim to the bank of a river. The heavens can bring one up to the serenity of contemplation only when they are not filled up. It is necessary that the page of the heart's surface be neither full of cares nor stretched tight with worries nor darkened by black passions. When these happen, then the teaching of such immense wisdom cannot be written on the page.

(3) We can take an example from trees. Here the liquid that provides nourishment, which has to be brought to the height of the branches, flows uselessly through the lower parts if the bark is severed and cracked. Love found in the soul is clearly to be called its liquid, which quickly wastes away in the lower parts when it is harmed through the wounds of carnal passions or worldly cares. Then the corrupted liquid makes its way, harming the love it would nourish, before it is lifted above in order to make heavenly desires grow.

(4) Some people want to calibrate the wings of their love for the heights of contemplation. But they sigh that the liquid of love immediately flows out in the place where the heart has found an inferior opening. This happens either when they have to devote themselves to domestic matters or are concerned about reward and punishment or are caught up in similar cares. Such people experience what the prophet deplores when he says "since my loins," meaning the affections, "are filled with illusions" (Ps 37:8). Indeed, they are illusions, which he otherwise calls "empty and false forms of madness" and "the inventions of the evil" (Ps 39:5; Ps 118:85). The lyric poet wished to resist them when he said: "If you do not dedicate yourself to study and decent actions, you will be tossed about by envy or lust."[30]

(5) But who, I ask, has been so completely freed from such assaults that he is not sometimes subjected to them? I think that

there is "no person alive," for "everywhere is vanity" (Ps 38:6). But it is one thing to give oneself over freely or out of duty or devotion to such occupations, and something else steadfastly to drive them away with all one's mental effort and in maintaining discretion. One can treat such concerns as if they were irritating stings of bothersome flies, or as the birds that flew around the evening sacrifice of Abraham.[31]

(6) Someone might ask about the occupations of many religious in their high-pitched psalmodies and canticles, which are multiplied beyond number. Do these activities get in the way of acquiring or exercising contemplation? I prefer that such people answer in terms of what they themselves experience. Indeed, Saint Augustine used to weep profusely amid the singing: "The sweet singing of the church moved me deeply. The music surged in my ears; truth seeped into my heart."[32] But I do not find here whether or not Augustine was one of those who sang.

(7) In order to obtain the tranquility of contemplation, grace has more effect than individual efforts. When additions are made in the singing, it is not hard to believe that some of those engaged in this activity, who invest all their effort in it, come to experience an extra-mental state of mind. This happens especially when they are become so filled in their animal being that the rational side is attained, and after both of these are filled up, then a spiritual awareness comes.[33]

(8) This extension of the self takes place perhaps more because the animal side of our selves is occupied for the time being, rather than if our spiritual side is busy, which is rare. Our animal part would not know how to meditate on higher things by itself in tranquility, nor how to make use of spiritual leisure. Through good training the religious life can perhaps be freed from being dependent on such a yoke. Otherwise it will be obliged to be like an ox that plows a field with an ass (Dt 22:10). Mary will never be found sitting at the feet of Jesus with them, but only Martha alone (Lk 10:39–40).[34]

(9) But if the victorious Lord and his Spirit lead you singing the psalms above these heights of flowing desires, then nothing is more powerful or more blessed. And so "blessed" is the one "who

knows jubilation" (Ps 88:16), who "sings a psalm in wisdom" (Ps 46:8), combining the meaning of God's word with affectivity. How happy is such a soul, good Jesus, which is not as a land without water for you (Ps 106:35). How salubriously the soul responds to this your dove, your bride, your lover (Sg 5:2), in gaining profit and receiving generosity. For the soul carries out the precept of religious praise when it says the hours but at the same time rejoices in the privilege of the one who, as it were, is the unique friend. Then it is taken in greatest devotion into the heights of silent contemplation. The more powerful the experience of contemplation, then the more blessed the soul is to be called.

(10) It is good if a time of prayer anticipates this process by meditation on the matters that are to be dwelt upon, so that one more freely can move into affectivity. It is useful to try to cultivate the activities spoken of, in order not only to reach a form of subtle and varied cognition but also to obtain the experience of tasting and rejoicing. For, often when there is less cognition, there arises more affection. "Love enters when knowledge remains outside."[35] Those who rejoice imitate the sound of the timbrel or harp. They do not know much about the harmony of the song, but they have enough in rejoicing through their exuberant dance. They keep to a beat which that melody calls forth.

(11) You, similarly, in that which you read, hear, see, speak, or think, convert it immediately into affectivity, as if you breathed it from within, smelled, or tasted it. So if you should hear "our Father," then let your mind rise up immediately and simultaneously to reverence and love, to a trusting request for your needs and those of your brothers, with whom the Father is shared. Show forth a magnanimous and noble contempt of all base and rustic behavior, you who glory in so royal a Father. Your exile from him should sadden you and make you sigh. For you has been reserved a heavenly heritage by title of sonship to the Father in heaven.

(12) We can find such forms of affection without number or end. From one day to the next they will be sweet and new, as if hidden in a honeycomb (Sg 5:1), in manna, or in a nut. These

affections will flow out copiously if the tooth of understanding draws them out.

The sixth consideration provides sixteen reasons for the dispensation of God toward the good and evil, accordingly as they make use of their benefits, and the punishment that is justly imposed or permitted for the evil.

(1) Curiosity is the pursuit of useless things, or greater concern for useful matters than is necessary, appropriate, or permissible.[36]

(2) Do not, I ask you, pursue the leisure of contemplation as if you were about to come to know or to show to others only its sublime content, in the way you have learned of it by faith in the most true witnesses of the saints. Instead, you should lower yourself and become more abject in your own eyes, once you have clearly perceived your own unworthiness in comparison to the divinity on which you have been dwelling. You should become stronger in resisting the javelins of temptations, so that you also become more fervent in the love of God and neighbor. In the end, by keeping to the path of God's commands, you will be found more fit for contemplation (Ps 118:32).

(3) Be attentive and feel sorrow that there are unfaithful and hostile sons (Dt 32:20; Ps 17:46), the evil servants (Mt 18:32), whom the heavenly Father for a time sustains with food from the richness of his granary and fills with honey from the rock (Ps 80:17). In the same way we see how some prelates or princes, soon after some people have been condemned to death, sometimes send to prison the remains of the best meats from their table.

(4) Therefore, "do not wish to know what is on high, but have fear" (Rom 11:20). Remember that the grace of contemplation is numbered among the graces that are freely given, as are faith and hope or prophecy or other similar powers.[37] They are given sometimes to the wicked and those who live without charity. Who then can glory unless he does so in the Lord (1 Cor 1:31)? Woe, woe to you, human presumption, for these and similar graces are found among the sons of malediction (2 Pt 2:14), either to increase their damnation for using God's gift with no

gratitude whatsoever, or in order to provide instruction for others, or for the temporal reward of some of their labors, which are essentially false and useless.

(5) For such a coin, corresponding compensation is given through God's hidden judgment, as the proverb says.[38] Have they tried only to fornicate against the gifts of God through base delight or rash presumption? What then? God has fulfilled their desire without their merits. He does so, but he is angered. Thus we have the passage in the gospels, "Take what is yours and go" (Mt 20:14).

(6) And so it often happens from the dispensation of God's mercy that he seems to turn away from his elect, but he does not do so in anger nor will he do so at the end. For he will remember his mercy when he has been angered. But who can probe the depth of his judgments (Ps 35:7; Wis 9:16; Sir 1:3)? From the sayings of the saints, who often spoke with God's inspiration (2 Pt 1:21), however, we can come to recognize some of the causes of this mystery.

(7) *Note how pride is cured by its opposite.* It happens sometimes and more often for the sake of our humility that pride is checked, either because it is in danger of dominating or so that the flesh not be allowed to deceive someone. Bernard experienced and testified to this process: "Truly nothing is so efficacious for finding, keeping, or recovering this grace, in meriting eternal life, than if you discover that you do not always know what is highest but taste it in sobriety."[39] And so "blessed" is the one "who always is fearful" (Prv 28:14) and stands on guard (Is 21:8).

(8) *The subtraction of grace causes desire.* This happens sometimes in kindling desire or making it burn more powerfully, just as fire when it is kept back by wind then can burst forth with more ardor. In this way we can learn to seek what is great with generosity of soul.

(9) *We learn to recognize our own wretchedness.* This happens when a man senses his own weakness and the abyss of his wretchedness in a profound manner and thus more clearly. He lowers himself and considers what he is in himself and what he can do with God's gift.

(10) *This change comes about when we console another person.* We put on the clothing of piety when others are desolate, in situations where consolation is not given to them or, once given, has been taken away.

(11) *We learn to remove presumption and sloth.* This grace is given in order to provide satisfaction for the time being for oneself or for others. We feel grief that we have been abandoned in such loss, just as the humanity of Christ was abandoned and was cast into a torrent of punishments in order to make satisfaction for sins, not his but those of others.

(12) *A devout person does not despise the one who lacks devotion.* This happens sometimes in order to prevent someone who is capable of aiding others by teaching or other activities from being allowed only to find rest in himself, and thus to cling to the embraces of Rachel.[40] This would be to reject the duty of charity and to pay no attention to the fertility of Leah (Gn 29:31–30:24).[41] Nature, which is fashioned for the good, detests indolence. Therefore, if it cannot be occupied in high matters, then at least it seeks occupation in the lowest. In this manner it happens that the soul, so weakened and so humbled, makes more progress. Thus the "voluntary rain" of divine re-creation is more gently instilled in the soul (Ps 27:10).

(13) *From temptation fraternal compassion can be learned.* This happens so that a man who has been tempted in many things can learn from them, in order that he experience obedience and other virtues, and thus can come to teach them more effectively. And so that Socratic saying is correct: We come to speak better about that which we know better.[42] And we know better that which we have experienced more intimately. For what does the inexperienced person know (Sir 34:9, 11)?

(14) *Community can be strengthened.* This sometimes happens so that a person not desert the obligation of action required by him for the sake of the extra gift of contemplation.

(15) *Sins can be remitted and greater reverence shown.* These take place in order to punish lesser faults, as if a most merciful father for a time turns his face aside from his wanton son and shows his sadness. From this time onward the son will be more attentive in

guarding every form of modesty and gradually decide that he must not neglect even the smallest matter.

(16) *We can acknowledge that God's gift is freely given.* This sometimes happens so that the Apostle's saying be known: "What matters is not our activity or will, but God's mercy" (Rom 9:16). A clear indication of the basis for this realization comes when a person says to himself: "You on this day, at that hour, will be free of all occupations; then you will most assuredly be ready for tasting the sweetness of contemplation; you should do so and so or act in such a way." But when that day comes, the person will feel a bitter aridity in his soul and a sense of revulsion toward the spirit. He will not only be repelled by prayer and spiritual reading but also will be plagued by darkness and confusion. In contrast, when a person has had no particular expectations, "it will come freely, though not hoped for at that time."[43]

(17) *A person will consider himself and his own value.* This happens in order to cleanse the great expanse of the spiritual sea. When there is too much tranquility, also of a material type, filth usually collects, but this is dispelled through stimulation and agitation.

(18) *We learn that the gift of God is not to be sought as if it could be merited.* This happens so that it become clear that if the soul freely chooses to fear God, then it is prepared to submit itself to its own burdens of tribulation and sorrows, as if it were receiving rewards of consolation and delights from him. This awareness is opposed to those who do not want to devote themselves to prayer or who believe it to be powerless unless they have experienced a sense of consolation. For such people it is as if God never imagined "the drudgery involved in following the command" (Ps 93:20).

(19) *Humility is also important so that perseverance be learned in the midst of changes.* In this way a person is weaned. One must be kept from always being a child or from starting to fornicate with God's gifts. Otherwise the person will love these things for his own sake and will cling to them and forget himself among them. Receiving here a temporal reward, such a person will lose a future reward. And so the ruler in this manner avoids immediately rewarding a knight, and a father does the same with his son in terms of a silver coin or a penny or a piece of fruit or a meal.

The knight or son will later be given rulership or a kingdom, even though the prince or father seems to give few even small signs of indulgence in order to console the son or to provide a sign of love. But this type of authority reserves for a later time rewards that are much finer.

(20) *The form of devotion will be maintained because of physical ailments.* It happens sometimes that such a great visitor delays coming to the soul in order that it not be burdened, as David said to his son Absalom (2 Sm 13:25). But what burdens? Tears, pious sighing, fasting, vigils, and other bodily sufferings. Or perhaps the soul that is still more youthful cannot sustain drunkenness of spirit, if the king brings it directly into the wine cellar (Sg 2:4). Therefore he has kept the key of devotion for himself, now closing and now opening the cellar.

(21) *In this way what is better and more pleasant can be hoped for.* This is done to provoke us to greater effort, "as the eagle stimulates its chicks to fly" (Dt 32:11) and a mother her son to walk. We see that a mother sometimes deserts her son with this purpose so that he, left to himself, will cry out for her. When he comes back, he will be more careful in keeping close to her. From that time onward, he will not let her out of sight and more happily will embrace the mother he has sought. He will embrace her the more sweetly when he has found her and fondle and kiss her.

(22) *Humility is also given so that we can remain patient when gifts are taken away.* This is done so that we exercise patience, which "has a perfect work" (Jas 1:4). For what tribulation is more bitter? What experience is more suited for instilling patience in the soul? Patience is needed when a foretaste of the joys of paradise is removed and turns into "the pains of hell" (Ps 17:6), in the image of "the shadow of death" (Ps 22:4; 87:7; 106:10, 14), for the tribulation of this exile. In the end we will be made to see what great bitterness there is in future eternal separation from God.

(23) Whoever you are, then, you who are dedicated to contemplation, approach it with energy, but in such a way that you wait for it to come from on high. Be prepared to make use of it in all humility and in thankfulness. Be ready also in a similar way to maintain a healthy spirit without contemplation if it does not

come. Love those who have it and do not spurn or judge those who lack it. Always remember that the kingdom of God exists in the love of God alone.

(24) In the end our land is cursed, even if it is spiritual, just as with that which is corporeal, for it does not bring forth fruit without thorns and thistles, and similarly the pregnant soul cannot give birth to the offspring of truth without pain (Gn 3:16–18).

The seventh consideration teaches us to show forbearance in our desire to attain an interior taste. We must seek earnestly. Though often repelled we are to persevere with what we have begun. He will not grow exhausted so long as he deserves to be heard in mercy and to be admitted.

(1) It might seem from the foregoing consideration that the devout person could, as it were, neglect the most salvific and gentle fruits of contemplation and say: "Why am I being tired out in vain? What am I trying to attain that my soul does not know? I have no idea if my efforts are profitable for my salvation or will be reputed to my damnation. And so let God's will be done (Mt 6:10). He will give me, if he wants, the sense here of a foretaste of his sweetness. Or if he wants, he will refuse it. My heart is ready for either one" (Ps 56:8).

(2) But you who speak in such a way, listen. Do you not know, I ask, that he who plants, according to the Apostle, is nothing, nor is he who waters (1 Cor 3:7)? Nevertheless, God wants us to show skill in planting and in watering, whether we understand this saying literally or figuratively. Otherwise, how can we be fellow workers for God (1 Cor 3:9)? How can we fulfill the command that "you will not tempt the Lord your God" (Mt 4:7; Dt 6:16) if we desert the task and obligation given us in a human context and count exclusively on divine aid?[44] Let it then be our task, our effort, our concern, to plant and to water. Christ will give growth as life-giving power infused from above. From him we will seek humbly and await faithfully.

(3) No one should fool himself by being negligent or inactive, unless he has no desire to seek the height of contemplation. The

prior consideration will confound him, for it says that "he is to reach for perfection."

(4) Moreover, no one should give up on this journey toward perfection, once it is begun, if such a person comes to feel, as is unavoidable, the traps of numberless temptations hidden "on the road on which he walks" (Ps 141:4). Even though he often is cast aside, he will not be confounded. Repeatedly exerting himself and not depending on his own judgment, he will not be thrown into confusion. He does his best, and tries in relying on the strong staff of the protection of the Almighty and not on the rod of his own labor.

(5) He who can understand this matter, let him realize how effort is expected, indeed required, for this purpose, although in themselves one's own exertions cannot provide the grace of contemplation. For we see this image in the generation of a person in the flesh: the fathers generate, the mothers nourish in their wombs. Otherwise how could it come about that a child is born? Nevertheless, what power would they have to do all these things if the soul were not given from above, by the will of the Creator alone? The soul will give life to all that was previously without form and that was, as it were, quite useless. Similarly, a person pulls up the window shades, lifts up his head, and opens his eyes. Otherwise, how can he see? But if the sun hid its rays, then all these efforts to see would be in vain. The same I think of the sun of justice, which is Christ.

(6) In the final analysis, God has given nothing to mortals without our expending great effort, as the poet says.[45] No one is crowned "except he who has competed according to the rules" (2 Tm 2:5), in accord with the words of the Apostle. Similarly, people learn the lesser arts, whose content it is unnecessary to enumerate, only through great effort, so that they miss sleep and experience anxiety. They do so because they want to escape poverty, to increase riches, to get praise from empty titles, or obtain something else. These goals are so mortal, perishable, and unstable that the poet thereby was inspired to say, "Dishonest work conquers all things, and indigence makes its way through harsh circumstances."[46] Such efforts ought to make us

ashamed that we are much less careful, patient, and eager when it comes to achieving what is most beautiful, great, and divine.

(7) Consider how you, in climbing this great mountain, prepare to attain contemplation. Eagerly rejoicing you set forth "like a giant to run the race" (Ps 18:6), firm in your step so that you do not fall backward. But if you fall, you will use all your strength, casting aside the millstone of worldly thoughts from your neck. This you can even learn from the fable of Sisyphus.[47] How can you, who are of royal descent, be satisfied with the poverty of this vale of tears? How can you be stuck in this deep mud and filth (Ps 83:7; 68:3; 39:3)? Aspire to rise above it, where there are riches, peace, and spiritual joy in the pure air. For how long will your soul be numbed by a frozen stiffness? For how long will "the burning fire" of devotion fail to ignite in it (Ps 38:4)?

(8) Blow on the fire, give it life, do not give up on reading, meditating, and praying until the spark of devotion, however tenuous, emerges. The smoke of temptations will erupt at the same time and in the beginning will disturb you, for it will be black and gloomy. I admit that it will sting the eye of the reason and will make the interior face wince. It will seem to you that now, more than before, you are being assaulted. You will say that they are happy who are content with a type of average life.

(9) But do not be afraid of this assault from the smoke. Stand firm and blow at it until the flame becomes stronger and thus purer. Finally, the most gentle and calm light, like that in a live coal, will overcome all the darkness of restless smoke. The Psalmist wanted to be lit up in such a way, and to be taken into such light, when he said, "Devour my heart and my mind" (Ps 25:2).

(10) But if in your efforts and quests you find nothing of the kind, then at least in your sorrow grieve for your misfortune and your frozen state.[48] You can say with the Prophet, "I have become wretched and am prostrate until the end; the whole day I have gone about in sadness" (Ps 37:7). Believe me: your effort is not worth less for God. It is not your earthly reward that matters, for "he considers the effort and pain."[49]

(11) But truly if God has granted to you the desire of your soul and has provided you with "blessings of sweetness" (Ps 20:3–4),

then you should concentrate most on this one pursuit. Thus when the fire of devotion has been lit with so much effort, then the sparks of humility keep it from the wind of arrogance. Now no one should seem great to you. Moreover, you will have strength in the face of this frozen state of inert neglect. Then you will not believe that you have obtained what you sought or allow yourself to overflow with all kinds of empty words or acts.

(12) There is truth in the statement provided in the verse: "There is no less virtue in seeking to protect what we have already acquired."[50] In French there is the common proverb, *Bon espargneur valt bon gangneur.* In Latin this is rendered *Bonus conservator par est bono acquisitori* (He who is good at keeping is the equal of the one who is good at getting).[51] But woe to the fools who waste their gains.

The eighth consideration is to think of the origins of the passions and affections. This procedure is treated under the triple mode of knowing in respect to divine judgment, in relation to how God shows mercy in an incomprehensible manner to sinners. The various powers of the soul are considered and exemplified in terms of how they lead to the excellence of virtues or the enormity of vices.

(1) Mystical theology has the property of being located in affectivity, while all other forms of knowledge are found in intellect. All affection either is love or arises from love. Therefore, according to philosophical deduction, is it not then in accord with reason that this mystical theology should be named the art of love or the science of loving?[52]

(2) But this is not love alone but also is the origin of the other affections or passions, so that it also gives birth to hatred.[53] We find, then, "that all things here are mixed up,/ Hope, fear, grief, joy," which come from affectivity.[54] But if God is loved above all things, then the consequence arises that whatever is perceived as being contrary to his love is hated. Again, since God becomes present to the soul through cognition as an object that is completely suitable for it, then there follow joy in his presence and sadness in his absence. Thus hope or fear arise.

(3) But concerning the number of the passions, different writers have had different teachings, such as Aristotle in his *Rhetoric*, Hugh of Saint Victor in his treatise *On Prayer*, William of Paris in his *Penitential*, while others have provided a greater or lesser number.[55] I remember that elsewhere I extended the number of passions to about twenty.[56] Hugh of Saint Victor is content with nine of them, although there is no doubt that they are without number.

(4) And since the way is more satisfying that counts fewer, for the present time we can conclude that the passions are threefold, in conformity with the three that are appropriated to the Trinity: power, wisdom, and goodness.[57] According to this criterion the venerable Richard of Saint Victor's distinction can be aptly used. He says that the grace of contemplation arises in a triple manner according to the three cries in the ascent of the soul in the Song of Songs.[58] They come from an abundance of devout compunction, which is like a "column of smoke" (Sg 3:6), from the greatness of admiration, "like the dawn peering forth" (Sg 6:9), and from the fullness of rejoicing, as it were "leaning on the one beloved" (Sg 8:5).

(5) And so if I consider more profoundly divine power and riches in comparison to my weakness and poverty, how can I in my misery and unworthiness avoid feeling remorse, or horror, or fear? I live as a failure under this "terrible" judgment "amid his counsels over the sons of men" (Ps 65:5). I have greatly offended such a great lord, and I have spurned such a Father of majesty (Ps 47:2; 76:14).

(6) Again, if I should consider before the eyes of this judge how "wonderful is your knowledge" (Ps 138:6), which has grown so strong that I cannot reach it, then come admiration, amazement, and incapacity. I cannot grasp how he foreknows that some attain glory, others perpetual unhappiness. Nor can I see how he denies many things to those who are grateful and use them well, while he gives them to those who are ungrateful and who will fight against him. And for what reason does he put up with many who are to be saved, even though they for almost all their lives have been involved in terrible crimes?[59] This happened with the thief on the cross (Lk 23:40–43), while others are lost for eternity, as Judas,

who was enriched with grace in a number of virtues (Mt 26:25; 27:3–4). Moreover, "no one can correct the one whom God has disdained" (Eccl 7:14), because "he shackled all things under sin" (Gal 3:22). For this reason the Apostle was made to cry out in amazement: "Oh, the height and riches of God's wisdom and knowledge, how unfathomable are his judgments and how inscrutable his ways" (Rom 11:33).

(7) Finally, the mind comes to think of the "torrent" of divine gentleness, and "how good the God of Israel is to those who are upright of heart" (Ps 35:9; 72:1). Does not my whole being in its need to rejoice cry out, "Oh, how gentle is your spirit, Lord" (Wis 12:1) and "How great the abundance of your sweetness, Lord, which you have hidden from those who fear you" (Ps 30:20).

(8) We have in these reactions three principal affections: compunction, in trembling; admiration, in amazement; exultation, in rejoicing, according to God's power, wisdom, and goodness, and according to the three powers of the soul: the irascible, the rational, and the concupiscible.[60]

(9) Furthermore, you will find nothing in all of scripture that is unsuited in this mode of reflection for use in the prayer with which God is pleased. You will be reminded of God's power in the face of your weakness and the tyranny of your adversaries. You will find the wisdom of God as opposed to your foolishness and the shrewdness of the enemy. And you will encounter God's goodness in contrast to your wickedness and that of others. Everything that is read in scripture, or everything that is understood there, does it not resound with one of these things: either our wretchedness, or the evil of our adversaries, or the majesty of God in power, wisdom, and goodness?

(10) Truly, if our thoughts are confused and worldly, if the fountain of love has become corrupt, immediately passions of a similar type rise up, but they are twisted and spurious. A sense of need comes over us, or else the tyrant passion threatens our sudden destruction because of our empty fear and useless compunction. From a deceptive cleverness emerges a sense of surprise; from a corrupt will comes false joy; and from the worst things comes an even more objectionable sense of glory.

(11) Do you wish, then, to generate only praiseworthy affections? Then keep the font of love pure. At the same time be aware that the source of this font draws its water from your pristine land of good faith and holy thoughts. Hence the Apostle warns us to renew our minds (Rom 12:2), cleansed from the corruption of feverish love. In this way our sense of sight will develop into the fullest beauty and clarity, our hearing into the highest harmony and resonance, our taste into the greatest savoriness, and our touch into the most pleasant and joyful state, all in pure union with God.[61]

(12) We can consider other matters here, so that we say that thoughts or affections and passions arise sometimes from change in external objects, sometimes from internal fantasy or the imagination. The reason can deal with them, or God from above can illuminate the mind or spirit with them. Similarly, good angels can elicit them, or fallen angels can do so. Against such passions "we must struggle," much more than "against flesh and blood" (Eph 6:12). Then our souls that have been purified and sanctified will sometimes have to bear the attacks of blasphemies and the most vile impurities, even in old age and in solitude. These temptations are of a type that is unknown to us so long as we live in the world among the average and more adolescent temptations of the flesh and the world.[62]

(13) Finally, our consideration could be appropriately extended, treating the natural and generative roots of this or that passion in conformity with the doctrine of the Philosopher in his *Rhetoric*.[63] Here he deals with the causes of the passions and the sources of modesty, boasting, despair, amazement, admiration, anger, envy, desire to flatter or to denigrate, reverential respect, and revulsion. In general, Aristotle considers the origin of the four passions to be hope, fear, sadness, and joy.

(14) That most keen investigator of thoughts, Augustine, noted in his *Confessions* that no vice is committed unless we want, as it were, to imitate some divine quality.[64] And so it is clear that "pride is the beginning of all sin" (Sir 10:15). For what is sin but disordered and intemperate affectivity? Pride, then, is the root

of any bad form of affectivity, just as, on the contrary, humility gives birth to every good form of affectivity.

(15) Therefore we have here a most simple but very effective rule for distinguishing between good and evil affections on the basis of this double root. One or the other, pride or humility, always can be sensed within the origins of thoughts, if you consider the matter carefully. Why do you think someone is envious? Because such a person wants to excel alone without any restraint. He grows angry, because he wants to win without being disturbed or held back. He is greedy, because he wants to outdo all, without lacking anything and taking no responsibility for his acts. He is slothful, because he wants to be first, without being restrained by any fatigue in his activity. He is cowardly and arrogant or disobedient, because he freely acts badly and does harm and wants to be the best without any restraints, according to his own judgment and by the choice of his own will. He caters to lust and serves gluttony because he wants to engage in pleasure, with no restrictions.

(16) If you take away this appetite, which desires one's own unimpeded success, then all the branches, fruits, and foliage of vices dry up.[65] Instead of envy, charity will germinate; instead of anger, gentleness; instead of greed, frugality; instead of laziness, activity; and the same with the other qualities. In these pursuits a person imitates Christ. In all others it is always Lucifer who is imitated.

The ninth consideration shows a suitable time and place to be sought for those who want to make progress. A rule is given because of the various dispositions people have. It is chosen from a teacher of theology and it is shown both that grace more abundantly flows from the Lord and that in tribulations we more quickly obtain solace and spiritual consolation.

(1) One person chooses a public place; another a secret one. One person prefers quiet, another noise. One person finds a dark corner, another a bright and spacious place in the open air. It is the same with the time of day: "God tempers the changing

day."[66] It is evening; it is late; it is night; it is cock-crow; it is dawn, morning, prime, terce, sext, nones.

(2) Even more so there are in these places various ways of preparing or adapting the body for contemplation.[67] One person stands, the other kneels, while a third is prostrate with the whole body. Another stoops forward or lies on his back. Yet another positions his face in between the knees, while someone else covers his face with his hand, and another sits supported by one or both elbows. Or a person lifts up his eyes, as much as he can; another turns them downward. Yet another marches around here and there; another stops in his tracks; and another person takes a stroll. Thus, as the Apostle says, each person "is fully convinced in his own mind" (Rom 14:5). As the Comic says, "To each is his own custom."[68]

(3) I have found this rule handed down for all these matters, that each should follow what seems good in his eyes in order to facilitate contemplation.[69] The only exception to this criterion of individuality is that a regular and common discipline binds us all to observe certain times, places, and bodily positions. Otherwise, "woe to the one through whom scandal comes" because of his singularity (Mt 18:7). For who "has fed upon" the Lord's "vine" (Ps 79:9,14)? Such a person is certainly a "singular wild beast" (Ps 79:14).

(4) There are those who find help by being in a hidden place. It is dark, narrow, low-lying, and dreadful in its horror, with a deep silence. Such persons live, as it were, in burial places "and in dens and caves of the earth" (Heb 11:38).[70]

(5) There are those for whom an open, light, spacious place is more fit, with the sky or the air surrounding it on all sides. Such people have lived in the deserts and in the mountains where, as Saint Jerome tells, everything shines forth more serenely than in the smoky cities.[71]

(6) You will find some people whom every sound offends, while for others, a noisy place is no hindrance, and in fact an incentive. They like the murmuring of falling water, or the whispering of leaves flying about, the rich singing of the birds, the strident whistling of the wind, the clashing confusion of rivers or seas, or especially the sweet resonance of the church sounding

315

forth with voices regulated by bells, organs, and singing choirs. What for others might lead to wantonness, for such people produces a sense of sober moderation.

(7) And so we see that there are some people, but only a few (and they are not to be imitated indiscriminately), for whom every element of nuptial joy in dancing, musical instruments, gestures, and the beauty of women "with gilded dress and a variety of cloth wrapped around" (Ps 44:10) is turned into a most genuine interior ecstasy. Here lust has no place and unclean impulses do not take over. Thus, "for those who love God, everything works together for the good" (Rom 8:28), and so in every way such people find what is good for themselves, just as bees find their honey. Lifted up from the earth, they draw all things to themselves (Jn 12:32).[72]

(8) What is then to be determined concerning the variety of situations, where now there is "a time to weep," now "to laugh," "to embrace," or "to be far from embraces," and so on, in comparison with other times (Eccl 3:4–5)? When the Psalmist is about to give glory in the Lord, he says, "Seven times in the day I have spoken your praise for the justice of your ways" (Ps 118:164), and in the same psalm he says, "At midnight I rose to acknowledge you" (Ps 118:62). Again he says, "In the morning" he has killed "all the sinners of the earth" (Ps 100:8), meaning that he has overcome the temptations leading us to sin. We cannot believe this is possible without prayer and vigilance. Again to the Lord he says, "You will rejoice in the gateways of the morning and the evening" (Ps 64:9). And who is it who dares to fix a time for God and not to expect him to do what is pleasing to him, accordingly as he wills, and with no less vigilance? "You visit man at daybreak," says the afflicted Job, "and immediately you test him" (Jb 7:18).

(9) Nevertheless, insofar as regards human effort, we think that the hour is more appropriate for this purpose after food has been digested and worldly cares put aside, and when there is no outside observer who can notice the heavy groaning, the sighing erupting from deep within the breast, the bitter cries, broken-off complaints, humble prostrations, teary eyes, the face now full of blushing shame, now of chalky pallor. Then both hands will be

clenched, with the eyes fixed on heaven, frequent beating of the breast, kisses pressed to the ground or onto altars, and other gestures and signs shown by the parts of the body to indicate supplication.

(10) In the end, a bodily condition or position is considered to be more efficacious when it is more apt for quietness of mind. For in sitting and finding rest the soul is made prudent.[73] It cannot be stable in its own peace unless the body learns to remain fixed in the same place.

(11) We should add that a sacred place is more suitable, other things being equal, for here the most powerful presence of Christ, solemn consecration, the offerings of the faithful, the deeds of the saints in pictures or writing, and the burial places of the dead make such a place more attractive.

(12) Similarly, who can be in doubt that at holy times of year and on great feasts it is customary for a more abundant flow of grace to be poured forth onto the great hospital of the living and the prison of the dead in need of cleansing? For then "on a good day we are to come" to God (1 Sm 25:8).[74] Then we say with great faithfulness to one of the saints: "May you prosper on your day of triumph." The remains of your gifts will be more abundant, as if from the most splendid table with holy guests, who decide that they are to be handed out to the poor and beggars who ask, seek, and knock for them. Does not the church sing for the union and nuptials of Esther, that is, of our humanity with divinity, that "today through the whole world the heavens have been made to flow with honey"?[75] Our bodies, which are like weak and infirm beggars, should thus teach us to observe the appropriate time. They should teach us when they are shut up in darkness and in prisons that sometimes from the table of the Judge we can deserve the leftovers and crumbs of delicious foods.

(13) Moreover, there remains what can be said about different times. For there is a time to weep and a time to laugh, a time of adversity, which is in the night, and a time of prosperity, which the scriptures often indicate by the daytime (Eccl 3:4).

(14) For the time being we can be silent about the perfect, who at both times know how to act "with the weapons of righteousness

for the right hand and for the left" (2 Cor 6:7), as if they were ambidextrous (Jgs 3:15).[76] They say with the Apostle, "I know how to possess in abundance, and I also know how to suffer want" (Phil 4:12), "rejoicing with those who rejoice, weeping with those who weep" (Rom 12:15). That of which Vergil spoke sometimes happens to them even amid their tears: "The mind remains unmoved, while empty tears are poured forth."[77] This is because the minds of such persons remain fixed on the one center of eternity, like the axis around which the changeable wheel of temporality revolves, or like a needle influenced by a magnet directs itself toward the pole.

(15) For both beginners and the advanced, experience, together with the authority of the scriptures, seems to be their teacher. A time of adversity profits them more, at least if it is moderated, so that the judgment of the reason does not shut off. Through the gift of God patience provides growth (cf. 1 Cor 10:13).

(16) For adversity of such a type admonishes them with its more powerful hand to tear themselves away from this "mud of the deep" (Ps 68:3), so that they lift themselves up from the earth. While they there find "pain and tribulation," they act with greater zeal, as the Prophet added, "And I called upon the name of the Lord" (Ps 114:3–4). They also feel that the Lord is close "to those who are troubled in their hearts" (Ps 33:19) and because he "is the one who hears them on the occasion of their tribulation" (Ps 9:10) and says, "Call on me in the day of distress, and I will rescue you and you will do honor to me" (Ps 49:15).

(17) For so the "dove" of reason, not having "where the foot" of desire "can rest" (Gn 8:8–9), returns to the ark of contemplation, for the same ark is lifted up higher when the waters of tribulation rise.[78] Similarly, those in tribulation "ascend to the upper regions of the house," which is their spiritual abode, as Judith and Peter (cf. Jdt 8:5; Acts 10:9). Here they have either to face some reproach, or the death of relatives, the affliction of their country, or a lack of material things.

(18) This is a kind of spiritual opposition,[79] which strengthens what is contrary to it. This is the flint that sharpens the iron; this is the wormwood for weaning children in taking them away from

breast milk; or this is the hammer whose task it is to flatten out and extend, as the Psalmist says: "In my distress you have flattened me out" (Ps 4:1). This is the file that polishes, cleanses, smoothes out, and purifies. This is the furnace that purges gold so that it glows red (cf. Prv 27:21). This is the rod that lifts up from hell those who have been knocked down, so that the one who has been in distress will speak out in expressing his thanks: "Lord, if by these things men live and in such is the life of my spirit, then take possession of me and give me life, for behold, my most bitter experience has given me peace" (Is 38:16–17). He also will say: "Let decay enter into my bones and abound beneath me, so that I will quietly wait for the day of tribulation and go forth to our armed people" (Hb 3:16), meaning the citizens of heaven.

The tenth consideration concerns moderation in sleeping and eating, and uses various examples, but especially from Saint Jerome, who provided letters to Rusticus, Paulinus, Furia, and Eustochium on keeping virginity, to Aleth and to Salvina, and several others.[80]

(1) In the first place we must take care, in order to understand what has been said or should be said, that some observances be maintained for beginners in contemplation, while others are for those who are more proficient, and others for those who are perfect. These perfect are they "who because of habit already have trained their faculties" (Heb 5:14). With the Apostle they "know how to have abundance and to suffer want" (Phil 4:12), and "in every place" to lift up "pure hands" (1 Tm 2:8). It is different among beginners, for whom supports are to be sought until a more solid structure is raised. For such persons we have spoken of the observation of places and times, as here concerning moderation in food and sleep.

(2) And indeed I contend that in this pursuit of contemplation's beginnings, an ardent and, as it were, continuous effort of the mind is required. This means that the vital and animal faculties will for the most part be used up and so will need more renewal through food and sleep. At least it will be necessary that such faculties be more frequently used. But you say that heavy eating burdens the

mind by tying it down and overwhelming it, for "the taste of flesh weakens the spirit."[81] You speak of heavy eating, while we mean moderate, even though in the moment of consumption a temperate intake can seem to be both heavy and burdensome, unless you take into account the full extent of the process.

(3) There have been those who, in order to merit the grace of contemplation or prophecy, have tried to imitate Elijah or John the Baptist or Daniel (cf. 1 Kgs 17:2–6; Mt 3:4; Dn 1:12), or else one of the Egyptian fathers in terms of abstinence and austerity. Such people have become not prophets but fantasts. They teach by their example that not anyone can soar with the perfect, to whom some graces have been given. Such people are more to be admired by posterity than to be followed in their way of life.[82]

(4) But if mental labor is added to this weakening of the body through fasting and excessive wakefulness, the vital and animal faculties, as we have said, are drained. What can follow from this condition except collapse and grave illness or fantasies and the pain of a disturbed mind? The body needs to be nourished in order to aid the mind. It should not be destroyed by overeating or self-starvation. A stomach that always is hungry and that takes in food normally is, according to Jerome, to be preferred to one that fasts for two days at a time.[83]

(5) If then a regular profession now holds someone bound under the authority of an indiscreet instructor who does not allow indulgence in food or sleep, then this beginner according to my counsel will find moderation through ardent meditation and contrition with tears in order to save himself. The danger is that he will be so weakened that his judgment will be less sound than it was when he set out on his quest. For such a person it is enough to follow what has been agreed, if he should find that the beast of burden, the body, which he is obliged to protect, is being quickly destroyed.

(6) I am not unaware that what is insufficient in terms of food or sleep for one person is more than enough for another. In this matter tradition according to doctrine cannot decide the right quantity or use, unless each person should test himself through a long process of individual discernment. Moreover, each person

should humbly trust in the counsel of the wise, and he will be taught in relation to his need, according to the anointing that will support him (cf. 1 Jn 2:20). For, as medical doctors and theologians say, indiscreet fasting harms more than intemperate eating. The latter is curable, while the former often cannot be remedied, even though nature is often content with a few things if gluttony does not insinuate itself.[84]

(7) We can take an example from plants. There are those that frequent watering greatly aids, while others are killed by this practice. There are those that benefit in their growth and fruitfulness when they are planted "by streams of water" (Ps 1:3) or even in marshy soil. Other plants require high mountains that are stony and arid in order to ensure that they are always green. There are plants that when they are set out have to be frequently watered, but less so as they grow up, and afterward rarely at all. But other plants require continual watering through their lifetimes.

(8) In summary, as superior virtue has more power from its nature or from good habits or from another source of strength that comes from above, then all the more easily can such virtue direct inferior and instrumental powers, even though they resist through their own weight or by perverse corruption. And so the wise man says, "The body that is corrupted burdens the soul" (Wis 9:15). This weight is increased if excessive consumption, drunkenness, and the cares of this world are joined. For just as the spirit of the virtuous person, who has contracted fortitude by God's gift and long exercise, is weakened if the body is burdened by food, drink, or excessive cares, so too all rational functions are completely shaken and disturbed beyond measure in a person who is less spiritually inclined or trained.

(9) Similarly, the untrained sailor is at a loss if the waves mount up so that he feels the ship now rising to heaven and now descending into the abyss (cf. Ps 106:26).[85] But the experienced and trained captain will remain unperturbed and practice the art of navigation with a steadfast mind. And so it is good that the Apostle insists, "Whoever abstains from food, let him not despise

the one who does eat" (Rom 14:3). And so in other matters understand that one acts rightly or wrongly according to a variety of circumstances.

The eleventh consideration shows how we are to concentrate in silence on pious forms of meditation that generate affectivity. It shows through probable reasoning that this procedure is worth more than concentration on reading or conversation. Moreover, it provides a procedure for meditation that arises especially from the emotions. This consideration gives several other good points necessary for this activity in terms of the effort involved.

(1) They are deceived who want always either to read or to pray aloud or to receive devotional encouragement from those who speak to them. Such people are wrong to believe that in this way the familiar grace of contemplation will appear to them as the companion of such activities. Such pursuits are profitable, but they are not enough. For if such persons sometimes feel remorse because of what they read or hear, then if you take away the book or the spoken word, the compunction that accompanied it also will disappear. Similarly, it will return when the book or the spoken word returns.

(2) Therefore it is necessary "in silence to await God's salvation" (Lam 3:26). A person should grow accustomed to praying in spirit and in mind (1 Cor 14:15), so that both the disturbance of talking and the need to look at a book are eliminated. The silent meditation itself should be his book and his sermon. He has to be careful so that he is not always trying to learn and never attaining wisdom (cf. 2 Tm 3:7).

(3) I know that some oppose this point of view and complain that they neither know their spirit nor are they able to get into contact with it through silence and meditation. It flies away, they say, immediately, carrying itself now here, now there. It slips quickly away unless held under constraint within the boundaries of reading or sermonizing. This is clearly what we have been saying. That is why to be with oneself is to be with oneself in silence, in keeping the spirit within. "This is the task; here is our effort."[86]

We insist that this goal be sought with all the energy of our affections. Sit alone and lift yourself beyond yourself, if you can (Lam 3:28). If you have been trying to do so for a long time but cannot, do not then quickly flee to the solace of reading or conversation, after you have given up on meditation.

(4) Let silence tire you out and let yourself become heavy with it (Jb 7:20). Because of this feeling you may think that it is a waste of time for you to keep silence. But wait: you will see that if you insist on waiting, you will overcome this weariness. You will avoid a situation in which the practice of immediately interrupting silence provides nourishment to the squeamish person, but not consolation. Your sense of fatigue will perhaps cease for a while but will return more harshly, as a dog who has been driven away later returns to a juicy bone.

(5) Why is there, alas, such a paucity of contemplatives, even among learned and religious churchmen, indeed even among theologians, unless because scarcely anyone is able to bear being alone with himself long enough so that he can come to meditate? And so, before the mind scarcely has had time to grow lukewarm in its meditation, either reading or conversation or exercises of this type are sought. They are sufficient to keep us from sinning. In a certain way such activities seem to restore us from a sense of lassitude in order vainly to keep the mind from fatigue. But the mind is not tired out as you think, for in the end God will have mercy on you, if you persevere, if you pray, if you seek and knock (Lk 11:8; Mt 7:9).

(6) Now that we have spoken of silence, we can pass over to pious meditations. Let us see what kind are most efficacious for engendering affective attachment. I doubt very much that we would be able to provide a universal formula for such a result. For as the Comic says, "There are just as many opinions as there are heads to be counted."[87] There are no less "just as many" ways of meditating, since we do not live according to one single vow.[88] Nevertheless, from so great an assembly, we can collect some procedures that provide help in giving rise to the emotion of fear.

(7) And so it was said truthfully and admirably, "The beginning of knowledge," meaning savory knowledge, "is the fear of

the Lord" (Ps 110:10; Sir 1:16). But since fear can immediately collapse into despair, we have to associate hope with it. Thus Bernard, *On the Song of Songs*, Richard of Saint Victor, *On the Twelve Patriarchs*, Hugh of Saint Victor, *On the Power of Prayer*, and almost all others we see as beginning in this manner.[89] This is surely so because "the Lord is pleased with those who fear him and with those who have hope in his mercy" (Ps 146:11). They sing to him of mercy and justice (Ps 100:1).

(8) But someone might object that it was said above that love is the beginning and root of any other affection.[90] If then love has not come first, how will fear and hope enter? But one thing is the love of God that is imperfect and remains in wonder before him. Faith in the existence of God is enough to engender such a love. This love precedes the other affections and, above all, faith, which moreover is secure in its certitude. Some people have contended concerning this love that without a preceding or concomitant knowledge, it cannot be brought to a good, as it were offering itself to the soul as its primary object. Similarly in the hierarchy of angels the Seraphim is prior to the Cherubim. This is contained in the book whose opening is "the roads to Zion weep."[91] Another fervent love is found that is ecstatic and perfect, able to join the lover with the beloved. This love can only be obtained after many other forms of affectivity have preceded it. The soul must first have its senses completely purified in their deepest dimension.

(9) In this purification from the feverish languor of an infecting sin, what is it that is more effective than "this fear of the Lord that drives out sin" (Sir 1:27) and makes the flesh tremble (Ps 118:120), meaning affections of the flesh? This fear neglects nothing. It provides consolation for the blessed who mourn (Mt 5:5). From this fear is conceived the spirit of salvation, which, together with other forms of virtue, scripture hands over to the blessed.

(10) This fear is usually divided by teachers into an original type, a mercenary one, and a filial fear. The original type tries to escape punishment; the mercenary one is afraid of losing reward; while filial fear is afraid only of being separated from the beloved.

(11) Do you wish to hear a meditation in fear? "I shall meditate," says the king, "as the dove" (Is 38:14). In what do you think the dove's meditation consists, except in complaint or sighing, which fear itself brings on? Thus perhaps another king will say, "Who will give to me the wings of a dove, that I might fly away and be at rest?" (Ps 54:7).[92] "Fear that goes on foot takes on wings," says another.[93]

(12) Thus in the image of the dove we can make meditations that are suitable for fear and to accompany hope. Let us say that this mystical dove is the soul. For thus God deigns to call the soul in the Song of Songs (Sg 2:10, 14; 5:3; 6:8). It has matching wings, the right ones of hope and the left of fear, so that it can fly up, and it is steered by a tail of discretion. Each wing, ten in number according to their makeup, bears "feathers covered with silver" (Ps 67:14), the silver of sacred eloquence. These make meditation possible, those on the left with fear, those on the right with hope. Each feather is made up of many little feathers positioned so that particular meditations can be taken from each of them. Finally, each wing supports this dove, as it were, with an equal weight, so that neither the wing of fear can pull it down into despair, nor the wing of hope lift it too high with presumption.

(13) Feathers are therefore placed in the left wing of fear. These are small feathers, according to their different positions. *Divine severity*: for this there are as many little feathers as there are examples of divine severity, as in the fall of the angels, that of Adam, the destruction of people in the flood, or that of Sodom, the calamity of the ungrateful servant and of Judas, and thence the cross of Christ, the judgment of the world, where few will be elect.

The endlessness of damnation: this has as many little feathers as there are different types of torments. There are inextinguishable fire, worms, filth, horrors, cries, shrieking, and weeping, and then hissing and cold, a multitude of tortures, the worst company, all things beyond understanding and with no end, the removal of all hope, which is something to be feared beyond all else, and the worst penalty in the absence of the vision of God.

The enormity of sin: there are as many little feathers as there are

325

sins committed, with circumstances making them all the more serious. *The individual's sense of weakness*: there are as many little feathers as there are dangers of future lapses into sin until death. *Seductive prosperity*: as many little feathers are found as occasions of sin in good times because of pride and luxury and the like. *Crushing adversity*: as many feathers are there as occasions for anger, disorder, and vindictiveness. *Familiar enmity*: it has as many little feathers as impure temptations that rise up out of the flesh.

The perversity of the demon: as many little feathers are here as tricks and traps set by demons. *Iniquity toward the living*: as many little feathers as lack of gratitude and scandals against one's neighbors, and especially those that arise against family members, benefactors, and dependents. *Cruelty toward the dead*: as many little feathers as loved ones who remain in torment or are kept from glory because we neglect what we promised to offer for them.

(14) On the right side follows the wing of hope, in proportion to the small and large feathers of fear. *Divine mercy*: there are as many small feathers as there are witnesses to divine mercy, as the glorified state of the angels, the salvation of Adam, of Noah, Lot, David, Peter, Paul, the good thief, Mary Magdalene (Lk 7:36–50), the Canaanite woman (Mt 15:22–28), the prodigal son (Lk 15:11–32), and the adulterous woman (Jn 8:1–11). Christ is savior, guarding over his elect through his holy angels. *Incomprehensible glory*: there are as many little feathers as there are gifts of soul and of body. *The grace of penance*: as many little feathers as there are acts of penance that are made for sins. *The continuous support of God*: there are as many little feathers as there are forms of assistance by God through virtues, gifts, beatitudes, through the sacrament of the Eucharist, which is most efficacious for this goal, through penance and the like. *Comforting joy*: there are as many feathers as there are acts of humility made in prosperity for the opportunity to do good for others. *Instructive sadness*: as many little feathers as benefits in adversity, when it is borne with fortitude. *Free will*: there are as many feathers as the number of ways by which free will can subjugate the flesh. *The good will of angels and of saints*: there are as many feathers as ways in which all male and female saints help us. *The help of the living*: there are as many wings as ways by which we aid the living

and are assisted by them. *Offerings for the dead*: there are as many wings as ways by which we help the dead and are helped by them.

(15) They who are eager to learn can follow this model in its fullness by daily exercise in meditations, according to what can be deduced at length in what is scattered throughout the entire body of Holy Scripture. They can, moreover, make corresponding wings for other affections. For the love of God and neighbor, they can provide for themselves meditations that lead to this goal. In order to hate sin, they can count the reasons in respect to God and neighbor why we ought to hate sin. On all these matters there is an abundance of materials in *The Summa of Vices and Virtues*, which is quite useful in the manner of its composition.[94] There is no doubt that meditations for the sake of fear will bring us to hate sin, just as those to engender hope will help us in the love of God and neighbor.

(16) Take on for yourself these "wings at daybreak" (Ps 138:9), meaning in vigilance. For as soon as you come to feel the love of divine illumination, like the dawn, radiating on the territory of your soul, then you will dwell "in the most distant parts of the sea" (Ps 138:9). You will, as it were, be on a shore that is secure amid the flow of thoughts and the agitation of desires. Even if your own efforts will not lead you there, the hand of the Lord will lead you and his right hand will hold you (Ps 138:10). You will say: "Perhaps the darkness will cover me," because it means forgetfulness of everything here below in its fog. The night over the lower world will be "my illumination in delights" (Ps 138:11) in the understanding that comes over you.

(17) Be careful, then, that unfaithfulness not remove those wings, nor despair cause them to go up in smoke, or lack of energy congeal them, avarice tie them together, lust burn them up, or gluttony weigh them down.

The twelfth consideration shows that the spirit must turn away from phantasms. It shows according to metaphysics that this can be done in various ways. Then it returns to greater matters that the grace of example brings into fulfillment.

(1) We must here remember those considerations we had when we dealt with the quiddity or meaning of mystical theology.[95] We showed that mystical theology is ecstatic love that leads to the understanding of its spirit. This understanding completely lacks any clouds of phantasms. Therefore it is necessary that a person who wants to be devoted to mystical theology try to attain this pure intelligence. Otherwise, how will such a person obtain the love that follows from it?

(2) Again, if we are to deal here with metaphysics, it is profitable to consider how the entire sensible world enters into the rational soul through the senses of the body. Through a kind of intelligible and most beautiful circle, this world, which is derived from God, is brought back to him. Therefore, whatever objects come forth from him and the further they proceed from him in imperfection, then the more fully they are found to be material and by a certain density belong more to what is bodily. This is apparent in the elements and in their mixtures. For we see in a ray of sun that it constantly grows thicker, as we would say, when it merges itself in a denser medium and in a certain way embodies itself in colors.

(3) But the converse situation takes place in the return to God. Matter passes away more and more into a form of spirituality. For example: light with the appearances of colors is brought to the eyes. These species then are regenerated and brought to a common center for the senses.[96] This discriminates among them and attenuates them with greater spirituality and purity so that they become imaginative power. But when reason is dealing with phantasms, it draws forth intelligible species, through which it conceives of an object without the phantasm that preceded it. Finally, a superior intellective potency, which we call spirit or mind, reaches, after cognition in the reason, the same object in the light of pure and simple intelligence. In doing so, spirit attains an order accessing on angelic cognition.

(4) If we want to go further, we can look at holy Dionysius, who was taught by Paul in the awareness of heavenly secrets. Dionysius, together with his interpreters, dealt with the mystical life. We will find that he showed how one can turn away from

bodily phantasms. In the negation of all things that can either be sensed or imagined or understood, the spirit brings itself through love into the divine darkness, where God is known ineffably and extra-mentally. He gives an example of a sculptor who makes a statue. The sculptor removes segments of wood or stone and forms a most beautiful statue, that is an image, solely by a process of removal.[97]

(5) In like manner the spirit removes through abnegation everything it can here know and whatever provides imperfection in terms of potentiality, dependence, privation, or changeableness. Finally, when everything has been removed, the spirit finds the image of God[98]: knowledge, as it were, of his completely actualized being without any potentiality, of his supreme power without dependence, of his purity without privation, of his necessary being without changeableness.

(6) But truly it would be very much worth consideration and inquiry whether that knowledge is only experimental in the highest affectivity united to God through love, or if it can be called intellectual, and not intuitive but abstractive knowledge, and not only connotative but absolute knowledge.[99] For each part has its own most lofty defenders.[100]

(7) There are those who in commenting on Dionysius maintain the first point of view. Others say that beyond the previously mentioned experimental or experimentative knowledge, a proper intellective concept can be reached. It is an absolute, and not an intuition, of the divine being, if from that being all imperfection is removed and abstracted. The same is true of the life, the goodness, the wisdom, the power, and similar predicated forms of perfection in God.

(8) An abstraction is made from the general concept of man that has been perceived concerning the position, movement, shape, and other accidental considerations on the exterior. And so there comes about what is the image of the man. This is the specific and absolute concept of man. In like manner, judgment is made concerning being, when its abstraction, which is being itself, is removed from any potentiality, deprivation, dependence,

or any other imperfection. Thus there results a concept of God that is appropriate and absolute.

(9) The argument is added that God responded to this concept as his proper name when he said to Moses, "You will say that He Who Is sent me to you" (Ex 3:14). It is affirmed that there is something similar to this view in the concept of goodness, as Christ who replies in the New Law, "Only God is good" (Mt 19:17). Augustine seems to be close to this point of view in many ways, especially in the eighth book of *On the Trinity*, where he shows how he was brought to an awareness of the absolute good.[101] Bonaventure follows him in his *Soul's Journey into God*, chapter six.[102]

(10) But see how in some way, I know not how, in dealing with the practical side of mystical theology, I fall back into its speculative dimension. But this is not superfluous. For it is necessary for you, my soul, that you seek to be brought into God through anagogical ecstasy, so that you can learn to turn yourself aside from phantasms. This you do through an innate abstractive power, just as an inferior abstractive power in brute creatures enables them to distinguish insensate from sensate species. And so you will know how to discern what is imperfect from what is perfect, so that finally a pure perfection will shine forth for you in essence and goodness.

(11) But let us speak for the less learned in metaphysics or theology, and we might say, if we can, in what manner or by what effort of observation the spirit can turn itself from phantasms while it seeks anagogical or extra-mental ecstasy. And perhaps this can be done if, in every thought and meditation on God, a person by no means stops in his cognition but aspires through affective power. He does so, as it were, with the mouth of the heart, which stands gaping before God's own power, wisdom, and goodness in order to savor and taste them. The person, as it were, perceives him who is "terrible in his counsels over the sons of men" (Ps 65:5), in the majesty of his power that rules and judges, "great" and admirable, in "whose wisdom there is no number" (Ps 146:5), and finally gentle and wholly desirable and truly lovable in his goodness and in "the torrent of his delights" (Ps 35:9).

(12) There will come to a person who is making this effort a great crowd of phantasms. I believe that these phantasms will rudely rush in and burst in on both your interior eyes. You must cast them away from you with fortitude and with all your strength, using the hand of devotion. Once the phantasm's head has been driven out, you must strive to escape it and be free. Otherwise, you can proceed as if these phantasms have gone into hiding and been spurned. Then in the midst of your journey, you can eagerly attack this unclean spirit. A spiritual thirst will goad you on. "As the deer yearns," being on all sides exposed to the attacks of dogs and running until it overheats, it seeks cool and safe "flowing streams" (Ps 41:3). Similarly, you must strive against the phantasms that hinder you, so that, warmed by the Holy Spirit's moisture, you also can say, "My soul longs for you, God; my soul thirsts for God," fountain of life. "When shall I come and appear before the face of God" (Ps 41:3)?

(13) But know that the instrument of fear must purge you through the most complete and genuine penance. Your mind must be cleansed from the dross of sin and shine forth pure through its reformation in newness of spirit according to the two first acts of divine hierarchy, which are to purge and to illuminate. Otherwise it will be completely "in vain that you get up before dawn" to reach this height of perfection (Ps 126:2).

"Get up," then, "you who eat the bread of toil" (Ps 126:2). This is the fear without which none can be justified before God (Sir 1:28). How can you dare in your impurity to rush forward to the kiss of the mouth (Sg 1:1), if you have not first taken care to bathe his feet with tears (Lk 7:38) and also to give thanks in kissing his hands?[103]

(14) Truly the mind must get to this place in being completely aware of God and purified, so that it thinks neither of its own enjoyment nor anything else, whether servile or mercenary. The mind will not find in God anything harsh, hostile, self-occupied, or agitated, as with a judge who requites or punishes. This one thing alone then comes into the mind, that he is wholly desirable, "sweet and gentle" (Ps 85:5), completely deserving of love, "even if he should kill" (Jb 13:15). He is most worthy, for only the

matter of love pleases him. Then fly securely into the embraces of the Bridegroom and draw tightly to yourself with the purest arms of friendship that divine breast. Place upon him the most chaste kisses of a peace that "surpasses all understanding" (Phil 4:7). Then you can say in the devotion of gratefulness and love, "My beloved is mine, and I am his" (Sg 2:16).

Here end the considerations or little books of mystical theology of the venerable Jean Gerson, once chancellor of the church of Paris, made by him in the year of the Lord 1407, and edited or reviewed and approved by him, as he wrote with his own hand in the exemplar. This treatise he sent to the Grande Chartreuse from the city of Lyon, in the year of our Lord 1427.

List of Some Teachers Who Have Spoken of Contemplation

The great Dionysius, who was taught by Paul, seems to be the first who dealt with this theology in a speculative manner, in his *On Mystical Theology*. He very often inserted it into his other books.[104]

The venerable Richard of Saint Victor was apparently the first after Dionysius who took this material, which was given to him by others in praise or warning, and brought it together in the manner of an art and teaching in his *On the Mystical Ark*.[105] All his other writings have the taste or resonance of nothing else but contemplation.

Cassian, in his *Collations of the Fathers*, especially that concerning charity.[106]

Augustine, in his *On True Religion*,[107] and his *Confessions*, and *On Loving God*,[108] and in his *On the Trinity*,[109] and elsewhere in a great many places, as through his entire *Commentary on the Psalter*.[110]

Climacus, in his book *On the Thirty Steps of the Ladder*.[111]

Gregory, scattered through his *Moral Commentary on Job*,[112] especially in the sixth book, and in his third *Homily on Ezekiel*.[113]

Bernard, *On the Song of Songs, On Loving God*, and *To the Brothers of Mont-Dieu*, and elsewhere.[114]

Hugh [of Saint Victor], in *On Noah's Ark*,[115] and *On Prayer*,[116] and *Commentary on Ecclesiastes*, especially in the prologue,[117] and *On the Celestial Hierarchy*,[118] especially the seventh chapter, and elsewhere.

Bonaventure, in his *The Soul's Journey*,[119] the whole of which was composed with a wonderful and most learned skill, and in his *The Goad of Love*.[120]

There are other treatises compiled more recently, as *The Goad of Love to the Passion of Christ*,[121] and another book on the triple path, whose beginning is *The Roads to Zion Weep*,[122] and another *On the New World*,[123] one on *The Seven Paths of Eternity*,[124] and one on *The Spiritual Espousals*, whose third part is suspect.[125]

Finally, there are some writings in the vernacular, and some sermons to the clergy, and smaller treatises, but it is not our task to list all of them here.

On Distinguishing True from False Revelations[1]

COVERING LETTER: JEAN GERSON TO HIS BROTHER NICOLAS[2]

Sent from Paris at the beginning of 1402

*L*ately I edited one of my lessons on how the Carthusians abstain from meat and sent it to them.[3] Now I have done the same in preparing another text and send it to you, my dear brother. This treatise opens with a certain image, that of the genuine coin of divine revelation, which can be distinguished from the counterfeit coin of diabolical trickery. The angel of Satan is not to deceive us by transfiguring himself into an angel of life. Instead, we are to test whether spirits are from God, and we are to keep to what is good, obeying the Apostle (1 Thes 5:21). This teaching, however useful it is to every Christian, is especially helpful, even necessary, for men dedicated to the religious life and to contemplation. For this path the heavenly Father has chosen you.

Be well, brother of my heart, in him who faithfully guards you and through whom I strongly desire the good of your Celestine fathers and brothers. I commend myself to their prayers and wish that what I hand over to you be held in common by them. I hope that my writings may become useful for you all.

Here then begins the treatise.

John was baptizing in the desert (Mk 1:4). In this phrase John the Precursor is recommended in three ways: from the reputation expressed in the name, John, which is interpreted as God's grace. From grace he begins. Only those of good reputation are called such. Second, John is recommended by the virtue of his activity, which is that of baptizing. In the third place, from the fitting setting, in the desert. Concerning his name, it seems that it was revealed from heaven, according to the version provided in Luke (1:13). And this is no small praise, to have a name "the mouth of the Lord has given" (Is 62:2) and that comes through an angel, and an angel such as Gabriel. Thereby can be seen the wondrous future perfection of his life, since he was given a miraculous name to indicate or prefigure this future. Otherwise the performance of a miracle in giving him his name would have been in vain, if it had not in reality indicated something magnificent and beyond the normal course of nature.

But let the curious questioner immediately interrupt and ask how it is known that this prophecy of his name was an angelic act rather than a diabolical illusion. Indeed, the angel of Satan according to the Apostle sometimes transforms himself into an angel of light (2 Cor 11:14). And this is the matter of doubt that was touched upon in my last treatise and delayed for another occasion, so that one can distinguish between angelic revelations and demonic illusions.[4] Concerning this matter, we can say first of all that as the true expression of religion comes under attack through heretics' sophistical and false arguments, so too lying angels try to abrogate the authority of true and holy revelations through sophistical deeds and the trickery of magicians.

As Saint Peter says to Clement of his journey, "Why is this so?"[5] It takes place so that men thereby might be led away from the knowledge of spiritual truth that has been handed over through the medium of miracles or revelations, when they see that similar means are being used to bring them to falsehood. We can also say that there is for human beings no general rule or method that can be given always and infallibly to distinguish between revelations that are true and those that are false or deceptive. If this were possible, we would not have to have only faith in our prophets, and consequently in our religion, for we would have the certitude of what was evident. Anyone who knew in this way that something was revealed by God or by his angel would be able to know its truth by a means other than by faith alone. Similarly, if someone had clear knowledge in order to refute those who sin against the truth of the faith and attack it with fallacies and arguments, such a person would have not only certain knowledge from faith, but also evident knowledge from demonstration of the articles of faith.[6]

It should thus be clear that an orthodox person does not need to try to obtain a complete and clear explanation for why the name of John was given in advance to Zechariah. Nor should he try to explain how this angelic revelation can be proven or known. This is a matter of faith, not of knowledge. And since the Apostle says that faith is not your own doing but is a gift of God [Eph 2:8], thus not everyone can distinguish a true from a false revelation. People can either spurn the true revelation and embrace a false one, or with sacrilegious impiety and incredulity, they can deny, castigate, and reject such things.

There is, nevertheless, another question, concerning how we the faithful, presupposing what belongs to faith, can come to know and to test whether spirits are from God (1 Jn 4:1), so that we not be deceived. In dealing with this question I have come across many illusions that have characterized our times. Even in the old age of the world, in this final hour, just before the Antichrist comes, the world is like a senile old man, which lets itself indulge in many fantasies and illusions that are like dreams.[7] Many say, "I am Christ," and leaving the truth, they turn to fables and seduce many. I have heard about a number of people that they were told for a fact that they would be future popes. Among them was a certain well-educated and well-known man who wrote such a thing in his own hand and whose writings I have read. He tried to make his assertion in many arguments and conjectures.[8]

Concerning another learned man of the same type, I heard that he was first persuaded that he would be pope, then Antichrist, and finally that if he was not Antichrist, at least he would be Antichrist's precursor. In the end he was violently tempted to kill himself, to avoid being the one who brought such great harm to the Christian people. Finally, through God's mercy

he came to a saner state of mind, and he wrote about these matters to instruct and warn others. But concerning many others who
follow lives of religion and austerity, incredible things have been
written down, which I have come to know from reliable witnesses.

If someone comes who claims to have had a revelation of the
type that Zechariah and other prophets in sacred history are
known to have received, what are we to do, and how are we to
act? If we immediately deny everything or ridicule the matter or
accuse the person, we will seem to weaken the authority of
divine revelation, which is just as powerful now as it once was.
God's hand has not been restricted so that it cannot show new
revelations. We will scandalize, moreover, ordinary people[9] if we
say that our revelations and prophecies can be falsehoods and
that they are but fantasies and illusions. We are obliged to find a
middle way. According to the witness of the Apostle John, we are
not to believe every spirit, but we are to test whether spirits are
from God (1 Jn 4:1). Obeying the Apostle we will hold fast to
what is good (1 Thes 5:21).

We are to be like spiritual moneychangers or merchants. With
skill and care we examine the precious and unfamiliar coin of
divine revelation, in order to find out whether demons, who
strive to corrupt and counterfeit any divine and good coin, smug-
gle in a false and base coin instead of the true and legitimate
one. In doing so they cause no small loss for the church's income
or treasury but also the imperial treasury of God. All the more
as a coin is more precious and quite rare, so too are acts of heroic
deeds and supernatural visitations. Just as all the more caution
and vigilance are to be shown in distinguishing among them, so
too all the greater is the loss when we fail to do so.

Since this metaphor is quite suitable for showing in a concrete
manner what we intend, we will continue to use it, saying first
that the one who investigates this spiritual coin ought to be a theologian who is trained by education and experience. He should
not be the kind of person who is an eternal student that never
comes to the knowledge of the truth, since he is wordy, garru-
lous, impudent, always making trouble and living in a bad way,
more given over to feasting and wine tasting rather than judging

his own actions carefully and conscientiously.[10] For such a person every mention of religious devotion is a fable or a bore. In the end his way of life, which cannot lie, blasphemes against and contradicts anything that his grandiloquent tongue trumpets forth. For such moneychangers, any coin of divine revelation is so obscure and foreign that when it is brought to them, they immediately reject it with a derisive laugh and great anger, ridiculing it and dismissing it.

There are others, I admit, who rush into the opposite vice. They ascribe to revelation even superstitious, vain, and illusory deeds and dreams of mad people, and they believe in the portents made up by those who are mentally ill or in depressed states of mind.[11] For such people the heart is too prone to believe, while for others it is too hard and harsh to be moved, and so I know that what Ovid said is absolutely right: "You are safest if you take the middle way."[12]

This coin of spiritual revelation, like gold, is to be examined mainly on five points: weight, flexibility or malleability, durability, conformability, and color. This can be done in accord with the five virtues from which the evidence is taken for legitimate spiritual coin. Humility provides weight; discretion malleability; patience durability; truth conformability; charity provides color. We read that Mary had these five virtues from the revelation the angel made to her. Similarly, we conclude from the account of the gospel of Luke, chapter 1, where the name of John was revealed, that Zechariah and Elizabeth also had these virtues.

Thus, insofar as the first sign is concerned, if you know anyone who because of arrogant curiosity and vain praise and presumption of sanctity is eager to have unusual revelations, if he thinks himself to be worthy of them and delights in boastful telling of such matters, then know that he deserves to be fooled. Do not pay attention if he affirms in boast that he has had some revelation or other. In his case the weight of humility is lacking. We have, moreover, many stories about the holy Fathers, concerning their careful attention to humility. To one of them a demon appeared, transformed not only into an angel of light but into Christ himself. He said that he had come into this world so that the Father would see and adore him. The holy Father remained lost in thought for a while, like the Virgin Mary. Thinking what this greeting could mean, he said to himself, "Do I not daily adore Christ? What can be the meaning of such an apparition?" Then taking refuge in humility, he said to the demon: "Consider to whom it is you have been sent, for I am not worthy to see Christ in this life." When these words were said in so humble a manner, the demon left, confused and shamed. Another Father shut his eyes in a similar manner: "I do not wish," he said, "to see Christ on earth. I will be happy to see him in heaven."[13] Also Saint Martin, from the arrogant dress of the demon, recognized the falsehood of diabolical speech in the one who said he was Christ.[14] It is therefore a most healthy counsel against the illusions of demons to take into account the weight of humility, and to consider oneself in terms of intellect and affectivity to be the most unworthy among all people to receive a revelation or ever be visited miraculously by God.

If such extraordinary revelations should happen to come to a person, then he should reject them with holy, humble, and diffident modesty. Such a person should think of such matters as resulting from an injury done to the imagination and should worry about being ill in the way that insane, manic, or depressive people are. Or the person is to fear that because of the enormity of previous sins, this revelation has been given in order to condemn him, so that he will be seduced by such falsities. If such things are machinations of the devil or temptations, then they will disappear in the face of such humility. But if God wants us to be tested in bearing them, they will not harm us. And if it is genuine divine revelation and not a figment of the imagination, this humility that gently rejects what has happened will better prepare us for receiving it. The person will deserve to hear the words, "Friend, go up higher" (Lk 14:10). This will happen all the more when the person is trying to take a seat in the lower place. You can read in the book of Exodus how often Moses rejected the divine order that he be sent to Pharaoh: "I beg you, Lord," he said, "send whom you will send, etc." (Ex 4:13). And Jeremiah cried out, "A, a, a, Lord God: I do not know how to speak, for I am a child" (Jer 1:6). Also John the Baptist did not dare touch the holy head of Christ but kept himself at a distance, saying: "I ought to be baptized by you, etc." (Mt 3:14). Likewise, the Apostle Paul placed himself first among sinners. "I am not worthy," he said, "to be called an apostle" (1 Cor 15:9). And if anyone should object that the Apostle boastfully made known and divulged his revelations, the holy doctors, including John Chrysostom, answer in this way: It is acceptable when it is necessary to counsel or aid one's listeners to make known one's secret graces or to make public one's powers.[15] This reaction is not the same as displaying empty glory in such revelations without doing any good for oneself or for others.

Thus the Virgin Mary, who treasured all words, keeping them in her heart (Lk 2:19), afterward conveyed to the apostles, especially to Luke, the sacred mysteries that had been given to her alone. She did so not to boast but to build up the church and religion. Otherwise she would not have held herself back for a long time, since every vice is impatient.

We have yet another example in Saint Bernard, who so often insisted that a person hide his virtues, even from his dearest and closest friends, rather than acting as others who try to hide their vices. But he did not think it to be pride that he not only openly spoke a great deal of his gifts and graces obtained through contemplation but also wrote of them.[16] How can this be so? It is because vanity did not force him to act in this manner, but charity. Deep in the soil of humility he planted the root of virtue, so that it would not be ripped up by the wind of bragging.

This charity and the requirement of edification absolve Saint Paul from any suspicion of presumption. He felt compelled to make known the weight of his authority because of false apostles who had appeared and were claiming glory for themselves. Even when he praises himself, there is much humility and recognition of his own weakness and ignorance. "Whether it was in the body," he says, "or outside the body, I do not know. God knows" (2 Cor 12:2). Again: "I am made a fool, etc." (2 Cor 12:11).

Thus to make known a revelation in itself is not arrogant or prideful. The fault lies in doing so in an empty way, with vanity, and with no benefit in terms of edification or guidance for others. It is shameful to allow a puffed-up mind to let go of the wind of boasting with which it is full.[17] It is wrong to titillate the prurient ears of bystanders with the curious tales of such vanities.

Even if this kind of loquacity does not create difficulties, it still consumes something great and invaluable, for time is wasted in this useless activity. And so it is quite relevant whether the subject of the revelation is useful for morals, for society, for the honor or increase of religion, or if it is full of empty matters or tales. Thus in secular histories and human acts we find that a man can praise himself without the fault of boasting, so long as he has to do so for his own defense. When Cicero gave a speech so that he not be driven into exile, he recalled how he had saved Rome, as well as other outstanding deeds of his consulship.[18] Thus Scipio Africanus laid claim to his triumph in subjecting Carthage. He did so to defend himself against his accusers.[19] In both cases there can be no charge of boasting.

It is of central importance whether one be a novice or a veteran in the exercise of virtue, for when virtue is formed, it can be knocked down by the slightest breeze, while virtue that has been established can stand up because of its own stability. You have in these matters some clarification of the first sign. Through it we can distinguish the spiritual coin of true revelation from the false one of diabolical illusion. The sign is the weight of humility.

Is this weight not present in the revelation made to Zechariah and Elizabeth on the naming of John? Read the story and you will see that neighbors and relatives called the boy by the name of the father, Zechariah, for the parents had not indulged in talkative and vain curiosity in spreading the news of the boy's name. Necessity alone forced them to say it when the boy was to be given his name at the circumcision (Lk 1:57–64). But also Elizabeth distinguished herself with holy, humble, and shy modesty when she went into hiding for six months.[20] And Zechariah is also shown to have had such great humility that at the word and sight of the angel he was struck dumb and frozen with fear and so scarcely believed what it told him (Lk 1:12, 20).

We should nevertheless add what Saint Gregory states in the

First Book of his *Dialogues*, that true humility is not stubborn but is tempered with fear, as he tells of a certain Libertinus, who was asked to raise a child from the dead and subjected to an oath for refusing to do so. There would have been no power in the heart, he said, if charity had not ruled it.[21] Clearly it is an indication not of humility but of pride in self-estimation if someone claiming to be humble spurns a church authority that is ordering one to do something difficult. For no one would react in such a way if he did not think himself wise in his own eyes and counted on his own prudence rather than the judgment of his superior. Such a person is not prepared to be subjected to the superior's judgment, good sense, and will. You can now see how lack of courage also arises from pride.

Gregory adds as a rule that miraculous deeds and humility are two signs that are sufficient to show the sanctity of a person.[22] Miracles in themselves are not enough, since God's just judgment permits the evil to perform them for the sake of the church. The mind that is filled with the divine spirit, says Gregory, has its own signs as the clearest evidence of its condition, and these are truth and humility. If both of these meet in one mind, then it is apparent that they bear testimony to the presence of the Holy Spirit. It still matters a great deal, however, whether the miracle is performed in order to bear witness to the true faith or to show the sanctity of a person. For even the evil can perform miracles of the first kind, as is written in Matthew (7:22), for truth can be spoken by any spirit and be from the Holy Spirit, and evil does not overcome it. But the operation of miracles in order to show someone's sanctity cannot take place for the evil without the clear and total rejection of the act by God. Otherwise God would be a false witness to a lie. Why is this so? Since God would then be attaching the seal of his own hand, meaning his power, to deeds that can be performed by him alone, to faked letters of pretended sanctity. He would make no objection. This phrase "no objection" is added because of the miracles of Antichrist, which some claim will be true in order to test the elect and seduce the damned. Nevertheless, Antichrist will be full of lies in making miracles and will live the most sinful of

342

lives. But so that Antichrist and his miracles not be believed, God through his own innumerable prophecies, as well as those of others, has uttered his objection and contradicted Antichrist. Therefore no one will have any excuse to believe in Antichrist.

The second sign for genuine spiritual currency is the discretion that provides flexibility. By this trait I understand a readiness to believe in that counsel which is the daughter of humility. You might happen to see someone following the example of Zechariah and Elizabeth and taking the royal road with a simple heart in all the just works of God. Such a person has no desire to walk with great or miraculous signs that are beyond him. He keeps to the middle ground in following the rules of life instituted by the fathers, nor does he transgress the boundaries his fathers made. Do not believe that such a person is easily fooled by the deceits of demons, for you see how he believes in good advice and maintains moderation of discretion in all other matters.

There are, however, others who take delight in following their own opinions and walk in their own inventions. A most dangerous leader guides them. More precisely, their own opinions compel them. They vex themselves beyond measure with fasts; they overextend their vigils; they tax and weaken their brains with excessive tears. In all these observances they have no faith in the warnings of others; also, they do not follow advice that they behave in more temperate manner. They do not take care in listening to or receiving counsel from the learned who are skilled in the law of God. Such people scorn the advice the learned give. Instead, because they have persuaded themselves that they are doing something magnificent, they think they know better than anyone else what is best to do. Of such persons I say that they will quickly fall for every demoniacal illusion. They will quickly become stuck on the rock of transgression, for they are caught in their blind haste and excessive speed. Therefore, be suspicious of any unusual revelations such people might pronounce.

A few months ago I was at Arras and heard of a certain married woman with children who sometimes for two days, sometimes for four or more, remained without food. For this reason many admired her. I arranged to speak with her. I questioned her at length and found that this abstinence was not a form of sobriety but showed empty and proud pertinacity. After such fasting, when she was drained by a terrible hunger, she would eat with unspeakable voracity. The woman could not produce any convincing reason why she acted in this way, except to say that she was unworthy to eat food. She also admitted that she had never received from her confessor or anyone else a rule of life. For more than six months she had not received the counsel or absolution of any confessor.

I admit that I was filled with fear and horror. Hiding my true feelings, I nevertheless began to point out that these are the traps of the demon, and that she was dangerously close to insanity. She had a frantic look on her face and her color was like that of someone close to death. I asked if she knew anyone whose authority, trustworthiness, and prudence were of greater weight and reputation with her than the judgment she herself made. She answered with a moan and sigh, with her eyes down on the ground, that she was a wretch, a sinner, and more ignorant and unlettered than anyone else.

I continued in my questioning: If she really felt this way about herself, how could she maintain a form of abstinence without the advice of someone else and do something so unusual and not regulated by others, who were holier and stronger than she was? She began to make up some vague answers, which I cannot remember. Although she could not avoid the question, humility was missing in her. Her attitude betrayed an element of arrogance, so that she was embarrassed to concede her defeat. Finally I insisted, in good faith and in view of the greatest danger for her soul and body, that she give up this foolish obstinacy in fasting. Without the counsel of experts she was to pursue nothing singular that others did not observe, especially because she upset her husband. Even worse was the compulsive eating that followed her fasting.[23] She did not respond to these concerns. I then left, and I do not know what afterward happened.

I brought up this matter in order to provide a clear example of how some people completely lack discretion. They do not allow themselves to be convinced so that they can follow advice. It is no wonder if the coin that is made by such persons is rejected as being made of iron rather than of gold. In this matter the advice of the wise man is most salutary, that a person not be wise in his own eyes, and not count on his own insight (Prv 3:5,7). One is to do all things with counsel, and there will never be any regrets.

It is not sufficient, however, to tire out the wise with daily questioning, but it is necessary to show faith and obedience. Otherwise such a person will behave stupidly, as the wise man says. This person does not accept words of prudence or of advice, unless they say exactly what he is contemplating in his own heart (Prv 18:2).

This is no small gift of the Holy Spirit, this gift of counsel. Through it good advice can be given or received or believed. And so John Climacus says, concerning the steps that lead to God, that an arrogant man, who has made himself his own God, does not need to have a demon to tempt him, for he has become a demon unto himself.[24] I think that in the end the accumulation of the greatest evils that we now experience and suffer from in the schism is the result of this disease of indiscretion, by which no one will let anyone else give advice. Concerning this virtue of discretion, John Cassian dealt at length in his *Collations of the Fathers*.[25] Ultimately, in the person of the great Anthony, Cassian concludes that this virtue alone leads by way of a route without obstructions to God's kingdom. It makes us safe from the ambushes and seductions of demons. Examples are added by which this is shown. The wretched outcome for those lacking in this virtue is recorded.

Excessive abstinence and drunken overeating both lead to a similar end, except that excessive abstinence is harder to remedy, for it brings incurable illness from brain damage and mental disorder. It happens then through mania or rage or other melancholy passions that phantasms become so deeply rooted and buried in the brain that they are thought to be true objects that appear outside the mind. A person believes that he or she can see or touch that which the external senses in no way perceive. This passion becomes stronger until sometimes in this insanity a person will judge himself to be something else than he or she is. Such a person has been found who believed he was a purple fish; another thought he was a cock; another an ass; yet another thought he was dead. Some doctors think that Nebuchadnezzar was struck by this illness, so that he thought he was a wild animal who had failed to put on an animal's body (cf. Dn 4:1–34). Medical books are full of such monstrous apparitions and disturbances in the power of judgment resulting from injury to the interior powers. Concerning such people, Jerome says that they are more in need of the remedies of Hippocrates than the counsel of others.[26]

I have seen many and also examined many who seemed in most matters to be of perfectly sound mind. In certain cases, however, they showed by their reactions that they were not sane, when damage to their powers of imagination manifested itself. But whoever considers carefully the evil practices of the magical arts will easily realize that many of its practices require excessive fasting and other acts that are intended for no other purpose than to disturb the senses and the mind. Thus it happens that people who dedicate themselves to such arts often become insane. Their faces and eyes betray a terrible trembling.[27]

But what I here have described should not be confused with John the Baptist and his abstinence. We must show constant awareness that people have different graces, both through their own natural goodness and from the gift of him who gives to each as he wishes (1 Cor 12:11). And so it can happen that a person without any fault or element of indiscretion will set out on a more austere way of life that is not fit for all. We have an example in our John. According to nature he had the best physical constitution, as well as a beautiful and complete harmony in the relationship of inferior to superior powers, to the degree fallen nature allowed.[28]

If this by chance should seem to be unclear to someone, let him know that according to the scriptures the works of God are perfect (Dt 32:4). But was not John the Baptist miraculously made by God? For the material seed from which his body was to be composed was neither too hard nor too fluid in its abundance.[29] It was made in such a way as was fitting for God its creator in fashioning and ministering to it. Imagine that some monstrous defect happened. What then would follow? Now such an imperfection would be blamed not on the operation of nature but on the causality of God in his miraculous working. This would be heinous to say. Therefore it is all the more clear that John's mental composition was not melancholy but sanguine.[30] In his conception and birth he was by no means subject to the heavenly constellations. The rules of the astronomers have failed or could have failed in conclusions about him and could not be extended to him.[31] The reason is obvious: the miracle of his conception. From these matters what more can be concluded? See now that John while he was a boy wanted to go into the desert and entered it (Lk 1:80). This he did neither because of a brain injury nor because of a melancholic temperament. Rather, he was led into the desert by the Holy Spirit. Similarly, the singularity of his food and similar traits, which also were announced before his conception (Lk 1:15), were maintained by John with his powerful wisdom, so that all others could admire them but not completely imitate them because of the virtue of discretion.[32] The flight of all birds is not equal to that of the eagle, nor can all animals in speed equal the tiger. Similarly, in virtues a different portion is given to each person.

Did not Saint Benedict as a youth dwell in a desert place?[33] And yet he made it clear that monks are not indiscriminately to be allowed at will to approach a life of solitude.[34] Not every inexperienced novice can bear the blows of the spiritual struggle, and so how can he safely hand himself over to a more serious match with a giant? Those who live together in society have more experience of conflict with the world and the flesh. These are the more rugged and more powerful struggles for those in a group. But those who live the solitary life have to fight the most awful giant of the devil and are attacked and tired out by its clever and powerful tricks.[35] If the grace of discretion did not help, they would come to a bad end. You see, then, how necessary the virtue of discretion is. Humility joined to true obedience gives birth, nurtures, and saves us. Let us consider the remaining matters with greater brevity.

The third sign in the spiritual coin, as we have said, is

patience, which provides durability. The coin is tested through the fire of tribulation, and insults and reproaches hammer on it. A man's learning, as the wise man says, is known by his patience (Prv 19:11). If those who describe what has been revealed to them speak of nothing but degradation, ridicule, and insults, then you will be able more easily to believe them than in a situation where there is good reason to suspect that they are trying to get hold of empty praise.

There is no doubt, however, that the sign is false, if it is not investigated with the very greatest of care, together with other signs. For obstinacy often imitates patience, and some people glory in foolishly suffering disgrace. Even their sordid clothes and hair shirts sometimes bring forth and nourish the most poisonous worm of pride. Such people think that they are like the just and holy, who experienced so many adversities or who acted in a similar way. Again, they think that in them is fulfilled the promise of Christ, "Blessed are they who suffer persecution, for theirs is the kingdom of heaven" (Mt 5:10). They do not take sufficiently into consideration that Christ added, "for the sake of justice." Their mental arrogance brings such great blindness that their rashness desires to be seen as something like virtue. Are there not also to be found those, I ask, who in the most base manner glory even in their own defects, failures, and needs?

It is quite absurd, but these people take pride in saying that such things have been granted to them by God in order to identify themselves with Paul in making sure that the greatness of their revelations and virtues does not make them arrogant (2 Cor 12:7). Imagine what a disaster such arrogance of conscience creates, for the defects of such persons do not humble them and so are not stripped away. For just as these people think that the prods of culpable negligence have been given to them as a useful service, so too they make no effort to get rid of them but instead use their presence in order to claim that they are perfect.

The fourth sign is truth, which provides proper design and the stamp of legitimacy. For Holy Scripture is the location or workshop where the royal mold of the spiritual mint is kept. If the coin in any, even the slightest matter, is different in its form and inscription from the royal mold, then without any doubt it is counterfeit. But sometimes the false coin can be so close in appearance to the true one that its counterfeit can only be detected by the most learned people. For with so many true lines on the counterfeit coin, it is hard to see the one point of falsity. Heretics have been seen who composed great books of catholic doctrine so that amid so many truths they might secretly insert one sole point of heresy and make it public by means of such a careful and effective fraud. This practice shows how necessary it is that the coin of extraordinary revelations first be examined by theologians, whose job it is to distinguish between true and false religion and to deal with morals. It is clear how evil it is to reject Holy Scripture. Such a step most certainly prepares the way for receiving Antichrist. This fourth sign is clearly given to us in the law, Deuteronomy, chapters 13 and 18.

In order to clarify this matter further, I want to repeat here the four requirements for a true revelation, in terms of the stamp of truth. These I set forth in a certain sermon on the angels.[36] The first conclusion is that no holy angel or prophet announces that anything will happen except that it exists truly in the future in the way which he himself or the Holy Spirit intended. This is not the way that demons reply, for they deceive and are deceived. This is the conclusion to be found in Deuteronomy, chapter 18: "If you answer in silent thought, how can I understand when the Lord has spoken?" The answer will follow: "Here you will have a sign. If the prophet of the Lord has foretold anything and it has not happened, then the Lord has not spoken, but the prophet has made something up in his inflated mind." Opposing this interpretation we have a powerful example with Jonah, who predicted the destruction of the people of Nineveh (Jon 3:4), and with Isaiah in regard to the death of Hezekiah (2 Kgs 20:16–21), and of Nathan (2 Sm 7:15–17).

Therefore a second proof is necessary. If what an angel or prophet foretold does not come about in the manner in which he predicted, first he will receive a revelation from the Holy Spirit concerning this matter about how the prophecy or revelation is to be understood: whether conditional, mystical, or literal. This is what happened with Jonah and Isaiah. Otherwise, they should have been stoned, according to the law written in Deuteronomy, chapter 18. This is what I meant before when I said that God can call back or even contradict a revelation, in order to use his understanding to provide for our salvation.

A third proof: Holy angels and true prophets do not preach or order anything that is contrary to good morals or sincere faith. This is not the case with demons or Antichrist, who are said to have signs of mendaciousness, for they make us come to believe in lies. This requirement is found in Deuteronomy, chapter 13. If someone insists on pointing to the order given to Abraham to sacrifice his son (Gn 22:2), I reply that if God had ordered it or given his dispensation, the killing of Isaac would not have been against the law. But someone who sacrificed sons and daughters to demons would be called wicked and idolatrous.

Therefore we need a fourth proof: Angelic or prophetic revelation in anything that departs from good living, unless God intervenes in ordering or dispensing, ought to take place in such a way that the one who receives the revelation on the matter or for whom the revelation is made in no way can be in doubt about it. For it is necessary that the revelation be perceived as something clearly coming from God in the same way as something that is in accord with Holy Scripture or right reason.

In such a case there is the greatest need for the gift that the Apostle calls discernment of spirits (1 Cor 12:10). Do you ask how this gift that we call discernment of spirits functions? It makes it happen that a person through a certain intimate taste and experimental illumination senses a difference between true revelations and deceptive illusions. This is what Saint Gregory says in his *Dialogues*.[37] This is what Saint Bernard acknowledged of himself in his own miracles. For he felt, or as I would express it, tasted, some kind of breath and odor within himself when the power of performing miracles came to him, such as with acts of healing.[38] He felt something of what the evangelist says of our Lord Jesus Christ, that the power went out of him when a woman was healed by touching the hem of his clothing (Lk 8:46). Otherwise Bernard and those like him would for no reason ever have been excused from rashness and from the sin of tempting God when they set out to perform miracles.

Augustine also tells in his *Confessions* that his mother in this way distinguished in the quiet of the night among true and false imaginings and visions.[39] Why then should someone be surprised if a universal rule or certain and infallible teaching cannot be handed over on this matter concerning discernment of spirits or the truth of revelations? This is more a matter of experience, dependent on a number of individual conditions, which are infinite, than a question of some technique.

We can consider the problem in a similar question, even though it is a far simpler one. Perhaps some people will laugh at the example, but they should watch out that they do not laugh at themselves. We can ask that we be given an ability and dependable way of knowing by which we can always know concerning ourselves or others whether we are having a dream or are in a state of wakefulness. Consider, first of all, that the visions experienced in dreams can follow a pattern, be rational, and reflect upon their own content. A man asks if he is asleep. He can argue both possibilities and finally conclude that he is awake. Add to this experience the fact that there sometimes can be so much similarity between sleeping and wakefulness that a person even though awake and considering his state of being will ask himself whether he was then truly asleep.

Furthermore, among some of those who sleep, as Aristotle writes[40] and experience tells, one can find the waking actions such as walking, speaking, and the like. Finally, so much happens that makes sleeping resemble wakefulness that only experience enables one to distinguish between the two states. Ask anyone who is awake how he knows whether he is awake. He will perhaps reply to the question as if it were an insult! But if you keep pushing, he will answer in anger: "I know quite well." Stick to the matter and say, "How do you know well?" He will say that there is the greatest difference between his dreaming and being awake.

If you point to the various similarities we have mentioned, I think there will be no other outcome in his response than for him to say, "Certainly I know, for I experience it." But persist in the matter and point out that a person frequently can think he is experiencing something while he is dreaming. He can believe that he is speaking, reading, and hearing, and by no means is dreaming. What will the person answer, except, "It is true, and in that case I am being deceived." But if you want to be even bolder and push the point even further, you can say, "And so now, my good man, you have no idea whether you are deceived?" Let him see whether he becomes speechless or if he can allege something of sufficient importance to free himself from this labyrinth. A person can only say that experiential knowledge alone of this wakefulness, which is quite different from dreams, is stronger and more vivid. Through this knowledge he does not so much have an opinion but knows and understands that he is awake.

Let this image, which might seem childish, be transferred to the more elevated subject matter being treated. Through such a concept, if I am not mistaken, the arrogance of human curiosity can be kept in check. This curiosity, which cannot even penetrate everyday and childish riddles, feels anger because it does not fathom the sacraments of the faith. Such a consideration should make us more careful, not only in judging about revelations but also in general in considering all our actions. How often a man thinks himself wise, just, humble, and tells himself how rich he is in virtue, and he does not know that he is a wretch, a miserable, blind, naked creature (cf. Rv 3:18). He excels in his vanity and glories in the multitude of his spiritual riches (Ps 48:7). In his madness he says, "I shall not be moved in eternity" (Ps 29:7). But it is certain that he is deceived, overwhelmed by a deep sleep, for he sees all these things not in the luminous wakefulness of truth but under the covering of somnolent vanity.

This deception man first senses when the good God rouses him from the sleep of sin. He finds nothing in his hands of the riches about which he had been dreaming. This conversion takes place when he returns to the light-filled and brilliant day of humility and himself awakes from the vanity in which he was sleeping. Then a person sees his mistake. He thinks over the matter for a long time and is astounded by what he had allowed himself or how he had been out of his mind.

In such a situation a person realizes that he truly had been proud, arrogant, puffed-up, or corrupt in other ways, even though he previously had thought differently of himself. Why is this so? Because iniquity lies to itself. And how can it be surprising if iniquity lies to itself, any more than if someone who is dreaming is to make judgments about dreams, or if a mad person is to judge madness, or the proud person pronounces on the subject of wisdom? Thus it is clear that the evil wrongly make conjectures about their own vices, just as the parsimonious person cannot judge niggardliness, nor does the proud person rightly know arrogance. As if overwhelmed by confusion,[41] such people will grope about at noon (cf. Dt 28:29). In order to obtain some enlightenment, it is absolutely necessary for them to be led by the advice of others and to follow it. Another person, who is awake, can better judge for the one who is dreaming. So, woe to the one who is alone, for when this person falls there will be no one to lift her up (cf. Eccl 4:10). Woe to the blind person if blind impious deception leads her, for both will fall into a ditch (Mt 15:14). Who will not tremble before you, you deceivers rightly to be feared? O you fallacious snares of a thousand deceptions, spreading everywhere, who can escape you? Who can keep to this narrow and dark footpath and be safe in this state of siege? Certainly only the one who is blessed and ten times blessed in being humble and poor, who obeys Wisdom, in always being fearful (Prv 28:14), and who keeps before himself the fear of God so that his house is not quickly overthrown (Sir 27:4).

Don't you think he experienced this who said, "The Lord watches over his children. I humbled myself and he freed me" (Ps 114:6)? The divine statement bears witness concerning what should always be remembered in an appropriate way concerning humility, as shown to Anthony.[42] In conformity, the devout Bernard swears that he had the fullest experience of such matters in his fifty-fourth sermon on the Song of Songs.[43] "In truth," he says, "I learned that there is nothing equally effective for meriting God's grace, or for keeping or recovering it, than to place yourself at all times before God, not in thinking you know his depth but in fearing it."[44]

"Blessed is the man who is ever fearful" (Prv 28:14). Anyone who has entered into the light of humility will walk safely amid whatever hidden snares of temptation there might be. The adversary will roar in vain as a lion (cf. 1 Pt 5:8). In vain he will go about seeking someone he can devour. In vain he will lay traps in his cave so that he can seize the poor and impoverished and contrite person, for that poor one has been left to you, Lord. You come to the aid of this orphan (cf. Ps 10:14).

This is the first and principal distinguishing sign among the indications of our spiritual coin. For I believe in all warnings that are given, all the strong instincts, every revelation, every miracle, every experience of ecstatic love, all contemplation, rapture, and finally every interior or exterior operation, so long as humility precedes, accompanies, and follows them, if nothing harmful is mixed in with them. If these conditions are met, you will not be deceived about their having the mark of being from God or his good angel. But if anyone takes his point of departure in such matters with pride and uses them as an excuse for displaying himself, then be suspicious of everything.

If the mark of humility is fully apparent, then other elements are added in vain. For pride and humility are sufficient to distinguish the coin of spiritual operations. This humility shows the most sublime pettiness and richest poverty. Existing in God, such humility betrays the most wise, if I may use the word, foolishness. It has no faith in itself, preferring itself to no one else, open to persuasion and detracting from no one. In its sense of indignity, such humility does all things in a gentle way (Wis 8:1). Whoever thinks that he acts and serves on the basis of his own power, efforts, or industry, he is very much in error and is most proud. I admit that a person can make himself ready for virtue, but this is freely given and guarded by him alone from whom every perfect gift comes (Jas 1:17). We should know and be aware that the great gift of God is also the beginning of humility. See then, venerable masters and beloved brothers, see how I have returned from the fourth sign to the first. So it is. But I cannot often enough or with sufficient words instill the praise of this virtue in the midst of our most incorrigible elevation of self. One can never sufficiently crush and obliterate in contempt beneath one's feet the enemy of pride. Oh, what a horrendous gigantic monster it is! How hideous is the work of pride. For alas, when it is stepped on, it rises again with more strength, like the fabled Antaeus.[45] When pride is plucked out, it sprouts forth again in greater abundance. But when it finally is cut away, like the head of the Hydra in poetry, it grows back all the more. Thus as much from its opposite, as from humility, low condition, fear, and even from its own death, pride returns to life.

But now let us return, if we can, to the fourth sign, which we were treating and which we spoke of as true, that provides the legitimacy of form or configuration to our spiritual coin. We can admit that some events, not being openly and directly opposed or contrary to the divine omnipotence that is extolled by Holy Scripture, can take place in absolute terms. But such things are still to be rejected as being empty and foolish, unfit for divine wisdom, and not shaped in accord with the mold of truth, but made in some other way. And this is the case if someone says that he has been told that the whole world tomorrow will be moved in straight line motion, that an angel will be destroyed and then recreated, and does not show any meaning in such an act. Or, for example, if someone claims that a church prelate will have to go alone and naked and carry a material cross on his shoulders or else the church will perish.[46]

Such assertions, I say, are to be rejected at once as mad and unworthy of divine revelation. For it is not power alone that shines forth in divine works. Goodness and wisdom are also present, for he fills all his deeds with them. "You have made all things in wisdom," says the Psalmist (Ps 103:24). To this consideration we should add what already was said about superfluous tales of fantastic apparitions and the time wasted on them.[47] On this matter we can depend on the outcome of learned discussions and the gloss on Matthew with the words, "If you are the son of God, throw yourself down" (Mt 4:6).[48] If a miracle lacks any devout purpose or meaning, for that reason it is to be suspected or rejected, as it would have been if Christ had flown through the air, and as with all sacrilegious stunts of magicians.

There was in our times a woman who was well known for revelations in such matters. This sign of truth has shown, unless I am mistaken, that she was out of her mind.[49]

Let us go now at last to the fifth and final sign. It is, if you remember, that of charity or divine love, which provides golden color to the coin. This sign is not immediately sufficient in all cases, because of the deceptive or fake golden color of empty or carnal love. Thus it has happened that certain women, although out of ignorance, have been affected by a harmful love toward God or toward other holy persons, rather than being moved by true, holy, and sincere charity. It is true of those who practice idolatry that they err in thinking that they love God. And so I conclude here that it is not safe for any holy women to live together and enjoy familiarity with men, even the most religious of them.[50]

Why is this so? Because it can happen that even though love begins from the spirit, it is to be greatly feared that through its charms it gradually gives way and is consummated in the flesh. As Jerome says, the devil will always have his birdlime.[51] For passion assaults even ironclad minds and tears away at their strength. As Vergil says, a man burns up just in seeing a woman.[52] On this matter a certain devout woman wrote that she suspected nothing as much as love, even more than the devil, and even when it was turned to God and to persons of proven sanctity.[53] This is by no means a foolish point of view,[54] for the more violent a passion or movement is, the more easily it leads to a fall and the more difficult it is to control. All the more for this reason the Beghards and Beguines are seen to have erred, because of their excessive love that was disguised as devotion.[55] The proof of this matter is found in a certain little book written by a woman with unbelievable cleverness. Her name is Marie of Valenciennes.[56] She treats the requirements and eminence of divine love. If anyone should come to it, she claims that he is released from all the precepts of the law. She supports her assertion with a phrase taken from the Apostle, "Have charity, and do what you want."[57]

I think you remember that Vergil in his *Bucolics* poses this question: whether those who love make up dreams for themselves.[58] And surely this is the case, for among all the passions of the soul, love is the one that penetrates deepest and alienates us from ourselves. And if love is true, chaste, and holy, it helps us inconceivably much in coming to know heavenly things. But if it is vain, in error, and lustful, it will fashion for itself different illusions, so that a person thinks he sees or understands matters of which he is wholly ignorant.

We experience the truth of this matter in those who love heresy. For if the Marie we have mentioned had not applied the love of which she wrote to those who are wanderers on earth, bound to fulfill God's commands, but instead to the state of the blessed, she could hardly have expressed anything more sublime about their enjoyment of God. But in her intellectual pride, combined with passionate love, she fell into error. And so she thought she would always enjoy God while this powerful passion for him grew in her soul, however far she was from following God's precepts.

I heard a Carthusian tell that he had heard from an important figure, who here showed his foolishness, that mortal sin does not always destroy charity, nor does it block out the love of God above all things.[59] Instead, it sometimes inflames with a divine sweetness and thanksgiving in admiration, praise, and desire. He gave as an example delight in fornication. This person was indeed out of his mind in his error when he fantasized in this way, for he called charity every passionate movement of love that made him think of God, whether it took place out of habit or otherwise. God's love does not take joy in evil (1 Cor 18:6). Charity does not make itself God's enemy through disobedience.

I know a man[60] who out of a devotion and a wisdom that were clearly praiseworthy took into the embrace of familiar friendship in the Lord a certain virgin living the religious life. At first there was present no trace of carnal love. Finally, through frequent contact, love slowly grew, but not wholly in the Lord, until the man could scarcely be separated from the woman, if she went away, without trying to visit her or thinking constantly about her. At that time he nevertheless thought that there was nothing carnal, devious, or indicating diabolical deception in the matter, until one time he had to be apart from her for a longer period.

357

Then the man felt for the first time that this love was not pure and completely sincere and chaste. He realized he was heading for great evil unless God in his goodness had averted it.

All passionate feeling is a most dangerous companion for virtue, as it is in love, zeal, correction of behavior, or similar matters. And so it is most true what someone said: Headstrong behavior deals badly with all things. This kind of deception is common with those who in cultivating or loving their neighbors are attentive to physical beauty, youth, riches, or other gifts of fortune. Such people should be on their guard to avoid burning up with sordid and carnal desires. It will be different if they love virtue alone, in its one dwelling place, the spirit, whatever kind of body it inhabits. They must love, cultivate, and associate themselves with virtues in such a way.

I am, nevertheless, not completely opposed to what the poet said, "Virtue is more pleasing when it comes from a beautiful body."[61] But I assert that even if it is more pleasing, virtue is not for this reason to be considered safer or more genuine. Furthermore, so that you will see that nothing is safe in the love of God itself, so long as we are on our pilgrimage from the Lord, regard carefully how a terrible deception can arise among those who are trained in God's love and in the other virtues. What deception is this? It happens that these devout persons, by the just but hidden permission of God, so that they are taught a lesson or are ruined, are deceived by the noonday demon of pride.[62] He changes himself into an angel of light in appearing to do great good. God then leaves these persons and takes away the nuptial garment of charity.

Such people presume, nevertheless, to believe that they have all the signs of their prior devotion and love, but they err on the question and in the experience of morals, just as the person who stumbles over his feet with his eyes open. Thus these people think that they act according to God's spirit, even though they are moved alone by the habit instilled in them and through the use of a virtue that they once possessed.

Who would not be amazed in hearing of such a phenomenon? Who would not be greatly repelled? Who would not obey the Apostle when he says, "Whoever thinks he stands, take care lest he fall" (1 Cor 10:12)? I believe that the wise man was contemplating on this matter when he said, "There is a way that seems right to a person, but in the end it leads to death" (Prv 16:25). And there is the one who says, "A person does not know whether she is worthy of love or of hate" (Eccl 9:1). In the face of this great abyss of the judgments of God, the Apostle took hold of the height of his contemplation when he cried out in fear, "Oh, the depth of the riches of the wisdom and knowledge of God! How incomprehensible are his judgments" (Rom 11:33). And another says, "He is terrible in his counsels over the sons of men" (Ps 65:5).

If such a consideration is not enough to humiliate us in our misery, then I do not know what else will succeed in doing so. For we must not forget that the same person who now may be good and decorous in charity quickly can descend into vice and again be converted from evil into justice. Similarly, it is possible that the same person now be visited by true revelations, but later be tried or tempted by false illusions. For also our prophets such as David, Elisha, and Nathan did not always have the prophetical spirit at their beck and call, as pointed out by Gregory and history.[63] And so Nathan from the frequent use of prophetic vision believed that his own judgments were revelations. When David asked him about the building of the Temple, he answered, "Do whatever you have in your heart, for the Lord is with you" (2 Sm 7:3). This example is valid for matters that are concerned with the use of divine love.

Whoever then believes he is able to make judgments in such matters on the basis of his own mental ability, skill, or efforts, let him know that he is in error. For if the spirit of presumption has crept in, the vanity of illusion will also easily enter. But be careful when you hear of this danger and are afraid that you will fall into the worse ditch of infidelity and despair, in thinking, as it were, that there is no certitude and that there can be no valid basis for hope in holy revelations. As the Apostle says of his own revelation, "I know a man, etc." (2 Cor 12:2), and of hope says, "I am certain that not death, etc." (Rom 8:38). He certainly has certitude, but from God's light and not alone from human investigation and judgment.

You know that the following statement is not logically correct[64]: We can be deceived and misguided in distinguishing between sleep and wakefulness, therefore there is no certitude about when we are awake, and so we can have no faith in those who are awake! The saints were awake in the divine light. We who are overwhelmed and covered by sins dream about many portents of vices and illusions. No wonder if we are deceived, while they are not. I know a man who, after being overwhelmed by temptation concerning an article of faith, was suddenly brought into such light of truth and certitude that there remained in him no trace of doubt, and no hesitation.[65] There was only a great calm, instilled in him by the one who commands the waves (cf. 2 Mc 9:8). This person added that his change did not come about from any new process of reasoning, which he had then been looking for and remembered seeking. The new faith he had merited alone from humbling his intellect and handing it over to the service of the faith and of the almighty God, so that he no more doubted that faith than he did his own existence. He asked what the basis could be for this great strength and peace in believing, and he found no other answer except that he experienced belief in such a way and did not know how to transmit it to someone else.

Perhaps the worldly wise will not believe that such illuminations take place, as has been most truthfully spoken to God through the prophet, "You wondrously bring light from the eternal mountains. All the foolish of heart are disturbed" (Ps 75:5). They do not know what belongs to the heart and the spirit, for they do not dwell with themselves in their hearts but live abroad on the plains of vanity. So it is clear that the just will be lifted up into the certain hope of their salvation. I speak of certainty not in relationship to themselves, but in him who breathes his secret to the soul, "I am your salvation" (Ps 34:3). In the midst of uncertainties and the temptations on the waves of human life, he secures the firm anchor of hope. It is he who also brings his beloved into the chamber of tranquility (cf. Sg 1:4), away from all the onrushing storms of human change.

Here we find the wonders of God in the depth of the human heart. These are seen by those who descend into the sea of bitter and strong contrition in the ships of virtue. Through a dedication to contemplation and meditation that is not idle, but pious and faithful, these wonders function amid the many currents of divine judgments as well as among human affections. Do you wish to see this great vision? Do you wish to go down to it? It is not necessary to use human strength. Your power is impotence; your knowledge, as Socrates said, is that you are ignorant.[66] Your justice is that you have no confidence in your own justice. How can this be? "Go to the deep heart and God will be exalted for you" (Ps 63:8).

You will see that you are not alone, but all the peoples, according to the saying of the prophet, are as nothing and empty in his sight (Is 40:17). Behold, you will see that you can do nothing. Nevertheless you will cry out with the prophet: "Your learning has become too wonderful for me. It is so high that I cannot attain it" (Ps 138:6). And so you will admit that you know nothing. Finally, with another prophet you will say, "All our acts of justice are like defiled garments in your sight" (Is 64:6). From this valley of weakness, from this darkness of ignorance, from this dust of humility and filth of bad reputation, the Lord will call you into his mountain, speaking to you from the darkness and lifting you up as a needy one from the dust, a pauper from the dung hill.

But perhaps you will say: I know already that I am nothing, know nothing, and so have no justice. I still experience nothing of what you promise. But, I ask, notice how you said you know; see to it that you do not hear that reproach: "From your mouth I judge you, evil servant" (Lk 19:22). For if you in truth and without doubt judge yourself to be such, perhaps it is through your intellect and your power of reasoning, as it is for almost all people. But then why do your affectivity and your actions contradict this point of view? Otherwise, why do you not feel and act in accord with your own words? Or why do you feel and act in such a way that you think yourself worthy of doing something through your own strength, efforts, and justice?

I praise the sense of justice you have described, but I demand to be able to experience its taste. Otherwise your judgments are like those of the uneducated, who in their ignorance never pay attention to the problems of any kind of knowledge. It is different for the wise and experienced person who considers, feels, and draws to himself the impossibility of knowing, due to the state of the matter itself or the complexity of the considerations involved.

In no way here do I accuse you or forbid you from making an attempt, from working hard, and using all your strength. But I am wholly repelled by your arrogance in these efforts and condemn it. Otherwise, do not be surprised if your hope hesitates and wavers, when even in small matters you find yourself unable to accomplish what you set out to do. It can so easily happen that your foot stumbles over pride and you fall, as all have fallen who have acted in iniquity (Ps 35:13).

In God, who alone is changeless, are we to place our hope, together with the one who says, "To cling to God is for me good, to place my hope in the Lord God" (Ps 72:28). You must understand, now that I return to my subject after my long digression on pride, what Solomon found when he tried by human effort alone to come to know matters divine, of the type that the present investigation of true and false revelations deals with. "I have tried everything," he said, "in wisdom. I have said, I am made a wise man, and that wisdom has left me and gone much further away from me than it was. It is a tremendous depth, and who shall find it?" (Eccl 7:24–25).

Do you not see, you most learned of men, do you not realize that there is something similar in the question proposed? For it seems to me that the higher the question, the deeper one must go in order to penetrate it. And here they who are supposed to make an inquiry can fail to inquire. Nevertheless, they do well. We have not wasted our efforts, you in listening, I in speaking, if we are distrustful of ourselves and not of God's gift. We must always have our hearts lifted up to the Lord in asking that we do not fool ourselves and do not get fooled. For God has given his wisdom and knowledge to the man who is good in his sight, as Solomon says (Eccl 2:26).

If it should happen that we become the official examiners of the coin of spiritual revelation, we should do our best to act in the way I have here described. We are to cling to God and to the scriptures, through which and in which God once and for all spoke to us. This revelation he will not repeat. It is my opinion that we are obliged in all matters, but especially in this investigation, not to make hasty conclusions. We are to delay our verdict until after the fullest investigation, unless it is easily apparent that deception or foolishness is involved. But when at first glance nothing false or silly is seen, then it is right not only to investigate what has been done but also to await the outcome of events.

For a demon can sometimes start out with many truths, and in the course of time when he has persuaded people, then he adds what is deceptive. This he can do either to deceive an individual person, or to attack miraculous events of our religion on which the faith is based. Or he can do so in order to show contempt for all devotion or to create a scandal that stands in the way of God's word. And so when someone falls who previously had a reputation as being outstanding in such revelations, then those lay persons who live in a worldly manner ridicule anyone who has decided to live a life of religious simplicity. Such a person is immediately singled out as a deceived and one who has been deceived. The worldly wise shout him down as a dreamer, or hiss that he is a Papelard, a Beguine, or Beghard.[67] If they get a chance, such people ridicule the simplicity of the just person. Ordinary people are clearly deceived in such matters and scarcely or never can be brought back to the way of truth. How can this be? For they do not listen to the clerics whom they believe to be weighed down by hypocrisy, jealousy, and evil. Nor can such common people be improved by lay persons whom they know to be as ignorant as they themselves are.

The result of all that we have here said is that the coin of divine revelation is to be examined. It must be seen whether it has the weight of humility without the vanity of curiosity and pride; if it contains the flexibility of discretion without superstitious stubbornness and lack of receptivity to advice; if it manifests the durability of patience in adversity, without any complaint or false imitation; if it shows the form of truth without mendacity or any undue attachment; if it has the bright and sincere color of divine love without the contamination or filth of carnality.

Since all these qualities were present in the revelation to Elizabeth and Zechariah concerning John and his name, it is not irrational to accept that John, as it were, had a name that was revealed and through "which the mouth of the Lord spoke out" (Is 62:2). We have considered this matter in the first part of our text: "John was baptizing in the desert, etc." (Mk 1:4). By his merits Christ Jesus, who is that truth, keeps us from error. He who is blessed forever. Amen.

On the Art of
Hearing Confessions[1]

*E*ven if a talent that develops through practice is carried out
more effectively than an activity based on a skill,[2] nevertheless it is still worthwhile to teach a skill for those who have not yet
completely mastered it. This is quite apparent in any art. Since
the art of arts is the direction of souls, especially in the hearing
of confessions, it is my desire to hand over in a brief and precise
manner some general considerations that I think can be profitable in directing experience.

I have been especially encouraged to do so by the fact that until
now I have discovered only a few persons who ever made complete
and full confessions. The cause of this condition lies in many cases
in either the negligence or the ignorance of confessors.[3]

First Consideration: Before all else the confessor should take
care that he is of pure life, since his task is to purify souls. He
should also place his hope in working to profit others not by his
own but by God's power. He must constantly remember that neither the one who plants nor he who waters is anything, but only
God who provides growth (1 Cor 3:7). Also, unless the Holy
Spirit is present in the heart of the one who listens, then the
tongue of the one who speaks acts in vain (cf. Ps 126:1). Let him
therefore frequently pray, just as the wise person consults the
body's doctor, that his work is directed by God so that he is
strengthened and grows in the Lord's virtue.

Second Consideration: The confessor is to recollect himself in the
fortress or watchtower of his reason, distancing himself as much
as he can from the exterior person, both in himself as in others,

so that he walks in the spirit and not in the flesh (Rom 8:4). Otherwise he might be enticed by the forms of bodies and these become a trap leading to his own perdition. He should keep a spiritual guard in considering the types of souls and not pay attention to difference of sex or physical appearance. Otherwise, what will it profit him if he wins the whole world but suffers the loss of his soul (Mt 16:26)?

Third Consideration: He is to fulfill the function of a careful confessor toward each who confesses to him. He is not to rush or to pass over anything in a superficial manner. With watchful care he is to examine and discern all matters. Through careful repetition he is to instill in the memory of the penitent what needs to be said and what actions are to be carried out. It is preferable that he listens to the confessions of a few people in a complete manner rather than those of many in an imperfect way. If priests do the latter, then they do not so much free penitents from scruples of conscience as abandon such people, who will still be greatly encumbered by their sins. In confession we are to imitate God, whose works are perfect (Ps 32:4). I should prefer, if I were a parish priest, to delay the confessions of many after Easter, even when some people would not return, rather than that I as a blind person lead astray the blind (cf. Mt 15:14).[4] Instead of being truly absolved from sin, these people show themselves to be incorrectly absolved.

Fourth Consideration: The confessor is to indicate through his acts that he seeks nothing from penitents but the salvation of their souls and their free release from the snares of sin. Therefore he is to do nothing that has the smell of gain. Freely you receive what is freely given (Mt 10:8). He is not to show off anything for worldly glory. The confessor is to offer himself to the poor in the same way as to the rich, to the base as well as to the beautiful, to the ignorant as well as to the learned. He is not to hope to gain a greater reward or recognition from the one or the other. This sincerity of right intention will manifest itself beyond measure, so that like some great spiritual iron magnet it will also draw all the more powerfully the hearts of the people to itself.

Fifth Consideration: It is best that a confessor who is zealous for souls obtains from his superior his power in reserved cases, especially when these are public and scandalous cases.[5] Very few priests are found who do not come across some such cases that in general are reserved. For the penitents themselves know that they ought not to be handed over to someone else in such matters, for they more freely and more often reveal themselves to their individual confessor. And this confessor likewise can be bold in more freely questioning them about individual matters. In this way he can also more fully cure them and trust in the absolution once given them.

Sixth Consideration: Let the confessor know all the varieties and species of sins, as a most learned doctor of spiritual illnesses.[6] Moreover, he is to be fully aware of how persons of different states and functions can sin. Small treatises have been written in order to spread this knowledge.[7] But there are some matters that cannot be safely committed to writing or public discourse, in order to avoid scandal to some people. Therefore confessors must secretly learn about those matters that it is their concern to know, just as for doctors it is important to know the different types of illnesses. Otherwise the confessor will hardly be able to question and instruct with care and prudence those who confess to him in recalling their sinful acts.

This is especially the case in exceptional sins of the flesh, in which it is known by experience that those guilty of such matters scarcely ever tell them in confession, unless they are encouraged by the most attentive artfulness, questioned, and finally taken captive in them.[8] Certainly it is necessary that the confessor have the spiritual art of the midwife in order to bring forth such a pernicious serpent, entangled and virulent in the soul that has conceived it. There is no doubt that the soul is endangered by the serpent and will time and again die an eternal death from it.

I do not think that in this matter we should listen to those who say that the confessor should not ask or inquire about anything from penitents.[9] Otherwise we do not take sufficiently into account the shame, ignorance, and weakness of sinners, nor do we carry out the saying of scripture that we are to bear one another's burdens (Gal 6:2) and many similar exhortations.

Seventh Consideration: Let the confessor make a guess, after some preliminary questions concerning age, status, condition, education, or office of the penitent, whether the person feels shame and is held back by great modesty, for it might be a child, or a woman, or someone of a weak constitution. Such persons are to be persuaded above all and in the first place to be convinced that confession is something completely secret and is made more to an omniscient God than to a human person. Sins are sought out not so that they may be revealed or that accusation be made but in order to avoid them, make amends for them, or absolve them, so that we can reach a state of perpetual relief from them. It would be better for the confessor to die than to reveal anything said to him.[10]

The confessor should remove every such suspicion, so that penitents do not fear that if they tell their sins, the confessor afterward will be hateful or contemptuous or accusatory toward them. Rather, he should love them the more tenderly as cherished offspring who have committed themselves totally to his trust.

Eighth Consideration: The confessor should strive, especially with young people and children, to get a general confession from them, for they hardly or never give full confessions unless they by chance have been instructed by the type of confessor whom we are describing.[11] Also this procedure would be useful among aged persons in the countryside, uneducated persons, and women. But if it is not easy to convince them, they can be made to do so by such questions as: Are you aware of this or that sin, for such an age, and in such company? According to their responses the prudent confessor can be aware if the confession otherwise was complete. If not, then the penitent can be convinced to make it complete.

Ninth Consideration: Let the confessor above all be careful not to be harsh, melancholic, and rigid from the beginning. If he does so, he will soon close the mouth of the terrified sinner. His speech should at first be affable, and if the situation sometimes requires it, he can show a certain familiarity concerning matters that are not sinful. Afterward let him point out how great an evil and terrible an act of hypocrisy it is to want to hide anything in confession before God, and how anyone who does so is basely deceiving himself. He should say that it would be better for him to depart unconfessed than to make an incomplete confession.

Tenth Consideration: The priest is to ask penitents whether they wish to be wholly purged from all their misdeeds. If they do not wish to do so, it is right that they depart, so that they do not spend their time in vain, or harmfully. If they wish to do so, they ought then themselves to help out. They can do so no better and no more quickly than by answering in complete truth the questions posed. But if they are found out in trying to lie or to hide the truth, as often happens, they are to be corrected by a discreet confessor or strongly and harshly reproached. They are to be immediately forced to seek forgiveness for a lie of this kind. Whatever they should then do, they again are to be encouraged in a kind and gentle way not to lie again or to hide the truth.

But if they have twice or more lied, they can be sent away and made to wait until another time, with the injunction that they then act better. It often happens that in a second confession people are more willing to reveal everything, when they think that their former lies were caused more by lack of care than through evil intent.

Eleventh Consideration: The confessor is to praise those who tell the truth about their offenses, and all the more as these seem to be substantial and detestable. They are to be praised for their truth, devotion, fear of God, zeal for their own salvation, their confidence in the priest, and similar things, and also because they boldly proceed to other matters without any hesitation.

It sometimes happens that it is not useless to question whether they elsewhere have confessed such matters. If not, then they should rejoice now all the more and thank God, who gave them the will and the opportunity to do so. It is also appropriate that the confessor should encourage them at that moment to give thanks. Afterward they can go on to other matters.

Twelfth Consideration: The confessor is to instruct penitents not to reveal the crimes of others by naming names or to indicate them by certain signs, unless perhaps the sins are such that they in no other way can be revealed, as when a brother has had carnal knowledge of his only sister or a man has sinned with his wife.

The priest should, moreover, not be curious in asking about particular circumstances of sins when these do not greatly increase or alter their gravity. Such a procedure can sometimes give birth to dangerous temptation, great turpitude, or harmful suspicion in the penitent. Nevertheless, we consider it to be useful in order to calm their consciences that penitents sometimes be stimulated by harsh goads, as if they had not fully and completely confessed their sins, so that they state in greater fullness whatever the confessor judges is required.

Thirteenth Consideration: The confessor is to make accusation and harshly blame them for the enormity of their sins, once he has come to recognize these in their fullness. He is to show how much punishment the sinner deserves. But he must be careful that the one confessing cannot again flee into denying what he already has admitted, something that very often has been discovered, even after the confession has been completed. Thus the description of the sins is to be most detailed.

Finally, whatever the priest has said in the confession, he is always in the end to be gentle and kind, pouring on the oil of consolation and compassion and good hope.[12] Furthermore, the confessor can sometimes say: In that you have confessed such and such, matters which are most grave, do not then hide anything but tell everything so that you may similarly benefit yourself.

Fourteenth Consideration: In the investigation of sins, and especially with carnal sin, which can only be extracted with the greatest difficulty from many, the confessor should go ahead first at a slow pace, concentrating on general matters and those that seem to imply no guilt or only a slight one. For if the sinner wants to lie and flee, he is often taken captive through those things that happen naturally to everyone, or in which the opposite is only rarely found. If he immediately denies such things, it is apparent that he is afraid of mentioning more substantial matters. In this way I know how many have been taken who when questioned denied that they ever had felt any heat in the genitals or any itch or erection, and who insisted that they had never been tempted or had any bad thought from a woman.[13]

And when they have been caught in this lie, they were asked: Was it not base to dismiss the problem in such a way? What were you then doing? Often they would reply to that which was asked, because they believed from the manner in which the confessor spoke that this act would be counted not as a fault but as something praiseworthy.[14]

Fifteenth Consideration: The confessor should know these and similar general questions: Were you ever, from the time you reached the age of reason, in the company of servants or friends, and especially in bed? If you were, did you ever hear anything evil said to you, as often happens, about impurity and women? If so, did you speak in a similar way? And did you desire such evils? If so, did you ever want anyone to touch you in an indecent way, or did he you? If so, then a further investigation is to be made under such a cover that the priest will understand whether masturbation or seminal emission has taken place.[15] And this sin can well be committed even before the age of puberty. It is always considered such, so long as one is awake, when delight is taken in the act, even if there is no seminal emission.[16]

Sixteenth Consideration: When impure matters are to be discussed, the confessor can say: Friend, you are not to be bothered by my speaking in a base manner, for it is necessary to say all things in confession. I would speak quite differently or certainly keep silence outside of confession. And let such things be said sufficiently slowly, and as if they were foreknown, or not considered

371

to be so grave. The confessor is not to stare into the face of the sinner but to look away, as if he were not worried, or almost as if he were telling a story. He should say: I can well see that you did such and such. Consequently tell everything in the Lord's name. I will be indulgent to you. And if you did not do anything else and even if you mentioned all the evils of the world, you would not be worse off, so speak boldly.[17] But it can be asked if he wishes that above all things he be questioned carefully, and if he does, it can be indicated that he is then to speak the truth.

Seventeenth Consideration: It sometimes happens, though it is quite rare with a conscientious and careful confessor, that a certain type of carnal sin or some vile circumstance is revealed, of which the sinner is not aware and of which he is not guilty. In this he will perhaps be scandalized or be taught in the future to do similar things. We do not accept that such a result is so much to be feared, as some experts claim, that a diligent investigation of sins therefore ought to be dropped. My desire is that the evils done by boys and others be confessed with the same diligence as they are known and done by them.[18]

We do not think they are to be asked as if they were ignorant. But they perhaps do not believe such matters are as serious as they in fact are for God, and they may wish not to make them known. But in this case the sin ought to be condemned with the most extreme detestation, as if it could not possibly happen for a person to do such a thing. But this should be said in order to find out whether the penitent knows how to distinguish between what he has done and what he has not done. For there are some people who wrongly respond affirmatively to everything that the confessor asks them.

Eighteenth Consideration: The confessor is to proceed, as we have said, from more general questions to more specific ones, from what is less base to what is base or worse, and thus, as it were, from general cases to their specific results. Once he has found out if the penitent ever tried to touch himself or a friend in a lustful manner, he is to be asked for how long and how often,

372

and with how many it happened, and at what time of his life, and if some were of his own family. Finally, he is to be asked in what part of his body his lust or that of the other person was fulfilled. In this way the investigation can move successively to other and worse manifestations of this sin.

Nineteenth Consideration: It is appropriate, as I have experienced, that children and male adolescents first be asked in the said manner about intimacy with male friends and servants, since they at first glance are less frightened, because such things are less unusual. Afterward they can be asked about intimacy with women. First of all, if they at the age of five or six years ever lay in bed with female servants, as is common for boys. If they are asked in conformity with what was said above, there will certainly also be found repulsive matters not only with servants but also with the more immediate family.[19] In such matters the confessor is only to proceed by being quick and indirect, in saying without changing his facial expression: Well then, I see that you did something similar with such and such. And if it is so, as alas often is the case, before anything more is said, then the priest should show practical consideration for the eleventh point above, in praising the sinner who makes known the sin.

Afterward the penitent will be convinced to want for his own good to speak of all the circumstances in detail, as he mentioned before about maidservants. The priest should show that the sinner's shame will give way to great merit and will provide tranquility of conscience in the future, for he will never again be forced to reveal these things to anyone else.

I think that with women the reverse order is to be followed in making investigations: First, they are to be asked about intimacy with each other; afterward with men or children. But I do not have complete experience on this matter.[20]

Twentieth Consideration: Perhaps someone might find fault with the boldness of a confessor who dares to reveal such matters, which scarcely seem believable and can hardly be imagined, except by those who have experienced them and have been seduced or have otherwise been informed about them. Let each person think what he wants.[21] I before God bear witness that I brought many persons to confession by such methods who admitted that they never, even at the moment of death, would say to anyone that they had done such things. But they praised God with all their hearts in giving thanks that they had revealed themselves in such a way. Some of them, but the smallest number, at times wanted to leave, but eventually they returned, admitting that they had been deceived by a demon who again tried to shut their mouth once they opened it. Others, who already had confessed but without such an investigation, were brought back to confession. They openly admitted to me that in their judgment, an investigation of this type is necessary.

Twenty-first Consideration: Someone might consider that he either does not know enough or does not wish to ask about such matters, because he perhaps is a shy and inexperienced surgeon, turning pale or unable to control himself in the face of such foul and terrible wounds. I will admit that caution is necessary, and one should not descend into these abominations with any sense of ease, and not unless the previous matters that have been confessed seem to lead to such a conclusion. But if someone does not know how to use such caution, then I counsel him to let the sinner go. Otherwise he will harm himself and scandalize the sinner, who, if he once has denied the matter and cannot be taken in it, will scarcely be able to be convicted of it in the future.

I do not yet know what kind of universal remedy should be used for all people. But I think that the general use of preaching is not sufficient. In this question, however, I am for the time convinced that such secret cases should not be reserved when they apply to youths of fourteen years and less or to women. Otherwise, I do not see how many of these will be kept from perdition because of the lack of a full confession. No one is more responsible for the healing of such people than church officials. They are in danger of damnation if they close the kingdom of heaven either through negligence or through a very rigid observance of reservation in hidden cases of this kind.[22]

Twenty-second Consideration: It seems quite necessary that in every prominent parish, the parish priest, if he is discreet, or another as his vicar or coadjutor, be appointed as the confessor for such cases and for such persons.[23] He thereafter should be diligent in hearing the confessions of children and youths at whatever time they want and when they are free, in summoning now one and now another. Since men of advanced age perhaps might be convinced to carry out this function, it should nevertheless be seen to that the confessor walk with care (Eph 5:15) and circumspection. It should be seen that none of those who are guilty and have seduced these youths can harass the priest directly or indirectly, through acts of particular evil or perhaps by putting ideas into the heads of the children.

The priest is to provide the greatest security around himself in having purity of conscience and intention. He is not to reveal by word or sign anything that has been said to him, and in no way is to be convinced to make it known. Nor is he to give a penance through which youths can be noticed in any way by those among whom they have their daily lives. In this matter it would seem better to have many confessors who are less expert in providing penances than to reserve many cases to a few experts and in this way to lead people, compelled by shame, never to confess such matters. Similarly it would be more bearable to complete one's penance in purgatory than to bear infinite penances in hell.

Twenty-third Consideration: Sometimes a scruple can remain in the priest concerning the confession of a sinner, a concern that he might not have said everything. This scruple the priest harbors either because he knows something that was not said in confession or because he is aware of certain basic facts, in what has already been confessed, that such and such a sin has been committed. Or the priest can have other reasons for doubt. In such a case he can either send away the sinner so that he can recollect himself, as has been said. Or, if he gives absolution, he will very often say to him, again and again, that if the sinner is hiding anything, his confession and the absolution are invalid and a mockery. Finally, he can say that if the person prefers to confess to another, he can go in the name of the Lord. He need only to make a full confession. This is enough, and nothing else is required. Or he can return if he wishes at another time to be more straightforward.

Twenty-fourth Consideration: The confessor is to ask the sinner if he intends with the help of God to abstain in the future from sin. Also, if he will cease from hatred toward another person. And if he in reality has the will, insofar as he is able, to make restoration. Likewise, if he intends to avoid the clear occasions of sin, as concubinage, usury, and the like. If any of these intentions is missing, the absolution has no validity and cannot be given. If the sinner admits a lack of will, he is still to be convinced that for the time being he is to do good insofar as he can, so that God will enlighten his heart. Likewise we say that in considering those who have been seduced by the sinner into evil counsels and bad habits, or with those who have been unjustly slandered by him, and in similar matters, it is not to be required that he make reparations beyond that which can reasonably be done.

Twenty-fifth Consideration: The confessor is to require a penance in harmony with the consent of the sinner and which the latter hopes to carry out, unless the sins are so public and scandalous, for which he ought to be compelled to provide reparation, even if he is unwilling.[24] But sometimes a penance can be given that he is not to commit one criminal act or another for a given future time under some punishment that can be effectively made in pecuniary or corporal terms. Or else he can be obliged to return to confession within two days after perpetrating the misdeed, or something else of this kind.

The penitent is still to be warned that he is not to accept this or any other penance if he does not firmly intend to carry it out. For he should realize that he will pay everything in a harsher way in purgatory than in this world. But he is to be told to hide his penance and whatever was done or said in the confession, and not to answer those who ask him out of curiosity.

Finally, many other matters could be treated, of which I have only written about some, partly in Latin and partly in French, in various treatises.[25] Other doctors have done so at greater length and to greater advantage. But let these few things be enough for the time being, so that their brevity will keep readers from disdaining them. And if anyone should approach this most salvific activity in good faith, he will learn and profit more by spiritual exercise and prayer than by reading.

Treatise Against
The Romance of the Rose[1]

*O*ne morning, not long ago, I woke up to find that my heart suddenly took flight on the feathers and wings of different thoughts. It went from one place to another and then all the way to the holy Court of Christianity, something to which it was accustomed. There it found Canonical Justice, the upright one, sitting on the throne of equity, sustained on one side by Mercy, on the other by Truth. Justice had in her right hand the scepter of reward and in her left the cutting sword of punishment. Her eyes were lively, dignified, and brighter than the lovely morning star, and even more than the sun.

The company around Justice was stunning. On one side was her very wise council, and on all sides were the knights and barons of all the virtues, which are God's own daughters and the offspring of Free Will, such as Charity, Strength, Temperance, Humility, and a great number of others. The head of the council and its apparent chancellor was Subtle Understanding, joined by the solid company of Lady Reason, the wise one. Her secretaries were Prudence and Knowledge; good Christian Faith and divine, celestial Wisdom were her closest advisors. Their assistants were Memory, Providence, Right Feeling, and many others. Theological Eloquence, which provided moderate and temperate language, functioned as advocate of the court. The prosecutor had the name of Conscience, for there is nothing she does not know or does not report.

CHASTITY MAKES HER CHARGES[2]

As I was delighting in greatly admiring all this fine display of the Court of Christianity and Justice in its equity, it seemed to me that Conscience rose up. Her function is to promote cases in the court. She went with Law as master of petitions. Conscience held in her hands and at her breast many supplications. Among these there was one I remember well, word for word, containing this sad complaint of most lovely Chastity, the purest creature, who would never allow herself to think any low thought:

> To Justice the upright one, holding the place of God on earth, and to all his court of religion, devout and Christian, Chastity, your weak subject, asks in humility and files complaint, that you quickly provide redress for the unbearable crimes committed against me and which are still being committed by one named the amorous Fool.[3] And these are the articles of my complaint:

The first article: This amorous Fool puts all his efforts into banishing me from the earth, I who have done nothing wrong. He does the same to my faithful guardians, Shame and Fear, as well as the good doorkeeper, Danger.[4] They would never dare allow one base kiss or lecherous look, any seductive smile or casual word. This Fool functions through a horrible old lady, worse than the devil, who teaches, demonstrates, and encourages that all young girls should sell their bodies often and at a high price without fear and without shame.[5] They are not to worry about deceiving or taking false oaths, so long as they can get something out of it. They are not to feel any compulsion or danger in quickly giving themselves, so long as they are beautiful, to all base acts of carnality, whether to clerics or lay persons or priests, without making any distinctions among them.

The second article: The Fool of Love wants to attack and chide marriage in all cases because of a suspicious, hateful, and angry jealousy. By himself and by some of the adversaries whom I have named, he advises that it is better to hang or drown oneself or to commit sins that cannot be mentioned rather than to commit oneself in marriage. He blames all women without exception, in order to make them so hateful for all men that none will want to take them in faith in marriage.[6]

The third article: He blames youths who join religious orders because, he says, they always try to get away from their true natures.[7] And this action especially harms me, for I am especially devout to those who enter the religious life.

The fourth article: He casts out everywhere a fire that burns more strongly and stinks more than Greek fire[8] and sulphur, a fire made of unbelievably prurient language, a fire consisting of astoundingly lecherous words, which are filthy and forbidden, sometimes in the name of Venus or of Cupid or Genius, often in his own name.[9] By such words my lovely houses and dwelling places as well as my sacred temples of human souls are ravaged by fire and burned down, and I am meanly cast out.

The fifth article: He defames Lady Reason, my good mistress, by reducing her to such rage and a low state that she advises one to speak openly, filthily, and graspingly, without shame in anything.[10] She will do so regardless how abominable and base these sayings and acts are, even among the most dissolute persons, who are my enemies. Alas, even if the Fool refuses to spare me, how has Reason ever harmed him? But this is the way he is; he is at war against all virtues.

The sixth article: When he speaks of holy, divine, and spiritual matters, he at the same time adds words that are most base and that encourage every kind of filth.[11] And yet such filth will never enter into paradise in the way he describes.

The seventh article: He promises paradise, glory, and praise to all the men and women who perform carnal acts even outside of marriage, for he counsels through his own person and his example that they try all types of women without distinction.[12] He curses all those who do not act in such a way, at least all who receive me and keep me with them.

The eighth article: He, in his person, names the private parts of the body and the sins of impurity and baseness with holy and sacred words, so that every such act becomes something divine and sacred that is to be adored, even outside of marriage, and by deceit and violence. He is not content with the above-mentioned abuses in publicizing them by word of mouth. The Fool has also written about and described them as well as he can in an attractive and effusive way in order the more to attract everyone to see them, hear about them, and accept them.[13] And even worse: In order to deceive people more cleverly, he has mingled honey with venom,[14] sugar with poison. Venomous snakes are concealed beneath the green grass of devotion. He does so in gathering together diverse materials that quite often are hardly in accord with his purpose except for the above motive. The Fool manages to gain more credibility and greater authority insofar as he seems to have a fuller grasp of things and to be more learned.

And so I ask you, Lady Justice, for quick remedy and suitable help in all these injuries, as well as others, too many for this little petition to contain. But his book provides material that is all too convincing in justifying my complaint.

REPLIES TO CHASTITY

After Chastity's supplication had been read out distinctly and clearly, you could have seen all the council and all the fine knights knitting their brows and appearing most indignant. Nevertheless, as wise and temperate persons, they ask that the other side be heard. But because the Fool of Love, who had been accused, was not there, for he had stepped over the high pass from which no one returns,[15] it was asked if he had in the Court of Christianity any legal representatives or supporters or well-wishers. Then you would have seen a great crowd and assembly of people without number, both young and old, male and female, of all ages. They came without keeping in any order and all at once, with one person trying to excuse him, another to defend him, the third to praise him. Yet another asks for pardon for the Fool because of his youth and folly in claiming that he had repented, for he had written, "I have made many sayings in my youth out of vanity."[16] Another supported him because he had been such a fine and noteworthy cleric and an excellent speaker of French, without any rival. Others defended him because he had spoken so well the truth concerning all classes without sparing nobles or non-nobles, country or nation, age or religion.

"What harm is there," says one of those who is most shrewd,[17] "what harm is there, I ask you, if a man of such intelligence, learning, and renown has desired to compose a book containing characters where he with great skill has each of them speak according to their own position and authority? Does not the prophet in the person of the fool say that there is no God (Ps 13:1)? And did not wise Solomon especially compose his book *Ecclesiastes* in this manner, through which one can absolve him from the hundreds of errors that there are written down? If the author has spoken in an offhanded way, it is the condition of Venus, or of Cupid, or of a Fool of Love that he wants to represent.[18] Furthermore, did not Solomon in his Song of Songs speak in the disguise of a lover and through words that might draw a person to evil? Nevertheless, one reads the book.

"If the author says in the person of Reason that everything should be called by its name, then his motives should be considered. Truly, what harm is there in names, if they are not understood? Names are names like anything else. If the same thing is meant by one name or another, then what difference does it make what name is given in order to denote something?[19] It is certain that in nature there is nothing ugly. The only ugliness is that of sin, of which in all cases one daily speaks in terms of its correct name, whether murder, theft, fraud, or rape. And in the end, if the Fool spoke of paradise and devout matters, how can he be blamed in something for which he ought to be praised?

"Even if we accept that there is some evil in his book, there can be no doubt that there is more good in it. Each should take the good and leave out the evil. He specifically protests that he accuses only evil men and women. Those who feel themselves to be guilty can improve themselves. Also, there is no one so wise that he does not sometimes fail, as even the great Homer was at fault.[20] Who could better move this wise Court of Christianity to pardon and clemency? We know that Saint Augustine and almost all other doctors of the church have erred on certain points.[21] Nevertheless, they are not accused or condemned but are held in honor. And truly he has quite a fine rose in his hat if he accuses this rose called "The Romance of the Rose."[22]

THEOLOGICAL ELOQUENCE ANSWERS

With these words it seemed to the friends and admirers of the Fool of Love that his cause had been wholly won without anyone knowing how to reply. They smiled and looked at each other or whispered or made various signs. At this point Theological Eloquence, which is the lawyer of the Court of Christianity, at the request of both Conscience and of Chastity, his beloved, and because of his office, got to his feet. Attractive in appearance, temperate in manner, and with great authority and grave dignity, a wise and learned person, he looked down, appearing as a man who was somewhat lost in thought. Then he lifted his face in a ponderous and grave manner and turned his eyes to Justice and all her entourage. Eloquence then opened his mouth. In a gentle, resonant but moderate voice, he began thus to speak his plea:

"I would like very much that it were the desire of God, whom you here represent, Lady Justice, that the author who is accused were here in person, returning from death to life. Then it would not be necessary for me to speak at length or to tire the court with long-winded accusation, for I truly believe that he would freely, quickly, and heartily confess his error or offense and ask pardon, beg for mercy, and do penance. My assumption is based on several indications, especially one that several have asserted: during his life, he repented and afterward made books of true faith and of holy doctrine.[23] I can bear witness to this fact myself. It is a pity that a foolish youth or some other evil disposition deceived such a cleric into directing with such skill and ignorance and with such wantonness his superb powers of mind, great knowledge, outstanding scholarship, and fine ability to speak in rhyme and poetry. Would to God that he had made better use of them.

"Alas, fine friend and clever cleric, alas! Were there not enough amorous fools in the world without your placing yourself in the crowd? Did they not have someone to guide them and teach them in their stupidity without your making yourself into their captain, leader, and master? He is a fool who acts foolishly, but in this foolishness there is no sense. He has too great a desire to be blamed who slanders himself and takes the position of someone who has been slandered.

"In truth you deserved some other expertise and status. Vices and sins, believe me, are too easily learned. One does not need any masters. Human nature, especially in youth, is too prone to trip and slip and fall into the filth of every form of carnality. There is no need that you lead it there and push it down. What are more quickly caught up and burned in the fire of base pleasures than human hearts? Why then do you breathe on this filthy flame with the breath of every flippant word and with the authority of your person and your example? Do you not then fear God and his vengeance? Why are you not made wiser by the punishment inflicted on Ovid?[24]

"The honor of your profession at least should have held you back. You would have been ashamed, I am sure, to have been found in the light of day in public together with the foolish women who sell themselves and to speak to them as you write. You do worse; you exhort them to worse things. You have by your folly, as much as is in you, sent to death and murdered or poisoned thousands upon thousands of persons by different sins and you continue to do so day by day through your foolish book.[25] I do not accept your excuse that you speak through your characters, as I will afterward prove with clarity. But I cannot explain everything at the same time.

"O God, who is all good and all powerful! If you, Fool of Love, since this is the name you want, if you repented in your life of the many writings that out of vanity you made in your youth, then why have you let these writings continue to exist? Should they not have been burned? It is a very bad safeguard to have venom or poison on the table, or fire in the midst of oil and cotton fiber. Who can allow himself to light a fire without putting it out? How can he abandon the houses that will be burned down by it? And what fire is worse and burns more than the fire of lust? What houses are more precious than human souls, as the petition of Lady Chastity so well expresses? For these souls ought to be the sacred temple of the Holy Spirit. But what burns up and inflames these souls more than lewd words and lecherous writings and pictures? We see that good, holy, and devout words, pictures, and writings move one to devotion, as Pythagoras said.[26] For this purpose sermons are given and statues made in churches. All too easily, on the contrary, bad objects lead one to damnation. Everyone experiences this fact, and many stories show it.

"But, good friend, I speak without cause to you, who are not here.[27] You are displeased by this development, and you would be displeased, as I have said, if you had been present.[28] And if at the time you had no knowledge, you have since learned by way of heavy costs and expenses, at least in purgatory or in this world through your repentance. Perhaps you will say that you were not able to recall your book after it had been published, and maybe it was stolen without your knowledge or in some other way. I do not know. But I do know of Berengar, once a disciple of the Peter Abelard whom you often remember.[29] When Berengar came to the hour of death, when truth shows itself to those who have lived well, and it was the day of the appearance of our Lord,[30] he sighed: 'My God,' he said, 'You appear today for my salvation as I have hope in my repentance, or for my harsh damnation as I fear, because those whom I have deceived through wrong teaching I have not been able to bring back to the right path of the truth of your holy sacrament.'[31] Perhaps this is what you say.

"In brief, this is no game here and there is no more dangerous act than to sew evil teachings in the hearts of people, insofar as the pains of the damned increase daily. And if they are in purgatory, their deliverance is hindered and delayed. Concerning Solomon, who was the wisest man in the world, the doctors of theology are in doubt whether he was saved. Why is this so? Because before his death he did not destroy the temples of the idols that he had made because of his foolish love for foreign women (cf. 1 Kgs 11:7–8).

"Repentance is not sufficient when one does not remove the occasions for one's own sins and those of others, insofar as it is in one's power. Nevertheless, regardless of your repentance, whether God accepted it or not (and I hope he did), I am speaking only of the deed in itself and of your book. Since you do not at all defend it as something wise, I will turn the whole of my complaint against those who go against your own judgment and will, in greatly prejudicing your good, honor, and salvation. These people try by any means, good or evil, to defend your book. They do not help you but instead render you a disservice and increase your vanity. Thinking they are defending you, they in fact ruin you. They offend and harm you when they wish to please you, like the hopeless doctor who wants to heal and instead kills, or the foolish lawyer who believes he is helping his master and instead destroys his case.

"I, on the contrary, will provide this service to your soul and give it this pleasure or benefit because of your clerical and learned status. I will provide all that you desire in every single matter. And what kind of ignorance is this here, my good friend?! What is this foolish presumption on your part, which I now see and hear mentioned? For you want to excuse from every folly and error this character who convicts himself, bearing on his forehead the title of his condemnation.

"His condemnation indeed! Do not look at me now. In your own words, he acts as a Fool of Love. Truly, when I want to say a number of terrible things about such an author, I could not call him anything worse than a Fool of Love. This name carries a great and heavy burden because of all the lewdness and carnality that kill all virtues and cause disturbances wherever they can. This is what Plato said, as did Archytas of Tarentum, Cicero, and many others.[32] Who once destroyed the great Troy by fire and flame?[33] The Fool of Love. Who once destroyed more than a hundred thousand good men: Hector, Achilles, Priam, and others? The Fool of Love. Who once chased out of Rome King Tarquin and all his line?[34] The Fool of Love. Who deceives through deceit and disloyal oaths upright girls and holy women in religion? The Fool of Love. Who forgets God and his saints, and paradise, and his end? The Fool of Love. Who pays no attention to family, friends, or to virtues whatsoever? The Fool of Love. From him come civil dissent, plunder, and larceny in order to support a foolish way of life. There arise bastard children, or the suffocation of children born in secret. Acts of hatred also, and the killing of husbands, and, in brief, every evil and every madness thereby arise. All through the Fool of Love.[35]

"But I well see, in this title and by this criticism, that you want to excuse him from his follies, because in a fool you ought to find nothing but madness. In the name of God, this is truth, my good friends. But one ought to show to the fool his madness, and the more so when he is wise and acts the fool. This is all the more the case when he brings great evil to a great country,[36] and basely destroys good customs, with Lady Justice and all her noble Court of Christianity.

"You see how Lady Chastity complains. Shame and Fear and Lady Reason my mistress go in mourning. In sum, all the council and the noble knighthood of the holy virtues, as you well now see from the way they look, are up in arms. And why should they not be? You say here that this actor does not say anything, but it is others who have been brought in here. That is all too small a defense for so great a crime.

"I ask you: If someone called himself an enemy of the king of France, and under this name and as such he made war against him, would this name protect him from being a traitor deserving of death?[37] You would not say so. If in the person of a heretic or a Saracen, or indeed of the devil, someone wrote and spread errors against Christianity, would he thereby be excused? Recently someone wanted to do so but was convinced by one of the chancellors of the church of Paris to come to his senses and be corrected in public before an audience. He nevertheless spoke this way among the listening clerics when he said, 'I speak as a Jew.' 'And you will remember as a Christian,' said the chancellor.[38]

"Another person, if he writes defamatory libels about a person, whether he is of low estate or not, no matter what his origins, even if he does so through fictional persons, will be judged in law as one worthy of punishment as a slanderer. And so what should the laws and you, Lady Justice, say, not concerning a leaflet but about a large book, full of all sorts of slanders, not only against men but also against God and all his saints who love virtue?

"Answer me. Has it ever been heard that someone said to a prince or a lord: 'Truly, sire, I speak to you in the person of a jealous man or an old lady or through a dream, that your wife is very evil and has broken her marriage vows. Look out for her and trust nothing about her. As for your daughters, who are so young and lovely, I counsel that they abandon themselves to every carnal act and to every man who wants to give a good price for them.' Tell me, you good friends, are you so impudent and ignorant that you would judge that such a man should not be punished, and that he should be tolerated, listened to, and let go? And all the more if besides his words he provides books and pictures? And what is worse: that a Christian cleric preaches in the person of a Saracen against the faith, or that he brings in a Saracen to speak and write? The second outrage would never be tolerated, but the first is nevertheless worse, for this is the act of a Christian. The enemy who is disguised is more dangerous than the one in the open, insofar as one receives, listens to, and believes the first in a more familiar way.

"I hand over poison covered with honey. If someone dies from it, will I be innocent of the crime? I strike in kissing; I kill in embracing: shall I be delivered of the act? I will say in public to a devout person: 'Truly those who envy and despise you say that you are a hypocrite and a Papelard,[39] as well as that you are a thief and a murderer, and they offer to prove it.'

"Will I be excused from this libel? An evil rake will act out and speak to a virgin of every form of lechery that can be found between man and woman. He will say, 'Do not act in the way that you see us acting, doing this and that; have a good look.' Would this behavior be bearable? Certainly not, for chastity, good reputation, one's vision, and one's faith are not toys. They are things that are all too easily harmed and corrupted.

"But I can hear what you are all murmuring together: you say, as one of you previously claimed, that Solomon and David acted in such a way. This is all too outrageous, in order to excuse an amorous Fool, to accuse God and his saints and to involve them in the dispute. This cannot be done! I heartily wish that this Fool of Love had not made use of these persons in a way other than Holy Scripture uses them. He should have condemned evil in such a way that everyone would be aware of the accusation against evil and the approval of the good. The most important aspect would be to do so without any misuse of sensuality.

"This procedure, however, was not followed. Everything seems to be said in the person of the Fool. Everything seems to be as true as the gospel, especially for the stupid fools of love to whom he speaks. What grieves me the most is that everything here incites the flame of lust, even when he appears to be reproving it. Even those who are quite chaste, if they let themselves study, read, or listen to it, will get into trouble.

"The doctors of theology say that the Song of Songs, even though its contents are quite sober, was of old read only by those who were over thirty years of age or more, in order that they not acquire from it any base sensuality.[40] What should silly and superficial young people then do with such a book, which is more like fire, which burns more strongly than Greek fire or some solid furnace? Fire, fire, my good people! For God's sake, get away; flee as fast as you can! Save yourselves and keep yourself safe, you and your children. This is the remedy. None is better. Whoever does not flee from the danger will stumble there and be captured like the rat in a trap and the wolf in a snare or the butterfly in a candle's fire because of its brightness, or as fools and children step on shining swords or burning coals because of their beauty, unless someone removes them.

"If you claim that there are many things inside, then I ask you, what about the evil on the outside? Is the fire thereby less dangerous? Does a hook harm the fish any the less when it is covered by bait? Does not a sword, if it is sticky with honey, cut just as well as when it is clean? Moreover, is there any lack elsewhere of good and pure teachings without some evil being attached to them? It is necessary that there be a good outer wrapping on what is evil so that it be held in respect and praised. Mohammed, I say, was most clever in his great malice by mingling the truths of our Christian religion with his filthy errors.[41] Why did he do so? In order better to attract Christians to his law and to hide his offenses. Does not the devil speak several truths at the same time? He does so through those possessed by demons, as by those who call on him, magicians, and also through heretics. But this is only a way to deceive in a more covert manner. Thus an evil teaching becomes worse when it has some good in it and so can do more harm.

"Believe me, and not only me but also the Apostle Saint Paul (cf. 1 Cor 15:33), and Seneca, and experience, that bad words and writings corrupt good habits.[42] In this way come sins without our feeling shame, and they remove every healthy bit of modesty, which is in young people the principal safeguard of their good status in the face of all evils. A young person without shame is completely lost. Why is it that Ovid, such a learned man and a most ingenious poet, was sent into harsh exile without the hope of returning? He himself bears witness that it was because of his wretched *Art of Loving*, which he had written in the time of Emperor Octavian.[43] He then wrote a book in opposition, *The Remedy of Love*, but in vain. Ovid would have well known how to speak through a dream or by characters if he had expected to be excused in this way.

"O God and all his saints! O devout court of Christian religion! O modern morals![44] Among the pagans an unbelieving and pagan judge condemns a pagan who writes down teachings that invite to mad love, while among Christians, and by them, a similar but much worse literary work is defended, praised, and supported. I can hardly express the anger and horror I feel. I lack words to express my disapproval. Certainly I maintain that this work is worse than that of Ovid, for the *Art of Loving*, which Ovid wrote, is not only wholly contained in this book, but the author has translated and brought together and inserted, as if by violence and without meaning, several more books by Ovid and others.[45]

"These writings are no less dishonorable and dangerous than the sayings of Heloise and of Peter Abelard, or those of Juvenal and all the idiotic fables, cursed for this end, of Mars and Venus, of Vulcan and Pygmalion, of Adonis and others.[46] Ovid expressly insisted that he did not wish to speak of good women and married ladies, nor of those who are not to be treated lightly in love. Do you do the same in your book? It includes all women, blames all, has contempt for all, with no exceptions. At least, since the author insisted he was a Christian and spoke of heavenly matters belonging to the faith, why did he not exclude the glorious virgin saints and others without number who even suffered most harsh torments and cruel death in order to guard their chastity or the temple of their hearts? Why did he not maintain some reverence for the saint of saints?[47] Not at all. He was the Fool of Love. He had no cure; he did not want to excuse anyone, in order to provide all the more encouragement that they abandon themselves. He could do so no better than by making women think that they all are this way and that they cannot restrain themselves.

"Necessity knows no law.[48] My God, what a doctrine, for it is not a doctrine but blasphemy and heresy. And so he insists on showing that young people will never be strong and stable in a religion that contains false teachings against human experience. But whoever wants to concern himself with criticizing everything in this book that is evil, he will find that the day comes to an end before his work is done. He might also find that such attention is more harmful to good habits than profitable for his cause. I might fall into the vice that I am rejecting.

"I will shorten my speech and speak only of the articles contained in the supplication of Lady Chastity presented by Conscience. Until now I think I have only dealt with the less weighty articles. It is now time that I consider those that are more grievous and inexcusable. This is an important matter, Lady Justice. Let your council listen and hear them carefully in order to be able quickly to reach a decision.

"Certainly in this book, if it deserves the name of book, we find the familiar proverb (In the tail lies the poison).[49] Here we find the story of Horace, concerning the painter who draws the head of a beautiful woman but completes her body as a fish.[50] It is said that the Harpies are such, with virgin faces but stomachs and other bodily parts that are quite filthy.[51] Alas, what filth has been dumped and collected here. What blasphemies have been spoken! What deviltry has been sown here! After having spoken of God, paradise, the sweet, chaste angel, the beautiful fountain, then in the person of the author he suddenly and immediately tells of his most dissolute life, in which nothing is so repulsive as his absence of shame. He encourages everyone to act in this way, to abandon themselves to all women, whether virgins or not, in order to try everything. And that which is the summit of evil, he says that such acts are sanctified and sacred works that are to be worshiped. He should rather have said that they are abominable and detestable.

"What can I say now? Truly, it is a great abomination merely to think of such matters. I do not want to fill my mouth with filth in speaking any more of this, nor burden your holy ears in fouling this court with having to listen. But I ask that my case not be jeopardized. If it is true as Augustine said that it is no less evil to despise the holy word of God than to have contempt for the body of Jesus Christ, then the author has shown less respect for God by speaking in this way and mingling base matters amid holy and consecrated words than if he had cast the precious body of our Lord under the hooves of pigs or onto a pile of dung.[52] Think how outrageous, hideous, and horrible this would be! It would not have been worse to cast the text of the gospels or the image of the Crucified into a huge, deep, filthy pile of waste.

"Aristotle says, as Seneca tells, that one should never maintain as much devotion and show as much respect as when one speaks of God.[53] And here we find someone throwing together in a filthy pile the precious and holy stone of Christian truth speaking of God. I will argue here that if he believed what he said about paradise, as I think, then it is a pity that he did not think about that in which he believed. If he did not believe it, he was a false and pretentious heretic. And so I charge him with a dissolute life in which he glorifies himself and boasts.

"I would continue to speak, if it were not for the fact that no one any longer can save him. I would speak about how in the person now of Nature, now of Genius, accordingly as Chastity has rightly pointed out, he exhorts and orders without distinction that we make use of carnality and curses all those men and women who do not. He makes no mention of marriage, which Nature nevertheless did ordain. He shows no restraint in his speech and promises paradise to all who act in the prescribed manner. He is a fool who does not believe or who does not comply with such doctrine and does not sing its praises everywhere.

"It is true that this poetic fiction was taken in a corrupt manner from the great Alan, in the book that he made, *On the Plaint of Nature*. A very great part of all that our Fool of Love asserts is hardly anything more than a translation of the writings of others.[54] I know well that he is humble who lets himself borrow from his neighbors and who decks himself out with every feather, as fables tell about the crow.[55] But this makes no difference for me. Returning to Alan, I insist that he never spoke through any of his characters in such a way. He would hardly have done so. He limits himself to speaking against and reproving vices against Nature, and by all rights. I do the same. Be cursed those who act in such a way, and may Justice burn them.

"It is not that Alan encouraged us to one sin in order to flee another.[56] It would be a ridiculous form of surgery to try to heal one wound by another or to extinguish one fire with another. And if someone wants to excuse these acts and outrages through having Nature speak, I respond for you, Lady Nature, that you never counselled anyone to sin, nor did you desire that anyone act against any of the ten commandments. These we call your commandments, Nature's commandments. To say the contrary would be to err in faith by claiming that according to the law of Nature, the natural act of man and woman is not sinful outside marriage.

"Dame Justice, I have spoken for a long time. I am indeed conscious of the time, but it seems brief in terms of the greatness of the crime, since you and your most wise and prudent counsel understand everything in a short presentation. You hate every manifestation of this vile filth; you know all the laws and rights and have long since heard about and spoken of this case. I can say so without hesitation, for I know to whom I speak, and before whom, and for whom. What I have said, then, should be enough to condemn this book and to ban it.[57] This has been done with others that threaten our faith and good morals, and the apostles did the same with the books of those who had been newly converted.[58] In the same way the ancients dealt with the books of a poet named Archilocus, even though they were works of great talent, but they did more to harm the good lives of young people than they profited their minds, just as is the case here.[59]

"I would stop here if it were not that Lady Reason the wise one and my good mistress is making a sign that I should keep speaking. This is no wonder, for her honor is greatly dependent on it. There is no doubt that she well knows how to defend herself, but because I have begun and it is her pleasure that I continue, I will do so gladly and briefly, and more so than the crime requires.

"If this error is outside the province of reason, then you who are here for the sake of the Fool of Love, who inflicts on Reason his madness, is it not then madness to say that one should speak nakedly, boldly, and without shame words that in the judgment of all peoples are so immoral, even for those who live without law or shame? If this teaching had not been long ago rejected by ancient philosophers, then this actor, or those of you who would defend him but actually accuse him, would not be so much to blame. But it is true that before the coming of Jesus Christ, Cicero in his book *On Duties*,[60] as well as other philosophers, and since them the holy doctors of the church, as you still can read and find out, castigated this madness. Moreover, the good behavior that imitates nature has contempt for, rejects, and despises this teaching.

"How then can one support ascribing to Lady Reason such a person, as if those who do not do so were totally lacking sense and reason? If this were so, then Reason would speak not as a sage but as a drunken fool. In God's name, such a person would have belonged more to pigs or dogs than to Reason. And do not disagree with what I say, for some of the ancients who called themselves philosophers were called dogs or dog-like because of this infamous teaching.[61] Was not Cham cursed and made into a low serf only for looking at the uncovered private parts of Noah, his father? (Gn 9:21–25) This was also the error of the Turlupins, who insisted that there was a state of innocence and complete perfection on earth.[62]

"How could one force something more unreasonable on Reason? How could one work harder at making everything irrational than by making Reason speak in such a way, so that in speaking she would tell of questionable matters leading to every form of sensuality? Would you now entrust and hand over your daughters and children to such a doctor, and, if they lack wisdom, would you send them to the school of such a Reason? They would be taught all evils if they did not know how to find them by them-selves, and they would be beaten if they did not speak of the mat-ters about which Reason gives orders.

"In this same way, moreover, it would be proven that one should go everywhere in the nude and without feeling shame.[63] You can be sure that he would support this idea according to his point of view. And see how now he goes into the streets, in order to show how Reason will defend him from being booed and jilted and covered with filth. Further, if Reason had spoken to a wise cleric who understands the nature of things, or to a great theolo-gian who knows that if it had not been for original sin, nothing would have given us shame, then Reason would have had some excuse. He could have pointed to the nakedness of Adam and Eve, although there is no resemblance between their state of inno-cence and ours. This is the difference between the healthy person and the ill one. A wine that does not harm a healthy person will make someone who is shaking with fever lose his senses.[64]

"So it is that in seeing or hearing of carnal matters in naked form or according to their basic condition, sinners who look to them are moved to the basest desires. In the state of innocence this would not have been the case. All of this is apparent because, before they sinned, Eve and Adam were naked without shame. But as soon as they sinned they hid and covered themselves with great shame (Gn 3:7).

"Thus there is no need to ask why one way of speaking is more reprehensible than another when one is talking of the same thing. Here it is not necessary that I pause in order to explain the natural cause, for experience demonstrates the case. It is because of the imagination, which is more suscepti-ble, and it is imagination that creates all desire. This is why Lady Idleness is the doorkeeper for the Fool of Love,[65] for she cannot find imagination and fantasies in a person who is busy. Otherwise she will send him carnal desires of one type or another. In such a situation there is no remedy as good as busy-ing oneself with some worthwhile concern. This is why a per-son who is melancholy, sickly, and of an unhappy disposition will at the same time be more harshly tempted by carnality than a person who is healthy and sanguine, one who laughs and enjoys himself. Everything comes from the imagination. What wonder is it that a fire covered with ashes does not burn as quickly as one that is found in the open? So it is with carnal matters that are talked about or seen in naked form.

"But I return to my intention and say that if the person of Reason had spoken to the wise and solid scholar, that would have been something. But no: he speaks to the Fool of Love. And here the author badly keeps the rules of my school, the rules of rhetoric that are supposed to consider who is speaking and to whom one speaks and at what time.[66] And this fault is not only apparent here, for in other places he attributes to the person who speaks a behavior inappropriate for him, as in introducing Nature speaking of paradise and the mysteries of our faith, and Venus swearing by the body of God.[67] But I am not so concerned with how much he has erred as with the fact that so many want to exalt him above all other authors who have ever existed. I grieve greatly for Lady Reason and for Chastity because of the obscene things that he has had wise Reason say to a young Fool of Love. Cupid, who calls himself god of love, once had forbidden these matters as low language and unfair to women, as if Cupid were more chaste and reasonable than Lady Reason and Chastity.[68]

"O God, I am wrong. There was not one author, as it was at the beginning when the author of whom I speak made all his work. Long ago the foundations were placed by the first author, by his own hand and material without begging here and there and without putting together there the filth and smelly substance that has been placed at the end of this work.[69] I do not know if his successor believed he was honoring him. If he truly did so, then he fooled himself, for after a beginning that possibly could be acceptable in its subject matter even among Christians, he went over to a most disgusting ending and an irrational presentation of Reason. Such a conclusion and such methods not even unbelievers, as I have said of Octavian and the philosophers, could ever have allowed in public affairs.[70] The holy doctors of the church themselves corrected the sayings of these pagans, something that is not at all the case here.

"So I conclude before you and your court, Lady Canonical Justice, that provision should be made, without possibility of appeal, for the arrest of the guilty party. I conclude nothing against the person of the author. But I speak of a crime that is too great. How can it be so? I have above made this point and repeat it here briefly. It is too grave in terms of occasions for errors, for blasphemy, for poisonous doctrines, in the destruction and desolation of impoverished Christian souls, in the unlawful waste of precious time, in contempt for Chastity, in the erosion of loyalty outside of and within marriage, in the banishing of Fear and Shame, in the defaming of Reason, in great dishonor to you, Lady Canonical Justice, and of your laws and statutes, and the whole of this religious Court of Christianity, and in fact of all good persons, and even of the bad ones, who thereby become worse.

"Thus this book should be removed and destroyed, without ever being used, especially in the parts where it resigns itself to dubious and unlawful persons, such as the damned Old Woman who should receive her deserts at the pillory,[71] such as Venus, which is lust, a mortal sin, and such as the Fool of Love, who should not be allowed to fool with his pleasures. One can hardly oppose him or hate him sufficiently. So my request is pleasing to God, reasonable for Lady Justice, agreeable to all your court, and most profitable and well-intended for fools of love, even if they complain for now. Once they are healed they will find my demands both pleasant and delightful. And so that no one may believe or complain that I am accusing persons or anything other than vices, I make in the name of Chastity and Conscience this request and summation against all paintings or writings or sayings that incite to lechery. Our weakness is already too inclined in this direction without thereby becoming more provoked and cast into the depth of vices, far from the virtues and the God who is our glory, our love, our salvation, joy, and happiness."

Eloquence had finished before I noticed that my heart took flight, as if it had been stolen from me. Without hearing the verdict, I found myself in my study at vespers, in the year of grace 1402, the eighteenth of May.[72] There I found many other less fickle matters to occupy my heart. I thought about the subject of the blessed Trinity in divine and simple unity,[73] then of the sacrament of the altar, etc.[74]

Notes

THE MOUNTAIN OF CONTEMPLATION

1. The French text of the *Montaigne de contemplation* is in Gl 7.1.16–55. It was written (according to Gl 10.585) between April and May 1400, while Gerson was at Bruges. He was ill and probably bedridden but had gotten over his depression about the value of scholarly life and wanted to return to Paris (see Gl 1.113–14). For this crucial period in Gerson's life, see my "Loving the Holy Order: Jean Gerson and the Carthusians," in James Hogg, ed., *Die Kartäuser und ihre Welt–Kontakte und gegensitige Einflüsse, Analecta Cartusiana* 62 (Institut für Anglistik und Amerikanistik, Universität Salzburg, and Edwin Mellen Press, Lewiston, New York, 1993), pp. 100–39, esp. 117–23.

2. The French is *aux simples gens*: those who read French but not Latin and so do not have a clerical background. There is nothing derogatory in the expression.

3. The French is *sans lettre*: in English, illiterate. Being literate in the Middle Ages meant being able to read Latin.

4. Bernard's work is translated to English in four volumes by Cistercian Publications. Richard of Saint Victor's mystical works are translated by Grover A. Zinn, *The Twelve Patriarchs, The Mystical Ark, Book Three of the Trinity*, CWS (1979).

5. For Gerson's sisters, see my "Late Medieval Care and Control of Women: Jean Gerson and His Sisters," RHE 92 (1997), pp. 5–37.

6. In the Vulgate, Paul speaks in both cases of how the woman thinks of or considers such matters (*cogitat*), while Gerson uses the verbs *s'estudie* and *s'efforce*. Especially in the second case, Gerson interprets the text so that the woman is compelled to act in such a manner.

7. The French word is *simplesse*, which indicates that the sisters did not know Latin. Gerson assumes that they could read French—and probably write it too.

8. For women's literacy in the fourteenth century, see Karen Scott, "*Io Catarina*: Ecclesiastical Politics and Oral Culture in the Letters of

Catherine of Siena," in *Dear Sister: Medieval Women and the Epistolary Genre*, ed. Karen Cherewatuk and Ulrike Wiethaus (Philadelphia: University of Pennsylvania Press, 1993), pp. 87–121.

9. This point is also made in Gerson's *Mystical Theology*, but here he was communicating directly to women and moving outside the circles of learned Latin culture.

10. Gerson can only be talking about himself. His devotion to his mother is apparent from Letter 9, to his brother Nicolas, where he called her another Monica.

11. The same observation is to be found toward the end of Gerson's *Treatise Against "The Romance of the Rose"* and is also to be found in the Epilogue of Boccacio's *Decameron*.

12. See *Moralia in Job* (6.37), ed. M. Adriaen, CC SL 143, 143A, and 143B (Turnhout: Brepols, 1979-85). The only translation I know is *Morals on the Book of Job by Saint Gregory the Great* (Oxford and London: Parker and Rivington, 1844–50), 1–3.

13. See Proverbs 3:32, in the Vulgate: *et cum simplicibus sermocinatio ejus* (God speaks with the simple).

14. Again one must turn to the Vulgate for Gerson's use of the Bible: *...et in simplicitate cordis quaerite illum* (Wis 1:1). The word *simplicitas* here means lack of cunning or reservation in one's commitment to God. It provides a bridge to the *simples*, the uneducated, who have no second thoughts about their devotion to God. They feel it without intellectualizing or rationalizing.

15. Saint Denis or Denys of France was the bishop of Paris martyred about 250. He became the patron of France. From the ninth century, thanks to Abbot Hilduin of Saint Denis Abbey, north of Paris, Denis was identified with Pseudo-Denis (or Dionysius) the Areopagite, a mystical writer of the fifth century, who had claimed to be the disciple of Paul named in Acts 17:13–34.

16. See *On the Song of Songs* Sermon 23.14. See also Bernard's Sermon 36.

17. The French word is *affection*, what for Gerson in Latin would have been *affectus*, a person's attachment, in this case, to God. See the helpful remarks on *affectus* in the vocabulary of Bernard in Bernard McGinn, *The Growth of Mysticism* (New York: Crossroad, 1994), pp. 500–501, note 212.

18. I think here Gerson is trying to sum up Aristotle's *Ethics*, which starts with the argument that to live well gives happiness: lines 95a18–19 in *Ethica Nichomachea* 1.4, p. 144 in *Translatio Lincolniensis.*

Recensio Pura, ed. R. A. Gauthier (Leiden and Bruxelles: E. J. Brill and Desclée de Brouwer, 1972). Aristotle said his purpose was not to provide knowledge but to make it possible "that we be made good" (2.1, lines 03b26–27, p. 164), anticipating Bernard's and Gerson's insistence on practice and experience as going beyond mere knowledge.

19. I cannot find any exact reference in Aristotle, but Gerson may have been thinking about the discussion of happiness and the contemplative life in the tenth book of the *Ethics*.

20. William of Auxerre was a distinguished Paris theologian from the early thirteenth century. See *Magistri Guillelmi Altissiodorensis Summa Aurea* 3.2, ed. Jean Ribaillier, Spicilegium Bonaventurianum 18B (Paris and Rome: Centre National de la Recherche Scientifique and Collegium S. Bonaventurae, 1986), Tractatus 34, pp. 664–65.

21. This is *Confessions* 8.8, the scene of Augustine's conversion, where he points to those who "have not had our schooling, yet they stand up and storm the gates of heaven while we, for all our learning, lie here grovelling in this world of flesh and blood!"

22. This is actually from William of Saint Thierry's *Letter to the Brothers of Mont-Dieu* (1.2.8), better known today as *The Golden Epistle*, from the thirteenth until the twentieth century attributed to Bernard.

23. The French is *mauvaise tristece*, similar to the *acedia* or immobility in depression against which the desert fathers warned.

24. See *On the Trinity* (9.3.3), on the power of the soul: if it does not know itself, it does not love itself (*Nam si non se novit, non se amat*). Augustine adds (9.4.4) that the soul, love, and knowledge are both three and one, a point of departure for his teaching on the Trinity.

25. Was Gerson writing on the basis of observation from real life or was he repeating what he found in a literary source?

26. Gerson also deals in the *Speculative Mystical Theology* with ways in which the experience of God (*cognitiones experimentales*) has been described, but in *The Mountain of Contemplation* he is even more specific about the sensory content of such experiences.

27. From where did Gerson get this example, literature, his own childhood experience, or "general knowledge" for a cleric in the early fifteenth century? His willingness to use such examples shows the breadth of his pastoral talent, drawing on areas of life with which a lay audience would have been familiar.

28. In French: *vie d'un saint ou sainte*. Gerson may well in this passage be talking about himself.

29. The French *doulceur* corresponds to the Latin *dulcedo*. Gerson

was thinking of God's sweetness as described in Psalm 30:20: *Quam magna multitudo dulcedinis tuae, Domine*. Recent translations often render this passage as "goodness."

30. Gerson may be thinking here of Gregory's story about a mother who gives birth in prison and in darkness. One day she tells her child of the existence of light. The child, having only experienced the darkness, doubts what his mother tells him. The same we do, for we are "born into the darkness of earthly exile" (*Dialogues* 4.1).

31. Again, an image of nourishment, or its lack, resulting in dehydration. Gerson probably knew what he was describing from street scenes in his Paris. Medieval people were acutely aware of hunger and thirst as spiritual concepts. They meditated on the verse, "Taste and see that the Lord is good" (Ps 33:9).

32. Gerson's image may be startling for us, but it was commonly accepted in the Middle Ages that physical force was to be used on children. In the twelfth century there was a debate about to what extent young monks were to be physically punished, but the general consensus was that childrearing involved some form of beating.

For Gerson's educational ideas, see his *On Bringing Children to Christ* (Latin text in Gl 9.669–86) and my "Education, Confession, and Pious Fraud: Jean Gerson and a Late Medieval Change," ABR 47 (1996), pp. 310–38.

33. I have not been able to find the source of this story in the *Vitae Patrum*, but Gerson could have gotten the anecdote from a later saint's *Life* or from an oral source.

34. Gerson attributes to Bernard what actually was written by Gilbert of Hoyland, one of the twelfth-century Cistercian writers who continued Bernard's *Sermons on the Song of Songs*. This is Sermon 7 (PL 184:43). Gerson again mentioned this sermon in a letter to his brother Nicolas (Letter 12, translated below) from Paris, 13 April 1402. In this letter Gerson recalled drawing on this sermon at the time when he had written *The Mountain of Contemplation* (Gl 2.54).

35. Gerson is apparently referring to the teaching of Bernard (or Gilbert of Hoyland) in the interpretation he has provided of Gilbert's (Bernard's) three stages of love in the spiritual life.

36. See Gregory's *Homiliae in Hiezechihelem prophetam* 3.9.

37. Especially in his *Letters to Lucilius*, Seneca considered solitude. In Letter 28, travel does not bring relief, for we have to live with ourselves. In Letter 55.5, those who flee human company find themselves weighed down by their own vices.

38. The French *oisiveté* (from the Latin *otium*). Gerson may be thinking of Seneca's Letter 55:5–8.

39. See Gregory the Great's description of Benedict's periods of isolation, *Dialogues* 2.1.3.

40. In his *Rule* (chap. 1), Benedict points out that hermits first spend time in a monastery, where they test themselves and learn to fight the devil. Only then can they leave and seek isolation.

41. Gerson was skeptical about male and female recluses and shared a deep suspicion in clerical circles toward informal communities of Beguines and Beghards in the Low Countries. These had been accused of heretical beliefs and practices. See Gerson's *On Distinguishing True from False Revelations* (translated below), note 55.

42. Gerson may be drawing here on his own experience, but more likely he was dependent on descriptions he had read. He was familiar with the revelations of Angela of Foligno. See *On Distinguishing True from False Revelations* (below), note 53.

43. The French is *comme en langueur*, close to the Latin *languor*, a sense of weariness or sluggishness.

44. This optimism of Gerson is summarized in a phrase, that man "does what he has in himself" in order to respond to God's grace, a grace that God certainly will give him.

45. This is from Jerome's famed epistle to Eustochium, 22.7.

46. These sentences are very difficult to convey. Gerson is balancing concepts of the interior life of the person and the exterior states she finds or creates.

47. See Ann K. Warren, *Anchorites and Their Patrons in Medieval England* (Los Angeles and Berkeley: University of California Press, 1985) and Sharon K. Elkins, *Holy Women of Twelfth-Century England* (Chapel Hill: University of North Carolina Press, 1988).

48. *Vitae Patrum* 5, *Verba Seniorum* 15.10 (PL 73:955BC).

49. *Confessions* 9.6.

50. Gerson seems to be drawing here on the advice contained in *Vitae Patrum* 5.2.9: "Go and sit in your cell and it will teach you everything" (PL 73:859C).

51. Gerson's term is *une femelete*, a "little woman."

52. One thinks inevitably of Virginia Woolf and *A Room of One's Own* as necessary for a woman's inner life and creativity.

53. Gerson is referring to *Ecloga de oratione, Homilia* 2, PG 63:585–86. Gerson was here summarizing arguments and not quoting directly. It is difficult to find Gerson's nonclassical references in data-

bases, for he rarely quoted word-for-word but instead remembered the essence of his sources. Gerson in his works refers many times to Chrysostom, and specifically in several places to *De compunctione* (as Gl 5.534).

54. See *Rhetorica divina*, chap. 26, in *Guilelmi Alverni Opera Omnia* 1 (Paris, 1674; reprinted Minerva, Frankfurt am Main, 1963), p. 365.

55. The term is *singularité*, from the Latin *singularitas*. In the monastic community no member exceeds accepted norms of behavior. Gerson transferred this idea to lay persons: no one is to act in a way that draws attention to himself or herself.

56. This saying is found in a collection of statements drawn from Aristotle: Pseudo-Bede, *Sententiae philosophicae ex Aristotele collectae* (PL 90:1009C) from his *Physics* 7.20: "In quiescendo et sedendo anima fit prudens."

57. In French: *N'est rien que labeur et diligence ne vinquist.* A typically Gersonian saying, indicating the life he had led until now, admired and rewarded for his diligence.

58. The French is *monseigneur*, a term of respect for nobility.

59. See *Sermons on the Song of Songs* 40.4.

60. French: *sa conversation es cieulx*, taken from the biblical *Nostra autem conversatio in caelis* (Phil 3:20), emblematic for Gerson (see Letter 40, Gl 2.199).

61. Bernard of Clairvaux, *On Precept and Dispensation* 20.60.

62. *On Sense and the Sensible*, part 7, par. 1.

63. *Il pense en ses amours.* Not found in Joseph Morawski, *Proverbes français antérieurs au XVe siècle* (Paris: Librairie ancienne Edouard Champion, 1925) but a well-known saying in French even today.

64. See Valerius Maximus, *Dicta et facta memorabilia* 8.7.7.

65. Ibid., 8.7.5.

66. Referring to *The Mystical Ark*, in Zinn (note 4 above), pp. 151–343, especially I.6, pp. 161–64. Gerson adeptly summarizes in this paragraph the whole of Richard's work. See McGinn, *The Growth of Mysticism* (note 17 above), pp. 398–99.

67. *The Mystical Ark* 5.2.

68. The image of the mountain now becomes central for Gerson's exposition. He drew on a familiar symbol in theological circles and in new vernacular forms of religious literature, as Dante's *Purgatorio*. But in using this image and relating it to problems of everyday life, Gerson left obvious theological sources and provided what appears to be his own exposition.

69. French: *la conversation du monde* (see note 60 above).

70. See Letter 1*, from winter 1399–1400, with very concrete advice about daily devotions. Gerson's remark indicates that there were other letters written prior to April 1400, when he wrote *The Mountain of Contemplation*.

71. *Confessions* 9.10.

72. Gerson did not return to the episode in this treatise but could have intended to do so elsewhere.

73. See Jerome's Letter 22:41.

74. The passage refers to Jerome's vision of Mary and other female saints coming in triumph to celebrate their deliverance, as Moses and the Israelites once did when they crossed the Red Sea.

75. Jerome's Letter 22.7, greatly simplified by Gerson.

76. The *Orloge de sapience* is probably the French translation of the Rhineland mystic Henry Suso's *Horlogium sapientiae*, which in turn is the Latin version of his own German *Little Book of Eternal Wisdom*. See *Henry Suso: The Exemplar, with Two German Sermons*, CWS (1989), p. 33, and Frank Tobin's translation, pp. 207–304.

77. A key passage in Gerson, indicating that he feared the contents of meditation based on images of marriage and sexual union in a way that his predecessors, such as Bernard of Clairvaux, had not done.

78. See *L'orloge de sapience*, chap. 21, concerning how one should learn to die and how it is when one is unprepared for death.

79. Ibid., chap. 17.

80. See *Sermon on the Song of Songs* 43.3.

81. Gerson could have gotten this anecdote from the liturgy for the feast of Saint Cecilia, Second Vespers (22 November). The same description, however, is also found in the *Golden Legend* by Jacobus de Voragine, trans. Granger Ryan and Helmut Ripperger (New York: Arno Press, 1969), p. 690.

82. Gerson's *L'esguillon d'amour* is the *Stimulus amoris*, by the Franciscan James of Milan, but by the end of the fourteenth century usually attributed to Saint Bonaventure. See *Walter Hilton: The Scale of Perfection*, CWS (1991), pp. 16–17.

83. There was an English version, which may have been translated by Walter Hilton (d. 1396). Note Gerson's interest in creating a vernacular literature of the contemplative life, both of his own composition and by way of translations of Latin texts. See Gilbert Ouy, *Gerson bilingue. Les deux rédactions, latine et française, de quelques oeuvres du chancelier parisien* (Geneva: Editions Slathine, 1998).

84. Gerson rarely considers the importance of what people do in community to heighten religious or contemplative awareness. Here he does, but he emphasizes the physical effort that people have to go through in order to sing: *pour la paine qui est en chantant.*

85. Gerson is probably here speaking of himself, following Saint Paul's use of the third person for humility's sake (2 Cor 12:2–3).

86. William of Auvergne, *Rhetorica divina* (note 54 above), chap. 38, p. 375.

87. Ibid., p. 376FG.

88. Ibid., p. 377B.

89. See *The Prayers and Meditations of Saint Anselm*, trans. Benedicta Ward (Penguin Classics, 1973). By Gerson's day many of the prayers attributed to Saint Anselm were not his. Like the work of Bernard, that of Anselm grew in the later Middle Ages.

90. Gerson had, of course, no great library to which he could go in order to check on translations. What was available to him in Paris would have been almost exclusively in Latin. He was a pioneer in seeing the need for religious texts in French. See Ouy, *Gerson bilingue* (note 83 above).

91. In French: *les hospitaulx.*

92. See *Pitieuse complainte* (Gl 7.1.213–16), later inserted into the *Mendicité spirituelle*, from 1401. The prayer is dated to about 1399 (see Gl 7.1.xiv).

93. Probably Gerson himself (see note 85 above).

94. Gerson quotes here in Latin, indicating that he expected his sisters to pray the psalter in that language.

95. Note 85 above.

96. *On Christian Doctrine* 7.9–11.

97. Gerson probably meant Pseudo-Dionysius's *Theologia mystica*, PG 3:997–1064, a major source for Gerson's own *Mystical Theology.*

98. See *Speculative Mystical Theology*, Second Consideration (5).

99. Printed in Gl 7.1.55–57 and dated to 1400–1401, the time of Gerson's writing *The Mountain of Contemplation.* For background, see "Late Medieval Care and Control of Women" (note 5 above).

100. Gerson wanted to make it clear that he had not forced his sisters into taking vows or making any other promises to live a religious life. He was aware of a possible charge that he converted them into an ad hoc Beguine community.

101. Gerson here seems to borrow from *The Rule of Saint Benedict*'s disciplinary provision (chap. 43) that a brother (or sister) who was dis-

obedient could be punished by being excluded from the daily functions of the monastery, and especially from sharing meals with the others.

102. This collection of good advice and examples, known as the *Summa virtutum ac vitiorum*, was written by the Dominican William Peraldus in the 1230s and 1240s.

103. Gerson's sisters would have had a psalter and would have followed a monastic routine, reading the psalms (and thus being able to read some Latin).

104. Notice that Gerson does not here recommend frequent communion.

105. This is similar to the remark found in *The Rule of Saint Benedict* on the need for manual labor (chap. 48): "Idleness is the enemy of the soul."

SERMON ON THE FEAST OF SAINT BERNARD

1. This sermon was probably delivered at the Cistercian College of Saint Bernard in Paris on the feast of Saint Bernard, 20 August. Glorieux dates it to 1402. The text is in Gl 5.325–39. For background and analysis, see my "Gerson and Bernard: Languishing with Love," *Cîteaux Commentarii Cistercienses* 46 (1995), pp. 127–57. Also Louis Lekai, "The Cistercian College of Saint Bernard in Paris in the Fifteenth Century," *Cistercian Studies* 6 (1971), pp. 172–79.

I am most grateful to Rozanne Elder of the Cistercian Institute, Western Michigan University, for checking this translation and providing many helpful suggestions, especially in terms of biblical references.

2. For the technique of medieval sermons, see D. Catherine Brown, *Pastor and Laity in the Theology of Jean Gerson* (Cambridge and New York: Cambridge University Press, 1987), pp. 12–14.

3. Gerson is citing directly from Bernard: *quoniam omnino non potest capere ignitum eloquium frigidum pectus*, from *Sermones super Cantica* 79.1.1 (SBO 2:272). Irene Edmonds, trans., *On the Song of Songs IV* (CP, 1980), p. 138: "It is vain for anyone who does not love to listen to this song of love, or to read it, for a cold heart cannot catch fire from its eloquence."

In order to save space, further references to Bernard's own works do not include volume or page numbers in the Latin edition of his work or in the translations, all available from Cistercian Publications, Saint Joseph's Abbey, Spencer, Massachusetts.

4. The reference here is not only to Isaiah but also to the ordinary of the mass, before the priest said the gospel: "Cleanse my heart and my lips, almighty God, who cleansed the lips of the prophet Isaiah with a burning coal" (for Latin text, see *The Liber Usualis*, ed. Benedictines of Solesmes [Tournai and New York: Desclee Company, 1959], p. 2.)

5. Gerson does not mean here that Mary is divine but is comparing her to the Greco-Roman goddesses of love.

6. See the *Tusculan Disputations* 4.6.11–14.

7. See PL 122:1136.

8. See *City of God* 14.28.

9. *City of God* 14.7.

10. Literally, "less prone to be imitated out of envy." Gerson apparently means that some writers or preachers try to imitate Bernard's style not because they seek his spirituality but because they want to be celebrated for their skill in words.

11. This rhetorical device of taking over the person of the saint who is described in a sermon is, as far as I know, unusual in Gerson's period and shows his rhetorical gift and power of imagination.

In what follows I have made titles, in order to facilitate the reading of the sermon. These do not appear in the Glorieux text.

12. Gerson's source may be Augustine, *City of God* 22.24. This teaching derives ultimately from Plato, but Augustine, especially *The Confessions*, would have been sufficient background.

13. Gerson's Bernard means that the soul in finding its divine image sees God and falls in love with what it sees, as Narcissus did in finding his human image (see Ovid, *Metamorphoses*, Bk. 3).

14. Cf. Juvenal 6.180.

15. Here the voice of Bernard returns, describing his own development.

16. The description of Bernard's sense of crisis in his own spiritual life may come from a passage in *Sermons on the Song of Songs* 14.6, but Bernard here spoke of how he needed a friend to help him, while Gerson's Bernard does not convey such a yearning.

17. In speaking to scholar monks of a school, Gerson used a double vocabulary: he referred to the schools of the University of Paris they visited, but also the school of the service of the Lord (*dominici schola servitii*) in the Prologue to *The Rule of Saint Benedict* (Prol. 45), the point of departure for all monastic life.

18. Gerson's term is *schola litteratoria, schola scientiarum variarum*

and clearly refers to university education, first in the liberal arts, and then in higher faculties, as theology.

19. The Latin is: *in his totus mergebatur intellectus; sed affectus procul erat*. I contrast intellect and emotions, but *affectus* means more than emotions in our sense. The word refers to the *affective* side of being, seeking loves and attachments.

20. This reference to a wilderness in Deuteronomy is a central phrase in early Cistercian literature, and Gerson may be displaying his knowledge of the tradition by referring to it here. See my *The Difficult Saint: Bernard of Clairvaux and His Tradition* (CP, 1991), p. 286.

21. This phrase from the epistle of Paul to the Philippians was one of Gerson's favored maxims, as can be seen in Letter 17 (Gl 2.199)

22. Gerson makes Bernard his mouthpiece for a critique of the intellectual life as an exclusive pursuit, divorced from affectivity.

23. The Latin is *schola religionis* and refers to allegiance to a "religion," which means a monastic order or religious congregation.

24. Again Gerson is close to *The Rule of Saint Benedict*, which looks upon the monastic way as necessary for those not strong enough to live as hermits and who need mutual support (*The Rule of Saint Benedict*, chap. 73).

25. Probably taken directly from the *Vita Prima* (VP) of Bernard of Clairvaux, 1.4.19 (PL 185:237C).

26. Gerson, like everyone else until recently, believed that Bernard wrote this work of spiritual advice, better known as *The Golden Epistle*. See *The Works of William of Saint Thierry: The Golden Epistle*, trans. Theodore Berkeley (CP, 1976).

27. This work, in Latin *De Diligendo Deo*, was one of Bernard's most popular. He actually described *four* steps of loving, the first being that in which a person loves himself. Gerson leaves this one out. See Robert Walton, *The Works of Bernard of Clairvaux 5: Treatises II* (CP, 1974).

28. Writing a few months earlier (April 1402) to his brother Nicolas (Letter 12), Gerson described the "ladder of contemplation" with three stages of contrition, solitude, and contemplation. He claimed to find them in Bernard's *Sermons on the Song of Songs*, but they are actually from the continuation of these sermons made by Abbot Gilbert of Hoyland, no. 7 (PL 184:43).

29. I cannot relate this reference to any particular passage in the book of Jeremiah.

30. This term refers to the summit of the soul's powers, having to do with conscience.

31. Gerson uses elsewhere the same formula for getting rid of the devil in sexual temptation, as *Phy, phy de vobis cogitationes vilissimae!* (Gl 9.60).

32. VP 1.3.7 (PL 185:231B).

33. VP 1.3.6 (PL 185:230C).

34. Gerson addresses here the youngest members of his audience, whose formation in the monastic life is not complete.

35. This last warning apparently does not reflect a particular passage in Bernard. It may be Gerson's own reminder to the older monks that they too are not safe from sexual temptation. See his *De cognitione castitatis*, also known as *De pollutione diurna* (Gl 9.50–64) for a detailed description of sexual temptation.

36. The earlier edition by Ellies du Pin has *eviratorum*, which would suggest homosexual men, while Glorieux prefers the reading *ejuratorum*, lawless men. The context, however, clearly refers to sexual sin and provides one of Gerson's central polemics against sexual activity between men.

37. For this passage in a fuller context, see my "Education, Confession, and Pious Fraud: Jean Gerson and a Late Medieval Change," ABR 47 (1996), pp. 310–38.

38. Again Gerson was drawing his illustrations from the *Vita Prima*, VP 1.4.22 (PL 185:239D) and VP 1.7.33 (PL 185:247B).

39. A reference to what was believed to be the behavior of the eagle as described in *Physiologus* or Bestiary literature: old eagles renew their sight and strength by flying toward the sun. Gerson, however, could have gotten his reference directly from Psalm 102:5: "You will be renewed as the eagle's youth."

40. For these terms, see Gerson's *Speculative Mystical Theology*.

41. The references to Bernard's ignorance of architecture are all taken from VP 1.4.20 (PL 185:238D), but Gerson slightly distorted the passage: Bernard was ignorant of the windows in the church, not in the cell of the novices. For Bernard and his saddle and his ignorance of the Lake of Geneva, see VP 3.2.4 (PL 185:305–6).

42. See VP 1.4.23 (PL 185:240D).

43. The text says *fugebam* (I fled), but this must be *sugebam* (I sucked forth, absorbed) in order to make sense in terms of the following verbs.

44. Gerson here uses the idea of a cow's *ruminatio*: what is absorbed into its system is subjected to several phases of digestion, so that it is chewed, regurgitated, and chewed again.

45. Note that we have no independent prayers or meditations from

Bernard's pen, but by the later Middle Ages his work had "grown" tremendously, in that other writings were attributed to him. Some of these are prayers and meditations (see PL 184).

46. This meditation is Gerson's own, but close to the approach of Bernard, as in *On Loving God*. For more detail, see "Gerson and Bernard: Languishing with Love" (note 1 above), pp. 145–46.

47. See *On Loving God* 5.15.

48. This identification of the soul with God's being is not far from the expressions of mystical union that Gerson questioned in John Ruusbroec (Letter 13 below). Gerson was attracted to such language but also wary (e.g., Bernard, *On the Song of Songs* 18.6).

49. See *The Golden Epistle* (note 26 above) 31.121.

50. This saying appears in the twelfth century, as in Thierry of Chartres, *De sex dierum operibus* 3: "Nam per visionem dilectio et benignitas aliquando designatur sicut in proverbio dicitur: ubi amor ibi est oculus," *Commentaries on Boethius by Thierry of Chartres and His School*, ed. Nicolaus M. Häring (Toronto: Pontifical Institute, 1971), p. 556. Gerson's source, however, is probably Richard of Saint Victor, whose imprint is evident in Gerson's *Mystical Theology*. See *Benjamin Minor* 13, where the saying is reduced to *ubi amor, ibi oculus* (PL 196:10A, *The Twelve Patriarchs*, trans. Grover Zinn, CWS, 1979, p. 65). I am grateful to Åge Rydstrøm-Poulsen for this reference to Richard.

51. Probably taken from *The Golden Epistle* 1.11.38.

52. Augustine, *Confessions* 10.27.

53. Gerson is apparently here following the structure of Richard of Saint Victor's *The Mystical Ark*, also called *Benjamin Major* or *The Grace of Contemplation* (see 5.12).

54. The Latin word is *subarratio*, from the verb *subaro*, to plough close to something.

55. The Latin is *verbigena*, from *verbum* and *gigno*, to be born of the Word, an expression already found in Prudentius, a Christian Latin poet of the fourth century. See his *Cathimerinon* 3.1 and 11.17, ed. W. Bergman, Corpus Scriptorum Ecclesiasticorum Latinorum 61 (1926).

56. See note 30 above.

57. Probably taken from Bernard's celebrated *On Conversion: A Sermon to Clerics* 13.25.

58. Gerson here describes the state of Christianity in the grip of the papal schism, which in 1402 had been going on for almost a quarter of a century and had undermined church authority.

59. Gerson is talking about cravings for food, wine, or sex.

60. Gerson may have been thinking of accusations made against the Avignon pope, Benedict XIII, by Jean Cortecuisse, and answered by Gerson in *Protestatio super statum ecclesiae*. For a review of the debate, see Gl 6.xlviii and John B. Morrall, *Gerson and the Great Schism* (Manchester: University Press, 1960), pp. 55–56.

61. Taken, like so much of Gerson's language, from the psalms: *Cogitavi dies antiquos, et annos aeternos in mente habui* (I thought of ancient days and remembered the years long past) (Ps 76:6).

62. See VP 1.1.1 (PL 185:227C).

63. Gerson's own mother had died a year earlier (8 June 1401). See Gl 1.114. For Gerson on teaching the young, there are several treatises. The *ABC for the Unlearned* is dated to this period (Gl 7.154–57).

64. Gerson is here in accord with *The Rule of Saint Benedict*, chap. 2, on the abbot, where it is said that he will have to answer on the day of judgment for every soul entrusted to him.

65. Gerson may be thinking of a Christmas vision of Jesus that Bernard was said to have had as a boy (VP 1.2.4, PL 185:229B).

66. Gerson felt attached to his sisters partly because he sensed that they were close to God. See "Late Medieval Care and Control of Women," RHE 92 (1997), pp. 5–36.

67. Gerson does not develop the thought because it is time for him to end the sermon, which must not become a treatise.

68. I have been unable to locate this saying in classical or patristic literature. Gerson may have been quoting something that a colleague or other contemporary contact had said. This attitude toward the conversation of friends is *not* a standard one in medieval thinking. Gerson here indicates a fear of involvements and a desire not to waste time on "empty talk." See the conclusion of my article on Gerson's use of Bernard, note 1 above.

69. See Seneca's Letter 28 to Lucilius.

70. Perhaps a reference to Hugh of Vitry (VP 1.3.13, PL 185:235C).

EARLY LETTERS

1. The Latin text of these letters is found in Gl 2.1–116. I have omitted the few letters in the collection sent to Gerson by others, such as Nicolas of Clémanges.

2. See Gilbert Ouy, "Une lettre de jeunesse de Jean Gerson," *Romania* 80 (1959), pp. 461–72, where the letter is dated between 1385 and

1390. Later Ouy put the date back further, perhaps to 1382. See Danièle Calvot and Gilbert Ouy, *L'oeuvre de Gerson à Saint-Victor de Paris* (Paris: Éditions du Centre National de la Recherche Scientifique, 1990), p. 204.

For the career of Pierre d'Ailly, who in 1384 became master of the College of Navarre and in 1389 chancellor of the University, see Alan E. Bernstein, *Pierre d'Ailly and the Blanchard Affair* (Leiden: E. J. Brill, 1978), esp. pp. 62–69.

3. Scylla was a sea monster in a cave opposite Charybdis, a whirlpool or maelstrom associated with the Straits of Messina. See OCD [185] and [820]. First found in *Odyssey* 12, but proverbial, since Horace, *Carmina* 1.27.19, and Augustine, *In evangelio Iohannis* 36.9: a two-sided and thus unavoidable danger.

4. According to the OCD [842], the Sirens were half-women, half-birds, who lived on an island close to Scylla and Charybdis and would lure sailors onto the rocks with their song. Ulysses (*Odyssey* 12) passed them in safety by following Circe's advice to keep his ears sealed and by having his men tie him down.

5. Gerson here is using the image of the underworld river Styx in the sense of the lower world or hell, as in Vergil, *Aeneid* 6.323.

6. The Acheron River disappeared from sight at many places in its course and "was, therefore, reputed to lead to Hades" (OCD [3]).

7. Gerson only barely implied here the use of Christian symbols. The fisherman's ship can refer both to his patron's protection at Paris, and to Christ, the fisher of men.

8. The comic Plautus used *cuculus* as a term of reproach for foolish men. See *Trinummus* 2.1.18. Here, as elsewhere in the letter, the very young Gerson displays his classical training.

9. A reference to the schism of the church.

10. Gerson's meaning is unclear here. He may be indicating that without Pierre d'Ailly's encouragement, he would have gotten nowhere at the University and would have returned home.

11. Palinurus was Aeneas's pilot. He fell asleep at the helm and tumbled into the sea off the coast of Lucania, in lower Italy (*Aeneid* 5.847, 871; 6.381).

12. Tiphys was pilot of the Argo. See *Aeneid* 4.34. For the Argonauts, see *Odyssey* 12.70.

13. The text speaks of two *lustra*, periods of five years each.

14. Again Gerson's meaning is obscure. Could he be referring to Pierre d'Ailly's teaching on how we perceive things? These sentences,

however, introduce the question of financial need. Pierre d'Ailly as Gerson's "doctor" can diagnose the disease and provide the cure.

15. Referring to Christ. Note how references to Christ and the Bible are submerged in the text, while classical names and stories are much more on the surface.

16. The word *deificari* is not found in the Bible, but see 1 Corinthians 6:17, "He who adheres to the Lord is of one spirit." For the New Testament bases for divinization, see Bernard McGinn, *The Foundations of Mysticism* (New York: Crossroad, 1992), pp. 78–79.

17. Not identified. Perhaps a mutual friend formerly at the College of Navarre.

18. Pirithous went with Theseus into the underworld to rescue Proserpine, but they were taken captive. Hercules delivered Theseus but could not save Pirithous (Ovid, *Metamorphoses* 8.302).

19. In the story of the Seven against Thebes, they were brothers-in-law. See OCD under "Adrastus," p. [7].

20. Cicero, *De amicitia* 7 and Ovid, *Remedium amoris*, where Pylades is celebrated as the faithful friend.

21. The biblical reference comes at the end of a string of classical ones. There seems to be more prestige here in displaying classical names than Biblical ones.

22. Gerson uses the word *plurificata* to describe his parents' poverty. Perhaps he is indicating that this poverty is multiplied by the number of children.

23. Gerson indicates here that he will do well, with God's and his patron's help. His success will reflect on his good parents.

24. Literally, "Let it come forth into the light." Notice the change in tone here, from self-abasement to self-assertion.

25. I am not completely sure of the translation here.

26. This is Jean the Benedictine, monk at Reims.

27. Not identified. Ouy, "Une lettre de jeunesse" (note 2 above), pp. 467–68, rejects an earlier surmise that Lord Ar was the archbishop of Reims.

28. Text in Gl 2.6–7.

29. There is a lacuna in the text here.

30. Gerson's mother was attributed the same remark that Saint Louis IX's mother, Blanche of Castille, was remembered as having spoken. See Joinville's *The Life of Saint Louis*, part 2, chap. 1, trans. M. R. B. Shaw, in *Chronicles of the Crusades* (Harmondsworth: Penguin, 1963), p. 182.

31. A reference, of course, to Gerson. The passage indicates that he had responsibility for the care of his brothers in Paris.

32. Poncete may have been born as late as 1385 (see the chart in Jadart, p. 131), but we know her only from this mention and so have no precise year of birth.

33. The hamlet of Gerson has long since disappeared. It was a few kilometers from the village of Rethel, about twenty-five miles northeast of Reims.

34. Text in Gl 2.9. We have this letter because it was quoted by Gerson in his *Discours de l'excellence de la virginité*, written to his sisters (see Gl 7.1.418).

35. The French is *et ne sont effraees nez qu elles estoient de six ans*. I am not sure of the translation, but I think the father is indicating that his daughters are more secure than they were six years earlier, perhaps the last time their brother saw them.

36. Text in Gl 2.14–17. See my "Late Medieval Care and Control of Women: Jean Gerson and His Sisters," RHE 92 (1997), pp. 5–37.

37. Gerson compares the spiritual life to a pilgrimage.

38. The French is *le saint ou la sainte*, more than just "saint."

39. For the gifts of the Holy Spirit, the *Catechism of the Catholic Church* (New York: Doubleday, 1995), no. 1831, and for the capital sins, no. 1866. An early expression of the former is in Gregory the Great, *Liber Homiliarum in Ezechielem* 2.7.7 (PL 76:6–17).

40. Gerson's sisters would thus recite the psalter in Latin.

41. Text in Gl 2.17–23.

42. Gerson is referring to his own "flight" from Paris, but the precise events to which he is referring are not clear.

43. A serious charge in view of recent scandal about corruption under the previous chancellor. See Bernstein, *Pierre d'Ailly and the Blanchard Affair* (note 2 above), pp. 82–114.

44. This admission indicates that Gerson, who made his name with several important sermons at the royal court in the early 1390s, had not been comfortable with that milieu. He found, however, the University almost as bad in terms of political intrigues.

45. Could Gerson be referring to Paris teaching on the movement of bodies, as in the works of Nicole Oresme, master of theology (1362–77)? See Etienne Gilson, *History of Christian Philosophy in the Middle Ages* (London: Sheed and Ward, 1955), p. 518.

46. Gerson's plea of poverty may be genuine. After the Blanchard affair, the income from fees to the chancellor was drastically reduced.

Gerson had to seek church prebends but ran into legal quarrels. See P. Glorieux, "Gerson au chapitre de Notre-Dame de Paris," RHE 56 (1961), pp. 424–48, esp. 428–33.

47. Gerson may be referring to pupils at the cathedral school of Notre Dame but also to arts students at the University, who became his boarders.

48. Gerson's temporary solution had been to accept a preferment by the duke of Burgundy to the deanship at the church of Saint Donatien in Bruges. In holding both this office and that of University chancellor, he was bound to cause some resentment, also because he was now absent from Paris. See E. Van Steenberghe, "Gerson à Bruges," RHE 31 (1935), pp. 5–52.

49. Gerson may be referring to a prebend at Notre Dame, which he had been trying to obtain since 1398. See P. Glorieux, "La vie et les oeuvres de Gerson," *Archives d'histoire doctrinale et littéraire du moyen âge* 25–26 (1950–51), pp. 149–92, esp. 158.

50. An attempt to gain a prebend at the Paris church of Saint-Merry. Gerson began in 1398 and was not successful until 1401. See Glorieux, "La vie et les oeuvres de Gerson" (note 49 above), p. 159.

51. Gerson prefers to stay at Bruges, despite the scandal, rather than giving up his peace of mind and returning to Paris.

52. *Bellum Jugurthinum* 3.3.

53. Gerson is vague but may be hinting at the "affair" of the Dominican Juan de Monzon, concerning the Immaculate Conception of Mary. See Gl 10.3–24. The reference to Plato cannot be traced to a single text but may be meant as a summary of his thought.

54. Possibly a reference to the rivalry between the king's younger brother Louis of Orléans and the duke of Burgundy, Philip the Bold (d. 1404). See Richard C. Famiglietti, *Royal Intrigue: Crisis at the Court of Charles VI, 1392–1420* (New York: AMS Press, 1986), esp. pp. 23–25.

55. Gerson is here playing with the word *beneficium*, referring to the prebends that had been causing so much trouble in his life.

56. Gerson often criticized University students for thirsting after novelties instead of concentrating on solid, established knowledge, as in *Contra curiositatem studentium*, Gl 3.238.

57. Perhaps in irony, Gerson contrasts *beneficium* and *praelatura*: the true benefits that can be accomplished at Bruges and the office that makes them possible.

58. This prophet was the only one to predict failure for the plans of King Ahab, and so he was imprisoned (1 Kgs 22:1–28).

59. A well-known proverb from Horace, Ep. 1.10.24.

60. As shown in the letters and treatises he wrote them.

61. *Heautontimorumenos* 4.3.41.

62. Gerson compares his own resignation from office with the attempt to get Benedict XIII at Avignon (1394–1417) to resign the papacy, the *via cessionis*. See John B. Morrall, *Gerson and the Great Schism* (Manchester: University Press, 1960), esp. pp. 10–13.

63. Gregory Nazianzen (329–89) resigned his bishopric of Constantinople a few weeks after he was made bishop. The former hermit Celestine V was pope for only five months before he stepped down from office in 1294, the only pope ever to do so.

64. Text and meaning are obscure. Gerson could be referring to his ambition to reform the University and the enemies he thereby made. A successor, he indicates, might have a better chance.

65. A prime canonical argument. Since 1394 Gerson had had a benefice at Bruges. He must take the position seriously and concentrate on it, instead of dividing himself between Bruges and Paris.

66. Gerson's basic self-assurance comes through here.

67. Probably irony. Gerson is here at a midpoint between earlier pride in intellectual abilities and later forms of spirituality (see my "Loving the Holy Order: Jean Gerson and the Carthusians," in James Hogg, ed., *Die Kartäuser und ihre Welt-Kontakte und gegenseitige Einflüsse* 1, *Analecta Cartusiana* 62 (Institut für Anglistik und Amerikanistik, Universität Salzburg, and Edwin Mellen Press, Lewiston, New York, 1993), pp. 100–139.

68. This citation meant a great deal to Gerson. See Letter 9, where he used it for his conflicting feelings about family.

69. I cannot find this reference: *Quae nocitura tenes, quamvis sint cara relinque.* Can Gerson have been thinking of a folk ballad?

70. Text in Gl 2.23–28.

71. Gerson seems to indicate here that anyone who sets out, as he is doing, to improve the situation of the church, must be mad!

72. This sentence may indicate that we have only a fraction of the letters that Gerson wrote from Bruges about his situation.

73. Pierre d'Ailly had been bishop of Cambrai since 1396.

74. Seneca, Letter 39.6.8–9.

75. See Gerson's attack on the feast of fools: *Contre la fête des fous*, Gl 7.1.410, dated about 1402.

76. The Catos of whom Gerson was thinking were Cato "Censorius" (234–149 B.C.), known for his conservatism in keeping Greek culture

from Roman life and his great-grandson, Cato Uticensis (95–46 B.C.), with a reputation for rectitude. In Plutarch the two Catos are called Cato Maior and Cato Minor (see OCD [173–174]).

77. Gerson spoke from experience; he had already had his troubles at Notre Dame of Paris, and at Bruges he did his best to reform the chapter, where he found many abuses. See Van Steenberghe, "Gerson à Bruges" (note 48 above), esp. pp. 15–20.

78. Gerson's criticism of preaching underlines an acute awareness in the later Middle Ages that it was essential to convey the teaching of the gospel to the laity in a convincing but sober way.

79. According to the Fourth Lateran Council of 1215, decree 11, every cathedral church was to maintain a theologian to instruct priests in everything having to do with the cure of souls. Each master of theology was to be given a living from a prebend.

80. Prophetic, and indicative of keen awareness of church abuses.

81. Gerson means that, formerly, the least rigorous clerics asked more of themselves than the "strictest" monks do in his time.

82. Glorieux mentions an epidemic that raged in both Paris and Bruges (see "La vie et les oeuvres de Gerson" [note 49 above], p. 160).

83. The Latin word is *schedula*: in classical Latin a small leaf of paper but in medieval usage it could mean a document or report, containing a list of things.

84. Gerson's word is *reformatio*, meaning restructuring and not separation. See Christoph Burger, *Aedificatio, Fructus, Utilitas: Johannes Gerson als Professor der Theologie und Kanzler der Universität Paris* (Tübingen: J.C.B. Mohr, 1986), pp. 45–48.

85. Seneca, Letter 88.37.3–4, also quoted below (note 104).

86. *City of God* 10.23.

87. See Etienne Gilson, *History of Christian Philosophy* (note 45 above), as p. 532: "The criticisms of scholastic theology in the fifteenth and sixteenth centuries will say nothing against it that Gerson has not already said."

88. Gerson may have been thinking about the opening passages in Thomas Bradwardine's *De causa dei contra Pelagium et de virtute causarum* (ed. Henry Savile [London, 1618]).

89. The Latin here is *in divinis*. Gerson's object in this erudite discussion seems to be to underline the freedom of God without sacrificing definitions of the Trinity in church doctrine.

90. The Latin term is *antiqui*, referring not to ancient philosophers but to scholastic theologians before about 1300.

91. Gerson made a similar point in *Against the Curiosity of Students* (Gl 3.239): Just as members of the arts faculty were not to deal with theology, so too theologians were not to dispute on questions of pure logic or philosophy.

92. Each bachelor of theology lecturing on the *Sentences* was to be under the supervision of a regent master in residence at Paris. See H. Denifle and E. Chatelain, *Chartularium Universitatis Parisiensis* 2.1 (Paris, 1891), no. 1189, statutum 11, p. 698.

93. Most commentaries on Peter Lombard's *Sentences* by now were limited to the more theoretical first book and skipped the more pastoral later books. See Burger (note 84 above), p. 46, note 25.

94. Gilson misunderstood what Gerson meant here when he wrote: "Gerson dreams of a simplified theology, the same everywhere, taught in each cathedral school by one single master, perhaps in one school only for all France, perhaps in one single school for the whole Church" (*History of Christian Philosophy* [note 45 above], p. 533). Gerson was referring to the necessity of a primer in religion for *simplices*: people with no Latin. They need to know the basics of the Christian religion. Gerson came to write various "basic books" of religion for those who read French but not Latin.

95. The Latin is *conviviis*, originally banquets, but Gerson was referring to convivial situations, as in taverns, when drink loosens the tongue and people express skepticism. Gerson did not believe in freedom of speech but insisted that the inquisition deal with those who challenged the church's teachings.

96. See note 79 above.

97. Gerson found the power of the chancellor to be too limited; he wanted to refuse the right to teach to doubtful theologians, but he admitted the importance of cooperation with the faculty. He had come a long way from the morbid thoughts of the previous letter and was again involved in the University.

98. Text in Gl 2.29–30

99. Terence, *Heautontimorumenos* 4.1.53.

100. In the book of Numbers, the donkey saw an angel of the Lord with a drawn sword and so turned off the road. Gerson became ill when he prepared to leave Bruges for Paris and so had to wait for recovery. The comparison to a donkey was perhaps meant to provide a touch of humor to his self-characterization.

101. Text in Gl 2.30–35.

102. Terence, *Heautontimorumenos* 56.

103. This may be a quotation from a lost letter to Gerson by the masters of the College of Navarre asking him to return to Paris.

104. The same quotation from Seneca as Gerson used at the end of Letter 3 (see note 85 above).

105. Gerson is summarizing *Ars poetica* 380–82.

106. Gerson's terms, almost intranslatable, are *flaccidum, illiberale, fluidum*. See Seneca's Letter 88, on the liberal arts.

107. Not found.

108. *Eunuchus* 8.

109. Gerson fails to admit here a central problem: that theological candidates were expected to contribute something new to the discussion, and so the search for originality often meant ignoring past contributions. See Hastings Rashdall, *The Universities of Europe in the Middle Ages*, ed. F. M. Powicke and A. B. Emden (Oxford: University Press, 1936 and later), 1:486.

110. Buridan's *Quaestiones super decem libros Ethicorum Aristotelis ad Nicomachum* (Paris, 1513). See Georg Wieland, "The Reception and Interpretation of Aristotle's *Ethics*," in *The Cambridge History of Later Medieval Philosophy*, ed. Norman Kretzmann, et al. (Cambridge and New York: Cambridge University Press, 1982), pp. 657–72, esp. 667–69; and Charles H. Lohr, "Medieval Latin Aristotle Commentaries, Authors G-I," *Traditio* 16 (1970), pp. 161–82.

111. Gerson repeats almost word-for-word the Latin Aristotle: *Aristoteles Latinus* xxvi 1–3, Fasciculus quartus, *Ethica Nichomachea*, ed. Renatus Antonius Gauthier (Leiden and Brussels: E. J. Brill and Desclée de Brouwer, 1973), p. 489, lines 43b12–14.

112. Bonaventure and Thomas are no suprise here, while the Dominican Durand of Saint-Pourçain (d. 1334) is. He ran into trouble because of his *Commentary on the Sentences*. See Gilson, *History of Christian Philosophy* (note 45 above), pp. 473–76.

113. *Quaestiones quodlibetales* were individual questions, taken by themselves and treated by the authorities. Henry of Ghent, a secular master in theology (d. 1293), can broadly be called Augustinian in his orientation. See Gilson, *History of Christian Philosophy* (note 45 above), pp. 447–54.

114. The *Dialogues* contain moralizing stories, *exempla*, about holy men, especially in Italy, in the sixth century. The second book is concerned with the life and sayings of Benedict of Nursia.

115. Gerson may be referring to the work of Eusebius from the fourth century, or to that of the Paris theologian and chancellor Petrus

Comestor (d. 1169), whose compendium on biblical history was known as the *Historia Scholastica* (PL 198).

116. The work of the fifth-century monastic writer John Cassian, of immense importance in Western ascetic literature.

117. The *Vitae Patrum* are brief accounts of the desert fathers of the fourth and fifth centuries, first collected in Greek and later translated into Latin; most easily available in PL 73.

118. Available in many editions; excellently translated by R. S. Pine-Coffin (Harmondsworth and New York: Penguin Books, 1961).

119. William of Auvergne, early-thirteenth-century bishop of Paris. See *Rhetorica divina*, in *Guilelmi Alverni Opera Omnia* 1 (Paris, 1674: reprinted Minerva, Frankfurt am Main, 1963).

120. *Saint Gregory the Great: Pastoral Care*, trans. Henry Davis (Westminster, Md.: The Newman Press, 1950). *Moralia in Job*, ed. M. Adriaen, CC SL 143, 143A, and 143B (Turnhout: Brepols, 1979-85). The only translation I know is *Morals on the Book of Job by Saint Gregory the Great* (Oxford and London: Parker and Rivington, 1844–50), 1–3.

121. *On the Song of Songs* 1–4 (CP, 1977–80). The Latin edition is by Jean Leclercq and Henri Rochais, *Opera Bernardi* 1–2 (Rome: Editiones Cistercienses, 1957–58).

122. Gerson probably meant Richard's *The Mystical Ark*, also known as *Benjamin Major* or *The Grace of Contemplation*, trans. Grover A. Zinn, CWS (1979), pp. 151–343. For William, see note 119 above.

123. For Orosius and his *History Against the Pagans*, see Beryl Smalley, *Historians in the Middle Ages* (London: Thames and Hudson, 1974), pp. 44–45. Third-century Lactantius, according to Peter Brown one of the great Christian apologists (*The World of Late Antiquity* [London: Thames and Hudson, 1971], p. 84), saw Christianity as saving the Roman Empire.

124. Even though it is usually said that medieval people had no sense of "private life," Gerson's term here, *in secreto*, suggests the intellectual who has learned something within himself.

125. Gerson's term is *colloquia*, normally a positive term in classical and medieval Latin. Gerson did not mean vicious gossip but everyday conversations.

126. This statement is one of the most revealing in all Gerson's writings, indicating his sense of distance from other people.

127. See note 120 above.

128. Text in Gl 2.36–42.

129. The phrase "to seek gold in the mud" is not to be found in

Vergil's works, as this reference might indicate. Gerson may be characterizing what Vergil does in *Georgics*, probing through the mud of rural life to find gold in knowledge and moral precepts.

130. Gerson was apparently referring to the mental and physical anguish he had experienced in the previous months at Bruges.

131. These sentences, however rhetorical, reflect Gerson's commitment to study and to the University of Paris.

132. Gerson was perhaps diplomatically implying that the cause of some University factions lay in political society, as the rivalry between the duke of Burgundy and Louis of Orléans.

133. Referring to the nations according to which the students of the University of Paris were divided. See Rashdall (note 109 above), 1:298–320.

134. Perhaps an indication of Gerson's sense of being a "foreigner," an outsider in terms of region and family who in Paris had not forgotten his origins.

135. Aristotle, *Ethica Nicomachea* (note 111 above), 2.1, 03b24–25.

136. *Ars poetica* 1.163.

137. Gerson himself had seen to it that the teachings of Jean de Monzon were condemned and the Dominicans exiled from the University of Paris after 1389 (Gl 10.7–24).

138. Gerson had gone with a legation of the University to the pope at Avignon in May to July 1388. They complained that the Dominican preachers refused to accept the church's traditional teaching on the immaculate conception of Mary (Gl 10.3–4). Gerson at that time was a *baccalareus cursor*, lecturing on individual books of the Bible (Rashdall [note 109 above], 1:475).

139. The Dominican friars were readmitted to the University of Paris on 21 August 1403 (Gl 1.118), probably with the help of Gerson, and in what Rashdall (note 109 above) calls "every circumstance of ignominious publicity" (pp. 550–51).

140. Lucan, *Bellum Civile* 2.142, but Gerson probably got the tag by way of Augustine, *City of God* 3.27.

141. The Dominican friars here indicated a flexibility they had not shown in the 1250s, when they refused to take an oath of loyalty to the University. See Rashdall (note 109), pp. 378–81.

142. Contained in the proverb collection *Polythecon*, ed. A. P. Orbain, Bk. 4, chap. 38, p. 128, found in CC CM 93 (Turnhout: Brepols, 1990).

143. Meaning the Dominicans, who had the conventual house of Saint James (Jacob) in Paris.

144. Assumedly the Dominicans.

145. Text in Gl 2.42–43.

146. See Letter 5 above. Gerson did not merely repeat what he wrote about authors who need to be read. Here he claimed concern with what happened to his own unfinished writings when they were distributed without his knowledge or desire.

147. As so often with Aristotle, Gerson was referring to the *Ethica Nichomachea* (68 a1), apparently in the translation of Robert Grosseteste (see note 111 above).

148. Gerson may have been thinking of the "little elevation" at the end of the canon of the Latin mass: "Through him and with him and in him, is to you God the almighty Father, in the unity of the Holy Spirit, *all honor and glory....*"

149. Gl 2.44. This letter accompanied the treatise "On Abstinence from Meat Among the Carthusians" (Gl 3.77–94). See "Loving the Holy Order" (note 67 above), esp. pp. 125–28.

150. Gerson is referring to Pierre d'Ailly. The term *religionem carthusiensium* describes the Carthusian way of life or discipline.

151. This hint that Jean de Gonnant might not be able to read Latin indicates that, for Gerson, the Carthusians at the time would have been willing to admit a knight with rudimentary Latin.

152. Text in Gl 2.45–48. My colleague Kirsten Grubb Jensen, at the Institute for Greek and Latin, Copenhagen University, has suggested that Gerson may have been influenced in this letter by reading Petrarch's letter to his brother Gerard, who had become a Carthusian. See *Familiarium Rerum Libri* 10.3: "To Gerard, his brother and Carthusian monk, on the happiness of his state and the miseries of the world, with the exhortation that he persevere in his intention." See Francesco Petrarca, *Opere* (Firenze: Sansoni, 1975), pp. 650–62.

153. The angelic society on earth experienced in the monastic order, here that of the Celestines, whom Nicolas had joined.

154. Gerson here leaves conventional piety and reveals himself.

155. See Letter 23 for similar expression of Gerson's concern about how another brother, Jean the Celestine, could manage the harshness of the Order's austerities.

156. Gerson's word for softness is *mollities*, the same word he uses for masturbation. Attachment to his brother is equated with weakness of the flesh, an illustration of Gerson's moral codex.

157. Gerson must have known quite well the *Life of Martin of Tours* by Sulpicius Severus. Its scene of temptation by the devil (chap. 6) fits perfectly Gerson's description of the temptation he imagines both he and his brother experienced.

158. An amazing assertion. Gerson almost goes so far as to assume that the taking of academic degrees in the arts would have been equivalent to choosing the path to damnation. For him, the University of Paris is part of the "evil world" from which his brother has saved himself. In the next sentence, however, Gerson pulls back and declares his conclusion to be only a conjecture.

159. Gerson used this same quotation from Matthew at the end of Letter 2, his list of complaints against his position at Paris.

160. I cannot capture the Latin play on words, since in that language *free* and *child* are almost the same term: *ut enim succurramus LIBERIS EORUM nunquam LIBEROS nos esse volunt* (Gl 2.47).

161. Gerson apparently felt that he as the oldest child and son had carried too much responsibility.

162. Hannah offered Samuel to the Lord: "As long as he lives, he is given to the Lord" (1 Sm 1:28). As with classical references and hagiography, Gerson was so well versed in Bible stories that he could almost always find parallels.

163. See Letter b above. The comparison to Monica is one that has been much noticed and quoted in treatments of Gerson (as James Connolly, *John Gerson: Reformer and Mystic* [Louvain: Librairie Universitaire, 1928], p. 22). Elisabeth la Chardenière had died a few months earlier, on 8 June 1401. Her death may have intensified Gerson's feeling of loss of his brother Nicolas.

164. *Enarrationes in Psalmos*, CC SL 40.

165. Text in Gl 2.48–49. For the Celestine Order, founded by the hermit pope, Peter Murrone, Celestine V, as one among many late medieval attempts to reform monastic life, see the article "Célestins," DTC (1910), 2:2064–68. Also DHGE (1953), 12:102–4. These treatments do not emphasize the severity of everyday life in the Order, but Gerson may have known better. Its founder was well known for his ascetic observances and would have been a model to his monks.

166. *Heroides* 1.12.

167. The Vulgate term is *in Christi visceribus*, literally, in his innards or guts, thus the love that comes from within Christ.

168. The term *orator* recalls the medieval conception of a society divided into those who pray, those who fight, and those who work.

169. Text in Gl 2.54–55. The letter shows Gerson's need to remain in contact with his brother after Nicolas joined the Celestines (Letter 9). It is unclear whether Gerson was addressing Nicolas or his superior.

170. This is *The Mountain of Contemplation*, translated above.

171. This is not Bernard's work but its continuation by Gilbert of Hoyland (Sermon 7, PL 184:43). The translation is my own, but see the full translation of Gilbert in Cistercian Publications, *Sermons on the Song of Songs* 1.

172. Gerson was very much caught up in this subject at this time. In winter 1402–3 he gave a course of lectures that became his *Speculative Mystical Theology* (see Gl 3.xii).

173. The ending is perhaps left deliberately unclear: the word *pupillum* indicates either that Nicolas remains Gerson's responsibility or is now in the Celestine superior's care.

174. Text in Gl 2.56–62. This letter shows, as does Letter 12, Gerson's interest at this time (1402) in questions of mystical theology.

175. The Latin title is *De ornatu spiritualium nuptiarum. John Ruusbroec: The Spiritual Espousals and Other Works*, trans. James A. Wiseman, CWS (1985). See André Combes, *Essai sur la critique de Ruysbroeck par Gerson* 1–3 (Paris: J. Vrin, 1945–59).

176. The term *idiota...sine litteris* means someone who cannot read or write Latin.

177. Note that Gerson read Ruusbroec in Latin translation, probably that of William Jordaens (d. 1372). See Wiseman (note 175 above), p. 32. The assertion of the "author" about the effort Ruusbroec had shown with the Latin probably came from Jordaens.

178. See Ambrose, *Expositio evangellii secundum Lucam* 2.19 (PL 15:1560). Also in CC SL 14, ed. M. Adriaen (Turnhout: Brepols, 1957), p. 39.

179. This is the fourth definition in constitution 28, *Ad nostrum qui*, at the Council of Vienne, 1311–12, condemning all teaching claiming that a spiritual person can obtain here the same perfect beatitude that he will realize in heaven. See *Conciliorum Oecumenicorum Decreta*, ed. Centro di Documentazione Istituto per le Scienze Religiose-Bologna (Basil: Herder, 1962), p. 359.

180. Perhaps a reference to Bernard of Clairvaux's statement that our absorption in God resembles the way a drop of water seemingly disappears when mingled with a cup of wine (*On Loving God* 10.28, in SBO).

181. The chapters in the CWS edition, based on the original Middle

Dutch text, are not quite the same as what Gerson had in the Latin translation. For this passage, see p. 147 in Wiseman's translation (note 175 above). I translate directly from Gerson's Latin, with a result slightly different from Wiseman's.

182. *Spiritual Espousals* (note 175 above), p. 149.

183. Ibid., p. 150.

184. Ibid., pp. 145–46.

185. Ibid., p. 150.

186. Probably referring to Augustine's *Retractationes*, written toward the end of his life in 426 in an attempt to admit and remove earlier errors in his writings. See PL 32:583.

187. Gerson's term is *apud exercitatos theologos in sacris litteris*. The term "sacred letters" refers to the study of the Bible, the point of departure for all theology.

188. Since Duns Scotus (d. 1308), questions of God's ordained or absolute power (*potentia ordinata seu absoluta*) characterized theological discourse. See Gordon Leff, *The Dissolution of the Medieval Outlook* (New York: Harper & Row, 1976), pp. 13–14.

189. No theologian would be able to put together a formal *quaestio* for the problems Ruusbroec creates. His point of view is beyond rational, intellectual, trained scholastic discourse.

190. For Gerson, Ruusbroec's removal of categories of being in order to emphasize the union of human with divine would abolish necessary distinctions between types of being.

191. If the soul is the formal principle of life, then it cannot lose itself in God as Ruusbroec has explained. Gerson requires absolute distinctions in modes of being.

192. Cf. Boethius, *Consolation of Philosophy* 3.10–11.

193. See Wiseman (note 175 above), pp. 139–41.

194. For the Beghards condemned at the Council of Vienne, see Robert Lerner, *The Heresy of the Free Spirit in the Later Middle Ages* (Berkeley and Los Angeles: University of California Press, 1972), pp. 78–84.

195. Chronologically impossible. The Council of Vienne took place in 1311–12. Ruusbroec's *Spiritual Espousals* probably belongs to the 1330s. Gerson's attempt, however, to exonerate Ruusbroec from the charge of heresy shows his sympathy and the attraction he felt to Ruusbroec's expression of the mystical life.

196. *City of God* 10.23.

197. A point to which Gerson regularly returns in his *Mystical Theology*.

198. *De Trinitate* 14.1.3.

199. *Hierarchia coelestis* 7, a favored quotation of Gerson (see also his *Notulae super Dionysium*, Gl 3.215, from this period).

200. Perhaps taken from the discussions about virtue and vice in *Ethics*. See *Ethica Nicomachea* 6.13, 44a34–37 (note 111 above).

201. See the *Heavenly Ladder* of John Climacus (late sixth century), abbot of Mount Sinai and known for his asceticism (PG 88:596–608). John Rupert Martin, *The Illustration of the Heavenly Ladder of John Climacus* (Princeton: University Press, 1954).

202. See *Collationes* 13.6. Gerson's word is "impassibilitates," the best Latin translation of the Greek *apatheia* or lack of passion or feeling in connection with the Stoic ideal practiced by some of the desert fathers.

203. See Gerson's warnings to the Celestine superior of his brother Nicolas against extreme asceticism (Letter 10 above).

204. Horace Ep. 2.1.115f. Jerome Ep. 53.6 (PL 22:544).

205. Text in Gl 2.63–64. The *De vita spirituali animae* (Gl 3.113–202) has six lessons on Mark 1:8, John the Baptist's "I baptized you with water, while he will baptize you in the Holy Spirit." These lessons are part of Gerson's commentary on the Gospel According to Mark, most of which has been lost.

206. *Epistolae ex Ponto* 4.1.28.

207. The letter could be looked upon as excessive praise by a disciple of his master, but at this point in his career Gerson probably had nothing to gain in being so devoted to d'Ailly.

208. Pierre d'Ailly had asked only for the lesson he had heard. Gerson sent him six lectures, in almost schoolboy enthusiasm to impress his master!

209. The Latin is *alium pro lectionibus, alium pro tractatibus stylum esse*. For Gerson's stylistic awareness, see Gilbert Ouy, "Gerson, émule de Petrarque," *Romania* 88 (1967), pp. 175–231. Also André Combes, "Gerson et la naissance de l'humanisme," *Revue du Moyen-Age latin* 1 (1945), pp. 259–84.

210. The terms *rationalis, irascibilis*, and *concupiscibilis* I render as the powers of reason, of emotion, and of desire.

211. The term *quidditatem* could be roughly translated as the "whatness" of a thing, but Gerson adds *a radice*, "from the root."

212. Gl 2.65–70. Gerson first treated the subject in May 1402, *Contre le Roman de la Rose*, translated below. For a chronological outline of the dispute, see Gl 10.25–26. Eric Hicks, however, dates this letter to winter

1402–3: *Le débat sur le Roman de la Rose* (Paris: Éditions Honoré Champion, 1977), p. liv. Pierre Col was a cleric, canon of Notre Dame and of Tournai, chanter of Saint Martin of Tours (Hicks, p. xii, note 17), with an important position at court as secretary to the chancellery. He was also responsible for diplomatic missions.

213. Gerson is referring to *The Romance of the Rose*.

214. According to Peter Brown, Pelagianism was invented by Augustine, not by Pelagius. See "Pelagius and Pelagianism," in *Augustine of Hippo: A Biography* (London: Faber and Faber, 1967), pp. 340–52, esp. 345. After Augustine, Pelagianism meant a belief that we are basically good at birth and only gradually are corrupted by the choice of sin.

215. *De nuptiis et concupiscentia* 2.3.9 (PL 44–45:440).

216. See Hicks (note 212 above), p. 92, for Pierre Col's claim that one cannot judge something unless one has experienced it.

217. *Satirae* 2.2.8–9.

218. See Hicks, p. 98.

219. *Eunuchus* 63.

220. See the *Disticha Catonis* 1.4.2, used as a Latin primer. Schoolboys would memorize its sayings.

221. Pierre Col predicted that Gerson in the future would go mad with love (Hicks, p. 97).

222. Hicks could not find the quotation but points out that Quintilian attributes it to Cato (*Institutio oratoria* 12) (Hicks, p. 230 166/93). See also Apuleius, *Apologia* 94.

223. Christine de Pizan, the first female author known to have supported herself through her writings. See Elizabeth Alvilda Petroff, *Medieval Women's Visionary Literature* (New York: Oxford University Press, 1986), pp. 303–7.

224. See Christine de Pizan's letter *A Maistre Pierre Col* (Hicks, p. 127, lines 405–10). Gerson shows his awareness of Christine de Pizan's contribution to the polemic against *The Romance of the Rose*, even though he does not mention her by name.

225. Christine de Pizan, *A Maistre Pierre Col* (Hicks, pp. 135–36).

226. *Adelphi* 643.

227. Pierre Col, *Responce aux traités precedens* (Hicks, p. 104, lines 540–45).

228. Pierre Col, *Responce* (Hicks, p. 107, lines 645–49).

229. Pierre Col, *Responce* (Hicks p. 102, lines 467–74).

230. Probably Ovid. He compensated for his *Art of Loving*, with the *Remedy of Love* (Pierre Col, *Responce*, Hicks, p. 105).

231. Pierre Col had argued, as fiction authors ever since, that his fictional characters did not necessarily reflect the author's point of view (*Responce*, Hicks, p. 100).

232. Ovid, *Amores* 3.4.17: *nitimur in vetitum semper.*

233. Gerson's reference is either to the Christian court described in his treatise attacking *The Romance of the Rose*, or to the royal court of France. He may here be purposely ambiguous.

234. Hicks (p. 230, 172/203) refers to the parts of *The Romance of the Rose* that are drawn from the classical and medieval authors mentioned here. The discourse of Nature is inspired by Alan of Lille's *The Plaint of Nature*. Terence and Martianus Capella are not among Jean de Meung's direct sources. But Gerson was also talking about himself and the sources of his knowledge. This list can thus be used as a guide to Gerson's readings in his youth.

235. Trans. by Ewert Cousins, CWS (1978).

236. See R. P. H. Green, ed. and trans., *Augustine: De doctrina christiana* (Oxford: Clarendon Press, 1995).

237. For Gerson, eloquence and truth belong together in theology, and so he can attack Jean de Meung for separating the two.

238. The Latin is *mediocri sermone*. Gerson is referring to his original attack on *The Romance of the Rose*.

239. Text in Gl 2.71–72. In early October 1403, Gerson left Paris with six other masters to visit the papal court of Benedict XIII. They obtained the privileges they sought for themselves and the University. On 18 November 1403, a papal bull incorporated the church of Saint-Jean-en-Grève under the chancellor of Notre Dame, a post Gerson earlier had been given but with which he had legal problems. His sermon of 1 January 1404, however, displeased the pope, who revoked the privilege. Gerson was back in Paris by 17 January. See P. Glorieux, "La vie et les oeuvres de Gerson" (note 49 above), pp. 149–92, esp. 167, and John B. Morrall, *Gerson and the Great Schism* (University Press: Manchester, 1960), pp. 65–68.

240. A town fourteen miles southwest of Avignon, on the Rhône River.

241. The duke was Louis (b. 1372), brother of the periodically mad king, Charles VI. On 23 November 1407 Louis was murdered by the duke of Burgundy's men. See Richard C. Famiglietti (note 54 above), pp. 23–37, and Richard Vaughan, *John the Fearless: The Growth of Burgundian Power* (London: Longmans, 1966), pp. 29–48.

242. Advocates of the *via cessionis* tried to convince both popes vol-

untarily to cede office, so that a new pope could be elected. See Francis Oakley, *The Western Church in the Later Middle Ages* (Ithaca, N.Y., and London: Cornell University Press, 1979), p. 62.

243. Benedict could at a later point, after his resignation, be reelected to the papacy.

244. Not "our lord the pope," but just "our lord." Gerson withheld recognition of Benedict XIII as rightful pope. According to Morrall (note 239 above), Gerson changed his position toward Benedict.

245. The new year did not begin on 1 January, and so Gerson still wrote 1403; our notation says 1404.

246. Text in Gl 2.72–73. The treatise Gerson sent was *Le miroir de l'âme*. It came to make up the first part of the very popular *Opus tripartitum*, which also included treatises on confession and on preparation for death. See Thomas Tentler, *Sin and Confession on the Eve of the Reformation* (Princeton, N.J.: Princeton University Press, 1977), p. 45. This letter was often included as an introduction to the *Threefold Work* (see Gl 7.1.xiii).

247. The word *speculator* (sentinel) can refer to the bishop's function as overseer or investigator of his flock's health, protecting it from the enemy, as by warnings given in pastoral literature and sermons.

248. Text in Gl 2.74–76. For the *Opus tripartitum*, note 246 above. The recipient does not necessarily have to be a prelate of the church. Gerson may have been looking to the new duke of Burgundy, John the Fearless, on the death of his father Philip the Bold, on 27 April 1404. Philip had been Gerson's patron.

249. The Maison-Dieu was the hospital where the local church provided for the care of the sick. See the visitation records (1248–69) of Archbishop Eudes of Rouen, trans. Sydney M. Brown and ed. Jeremiah F. O'Sullivan, *The Register of Eudes of Rouen* (New York and London: Columbia University Press, 1964), at pp. 183–84.

250. For the corporal works of mercy, *Catechism of the Catholic Church* (New York: Doubleday, 1994), no. 2447.

251. *Locis religiosis* could also be holy places, as those of pilgrimage.

252. The greater part of the letter's contents are then repeated in French, in addressing parish priests themselves.

253. Text in Gl 2.76–77. Glorieux (2.xv) assumed the recipient was Gerson's father, who died at the Benedictine abbey of Saint Rémy, Reims, in September 1404. Gerson's failure to mention the brother Jean the Benedictine, as well as the rather formal tone of the address, however, point elsewhere. Max Lieberman (*Romania* 81 [1960], pp.

338–79) thinks the recipient was Philippe de Mézières and dates the letter to 1403. Philippe was a well-known writer attached to the court of the duke of Burgundy, Philip the Bold, and died in 1405 (Richard Vaughan, *Philip the Bold: The Formation of the Burgundian State* [London: Longmans, 1962], p. 200).

254. *La science de bien mourir*, also known as *La médecine de l'âme*, the third part of the *Opus tripartitum* (Gl 7.1.404–7).

255. From the *Lives of the Fathers* (*Vitae Patrum* 15.1, PL 73:953), the story was concerned with humility. Gerson changed the moral, encouraging his correspondent to concentrate on his own salvation and to stop being concerned with other people!

256. Perhaps a reference to Jacobus of Voragine's *Golden Legend*, 23 January: An emperor had a tomb made of marble and precious metal, and John the Almsgiver also had a tomb built, but left unfinished. John was to be told daily to hurry and finish his tomb, for we do not know when the thief will come to claim us.

257. There is a lacuna in the text here.

258. The name Robert without any title indicates that the man is a servant of the letter's recipient. For Gerson, such a person could have read French but not Latin.

259. Gl 2.78–80. Glorieux points out (2.xv) that it is difficult to determine the precise date of the letter. See Letter 16 above.

260. Again, Gerson does not use the title "the pope" for Benedict XIII (see note 244 above).

261. Terence, *Phormio* 697.

262. Gerson was probably thinking of the third part of Gregory the Great's *Pastoral Care*, with a guide to the art of preaching. For the fifth-century Greek theologian John Chrysostom, see his imposing *De sacerdotio* (*On the Priesthood*), PG 48:627–92.

263. See note 236 above.

264. The closest equivalent in Apuleius is in *De Deo Socratis* 2.30 (*non animo sed auribus cogitant*).

265. Apparently not biblical. The closest I can come, thanks to Mark F. Williams, is the remark by a Spartan, Dieneces, before the battle of Thermopylae. When told that the Persians would shoot so many arrows that they would blot out the sun, he replied that if the Persians hide the sun, "we shall have our battle in the shade" (Herodotus, *The Histories*, Bk. 7.226).

266. The Latin is *poena et culpa*. In one of the central manuscripts these last words are missing, so Gerson would have been understood to

claim something far more dangerous, that the power of the parish priest is equal to that of the pope.

267. An allusion to the question of reserved cases for confession. See Tentler (note 246 above), pp. 304–13. Gerson indicates that parish priests in extreme situations can give absolution for sins normally reserved for special confessors.

268. Text in Gl 2.80–84. In the Latin text the geographical term is *in monte vallis,* which is not absolutely clear. In the earlier edition of Gerson, that of Louis Ellies du Pin (2.773), this place name is rendered as Mont-Valérien, which is a hill on the outskirts of Paris. Glorieux followed this reading without comment.

269. A common maxim found, for example, in Jerome, Letter 54.6, to a woman on the duty of remaining a widow: *Arripe, quaeso, occasionem et fac de necessitate virtutem.*

270. In the Vulgate the word is *curam,* not Gerson's *cogitatum.*

271. *Salus* can mean physical health or spiritual salvation. Gerson seems to be using both senses of the word.

272. Compare with Aelred of Rievaulx's *Rule of Life for a Recluse,* which Gerson almost certainly did not know, but which reflects the mainstream of "literature of advice" for hermits.

273. The Latin term is *acedia* (also spelled *accedia*). The translation *depression* is a very imprecise one. *Acedia* is a state of mind associated with loss of courage, belief, or conviction, especially for a person in the ascetic life. See *The Sayings of the Desert Fathers,* trans. Benedicta Ward (London and Oxford: Mowbrays, 1977), pp. 1, 61, 71, 158, 197.

274. Gregory the Great's *Moralia in Job,* ed. M. Adriaen, CC SL 143, 143A, and 143B (Turnhout: Brepols, 1979-85). The only translation I know is *Morals on the Book of Job by Saint Gregory the Great* (Oxford and London: Parker and Rivington, 1844–50), 1–3. For Benedict, see *RB 1980: The Rule of Saint Benedict,* ed. Timothy Fry (Collegeville, Minn.: The Liturgical Press, 1980). For the *Rule of Saint Augustine,* George Lawless, *Augustine of Hippo and His Monastic Rule* (Oxford: Clarendon Press, 1987). The *Institutes* of John Cassian are edited and translated by Jean-Claude Guy, *Institutions cénobitiques* (Paris: Les éditions du Cerf, 1965). The *Sermons on the Song of Songs* by Bernard are translated in Cistercian Publications.

275. A common proverb: Hans Walther, *Lateinische Sprichwörter and Sentenzen des Mittelalters und der Frühen Neuzeit* 3 (Göttingen: Vandenhoeck and Reiprecht, 1965), p. 75, no. 95c (Matthew of Vendôme, *Poetria* 2.3); also vol. 8 (1983), p. 567.

276. Text in Gl 2.84–86. See Morrall, *Gerson and the Great Schism* (note 239 above), p. 74.

277. The title (*qui se facit Romae Gregorium XII appellari*) shows that Gerson and d'Ailly did not recognize Gregory XII as pope.

278. Referring to Gregory XII, who seemed to offer hope of reconciliation: he suggested a personal meeting at a place chosen by the Avignon pope. See Morrall, *Gerson and the Great Schism* (note 239 above), pp. 69–70.

279. The text of the unique manuscript is corrupt here. Glorieux had to provide alternative readings. I substitute *animarum* (souls) for *animalium* (animals) to make sense of the passage.

280. Minerva cannot be taught. She is wisdom itself. Similarly, a theologian should not teach a pope, who should be theological wisdom itself. Gerson may have gotten the saying through Jerome (*Apologia contra Rufinum* 1.17).

281. "Apostles" means the heretical Beghards. See Robert Lerner, *The Heresy of the Free Spirit in the Later Middle Ages* (note 194 above), pp. 66–67.

282. Rachel (Gn 29) for the medieval church represented contemplative life.

283. Text in Gl 2.86–90. This is the last of what we can call the "personal letters." Hereafter Gerson concentrates, in Abelard's pattern, on "letters of advice." An absolute distinction between the two categories, however, cannot be made.

Glorieux is very uncertain about the dating, but 1408 is a good guess. By now Gerson had returned to Paris, with no success in ending the schism. He was concentrating on teaching and preaching. Family involvements remained important for him.

284. Gerson had been with d'Ailly in Italy (Genoa) in January. They could have visited Nicolas at the Celestine house of Villeneuve near Avignon on the way home. Jean was about to make his profession at the monastery of Limay, near Mantes in the diocese of Rouen. See Gl 1.122.

285. Almost a commonplace from the *captatio benevolentiae* as used in medieval letterwriting. Gerson rarely expounds on the virtue of friendship in such a manner.

286. Gerson was probably about forty-five when he wrote this letter. In the usual Roman categories, old age begins in the sixty-first year, so Gerson is stretching the criterion a bit.

287. A paraphrase from *Heautontimorumenos* 503–4.

288. The same biblical reference is also in Letter 20.

289. Could Gerson be referring to the fact that both brothers, who once lived with him at Paris, had now left him (Letter 9)?

290. *Religionem* refers both to the Celestine Order and its way of life, which Gerson found too harsh for his brother.

291. Cf. 1 Jn 3:18: "...non diligamus...lingua, sed opere et veritate" (let us not love with speech but in deed and truth).

292. We lack the letters of advice that apparently so upset the youngest brother. I think they touched on sexual matters.

293. There is word play on the terms *genus* and *species* here.

294. A good indication of how much Gerson resented the fact that his brothers had left him to join the Celestines. So long as Jean was with Gerson in Paris, there were no mental problems.

295. Gerson was skeptical about forms of religious life and experience that were so extreme that they could bring their practitioners to the verge of madness. But Jean persisted in his vocation and welcomed his exiled brother to his house at Lyon in the 1420s. After Gerson's death, Jean the Celestine became the keeper of his brother's literary legacy and preserved his works.

296. I have been unable to locate the saying.

297. Text in Gl 2.90–93. For background, see Tentler (note 246 above), pp. 308–9. Tentler points out (p. 311) that Gerson's teaching here is different from that in the second part of the *Opus Tripartitum*, dealing with confession, where a wide number of sins, especially of a sexual nature, are taken out of the jurisdiction of the parish priest. Tentler's explanation is that this work is a conservative one, meant for wide distribution, and so Gerson was careful not to challenge the prerogatives of the church hierarchy (pp. 312–13). I would add that this work was originally written in French, and so Gerson felt obliged to be more cautious than when he was writing in Latin, for a more limited public, as in the letter translated here.

298. See Gerson's *Sur l'excellence de la virginité*, only partly available in Gl 7.1.416–21. The full text contains a graphic description of the dangers of married life for women. See my "Late Medieval Care and Control of Women" (note 36 above).

299. For candles.

300. William of Auvergne, *Rhetorica divina* (note 119 above), chap. 12, col. 348G, comes close to this statement. Tentler (note 246 above), p. 334, notices this quote at least four places in Gerson but does not indicate its source.

301. Gerson may have been alluding to his own experience.

302. Gerson indicates an economic motive for priests to whom reserved cases are entrusted.

303. Cf. the parable of the lost sheep. The sheep has no choice but to allow itself to be brought back to the fold (Mt 18:10–14).

304. Representatives of each of the former popes.

305. Gerson was still hoping that both popes voluntarily would give up office (*via cessionis*) and that this would happen soon.

306. Juvenal, *Satirae* 6.300.

307. In connection with usury or cheating (Tentler [note 246 above], p. 308).

308. Text in Gl 2.93–96. Ermine of Reims received visions from 31 October 1395 until her death on 25 August 1396. An account of her life was written by her confessor, Jehan le Graveur, under-prior of Saint-Pol at Reims. Jean Morel, prior of the abbey of Saint-Denis at Reims, sent it to Gerson for his approval (see Gl 2.xvi). Gerson had been in Reims in April 1408 for a synod convoked by the archbishop. See the translation below of Gerson's *On Distinguishing True from False Revelations*.

309. Gerson is referring to the immensely popular collection known as *Vitae Patrum* (PL 73).

310. The Latin word for "discourse" here is *conversatio*, which until now in medieval Latin has meant one's way of life. It was used for the most part in a monastic context, and so here we find Gerson opening it into a larger context and moving toward the modern sense of communication by speech.

311. The statement is a variant of the golden rule, cf. Mt 7:12, Lk 6:3.

312. God can always make miracles happen. What he once did, as in the Bible and the lives of early saints, he can repeat.

313. Gerson emphasized in his *Mystical Theology* that training in scholastic theology is by no means necessary for someone to whom God chooses to reveal his truth.

314. Cf. Is 14:12–17. For the fall of Lucifer, Rv 12:9.

315. See *Vitae Patrum* (PL 73:953B), Bk. 15.3: "Again Abbot Anthony said: I saw all the traps of the enemy set up on earth. I moaned: Who can one imagine will be able to get past them? And I heard a voice saying: Humility."

316. I cannot find a precise equivalent among the many sayings under the headings of humility and discretion (note 315 above). The closest equivalent is the assertion that "our own wills become demons" (PL 73:923A: *Verba Seniorum* 10:62).

317. *The Life of Ermine.*

318. Text in Gl 2.97–102.

319. John of Schoonhoven entered Ruusbroec's religious community at Groenendaal in 1378, four years before the mystical writer's death (*John Ruusbroec: The Spiritual Espousals and other Works*, trans. James A. Wiseman, CWS [1985], p. 3). The Latin original of Schoonhoven's letter is in André Combes, *Essai sur la critique de Ruysbroeck par Gerson* (Paris: J. Vrin, 1945), 1:729.

320. See Letter 13 above.

321. *City of God* 10.23, already used in Letter 13.

322. Probably referring to the opening of Basil the Great's treatise on the Holy Spirit, *Liber de Sancto Spiritu* (PG 32:67–71), emphasizing the extreme importance even of prepositions in describing interrelationships of the persons of the Trinity.

323. The Nicene Creed established, against the Arians, that the Father and Son are identical in essence, *homousious.*

324. Gerson's point is that theological language can be used figuratively without being distorted. He is referring to verse 16 of the great hymn of thanksgiving, *Te Deum laudamus*: "You in receiving humankind to liberate it did not reject the womb of a virgin."

325. Gerson's explanation for the rigid procedure of question, objections, and answers in scholastic theology is perhaps the best defense for its dry formulae, which make it almost unreadable for us. The very structure of language and expression was meant to make statements more liable to control and verification.

326. Despite his concession of the possibility of special revelations to the uneducated (Letter 25), Gerson remained a champion of scholastic training for theological discourse.

327. Gerson is apparently referring to Albert the Great's *Commentary on Dionysius' Mystical Theology*, trans. Simon Tugwell, *Albert and Thomas: Selected Writings*, CWS (1988), pp. 131–98.

328. For William of Saint Thierry's use of this expression, see Bernard McGinn, *The Growth of Mysticism* (New York: Crossroad, 1994), p. 266.

329. Cf. the famous Thomistic adage: "Grace does not suppress nature but perfects it" *(gratia non tollit naturam sed perficit)* (*Summa theologiae* Ia.i.8, ad 2).

330. At the Fourth Lateran Council (end of the second article), the teaching of Amaury of Benes was called "insane" (*Conciliorum...Decreta* [note 179 above], p. 209). Hostiensis (Henry of Segusio, d. 1272) was

cardinal bishop of Ostia and is best known for his defense of papal power. See his *Lectura in quinque decretalium, De summa Trinitate*, §6, Reprobamus. Also DHGE 24, fasc. 142 (Paris, 1992), col. 1248. The image of the drop in water is found in Bernard of Clairvaux, *On Loving God* 10.28 (note 180 above), 3.143. Gerson also used this image in Letter 13. See the discussion in McGinn (note 328 above), pp. 213–14, with reference to Gerson's attack. Also, see the *Speculative Mystical Theology* 1.41.

331. I have been unable to find the identity of this Augustinian theologian, but one possibility would be a successor to Henry of Ghent, who died in 1293. According to Etienne Gilson (*History of Christian Philosophy in the Middle Ages* [note 45 above], p. 449), Henry's doctrine of our knowledge of God creates problems of the type Gerson here criticizes: "In a doctrine in which all infallible truth is known in the divine light and for which the first object known in this light is divine being itself, to see truth in the light of God grows perilously near to seeing God in the light of God."

332. The Latin text says *in capitulo vitis*, a reference that I have not succeeded in finding.

333. Such people belong to the heresy of the free spirit, but the term does not apply to a well-organized heretical movement. See Robert Lerner, *The Heresy of the Free Spirit* (note 194 above).

334. This is a quotation from Gerson's own earlier letter on Ruusbroec (Letter 13 above).

335. Gerson's *Mystical Theology*.

336. *Bucolics* 8.108.

337. See Letter 13 above.

338. Robert Lerner (note 194 above), p. 166, where he disagrees with Gordon Leff's interpretation of this passage (*Heresy in the Later Middle Ages* [Manchester: Manchester University Press; New York: Barnes and Noble, 1967], 1:357).

339. I cannot replace the Latin pun: *amantium immo et amentium*.

340. Translated below.

341. *Ars poetica* v. 438–44.

342. The Arian heresy claimed that the Son was not equal to the Father.

343. Gerson treated this question in detail in his *Against the Curiosity of Students* (Gl 3.245), from 1402, on the importance of using terms that are both certain and agreed upon in speaking of God: "On the basis of this consideration our masters [at Paris] and I were greatly concerned

that the teaching of Raymund Lull not be published, for he has terms that have been used by no other doctor [of theology]."

344. Note the self-assuredness in Gerson's tone here, a stark contrast with his self-doubt a few years earlier.

345. Text in Gl 2.103–105. Saint Denis was the great abbey church just outside Paris, the burial place of the French kings and of Saint Denis, bishop of Paris and martyr (third century). Gerson and others in his time still confused Saint Denis with Pseudo-Dionysius the Areopagite and with the disciple of Saint Paul (Acts 17:13–34). Apparently the cathedral church of Notre Dame in Paris claimed to have the head of Saint Denis. For more than four years, from 16 October 1406 to July 1410, there was vigorous controversy between the two churches concerning this relic of Saint Denis. On 7 November 1407 Gerson preached at the church of Saint Catherine and defended the relic of Saint Denis at Notre Dame (see Gl 1.121). See also Gl 10.498–500 for further developments after Gerson's letter to the abbot.

346. The panel may have been a painting on wood, perhaps part of an altarpiece, and seen by Gerson and his fellow canons as challenging the authenticity of their relic of Saint Denis.

347. Gerson contrasts the heads of the superiors, which the abbot of Saint Denis lacks on his side, with the missing head of the saint, which Notre Dame of Paris claims to have!

348. Gerson was probably referring to, among other things, his now lost sermon from 7 November 1406 on the head of Saint Denis.

349. Gerson was much more permissive in allowing multiple relics of the same bodily parts for saints than the twelfth-century abbot Guibert of Nogent (*De pignoribus sanctorum*, PL 156:607–80).

350. Gerson's argument for not challenging the veracity of relics was perhaps shored up by a consideration he articulated a few years later at the Council of Constance, concerning the veracity of Birgitta of Vadstena's (Bridget of Sweden's) revelations: "To denounce these revelations, which are declared authentic in many places and by different peoples, after various and numerous examinations, would pose a threat, perhaps great, of spiritual harm to the Christian religion and the devotion of the faithful" (*De probatione spirituum*, trans. Paschal Boland, in *The Concept of Discretio Spirituum* [Washington, D.C.: Catholic University of America Press, 1959], p. 28).

351. Text in Gl 2.105–7. Compare this letter with Gerson's previous letters to Pierre d'Ailly (such as Letters 3 and 14, and possibly also Letter 1). In these earlier letters he tried to impress his teacher with his

knowledge, especially in terms of classical allusions, while here Gerson writes purely in religious terms and language.

352. This Pauline phrase, *Nostra conversatio in coelis est*, became Gerson's motto. See the description of his shield and its text, made in 1417 to his brother Jean the Celestine, Letter 49 (Gl 2.199).

353. This amazing assertion, apparently theologically unique, indicates a great deal about Gerson's search for isolation from the people around him. See Colleen McDannell and Bernhard Lang, *Heaven: A History* (New Haven, Conn.: Yale University Press, 1988).

354. Gerson may here be paraphrasing the hymn *Iste Confessor Domini*, sung at Second Vespers on the feast of a confessor who was not a bishop.

355. Given on the feast of All Saints, 1 November 1402. See Gl 5.91–107 and Max Lieberman, "Gerson et d'Ailly," *Romania* 78 (1957), pp. 433–62, esp. 443. The other sermon for All Saints that Gerson here mentions is apparently lost.

356. The octave is the eighth day following a church feast. Saint Denis's feast was 9 October, so this letter would have been written on 16 October.

357. *De divinis nominibus*, chap. 8 (PG 3:598).

ON MYSTICAL THEOLOGY: THE FIRST AND SPECULATIVE TREATISE

1. Gerson's original title for the work seems to have been *Six Lessons on Mystical Theology*, but I chose the title by which it is best known, in order to distinguish this *Speculative Mystical Theology* (SMT) from the *Practical Mystical Theology* (PMT). Gerson wrote this first work as lectures for the faculty of theology at Paris University in the winter of 1402–1403. According to Glorieux (3:xii), Gerson added the *Practical Mystical Theology* in September-November 1407 and then published the two treatises together at Paris at the end of March 1408. Minor revisions were made while Gerson lived in exile at Lyon in the 1420s. I follow the critical edition by André Combes, *Ioannis Carlerii de Gerson de Mystica Theologia* (Lugano, Switzerland: Thesaurus Mundi, 1958). Combes's edition is almost too richly footnoted, and I will only reproduce references to the extent that they are of central importance for understanding Gerson's meaning.

I originally translated all of the SMT but because of space must limit the translation here to the introductory segment and a discussion on love, rapture, and ecstasy.

2. Gerson is quoting here from the last lines of his treatise *Against the Curiosity of Scholars* (Gl 3.249), written on 8 and 9 November 1402, just before the composition of the *Speculative Mystical Theology*. A part of the former work has been edited and translated by Steven E. Ozment in *Jean Gerson: Selections*, Textus Minores 38 (Leiden: E. J. Brill, 1969), pp. 26–45.

3. For Dionysius, see Bernard McGinn, *The Foundations of Mysticism* (New York: Crossroad, 1991), pp. 157–82. The phrase "mystical, thus hidden" is perhaps taken directly from Albert the Great's treatise *Super Mysticam Theologiam Dionysii*, chap. 1 (*Opera Omnia*, 37, 2, ed. Paul Simon [Cologne: Aschendorff, 1978], p. 453). See the translation by Simon Tugwell, *Commentary on Dionysius' Mystical Theology*, in *Albert and Thomas: Selected Writings*, CWS (1988), p. 135.

4. Each of the terms given here (*contemplatio, meditatio, raptus, extasis*, etc.) has a long tradition in Christian theology and deserves an essay by itself. These words, nevertheless, have acceptable modern equivalents. The phrase *mentis excessus* implies a more cognitive and less affective state of elevation than rapture or ecstasy. I have chosen to follow David Schmiel's translation, *extra-mental projection*. See his helpful *Via Propria and Via Mystica in the Theology of Jean le Charlier de Gerson*, Graduate Study no. 10 (St. Louis, Mo.: School for Graduate Studies, Concordia Seminary, 1969), p. 6.

5. The passage is both difficult to translate and to understand. I do not think Gerson is here indicating that he had had what we loosely can call "a mystical experience." He is saying that in trying to understand and describe the phenomena associated with the mystical life, he meets intellectual and perhaps also spiritual difficulties.

6. Gerson's meaning is that by trying to look at the meaning of mystical experience, he will because of pride lose sight of God in the light of glory (*lumen gloriae*) promised in the beatific vision.

7. Cf. *Against the Curiosity of Scholars* (see note 2 above).

8. Gerson is apparently referring to his offices as teacher at the faculty of theology and chancellor of the University. He is saying that despite his obligations here, he cannot allow himself to hide the "talent" he has been given in order to describe another kind of theology.

9. Bernard of Clairvaux speaks of the hidden manna in terms of the spiritual kiss of Christ: "I think no one can even know what it is, except the one who receives it." See *Sermones super Cantica* 3.1 (SBO 1:14).

10. Gerson is referring to the great Sequence, formerly used in masses for the dead, the *Dies irae*, the *Day of Wrath*.

11. Gerson deliberately uses the term *vacate* (to rest) instead of the Psalm's word *gustate* (to taste). His meaning is that in the leisure of contemplation, one comes to taste the sweetness of the Lord.

12. The word *affectus* represents for Gerson all that lies in the emotional and spiritual side of one's being, as opposed to the *intellectus*, the rational and intellectual identity. "Affectivity" is probably a better translation than "affections."

13. Gerson's remark is aimed at theologians who would ban discussion of the mystical life from university discourse. Even though he was willing to admit the possibility of mystical experience for the unlearned, Gerson insisted that there must be a theological language that could deal with mysticism.

14. This is the Hebrew Psalm 10, placed as a continuation of Psalm 9 in the Vulgate version, and usually marked as (10).

15. See Pseudo-Dionysius Areopagite, *De divinis nominibus (On the Divine Names)*, PG 3:679. Notice that Gerson has indeed just completed a prayer, in crying out his insufficiency to God. However "familiar" such a beginning might sound, it was highly unusual as the opening of a scholastic-style treatise. Gerson hearkens back to the pre-scholastic theology of the eleventh and early twelfth century. One thinks, for example, of the prayer with which Anselm of Canterbury's *Proslogion* begins.

16. Gerson may have known Hilduin's *Life of Dionysius* (PL 106:13–50), esp. chaps. 6–8 about the relationship between Paul and Dionysius, but the story was well-known and generally accepted in the medieval period.

17. Gerson's word here, *omninomius*, refers to symbolic theology as expressing God's "possession of every name" (*omninomininabilis*).

18. For this distinction between *theologia propria* and *theologia mystica*, see David Schmiel's work (note 4 above).

19. This means that Gerson did not possess Dionysius's *Symbolic Theology*—nor do we. Modern scholars have doubted its existence. See *Pseudo-Dionysius: The Complete Works*, trans. Colm Luibheid, CWS (1987), p. 57, note 89.

20. See, for example, Albert the Great, *Super mysticam theologiam*, in *Opera Omnia* (note 3 above), 37, 2, p. 466.

21. Cf. Pseudo-Dionysius, *De mystica theologia* 2 (PG 3:1026): "et supranaturalem illam caliginem intueamur...."

22. For this last phrase, see Augustine's *Confessions* 9.4.11, as well as

Richard of Saint Victor, *Adnotatio in Psalmum XXX* (PL 196:273). For the earlier terms, Combes gives a great number of references, including William of Saint Thierry's *Epistola ad fratres de Monte Dei*, known as *The Golden Epistle*, Pseudo-Dionysius, Richard of Saint Victor, Thomas Aquinas, and Bonaventure.

23. More so than *theologia propria*, the theology of the schools, which proceeds by rational investigation.

24. Gerson's emphasis on experience goes back to the affective theology of the twelfth century, as seen, for example, in Bernard of Clairvaux's *Sermons on the Song of Songs* and in Hugh and Richard of Saint Victor. See Hugh's famous dictum, "Experience is the teacher of understanding" (*magistra intelligendi experientia est*), in *Expositio in hierarchiam coelestem S. Dionysii areopagitae* (PL 175:1061BC).

25. Paul as "our philosopher" is called such in Duns Scotus, *Reportata Parisiensia* (*Opera Omnia* 24, Bk. 4, d. 49, p. 625).

26. Gerson could have gotten this reference either from Seneca's *Letters to Lucilius* (no. 52.10) or from Saint Jerome, *Commentarium in Ecclesiasten* 3:6/7.

27. Combes could not find a reference in Plato. I think Gerson may have been thinking about the arguments for the immortality of the soul, which Socrates toward the end of the *Phaedo* characterized as "a belief worth risking." See the Penguin Classic translation (Harmondsworth: Penguin Books, 1966 and later), p. 178.

28. See Thomas Aquinas, *Summa theologiae* IIaIIae, q. 2, a. 3, where reference is made to Aristotle's *De sophisticis elenchis* l. I, c. 2, n. 2.

29. Gerson is referring here to the Augustinian tradition of belief leading to understanding, which was especially summed up in Saint Anselm's famous dictum *Credo ut intelligam* ("I believe so that I may understand").

30. This is an alternative reading to the more common Vulgate text, "Si non credideritis, non permanebitis" (If you do not believe, you will not stand fast).

31. See Bonaventure, *In Hexaëmeron Collatio* 20:10 (*Opera Omnia* 5, p. 427): "This is perfect contemplation...which...no one can explain."

32. I have translated Gerson's *ratiocinatores* as "theorists," people who develop rational explanations for phenomena.

33. *De viris illustribus*, chap. 109 (PL 23:743).

34. Thus the great divide in Gerson's thought is not between "proper" theology and mystical theology, but between theological knowledge obtained in direct mystical experience and theological

knowledge obtained through the processes of reason. Those who have the latter can rightfully deal with mystical theology, even though they personally have no experience.

35. By these terms Gerson refers to mystics or pseudo-mystics who followed their own inclinations (*affectus*) and had no respect for the authority of the church. Robert Lerner deals with all the passages in Gerson using this term (*The Heresy of the Free Spirit in the Later Middle Ages* [Berkeley and Los Angeles: University of California Press, 1972], pp. 164–68) and concludes that Gerson did not have personal experience of these heretics and for the most part saw them as a phenomenon of the past.

36. Gerson is referring to William of Auvergne, master in theology at Paris from 1223 and bishop there from 1228–49.

37. The Latin word here is *quidditas*, indicating the essential quality of something, that which makes it what it is.

38. By the word *formalizantes* Gerson apparently means that he will make formal distinctions among his concepts in order to make his definitions visible and understandable, but without claiming that these distinctions reflect actual differences in reality.

39. Gerson is attacking those who would multiply abstract entities and claim for them a real existence. His purpose is to maintain God's simplicity, and his point of view brought him into conflict with the followers of Duns Scotus. See Louis B. Pascoe, *Jean Gerson: Principles of Church Reform*, Studies in Medieval and Reformation Thought 7 (Leiden: E. J. Brill, 1973), p. 83, note 8.

40. The statement could be taken from Pseudo-Bede's *Philosophical Sentences Collected from Aristotle*: "Non est mendacium abstrahentium" (PL 90:1022A), referring to Aristotle's *Physics* 2, t.18.

41. Here again it is clear how Gerson argues in a mild form of the so-called nominalist mode, warning against the multiplication of entities. For him the mental process of definition of the powers of the soul is not to be used to divide up the soul into "real" compartments.

42. See the Pseudo-Aristotelian *Liber de causis* §16, ed. O. Bardenhewer (*Die Pseudo-aristotelische Schrift über das reine Gute* [Freiburg im Breisgau, 1882]), p. 179. Similar statements are to be found in Robert Grosseteste and Pseudo-Bede.

43. *De Trinitate*, esp. 15.5.8.

44. *Synderesis* is defined by Thomas Aquinas as a "special natural habit of mind" that has a moral sense (*Summa theologiae* 1.79.12). For Gerson, it is a faculty at the "apex of the mind" in terms of the affective

powers. See the helpful note by D. Catherine Brown, *Pastor and Laity in the Theology of Jean Gerson* (Cambridge and New York: Cambridge University Press, 1987), p. 309.

45. See Thomas Aquinas, *Quaestiones disputatae de veritate* 2, q. 2, a. 1.

46. As in Albert the Great, *Summa de homine*, as cited in Odo Lottin, *Psychologie et morale aux 12e et 13 siècles* 2:1 (Louvain/Gembloux, 1948), p. 213. See also Bonaventure, *In libros sententiarum* 2, d. 39, a. 1, q. 2 (*Opera Omnia* 2, p. 903).

47. As in William of Auvergne, *De anima* 7.13, in *Opera Omnia* 2, pp. 219–20 (Orléans-Paris, 1674).

48. This medley of sayings is taken from various sources, including possibly Boethius's translation of Aristotle's *De interpretation vel Periermenias* (Bruges/Paris, 1965), p. 9, on affirmation and/or negation, and the Aristotelian sayings contained in Pseudo-Bede, *Philosophical Sentences Collected from Aristotle* (PL 90:1031): "Omne totum est majus sua parte."

49. See *Liber de intelligentiis* 10, in Clemens Baeumker, *Witelo. Ein Philosoph und Naturforscher des XIII. Jahrhunderts* (1991). Also Bonaventure, *Sententiarum libri* 2, d. 39, a. 2, q. 1.

50. See especially §3 in chap. 7 of *De divinis nominibus* (PG 3:870–71). Also Thomas Aquinas, *Quaestiones disputate de veritate* 15, a. 1, and 16, a. 2, in discussing Dionysius.

51. *De quantitate animae* 34.77 (PL 32:1077–78). For the relationship between the human soul and God in terms of divine illumination, see Etienne Gilson, *The Christian Philosophy of Saint Augustine* (London: Victor Gollancz, 1961), pp. 79–80.

52. Pseudo-Dionysius, *De caelesti hierarchia* 4, §4 (PG3:181B).

53. For the shadow, see Albert the Great, *De causis et processu universitatis a prima causa*, lib. 1, tract. 4, cap. 5, in *Opera Omnia* (note 3 above), 17.2, p. 48.

54. Once again Gerson uses the word *quidditates*, which I have translated as "the essences of things."

55. Gerson here follows the teaching of Thomas Aquinas. See his *Summa theologiae* Ia, q. 77, a. 5.

56. Cf. Augustine, *De Trinitate* 12.3.3.

57. This fundamentally Augustinian position was available to Gerson from many sources, e.g., Bonaventure, *Breviloquium* 2.9.7.

58. Combes noticed closeness of language here to that of Isaac Israeli, *Liber de definitionibus*, ed. J. T. Muckle, *Archives d'histoire doctrinale et littéraire du moyen âge* 11 (1938), p. 313: "...anima racionalis, quoniam

ipsa in horizonte intellicenciae...." But the more probable source is William of Auvergne, *De anima* 6, in *Opera Omnia* 2 (Orléans-Paris, 1674), p. 211.

59. For what follows here, see Thomas Aquinas, *Summa theologiae* Ia, q. 78. a. 3 and 4.

60. This is the *sensus communis*. See Aquinas, *Quaestiones disputatae de veritate*, q. 15, a. 1.4.

61. For synderesis, see note 44 above.

62. Cf. Bonaventure, *Sententiarum libri* 2, d. 39, a. 2, q. 1: "Dico enim, quod synderesis dicit illud quod stimulat ad bonum."

63. By this awkward definition Gerson wants to consider synderesis as a mental power, as opposed to the following definitions of act and habit. The fullest treatment of teaching on synderesis is perhaps in Lottin (note 46 above), pp. 103–350, "Syndérèse et conscience aux 12e et 13e siècles."

64. Cf. Bonaventure, *Sententiarum libri* 2, d. 39, a. 2, q. 2.

65. Bonaventure, *Sententiarum libri* 2, d. 39, a. 2, q. 1. See also Thomas Aquinas, *In Secundo Sententiarum*, d. 24, q. 2, a. 3.

66. For synderesis as a spark of intelligence, see Jerome, *In Hiezechielem* 1.i (CC SL 75, p. 12).

67. See Bonaventure, *Itinerarii mentis in Deum* 1.6, in *Bonaventure: The Soul's Journey into God*, trans. Ewert Cousins, CWS (1978).

68. The word here is *affectio*, and once again it seems that Bonaventure's teaching lies behind Gerson's considerations. See *Sententiarum liber* 2, d. 39, a. 1, q. 1.

69. Gerson may be thinking of Aristotle's *De anima* 3.9, as quoted in Aquinas, *Summa theologiae* Ia, q. 82, a. 5. Gerson's source in Augustine may be the Pseudo-Augustinian *Liber de spiritu et anima*, chap. 13 (PL 40:788–89).

70. See Thomas Aquinas, *Summa theologiae* IaIIae, q. 9, a. 2.

71. See Thomas Aquinas, *Summa theologiae* Ia, q. 80, a. 1.

72. The example of the ant is known from classical literature, as in Aesop's Fables. See also Vergil's *Aeneid* 4.402–3.

73. Augustine's *City of God* has similar considerations, but centered on the creative power of God. See *De civitate dei* 7.30.

74. Cf. Thomas Aquinas, whether union be the effect of love (*Summa theologiae* IaIIae q. 28, a.1), and whether ecstasy be the effect of love (a. 3).

75. Contrast with Thomas Aquinas, *Summa theologiae* IIaIIae. q. 175,

a. 2, *ad primum*. For Bonaventure's view, see Ephrem Longpré, "Bonaventure," in *Dictionnaire de spiritualité* (Paris, 1937), 1:1838–39.

76. Gerson may have gotten his interpretation of the Sheba and Solomon story from Richard of Saint Victor, *Benjamin Major* 5.12 (PL 196:181BC, translated by Grover Zinn as *The Mystical Ark*, CWS [1979], pp. 326–29).

77. This is a direct quote from Augustine's *Confessions* 13.9.10.

78. The idea of the "weight of love" is developed in Hugh of Balma, *The Roads to Zion Weep* III.45, *Carthusian Spirituality* (trans. Dennis Martin, CWS [1997], p. 124).

79. Again Augustine, *Confessions* 13.9.10.

80. Apparently a reference to Aristotle, but Combes refers to William of Auvergne, *De retributionibus sanctorum* 321aC, in *Opera Omnia* 1 (Orléans-Paris, 1674).

81. See Thomas Aquinas, *Quaestiones disputatae de veritate*, q. 13, a. 1, *responsio*.

82. *Factorum et dictorum memorabilium* 8.7, pp. 383–93, ed. C. Kempf (Leipzig, 1888; reprint Stutgardiae: Teubner, 1966).

83. For the term "ecstatic love," see Bonaventure, *Sententiarum libri* 3, d. 24, a. 4.

84. Gerson is here summarizing the vocabulary especially of Dionysius and Richard of Saint Victor. For the death of Rachel as an image of the mystical life, see *Benjamin Minor* 73 (PL 196:52D and 86, PL 196:61D-62B, translated by Grover Zinn as *The Twelve Patriarchs*, CWS [1979], pp. 130–31 and 145).

85. Gerson was ever wary about suggesting connections between physical and spiritual unions. See his remark in the *Mountain of Contemplation*, chap. 37, on Bernard's *Sermons on the Song of Songs*: "When one believes one is thinking about spiritual marriage, one easily can slide into thoughts about carnal marriage."

86. For this process of spiritual union, see Hugh of Balma (note 78 above), section III, "Concerning the Unitive Way," the first paragraphs.

87. *Aristoteles Latinus* xxvi.3, *Ethica Nichomachea* 9.9, chap. 11, line 70b6, p. 339, ed. Renatus Antonius Gauthier (Leiden and Brussels: E.J. Brill and Desclée de Bouvwer, 1972).

88. As Combes rightly points out, this famous saying about friendship actually comes from Sallust, *Catilina* 20.4, and so Gerson must have been following the attribution to Aristotle in William of Auvergne, *De retributionibus sanctorum* 328aE (note 80 above).

89. See Hugh of Balma (note 78 above) on the petitions of the Our

Father, the sixth petition, referring to friendship in union with God, II, chap. 38, p. 100.

ON MYSTICAL THEOLOGY: THE SECOND AND PRACTICAL TREATISE

1. The same point is made by Hugh of Balma in the prologue to his *Mystica theologia*, which Gerson from its first words calls *Viae Sion lugent (The Roads to Zion Weep):* "This wisdom differs from all other areas of knowledge, because it has to be put to use in oneself before its words can be understood. In short, the practical precedes the theoretical" (*Carthusian Spirituality*, trans. Dennis D. Martin, CWS [1997], p. 72).

2. The Latin is *ecclesiasticus* and could be translated to English as the indeterminate "ecclesiastic," but Gerson apparently meant someone who holds a certain rank or position.

3. The idea of Christ's mastery of mystical theology is found in Richard of Saint Victor, *Benjamin Minor* 77–80 (PL 196:55–57), a text Gerson knew well (translated by Grover Zinn as *The Twelve Patriarchs*, CWS [1979], pp. 135–38).

4. William of Saint Thierry used the same passage in his *Epistola ad fratres de Monte Dei* 110 (ed. M. M. Davy [Paris, 1940], p. 147).

5. Gregory the Great, *Moralia in Job* (14.27), ed. M. Adriaen, CC SL 143, 143A, and 143B (Turnhout: Brepols, 1979-85). The only translation I know is *Morals on the Book of Job by Saint Gregory the Great* (Oxford and London: Parker and Rivington, 1844–50), 1–3.

6. The Latin term here is *coadjutores*, which implies assistants or helpers, not necessarily in the sense of "servants."

7. For the natural desire for beatitude, see especially Augustine, *On the Trinity* 13.8.11 and 13.20.25, as well as *Confessions* 10.20.29 and 10.21.30.

8. For the gifts of the Spirit, see Bernard of Clairvaux, *Sermones super Cantica* 18.1 (SBO 1:103). Also Alexander of Hales, *Summa theologica*, Tomus 4, ed. Quaracchi (1948), for the various types of graces (see iv, p. 3, inq. 1, tr. 2, q. 1–2, nos. 646–72, pp. 1023–60).

9. Vergil, *Ecloga* 8:63. This was a popular quotation, found, for example, in Jerome (Letter 52.9) and John of Salisbury (*Polycraticus* 7.8).

10. The threefold division of the powers of the soul goes back to Plato. See *Timaeus* 69D.38 and *Republic* 439–41, and Bernard McGinn, *The Growth of Mysticism* (New York: Crossroad, 1994), p. 288.

11. The distinction here and in the following sections among servants, mercenaries, and sons may come from Bernard of Clairvaux's Letter to the Brethren of La Grande Chartreuse (Ep. 11:3–9), also in his *De deo diligendo* 12.34–14.37 (SBO 3:148–51).

12. See Thomas Aquinas, *Quaestiones disputatae* 2, *De anima* a. 2, ad 19. Also *De anima* a. 8 and *In Aristotelis librum de anima commentarium* 3, lectio 4, 621.

13. See *Moralia in Job* (note 5 above) 6.37.57.

14. Gerson's awareness of religious experience in women is apparent in his *Mountain of Contemplation*, translated above.

15. See Aristotle's *De anima* 3.2, as commented by Thomas Aquinas, *In Aristotelis librum de anima*, lectio 2. Gerson could have gotten his statement from the Aristotelian sentences found among the works of Pseudo-Bede: *Sententiae philosophicae ex Aristotele collectae* (PL 90:967D): "Actus activorum sunt in patiente praedisposito."

16. *Sermones ad Cantica* 32.7.

17. The three types of vocation listed in the first consideration.

18. *Moralia in Job* (note 5 above) 19.25.43.

19. *Regulae pastoralis liber* 1.5 (PL 77:19C), translated by Henry Davis, in *Saint Gregory the Great: Pastoral Care* (Westminster, Md: Newman Press, 1950), pp. 29–31.

20. Gerson may have the term *ambidexter* from William of Saint Thierry's *Epistola ad fratres de Monte Dei* 12 (note 4 above), p. 74.

21. Cf. Gregory, *Moralia in Job* (note 5 above) 19.25.43.

22. See Augustine, *On the Trinity* 1.8.17.

23. See Gerson's *Treatise Against "The Romance of the Rose"* (translated below) for this concern. Also his *On Bringing Children to Christ* (Gl 9.477).

24. Horace, Ep. 2:69–70. The same expression is in Jerome, Letter 107.4.

25. See Jerome, Letter 14.7: "Perfectum autem esse nolle delinquere est." Also Bernard of Clairvaux, Letter 254.4 (SBO 8:159): "...quia nolle proficere, non nisi deficere est"; and Pelagius, *Ad Demetriadem epistola* 27 (PL 30:44A): "...nostrumque non progredi, jam reverti est."

26. See Bernard of Clairvaux, *De consideratione* 1.5.6 (SBO 3:400).

27. *City of God* 19.19.

28. *Epistulae morales* 53.9.

29. Cf. Vergil, *Aeneid* 12.592.

30. Horace, Ep. 2:35–37.

31. See Gregory the Great, *Moralia in Job* (note 5 above) 16.42.53. The

same image is in William of Saint Thierry, *Epistola ad fratres de Monte Dei* (note 4 above), 33, p. 89.

32. *Confessions* 9.6.14 (translated by R. S. Pine-Coffin [Harmondsworth and New York: Penguin Books, 1961], p. 190).

33. William of Saint Thierry, *Epistola ad fratres de Monte Dei* (note 4 above) 24 and 25, pp. 81–83.

34. The meaning seems to be that our animal selves must be occupied with some good activity, while our spiritual selves need to be at leisure, so that we can experience contemplation.

35. Taken from Hugh of Saint Victor, *Expositio in hierarchiam coelestem S. Dionysii areopagitae* 6 (PL 175:1038D): "...et intrat dilectio, et appropinquat, ubi scientia foris est."

36. Combes (p. 154 in his 1958 edition of *Mystical Theology*) refers here to Bernard, *The Steps of Humility and Pride* 10.28, where curiosity is defined. Bernard's definition is much more concrete than Gerson's and I see no connection.

37. Thomas Aquinas, *Summa theologiae* 1a2ae, q. 3, a. 4.

38. The Latin is *Pro tali nummismate talis merces redditur occulto Dei iudicio, dicit enim proverbium.* Gerson may be referring to the laborer's reward, as mentioned several places in the gospels, but no single quotation fits completely here.

39. *Sermones in Cantica* 54.9. Gerson's quotation ends with a word play on *sapere*: "quam si semper inveniaris non altum sapere, sed sapere ad sobrietatem," while the critical edition of Bernard (SBO 2:108) has "non altum sapere, sed timere."

40. See Richard of Saint Victor, *Benjamin Major* 1.2 (PL 196:66A, translated by Grover Zinn as *The Mystical Ark*, CWS [1979], pp. 153–55). For the same image of embracing Rachel, see also Gerson's Letter 22 (translated above).

41. Bernard of Clairvaux, *Sermones ad Cantica* 46.5.

42. The closest approximation I can find to this saying is in Cicero, *On the Orator* (1) 58, in *Cicero: On the Good Life*, trans. Michael Grant (Harmondsworth: Penguin Books, 1971), p. 329.

43. See Horace, Ep. 4:14: "grata superveniet quae non sperabitur hora." *Superveniet* in Horace has become *veniet* in Gerson.

44. Here is a central difference between Gerson's theology and Martin Luther's. For Gerson, we have to do what we can (*facere quod in se est*). See D. Catherine Brown, *Pastor and Laity in the Theology of Jean Gerson* (Cambridge and New York: Cambridge University Press, 1987), pp. 65, 71, 101, 107, 109. For Luther, our own efforts by definition are com-

pletely inadequate, and we must put ourselves in God's hands, in the way Gerson describes in (1) and rejects.

45. Horace, *Sermonum libri* (*Satires*, OCT [1959], 1.9.59–60): "nil sine magno vita labore dedit mortalibus." Horace's *vita* is substituted with *Deus*.

46. Vergil, *Georgics* 1.145–46.

47. The man tormented in Hades, whose fate it was eternally to roll a rock to the top of a hill, only to see it roll down again. First mentioned in *Odyssey* 2:593 (OCD [842]).

48. For the pain (*dolor*) the sinner experiences, see "Concerning the Path of Cleansing" in the opening pages of Hugh of Balma, *The Roads to Zion Weep* (note 1 above), pp. 73–78.

49. This quotation is from the Hebrew psalm 10:14, in the Vulgate placed after psalm 9 and before psalm 10.

50. Ovid, *Ars amatoria* 2.13.

51. Joseph Morawski, *Proverbes français antérieurs au XVe siècle* (Paris: Librairie ancienne Edouard Champion, 1925), no. 1251: "Meauz vaut bons garderres que bons gaaignierres," a slightly different variant.

52. See William of Saint Thierry, *De natura et dignitate amoris* 1.1 (PL 184:379C): "Ars est artium ars amoris."

53. See Thomas Aquinas, *Summa theologiae* 1a2ae, q. 29, a. 2: "Whether hate has its cause from love."

54. This is a quotation from a Sequence by Adam of Saint Victor, which Gerson already used in the *Speculative Mystical Theology*.

55. *Rhetorica* 2:2–17, see *Aristoteles Latinus* xxxi 1–2. *Translatio anonyma sive vetus* (Leiden: E. J. Brill, 1978), pp. 66–95. Hugh of Saint Victor, *De modo orandi* 7 (PL 176:985BC). William of Auvergne, *Tractatus novus de poenitentia* 15 (*Opera Omnia* 1 [Paris, 1674], p. 590bFG) and *De virtutibus* 9 (p. 119). Also Richard of Saint Victor, *Benjamin Minor* (note 3 above) 7 and 60 (PL 196:6BC and 43D), pp. 59–60 and 117.

56. See Gerson's *De passionibus animae* (Gl 9.1–25).

57. See Hugh of Saint Victor, *De sacramentis christianae fidei* 1.3.26 (PL 176:227D).

58. *Benjamin Major* (note 3 above) 5.5 (PL 196:174A-175A), pp. 316–17.

59. See Gregory the Great, *Moralia in Job* (note 5 above) 5.18.35.

60. For this division, see note 10 above.

61. See Bonaventure, *Sententiarum libri* 3, d. 13, dub. 1 (*Opera Omnia* 3, p. 291). Also William of Saint Thierry, *De natura et dignitate amoris* 6.15

(PL 184:390–91), and Richard of Saint Victor, *Benjamin Major* (note 40 above) 2.15 (PL 196:93D), pp. 195–97.

62. Gerson was probably to a certain degree referring to himself and what he experienced in terms of temptation.

63. See note 55 above.

64. *Confessions* (note 32 above), 2.6.13–14, p. 50: "All who desert you and set themselves up against you merely copy you in a perverse way; but by this very act of imitation they only show that you are the Creator of all nature."

65. The definition of pride as love of one's own excellence comes from Augustine, *De Genesi ad litteram* 11.14.18 (PL 34:436) and is used by Bernard of Clairvaux in *De gradibus humilitatis et superbiae* 4.14 (SBO 3:27).

66. According to Combes, this is a line from a hymn sung at Sext. Similar considerations are in Hugh of Balma (note 1 above), pp. 132–33. Gerson also talks above the secret place for meditation in his *Mountain of Contemplation* 24 (see translation above).

67. Gerson may have been dependent here on William of Auvergne, *Rhetorica divina*, chap. 26, in *Guilelmi Alverni Opera Omnia* 1 (Paris, 1674; reprinted Minerva, Frankfurt am Main, 1963), p. 365.

68. A variant of Terence, *Phormio* 2.4.454.

69. William of Auvergne, *Rhetorica divina* (note 67 above), chap. 26.

70. See Athanasius's *Vita Sancti Antonii* 8 (PG 26:854C-855A), translated by Robert C. Gregg, *Athanasius: The Life of Antony*, CWS (1980), p. 37.

71. Jerome, Letter 14.10.

72. This image is used in Bernard of Clairvaux, *Sermones in Cantica* 21.4.7 (SBO 1:126).

73. This saying is in Pseudo-Bede, *Sententiae philosophicae ex Aristotele collectae* (PL 90:1009C), taken from Aristotle's *Physics* 7.20: "In quiescendo et sedendo anima fit prudens." A variant is in Thomas à Kempis, *De imitatione Christi* 1.20. Also see *The Mountain of Contemplation*, note 56, for the same saying.

74. See William of Saint Thierry, *Epistola ad fratres de Monte Dei* (note 4 above), 102, p. 143.

75. From the second response at first nocturns during matins on Christmas morning: "Hodie per totum mundum mellifui facti sunt caeli." See *The Liber Usualis*, ed. Benedictines of Solesmes (Tournai and New York: Desclee Company, 1959), pp. 376–77.

76. See note 20 above.

77. *Aeneid* 4.449.

78. See Hugh of St. Victor, *De arca Noe morali* 4.8 (PL 176:675CD).

79. Gerson here uses the Greek term *antiperistasis*.

80. See Jerome's letters 122, 58, 54, 79, 22, and 107.

81. See William of Auvergne, *De retributionibus sanctorum*, 328bH, in *Opera Omnia* 1 (Orléans-Paris, 1674): "...quia gustata carne, hoc est admissa, sive recepta carnalis voluptate, deficit omnis spiritus."

82. A commonplace of medieval hagiography is that the saints in their extreme observances are to be admired rather than imitated. This opposition is already found in Augustine, *Soliloquiorum* (PL 32:878): "...quisquis rei hujus tantum gratia concumbit, mirandus mihi videri potest, at vero imitandus nullo modo."

83. Jerome (Letter 54.10) speaks of fasting for three days at a time, not two, an indication that in such references to patristic writers, Gerson "remembered" a text and did not always look it up.

84. Boethius, *Philosophiae consolatio* 2.5. Gerson writes: "...natura paucis contenta est," while Boethius has "...paucis enim minimisque natura contenta est." The saying is also included in the collection attributed to Aristotle (PL 90:1024A).

85. The image of shipwreck is a favorite for Gerson, as seen already in the first letter we have from his hand.

86. *Aeneid* 6:129.

87. Another variant of Terence, *Phormio* 2.4.454 (see note 68 above).

88. This saying, *non voto uno vivitur,* is probably taken from a satirist of the first century A.D., Persius Flaccus, *Satura* 5.53, in OCD (1966), p. 20.

89. Bernard, *Sermones super Cantica* 3.2 (SBO 1:14–15); Richard of Saint Victor, *Benjamin Minor* (note 3 above) 8–10 (PL 196:6D-7D) and *Benjamin Major* (note 40 above) 2.17 (PL 196:98BC); Hugh of Saint Victor, *De modo orandi* 2, 3 (PL 176:980B, 981A), as well as *De sacramentis christianae fidei* 2.13.3–4 (PL 176:527C-528) and *De arca Noe morali* 3.1 (PL 176:647).

90. See the eighth consideration, §1, above.

91. This is the *Viae Sion lugent (The Roads to Zion Weep)* by Hugh of Balma (note 1 above). For the controversy about love and knowledge, and Gerson's rejection of Hugh of Balma's view that love precedes knowledge, see James L. Connolly, *John Gerson: Reformer and Mystic* (Louvain: Librairie Universitaire, 1928), pp. 307–14. See also Dennis D. Martin's excellent introduction to the CWS translation of Hugh (note 1 above), pp.19–25.

92. Richard of Saint Victor also makes use of this quotation from Paul

to represent contemplative experience. See *Benjamin Major* 1.10 (PL 196:75B) and 5.4 (PL 196:173C), trans. as *The Mystical Ark*, CWS (1979), pp. 168 and 315.

93. *Aeneid* 8.224.

94. The *Summa de vitiis et virtutibus*, an important thirteenth-century collection of ethical teaching with examples compiled by a Dominican, William Peraldus, to my knowledge not available in a modern edition. Combes refers to a version from Cologne in 1479. According to Jacques Berlioz and Marie Anne Polo de Beaulieu (*Les exempla médiévaux* [Carcassonne: Garae/Hesiode, 1993], p. 47), a new edition is being prepared by Heinz Martin Werhahn.

95. In the *Speculative Mystical Theology*, consideration 27.7, at the end, as well as consideration 28.2.

96. The Latin is *sensus communis*, which directly translated sounds too much like banal "common sense." Gerson meant a kind of clearing house in the mind where the data of all the senses are brought together.

97. Pseudo-Dionysius, *De mystica theologia*, 1.2 (PG3:1018–19). Also Bonaventure, *In Hexaëmeron Collatio* 2.33 (*Opera Omnia* 5, p. 342) and *De triplici via* 3.13 (*Opera Omnia* 8, p. 17).

98. Gerson here uses the Greek term *agalma*, which comes ultimately from Plotinus, *Enneades* 1.6.9. See the translation by Stephen MacKenna (London: Faber and Faber, 1969), pp. 63–64.

99. See Gerson, *Notulae super Dionysius* (Gl 3.98.214–15), and André Combes, *Jean Gerson. Commentateur Dionysien* (Paris: Librairie J. Vrin, 1940), p. 257.

100. For an excellent summary of this discussion, see Brown (note 44 above), pp. 175–82.

101. *De Trinitate* 8.3.4.

102. *Itinerarium mentis in Deum* 6, p. 310 in *Opera Omnia* 5. Cousins (note 67 above), pp. 102–3.

103. Bernard distinguishes between the first kiss, of the feet; the second, of the hands; and the third, of the mouth. See *Sermones super Cantica* 3 (SBO 1:14–17). The same distinction is in the *Viae Sion lugent* (note 1 above), p. 71.

104. For an excellent treatment of Dionysius, see Bernard McGinn, *The Foundations of Mysticism* (New York: Crossroad, 1991), pp. 157–82.

105. Gerson usually calls this treatise *Benjamin Major*, the name given in PL 196, but it is also known as *The Grace of Contemplation* or *The Mystical Ark* (note 40 above), pp. 151–343.

106. This is Collation 11, on the perfection of charity. See E. Pichery, *Jean Cassien. Conférences* 2.8–17. SC 54.

107. Dated to 389 and found in PL 34:121ff. Translated in *Augustine: Earlier Writings*, Library of Christian Classics (London: SCM Press, 1953).

108. This is a Pseudo-Augustinian treatise, printed in PL 40:847–64.

109. For the various translations, see Peter Brown, *Augustine of Hippo: A Biography* (London: Faber and Faber, 1969), Chronological Table C, p. 185.

110. *Enarrationes in Psalmos* (*Homilies on the Psalms*) are in PL 36:67ff. and 37:1ff., translated as *Expositions on the Book of the Psalms* 1–6 (Oxford, 1847–57). Available in CC SL 38–40, ed. E. Dekkers and J. Fraipont (Turnhout: Brepols, 1956). See also *Saint Augustine on the Psalms*, trans. Scholastica Hebgin and Felicitas Corrigan, vols. 1–2 (to Psalm 37), Ancient Christian Writers 29–30 (Westminster, Md.: Newman Press, 1960–61).

111. What Gerson calls *De 30 gradibus scale* is better known as *The Ladder to Paradise*, by John Climacus (d. 649), monk and abbot of Mount Sinai. His works are in PG 88. Translated by Colm Luibheid and Norman Russell, *The Ladder of Divine Ascent*, CWS (1982).

112. *Moralia in Job* (note 5 above).

113. Charles Morel, ed., *Grégoire le Grand: Homélies sur Ezechiel*, SC 327 and 360. Latin text also in CC SL 142, ed. Marcus Adriaen (Turnhout: Brepols, 1971).

114. For Bernard's works, see volumes 1–3 of the SBO edition and the translations provided by Cistercian Publications. *To the Brothers of Mont Dieu* is William of Saint Thierry's treatise, at an early point attributed to Bernard, and best known as *The Golden Epistle*, trans. Theodore Berkeley (CP, 1976).

115. *De arca Noe morali* (note 78 above) and *De arca Noe mystica* are in PL 176:617ff. Anonymous translation as *Hugh of Saint Victor: Selected Spiritual Writings* (London: Faber and Faber, 1962).

116. *De modo orandi*, a brief treatise found in PL 176 and apparently not translated into English.

117. *In Ecclesiasten homiliae* or *In Salomonis Ecclesiasten*. The prologue is in PL 175:115, where Hugh discusses the mystical understanding of scripture.

118. *In hierarchiam coelestem commentaria* (PL 175:928ff.). See McGinn, *The Foundations of Mysticism* (note 104 above), pp. 371–95.

119. *Itinerarium mentis ad Deum* (note 102 above).

120. The *Stimulus amoris* is better known as *De triplici via*, ed. in the

Quaracchi edition, v. 8, pp. 3–27, and described by Ewert Cousins as Bonaventure's "systematic treatment of the stages of the spiritual life" (p. 10 in the introduction to his translation, note 67 above).

121. Two of the manuscripts add here that the author of the work is Hugh of Balma. Gerson, however, is probably referring to the work of James of Milan, a Franciscan. The treatise was once attributed to Bonaventure. See *Dictionnaire de Spiritualité* 8:48–49. For the text: *Stimulus amoris Fr. Iacobi Mediolanensis*. Bibliotheca Franciscana Ascetica Medii Aevi 4 (Quaracchi, 1905; reprinted 1949). It has been argued that Walter Hilton is the author of an extant English version, *The Pricking of Love*. See J. P. H. Clark, "Walter Hilton and the *Stimulus Amoris*," *Downside Review* 102 (1984), pp. 79–118. I am most grateful to Paul Chandler of the Melbourne College of Divinity and Stephen Hayes of the University of Kansas for their assistance here via the MEDTEXT network.

122. See note 1 above.

123. The *De novo seculo* was written by the Franciscan Bertram de Alen in the first half of the fourteenth century. This work is known under many different names, which all point to its concern for mystical theology: *Tractatus de laude novi saeculi, Excerptus de dictis beati dionysii; Tractatus de via contemplacionis et cognicionis Dei secundum libros divini Dionysii factus;* and *Libellus sive hymnus de rege novi saeculi id est de materia librorum B. Dionysii*. See Jean Hoffmans and Auguste Pelzer, *Les philosophes belges* 14 (Louvain, 1937), pp. 250–53.

124. *De septem itineribus eternitatis*. Not identified. Two of the manuscripts of Gerson add the work's *incipit* or opening words: "He who comes to me I shall not cast outside" (*Eum qui venit ad me non eiciam foras*).

125. John Ruusbroec's work, called by Gerson *De ornatu spiritualium nuptiarum. John Ruusbroec: The Spiritual Espousals and Other Works*, trans. James A. Wiseman, CWS (1985), pp. 41–152. See Gerson's critique in his Letters 13 and 26.

ON DISTINGUISHING TRUE FROM FALSE REVELATIONS

1. The Latin text is in Gl 3.36–56. The treatise is associated with the lectures (many now lost) given by Gerson on the gospel of Mark, here Mk 1:4, on John the Baptist. This lesson was given in November or December 1401, while the letter (text in Gl 2.49) was probably written

in early 1402 (Gl 2.xiii). See the translation by Paschal Boland in *The Concept of Discretio Spirituum in John Gerson's De Probatione Spirituum and De Distinctione Verarum Visionum a Falsis* (Washington, D.C.: Catholic University of America Press, 1959). This work, here abbreviated as "Boland," was for its time a significant venture into Gerson, but the translation is neither complete nor reliable, and the notes only occasionally reveal Gerson's sources.

2. This is the Nicolas who joined the Celestines, much to Gerson's distress. See Letter 9 above.

3. Gerson was referring to his *De non esu carnium apud Carthusienses*, from December 1401 (Gl 3.77–95), which also has a covering letter (Letter 8, translated above). I translate *lectio* as "lesson," but one might also say "lecture."

4. Boland (note 1 above), p. 77, thought this was a reference to the *De probatione spirituum* (which he translated as *On the Discernment of Spirits*). This is chronologically impossible, for this work is from 1415. Gerson meant his treatise for the Carthusians, *De non esu carnium (On Abstinence from Meat)*, Gl 3.95.

5. This is the apocryphal epistle of Saint Peter to Clement of Rome. See Henry Chadwick, *The Early Church*, Pelican History of the Church (Harmondsworth: Penguin Books, 1967), pp. 43–44.

6. Gerson means that knowledge of spiritual truth as given by miracles would wipe out the necessity of faith.

7. This is a commonplace or topos in Christian thinking, going back to the gospels, and present all through the Middle Ages (see, for example, the letter of Pope Gregory I to King Ethelbert, included in Bede's *History of the English Church and People* 1.32).

8. People with such beliefs were often called *Beghards* or *Turlupins*. See Robert Lerner, *The Heresy of the Free Spirit in the Later Middle Ages* (Berkeley and Los Angeles: University of California Press, 1972), esp. pp. 165–68. Lerner argues here that Gerson until this time (1402) had no contact with people of these beliefs, an assertion that is undermined by Gerson's own statement here.

9. The Latin term is *simplices*, those who have no training in reading and writing Latin.

10. Gerson here describes the type of Paris student who was at university in order to have a good time and did not take the content of the Christian religion very seriously.

11. The Latin *melancholicorum*, people in a state of depression.

12. *Metamorphoses* 2.137: *medio tutissimus ibis.*

13. These stories probably come from the Latin version of the *Vitae Patrum, Verba Seniorum* (PL 73:965, 68, and 70). Gerson apparently replaced a vision of a false angel Gabriel in the first story with a vision of a false Christ. If this is true, he "remembered" the stories without checking them, an indication of how he used *exempla* in his writing and preaching.

14. See Sulpicius Severus, *Life of Saint Martin of Tours*, chap. 24.

15. John Chrysostom, *De laudibus Sancti Pauli Apostoli, Homilia* 5 (PG 50:500).

16. Bernard revealed the contents of his contemplative experience in his *Sermons on the Song of Songs* (74.5). Also VP 3.20 (PL 185:314–15).

17. Gerson seems to be suggesting here the creation of a fart.

18. Cicero, *Philippicae* 2.5–6.

19. Gerson's source here is probably Valerius Maximus, *Facta et dicta memorabilia* 3.7.1e; Scipio defended himself against the charge of receiving public funds by saying that the only thing he gained from the conquest of Africa was his surname.

20. The text says six months, not five (Lk 1:24), but Gerson counted the sixth month in seeing Elizabeth as emerging from her seclusion only at the Visitation.

21. Gregory the Great, *Dialogues* 1.2.

22. *Dialogues* 1.1.

23. "Compulsive eating" is my translation of *edacitas insaturabilis*. The Latin phrase indicates loss of self control. See Rudolph M. Bell, *Holy Anorexia* (Chicago and London: University of Chicago Press, 1985) and Caroline Walker Bynum's more careful and profound study, *Holy Feast and Holy Fast: The Religious Significance of Food to Medieval Woman* (Berkeley, Los Angeles, London: University of California Press, 1987).

24. This is from *The Ladder to Paradise* 23 (PG 88:970).

25. The second collation or conference of John Cassian deals with the virtue of discretion. See E. Pichery, *Jean Cassien. Conférences* 1:1–7, SC (1955), pp. 109–37.

26. See Jerome's letter to Rusticus (no. 125.16, dated to 411), on good and bad monks. F. A. Wright, *Select Letters of Jerome* (Cambridge, Mass., and London: Loeb Library, 1975), pp. 426–27.

27. The Latin term *horrorem terrificum* was translated by Boland (note 1 above), p. 90, as "twitching." This is too precise for Gerson's meaning.

28. This theological interpretation of John the Baptist goes back to Luke 1:15 and 1:41. Through the Middle Ages theologians discussed if

John at this moment was freed from original sin, but they agreed that John was born as among the most perfect of human beings.

29. I have not been able to find a source for this statement about semen in Galen, but a possible source is the so-called *Prose Salernitan Questions*. According to John Baldwin (*The Language of Sex: Five Voices from Northern France around 1200* [Chicago and London: University of Chicago Press, 1994], p. 10 and note 35), one of the important manuscripts in this collection, *Questiones Alani* "was copied for the chapter of Notre-Dame in Paris by the fourth decade of the thirteenth century" and would have been accessible to Gerson, who had a keen interest in medical explanations for human behavior.

30. According to *Webster's Dictionary*, "in medieval physiology, having the warm, passionate, cheerful temperament and the healthy, ruddy complexion of the one in whom the blood is the predominant humor of the four."

31. Gerson did not completely reject astrology as a science, so long as it respected the preeminence of theology. See his *Trilogium astrologiae theologizatae* (Gl 10.90–109).

32. This is one of the most familiar commonplaces of medieval hagiography: many of the saints' most spectacular deeds are to be admired but not necessarily imitated (*admiratio, non imitatio*).

33. See Gregory the Great's portrait of Saint Benedict, *Dialogues* 2.1.

34. *Rule of Saint Benedict*, chap. 73.

35. For the image of fighting, see *Rule of Saint Benedict*, chap. 1. Gerson knew the stories in the *Lives of the Fathers* and Gregory's *Dialogues*, where holy men battle with the devil.

36. Gerson's collation for 29 September 1392, on the feast of Saint Michael the Archangel (Gl 5.309–24).

37. See *Dialogues* 4.50.

38. I cannot find any reference in the *Vita Prima* to this process. There is, however, a passage in the *Sermons on the Song of Songs* (14.6), where Bernard spoke of a breath or odor that could come over him, but he related it to periods of depression in his life, not to a sense of ability to perform miracles.

39. *Confessions* 6.13.

40. *Parva naturalia*, chap. 2, 456a, and chap. 3, 462a.

41. Gerson uses the Greek term *akrisia* here.

42. See Book 17, on humility, especially the first four anecdotes, in *Vitae Patrum, Verba Seniorum* (PL 73:953BC).

43. In *Sermons on the Song of Songs* 54.8 Bernard admitted that he occasionally had been trapped by pride.

44. *Sermons on the Song of Songs* 54.9.

45. Antaeus rose up stronger from the ground onto which he was thrown, for there he came into contact with his mother, the Earth.

46. Such discussions were connected both with assertions of God's absolute power and debates about how the church could be saved from destroying itself in the schism.

47. See Gerson's considerations above (p. 341–42), concerning the *Dialogues* of Gregory the Great and their teaching on revelations and miracles.

48. See the *Glossa ordinaria*, on this passage in Matthew (*Biblia Latin cum Glossa Ordinaria* [Turnhout: Brepols, 1992; reprint of the 1480/81 edition]).

49. It is not clear to whom Gerson was referring. Both for Ermine at Reims and for the much better known Birgitta of Vadstena (Bridget of Sweden) he gave his approval (Letter 25 above).

50. This polemic goes back to Jerome's letter 22:13 to Eustochium, where he warned her against the dangers involved when spiritual men and women lived together. Also his Letter 117.

51. The original expression comes from Pseudo-Jerome, Letter 42.3 (PL 30:293C): *Ego judico, si cum viris feminae habitent, viscarium non deerit diaboli* (I judge that if women live together with men, the birdlime of the devil will not be lacking). This is part of a long polemic against women. Birdlime was made from the berries of the mistletoe and was thought to have aphrodisiac powers. The sticky substance was also spread on twigs to catch birds.

52. *Georgics* 3.215: *carpit enim viris paulatim uritque videndo femina*.

53. See *The Book of Blessed Angela: The Instructions* 2, "The Perils of Spiritual Love," in *Angela of Foligno: Complete Works*, trans. Paul Lachance, CWS (1993), p. 221.

54. Gerson actually says: "This has been handed down in a way that is not womanly (*muliebriter*)."

55. See Malcolm Lambert, *Medieval Heresy: Popular Movements from Bogomil to Hus* (London: Edward Arnold, 1977), pp. 174–81.

56. According to Lerner (note 8 above), pp. 165–66, this must be Margaret Porete, the mystic burnt as a heretic at Paris in 1310. See her *Mirror of Simple Souls*, trans. Ellen L. Babinsky, CWS (1993).

57. This famous quotation comes from Augustine (*Homilies on 1 John*

7:8), not from Paul (Gerson uses the term *ab Apostolo*). For Marguerite's use of the phrase, *Mirror of Simple Souls* (note 56 above), chap. 13, p. 95.

58. *Bucolics* 8.108.

59. It was about this time that Gerson began making contacts with members of the Carthusian Order. See Letter 8, translated above.

60. This phrase is a rhetorical signal that Gerson could be talking about himself (cf. Paul on his own experience, 2 Cor 12:2–3). Johan Huizinga already noticed this anecdote in his brilliant chapter, "Religious Sensibility and Religious Imagination," in *The Waning of the Middle Ages*.

61. Vergil, *Aeneid* 5.344.

62. See Ps 90:6. The noonday demon was a familiar concept for medieval clergy and religious.

63. The word *historiam* probably points to the history of salvation as drawn from the Bible. Gregory, *Dialogues* 1.4.

64. Gerson calls it a *non sequitur*.

65. Again Gerson is probably referring to his own experience.

66. Gerson's immediate source may have been Jerome, who in *Apologia contra Rufinum* 1.17 says: "Should he not have known that saying of Socrates: I know that I do not know?" (*S. Hieronymi presbyteri Opera. Pars III. Opera Polemica 1*, ed. P. Lardet, CC SL 79 [Turnhout: Brepols, 1982], p. 15).

67. For the term *Papelardi*, seen in the writings of Robert of Sorbonne (d. 1274), and its equation with the Beguines, see Ernest W. McDonnell, *The Beguines and Beghards in Medieval Culture* (New Brunswick, N.J.: Rutgers University Press, 1954; reprinted New York: Octagon Books, 1969), pp. 472–73.

ON THE ART OF HEARING CONFESSIONS

1. This brief treatise was enormously popular in the fifteenth century, as seen by the number of manuscripts that Glorieux used. See Gl 8.xii, where he dates the work to about 1406. It is impossible to give a precise dating, but the work belongs to the period before about 1408, when Gerson was teaching in Paris and was devoted to pastoral issues. Text in Gl 8.10–17.

2. Gerson's word is *ars*, and the Latin title of the treatise is *De arte audiendi confessiones*. This is not our modern conception of "art," but the medieval idea of a skill, going back to the Greek *tekné*.

3. For Gerson's remarks in a full historical context, see Thomas Tentler's landmark study, *Sin and Confession on the Eve of the Reformation* (Princeton, N.J.: University Press, 1977). Also D. Catherine Brown, *Pastor and Laity in the Theology of Jean Gerson* (Cambridge and New York: Cambridge University Press, 1987).

4. Gerson referred to the decision of the Fourth Lateran Council in 1215, canon 21, *omnis utriusque sexus*: every Christian had to make his or her confession once yearly, usually in connection with Eastertide, before receiving holy communion. See Colin Morris, *The Papal Monarchy: The Western Church from 1050 to 1250* (Oxford: Clarendon Press, 1991), p. 436.

5. Reserved cases involved those sins of great magnitude for which the parish priest could not give absolution. For an analysis of Gerson in this area, see Tentler (note 3 above), pp. 304–13. See also Gerson's Letter 24 (translated above).

6. This image of the confessor as a doctor is one that goes far back in the literature of confession. It was used at the Fourth Lateran Council: "Let the priest be discreet and cautious...after the manner of a skillful physician" (Edward Peters, *Heresy and Authority in Medieval Europe* [Philadelphia: University of Pennsylvania Press, 1980], p. 177).

7. Gerson may be referring to his own work, as well as to well-known manuals for the confessor, such as John of Freiburg's *Summa confessorum*, mentioned in a letter of Gerson to his brother Nicolas, dated to Paris in 1410 (Gl 2.133). See Brown (note 3 above), pp. 116–17.

8. Cf. Gerson's remarks at the opening of his little work *On the Confession of Masturbation* (*De confessione mollitiei*) (Gl 8.71).

9. Gerson's remark attacks the tradition represented by Thomas of Chobham's *Summa Confessorum*, according to which the confessor is not to ask his penitents too specific questions, especially in sexual matters. Otherwise he might give them inspiration. See my "Education, Confession, and Pious Fraud: Jean Gerson and a Late Medieval Change," ABR 47 (1996), pp. 310–38, esp. 325–26.

10. The so-called seal of confession, the subject of more than one Hollywood film, but also a very real phenomenon in the history of the sacrament of penance. See *Catechism of the Catholic Church* (New York: Doubleday, 1995), no. 1467.

11. For more detail, see Gerson's *On Bringing Children to Christ* (*De parvulis trahendis ad Christum*) (Gl 9.669–86). Also Brown (note 3 above), pp. 245–47.

12. Reminiscent of Psalm 22:5: "My head you have anointed with oil."

13. Gerson uses the term *membrum pudendum* (shameful part). He is more specific about this method in the little treatise *On the Confession of Masturbation*, where the priest is told to ask the young male penitent, "Friend, do you remember in your childhood, around ten or twelve years of age, that your rod or shameful part ever was erect?" If the youth answers no, then "he will be immediately convinced of a lie," because "it is certain that this is the case in all boys whose bodies are not malfunctioning." See *De confessione mollitiei* (Gl 9.71).

14. The confessor is almost to lure the youth into admitting sexual activity, by acting at first as if genital excitement is quite natural. See my "Education, Confession, and Pious Fraud" (note 9 above), pp. 323–26.

15. The Latin terms are *mollities sive pollutio*.

16. Gerson's point is that any consent to sexual pleasure outside of the act of procreation in marriage is mortal sin: "Any pleasure or enjoyment that resulted from sexual thoughts and feelings was clearly sinful according to the teaching current in the period" (James A. Brundage, *Law, Sex, and Christian Society in Medieval Europe* [Chicago: University of Chicago Press, 1987], p. 204, referring to Ivo of Chartres, *Decretum* 9.123 [PL 161:689], who in turn cited Augustine, *City of God* 1.25).

17. The confessor's point here seems to be that since the penitent already has mentioned material for mortal sin, then he could not be worse off, so he might as well tell everything.

18. See Tentler (note 3 above), pp. 91–93, for Gerson's technique of investigation, especially with sexual sin. However correct Gerson may have been in insisting on the need for the confessor to know specifics, I find it ethically unacceptable for a confessor to probe in such detail.

19. Such passages deserve more attention from historians dealing with the history of the family and of sexuality. Philippe Ariès, for example, was aware of Gerson's teaching on the confession of masturbation but not on these other matters. See his masterful but flawed *L'enfant et la vie familiale sous l'Ancien Régime* (Paris: Editions du Seuil, 1973).

20. Gerson indicates that the confessions he heard were almost exclusively those of men and of boys; his world, being limited for the most part to academic Paris and the church of Notre-Dame, contained hardly any women.

21. Notice Gerson's almost Pauline passion here, followed by the assertion that he almost performed miracles in extracting sin from ini-

tially unwilling penitents. For Gerson it was a matter of life or death to get to specific, concrete truths.

22. It is such passages, and not those about Gerson's technique of extracting information about sexual behavior, that earned him the title "consoling doctor."

23. Gerson was here thinking of urban and well-provided parishes.

24. Gerson generally favored a light penance, no matter how serious the sin, to avoid a situation where a sinner forfeits absolution because he fails to carry out the penance given. See Tentler (note 3 above), pp. 333–34; also Brown (note 3 above), p. 68. For the question of restitution, see Tentler, pp. 340–43.

25. Gerson's related treatises in French are *Doctrine contre conscience trop scrupuleuse* (Gl 7.1.140–42), dated 1400–1401; *Le prouffit de scavoir quel est peche mortel et veniel* (Gl 7.1.370–89), dated 1400–1401. The most widespread of his works on this subject was probably the *Examen de conscience selon les sept péchés mortels*, from this same period. This work became the second part of the much-read *Opus tripartitum* (Gl 7.1.393–400). Latin treatises include *De pollutione nocturna et praeparatione ad missam*, also known as *De dignitate celebrationis* (Gl 9.35–50) and *De cognitione castitatis, seu De pollutione diurna* (Gl 9.50–64), which could be from 1408. Also the letter-treatise, *Super moderatione casuum reservandorum in foro*, Letter 24, translated above. The sacrament of penance was one of Gerson's major pastoral concerns.

TREATISE AGAINST *THE ROMANCE OF THE ROSE*

1. Text in Gl 7.1.301–16. The full title in the manuscripts is *Le Traictié d'une vision faite contre Le Ronmant de la Rose par le Chancelier de Paris*. The treatise is also found in Eric Hicks, *Le débat sur le Roman de la Rose*, Bibliothèque du XVe Siècle 43 (Paris: Éditions Honoré Champion, 1977), which adds contributions by Christine de Pisan, Jean de Montreuil, Gontier and Pierre Col. Gerson's treatise is dated to 18 May 1402. See the chronology in Hicks, pp. lii–liv; also Glorieux's more schematic dossier, "Autour du Roman de la Rose" (Gl 10.25–26). I have made use of Hicks's excellent notes.

This treatise was translated by Diana Elizabeth Adams-Smith, *Some French Works of Jean Gerson: An Introduction and Translation*, Ph.D. diss., University of South Carolina, 1976 (available from University Microfilms, Ann Arbor, Michigan 48106), pp. 118–79. This translation makes several interesting comparisons between the original French version of Gerson's work and later Latin translations, information that I do not repeat here. Dr. Adams-Smith gives few references to Gerson's sources.

2. The headings given here are my own.

3. The *Fol Amoureux* refers to the central author of *The Romance of the Rose*, Jean de Meung. See the standard edition of the *Roman de la rose*, ed. Ernest Langlois (Paris: Société des anciens textes français, 1914–24), vols. 1–5, lines 7181–82. The work is translated into English verse by Harry W. Robbins and edited by Charles W. Dunn (New York: E.P. Dutton & Co., 1962). Hereafter, references to the Langlois edition will give the line in the poem, while references to the Robbins translation will give the page.

4. Line 2824, p. 59.

5. Gerson here is apparently referring to the Duenna, the old woman who provides advice about how women are to gain the love of men (lines 13281–13846, pp. 277–88). Gerson exaggerates the content of her advice.

6. Lines 8455–8744, pp. 171–76, is indeed an attack on marriage and on women.

7. "Just such a life does young man seek who takes/The monkish vow; he'll never learn to make/Shoes large enough, or cowl, or broad-brimmed hat/To hide what nature's planted in his heart....Each creature to its nature will return,/Nor can relinquish it for violence/Or force or covenant" (p. 292).

8. A material that was supposed to burn on water, used by the Byzantines to great effect in the defense of Constantinople. See *The Alexiad of Anna Comnena* (Harmondsworth: Penguin Books, 1969), 11.10.360–61.

9. For these *paroles luxurieuses* in the *Roman de la Rose*, see Hicks (note 1 above), p. 208. Gerson may have been thinking especially of the poem's ending, where the sexual imagery becomes almost explicit.

10. The French adverbs are *nuement, deslaveement et goliardement*, pointing to the Goliards, ribald twelfth-century student poets. By the fifteenth century the word meant entertainers of a dubious sort. See "goliard" in Algirdas Julien Geimas and Teresa Mary Keane, *Dictionnaire du moyen français. La Renaissance* (Paris: Larousse, 1992). Also see *Roman de la Rose* (lines 6901–7230, pp. 142–48), where the Lover accuses Reason of using foul language.

11. Gerson may be thinking, for example, of Genius's exhortation

to sexual reproduction, when he dresses like a priest in a chasuble (lines 19505–19906, pp. 413–23).

12. Lines 19907–20036, pp. 423–25.

13. Again, Gerson seems to be thinking especially about the end of the poem, where the Lover makes his way into the tower and male sexual potency triumphs through images of the sacred (as "The sacred relics of the ivory tower/I hoped to touch with all my equipage" [p. 459]).

14. A proverb ultimately derived from Ovid, *Amores* 1.8.104.

15. Jean de Meung probably died in 1305. See Hicks (note 1 above), p. 209.

16. This is from the *Testament maistre Jehan de Meun*, the first line of the second quatrain: *J'ay fait en ma jeunesce mainz diz par vanité*, contained in M. Méon, *Le Roman de la Rose* (Paris, 1814), vol. 4, *Testament et Codicile*.

17. This may be a reference to a lost treatise by the humanist secretary of the French king, Jean de Montreuil. See Hicks (note 1 above), p. 210.

18. As Hicks has pointed out, this argument has been repeated in modern literary criticism of *The Romance of the Rose*. See, for example, Alan M. F. Gunn, *The Mirror of Love: A Reinterpretation of "The Romance of the Rose"* (Lubbock: Texas Tech Press, 1952).

19. See Cicero, *De officiis* 1.35.128.

20. Gerson may have been thinking of the passage in Horace, *Ars poetica* 359: "I get angry that the good Homer sometimes fell asleep" (*Indignor quandoque bonus dormitat Homerus*).

21. Augustine himself listed in his *Retractions* (PL 32:583) what he considered his errors to be.

22. For this passage, see Adams-Smith (note 1 above), p. 177, note 9.

23. See note 16 above.

24. Ovid was sent into exile by Augustus, partly because of his erotic poetry. See OCD [631].

25. For Gerson (using here the *persona* of Theological Eloquence), it was a matter of life or death to stop the circulation of such works, which he believed would corrupt youth.

26. See Seneca, Letters to Lucilius 15.94.42.

27. Theological Eloquence is referring to Jean de Meung, long dead, who is supposed to have repented. He will have had to pay his debt in purgatory.

28. Theological Eloquence gives Jean de Meung the benefit of the

doubt and believes the author never intended his poem to be used to corrupt morals.

29. Gerson confused the eucharistic heretic, Berengar of Tours (d. 1098), with Abelard's disciple, Berengar of Poitiers. See David Luscombe, *The School of Peter Abelard* (Cambridge: Cambridge University Press, 1969), p. 49, note 3. *The Romance of the Rose* retells the story of Abelard and Heloise (lines 8745–8956, pp. 177–83).

30. Referring probably to Low Sunday, the First Sunday after Easter, where the gospel (Jn 20) describes the first appearance of Jesus after his resurrection.

31. The story of the repentance of Berengar of Tours is in William of Malmesbury, *Gesta Regum Anglorum* 3 (J. A. Giles, trans., *William of Malmesbury's Chronicle of the Kings of England* [London, 1847; reprinted New York: AMS Press, 1968], p. 314). Gerson's source was more likely to have been the *Speculum historiale* by the Dominican scholastic encyclopedist Vincent of Beauvais: 25.30, p. 1012 (reprinted Graz, Austria: Akademische Druck u. Verlagsanstalt, 1965).

32. Archytas of Tarentum, from the fourth century B.C., is known as the founder of mechanics and was also known as a mathematician. See OCD [85]. Plato is supposed to have visited him. Gerson's reference, however, probably comes from Cicero's *On Old Age* (*De Senectute*) 12.41.

33. Later in 1402 Gerson preached a sermon against sensuality, on the Second Sunday of Advent, the first of a series of three, and also mentioned the destruction of Troy (Gl 7.2.812).

34. Livy, *Annales* 1.58–60. King Tarquin's ravishing of Lucretia is in *The Romance of the Rose* (p. 174). These lines of Gerson are quoted verbatim by one of his opponents in the debate. See *La response maistre Pierre Col, chanoine de Paris, aux deux traitiés precedens*, Hicks (note 1 above), p. 92. Gerson reused the story of Tarquin in his third *Poenitemini* sermon on sensuality (Gl 7.2.825).

35. However extreme Gerson's views might sound, they are already contained in Cicero's *On Old Age*, chap. 12: *Nullam capitaliorem pestem quam corporis voluptatem hominibus a natura datam* (There is no more fatal disease than the bodily desire given us by nature), words spoken by Archytas but reflecting Cicero's own view of human sexuality.

36. The phrase *grant pais* hints at a proto-patriotism for France found elsewhere in Gerson's work. See Gilbert Ouy, "Humanism and Nationalism in France at the Turn of the Fifteenth Century," *The Birth of Identities: Denmark and Europe in the Middle Ages*, ed. Brian Patrick McGuire (Copenhagen: C.A. Reitzel, 1996), pp. 107–25, esp. 112–14.

37. A timely question in view of a continuing war with England and rivalries between the king's brother, the duke of Orléans, and the duke of Burgundy.

38. Gerson was almost certainly referring to an incident he himself experienced, but there is no reference in the rich dossier *Actes et documents* from Gerson's life prepared by Glorieux (vol. 10).

39. The French word *papelart* in the thirteenth century referred to the religious associations of the Beguines and was not necessarily pejorative (see Ernest W. McDonnell, *The Beguines and Beghards in Medieval Culture* [New York: Octagon Books, 1969], p. 433, citing a sermon by Jacques de Vitry). By the later fourteenth century, however, the word meant a hypocrite, who feigned religious devotion. See "papelard" in *Dictionnaire du moyen français* (note 10 above).

40. See Origen's prologue to his *Commentary on the Song of Songs* (E. Ann Matter, *The Voice of My Beloved: The Song of Songs in Western Medieval Christianity* [Philadelphia: University of Pennsylvania Press, 1992], p. 28). Origen's work is translated by R. P. Lawson, *Origen: The Song of Songs, Commentary and Homilies*, Ancient Christian Writers Series 26 (New York: Newman Press, 1957).

41. This view of error has a long history in medieval Christian thought. In the eighth century Bede wrote that "there is no false doctrine which does not mix in something of truth" (*Commentarium in Lucam* 5.17.12) and this tag was attributed to Augustine. See Norman Daniel, *Islam and the West: The Making of an Image* (Edinburgh: University Press, 1980), pp. 164–66. I am grateful to my friend and colleague at the Department of History, Odense University, Kurt Villads Jensen, for this reference.

42. This is Pseudo-Seneca, actually the *Libellus de moribus* attributed to Saint Martin of Braga (d. 580), in PL 72:31. For a fuller reference, see Hicks (note 1 above), p. 231.

43. See Ovid's *Tristia* 2.211–12. Also OCD [631].

44. The exclamations remind one of Cicero's *O tempora! O mores!* in his speech against Catiline. Gerson may well have consciously imitated this polemical style, an indication of his attraction to humanist prose. See Ouy (note 36 above).

45. Hicks (note 1 above, pp. 212–13) agrees with Gerson and says that *The Art of Loving* provides the basis for the speeches of the Friend and of the Duenna. He refers to E. Langlois, *Origines et sources du Roman de la Rose* (Paris: Thorin, 1891), pp. 119–21.

46. In *The Romance of the Rose*, the story of Abelard and Heloise, with

the latter's polemic against marriage, is told by the Jealous Husband, lines 8745–8802, pp. 177–78. For the original in translation, see *The Letters of Abelard and Heloise*, trans. Betty Radice (Harmondsworth: Penguin Books, 1974). *The Romance of the Rose* borrowed from the sixth book of Juvenal's *Satires* (see, for example, the Dutton translation, pp. 167–68). The examples of Mars, Venus, and Vulcan are recorded by the Duenna (lines 13810–38, 14131–56, pp. 288–89), in accord with Ovid's *Art of Loving* 2.561–92. Pygmalion (pp. 441–50) and Adonis (pp. 332–34) are from Ovid's *Metamorphoses*, Book 10.

47. Mary, the mother of God.

48. A common proverb in Old French. See Joseph Morawski, *Proverbes français antérieurs au XVe siècle* (Paris: Librairie ancienne Édouard Champion, 1925), no. 237: *Besoing ne garde loi*.

49. See Morawski (note 48 above), no. 661.

50. *Ars poetica* 1–5.

51. Vergil, *Aeneid* 3.216–17.

52. Pseudo-Augustine, *Homilia 26 in Psalmos*, also called *Sermo* 300 (PL 39:2319).

53. *Ethica Nichomachea* I.12, 01b19–01b26. Seneca *Naturales quaestiones* 7.30.1.

54. See W. Wetherbee, "The Literal and the Allegorical: Jean de Meung and the *De planctu Naturae*," *Mediaeval Studies* 33 (1971), pp. 265–91. This is Alan of Lille, who died in 1202 or 1203 as a Cistercian monk but had first been student and teacher at Paris: *The Plaint of Nature*, trans. James J. Sheridan (Toronto: Pontifical Institute of Mediaeval Studies, 1980).

55. Aesop's *Fables* existed in innumerable medieval variants. See Hicks (note 1 above), p. 213, *la cornaille*. Also *Fables of Aesop*, trans. S. A. Handford (Harmondsworth: Penguin Books, 1979), no. 72, "Borrowed Plumes," where the crow is called a jackdaw. It collected all the feathers of other birds and then presented itself before Zeus as the finest of all birds. But the others attacked him and took back what belonged to them.

56. Gerson claimed Jean de Meung misinterpreted Alan of Lille as having argued that in order to avoid sexual contact among males (the sin "against nature"), nature demands that men practice heterosexual sex.

57. The word is "excommunicate," but the idea is to forbid the book and thus separate it from the company of all good Christians.

58. See *Acts of the Apostles* 9:19: "A number of those who practiced magic collected their books and burned them publicly."

59. The story of Archilocus is in Valerius Maximus, *Factorum et dictorum memorabilium libri novem*, ed. Carolus Kempf (Stuttgart: Teubner, 1966), 6.3.Ext.1.

60. *De officiis* 1.35.126–28.

61. This is a play on the linguistic resemblance between Cynic philosophers (*cynici*) and dogs (*canes*). According to Hicks, Gerson's source is probably Augustine, *De nuptiis et concupiscentia* 22.24 (PL 44:428).

62. According to Robert Lerner the word *turlupin* was "a French synonym for beghard" (*The Heresy of the Free Spirit in the Later Middle Ages* [Berkeley and Los Angeles: University of California Press, 1972], p. 52).

63. According to the Cynics, we should not be ashamed of the appearance of our bodies or of their natural functions, the doctrine of shamelessness. See "Cynics" in OCD [248].

64. As Hicks (note 1 above) points out, Boccaccio in the Epilogue of his *Decameron* makes almost the same observation.

65. See *The Romance of the Rose*, lines 573–81, p. 13.

66. Probably a reference to Augustine's use and interpretation of Cicero in *On Christian Doctrine*, Bk. 4.

67. *The Romance of the Rose*, lines 19041–74, pp. 404–5, for Nature; and for Venus, "by the flesh of God," line 20696, p. 439.

68. This is a reference to the Commandments of Love found in the early part of *The Romance of the Rose* (lines 2096–107, p. 45).

69. Gerson was referring to the split between the relatively naïve and gentle first section of the poem, authored by William of Lorris in the twelfth century, and the much more clever and cynical bulk of the poem, written in the thirteenth century by Jean de Meung.

70. Gerson was again referring to Emperor Augustus (Octavian), who was believed to have exiled Ovid for his salacious writings (note 24 above).

71. Referring to the woman called the Duenna in the English translation I have used.

72. This theme of awakening from a dream in which one has experienced moralizing characters was common in late medieval vernacular literature, as can be seen in the last line of *Piers the Ploughman*. Gerson's use of himself as the dreamer was meant as a counterpart to the Dreamer in *The Romance of the Rose*.

73. An allusion to Gerson's sermon, delivered three days later, 21

May 1402, at Saint-Jean-en-Grève church, on the Holy Trinity: *Videmus* (Gl 7.2.1123–37).

74. The feast of the Blessed Sacrament, Corpus Christi, fell in 1402 on 25 May, so again Gerson was probably referring to a sermon he was preparing (see Gl 7.2.698–709).

Abbreviations and Select Bibliography

(includes only works specifically on Gerson
or of general interest for the period)

ABR = *American Benedictine Review*. Assumption Abbey, Richardton, North Dakota, 1950–.

Bernstein, Alan E. *Pierre d'Ailly and the Blanchard Affair: University and Chancellor of Paris at the Beginning of the Great Schism*. Leiden: E. J. Brill, 1978.

Boland, Paschal. *The Concept of Discretio Spirituum in Jean Gerson's De Probatione Spirituum and De Distinctione Verarum Visionum a Falsis*. Washington, D.C.: Catholic University of America Press, 1959.

Brown, D. Catherine. *Pastor and Laity in the Theology of Jean Gerson*. Cambridge, England: Cambridge University Press, 1987.

Burger, Christoph. *Aedificatio, Fructus, Utilitas: Johannes Gerson als Professor der theologie und Kanzler der Universität Paris*. Beiträge zur historischen Theologie 70. Tübingen: J.C.B. Mohr, 1986.

Burrows, Mark Stephen. *Jean Gerson and De Consolatione Theologiae*. Beiträge zur historischen Theologie 78. Tübingen: J.C.B. Mohr, 1991.

Bynum, Caroline Walker. *Holy Feast and Holy Fast: The Religious Significance of Food to Medieval Women*. Berkeley, Los Angeles, and London: University of California Press, 1987.

Calvot, Danièle, and Gilbert Ouy. *L'oeuvre de Gerson à Saint-Victor de Paris. Catalogue des manuscrits*. Paris: Éditions du Centre National de la Recherche Scientifique, 1990.

ABBREVIATIONS/SELECT BIBLIOGRAPHY

CC CM = Corpus Christianorum. Continuatio Mediaevalis. Turnhout, Belgium: Brepols, 1966–.

CC SL = Corpus Christianorum. Series Latina. Turnhout, Belgium: Brepols, 1954–.

Combes = André Combes, ed. *Ioannis Carlerii de Gerson de Mystica Theologia*. Lugano, Switzerland: Thesaurus Mundi, 1958.

Combes, André. "Gerson et la naissance de l'humanisme." *Revue du Moyen-Age latin* 1 (1945), pp. 259–84.

———. *La théologie mystique de Gerson. Profil de son évolution* 1–2. Rome: Desclée et Socii, 1963–64.

Connolly, James L. *John Gerson: Reformer and Mystic*. Louvain: Librairie Universitaire, 1928.

CP = Cistercian Publications, Kalamazoo, Michigan, 1971–. (In order to save space, Cistercian translations of Bernard of Clairvaux and other Cistercian writers are normally not specifically mentioned in the notes.)

CWS = Classics of Western Spirituality. New York and Mahwah, N.J.: Paulist Press, 1978–.

DHGE = *Dictionnaire d'histoire et de géographie ecclésiastiques*. Louvain, 1912–.

DTC = *Dictionnaire de théologie catholique*, ed. A. Vacant, E. Mangenot, and E. Amann. Paris, 1903–50.

Famiglietti, R. C. *Royal Intrigue: Crisis at the Court of Charles VI, 1392–1420*. New York: AMS Press, 1986.

Gilson, Etienne. *History of Christian Philosophy in the Middle Ages*. London: Sheed and Ward, 1955.

Gl (with volume and page number) = Palemon Glorieux. *Jean Gerson. Oeuvres Complètes*. Paris: Desclée & Cie, 1960–73, vols. 1–10.

Glorieux, Palemon "La vie et les oeuvres de Gerson." *Archives d'histoire doctrinale et littéraire du moyen âge* 25–26 (1950–51), pp. 149–92.

————. "L'ensiegnement universitaire de Gerson." *Recherches de Théologie ancienne et médievale* 23 (1956), pp. 88–113.

————. "Gerson à Bruges." *Revue d'histoire ecclésiastique* 31 (1935), pp. 4–52.

————. "Gerson au chapitre de Notre-Dame de Paris." *Revue d'histoire ecclésiastique* 56 (1961), pp. 424–48 and 827–54.

Grosse, Sven. *Heilsungewissheit und Scrupulosita im späten Mittelalter. Studien zu Johannes Gerson und Gattungen der Frömmigkeitstheologie seiner Zeit.* Beiträge zur historischen Theologie 85. Tübingen: J.C.B. Mohr, 1994.

Hicks, Eric. *Le débat sur le Roman de la Rose. Édition critique, introduction, traductions, notes.* Bibliothèque du XVe Siècle 43. Paris: Éditions Honoré Champion, 1977.

Huizinga, Johan. *The Waning of the Middle Ages.* London: Penguin Books, 1968 (first published in English in 1924).

Jadart, Henri. *Jean Gerson. Recherches sur son origine, son village natal et sa famille.* Reims: Deligne et Renart, Libraires de l'Academie, 1881.

Kretzmann, Norman, Antony Kenny, Jan Pinborg, and Eleonore Stump. *The Cambridge History of Later Medieval Philosophy.* Cambridge and New York: Cambridge University Press, 1982.

Lambert, Malcolm. *Medieval Heresy: Popular Movements from Bogomil to Hus.* London: Edward Arnold, 1977.

Lerner, Robert. *The Heresy of the Free Spirit in the Later Middle Ages.* Berkeley and Los Angeles: University of California Press, 1972.

McDonnell, Ernest W. *The Beguines and Beghards in Medieval Culture.* New Brunswick, N.J.: Rutgers University Press, 1954; reprinted New York: Octagon Books, 1969.

McGinn, Bernard. *The Foundations of Mysticism: Origins to the Fifth Century.* Vol. 1 of The Presence of God: A History of Western Christian Mysticism. New York: Crossroad, 1991.

————. *The Growth of Mysticism: Gregory the Great Through the Twelfth*

Century. Vol. 2 of The Presence of God: A History of Western Christian Mysticism. New York: Crossroad, 1994.

McGuire, Brian Patrick. *Friendship and Community: The Monastic Experience 350–1250.* Kalamazoo, Mich.: Cistercian Publications, 1988.

————. *The Difficult Saint: Bernard of Clairvaux and His Tradition.* Kalamazoo, Mich.: Cistercian Publications, 1991.

————. "Loving the Holy Order: Jean Gerson and the Carthusians." Pages 100–139 in James Hogg, ed., *Die Kartäuser und ihre Welt–Kontakte und gegensitige Einflüsse. Analecta Cartusiana* 62. Salzburg, Austria: Institut für Anglistik und Amerikanistik, Universität Salzburg; Lewiston, N.Y.: Edwin Mellen Press, 1993.

————. "Gerson and Bernard: Languishing with Love." *Cîteaux Commentarii Cistercienses* 46 (1995), pp. 127–57.

————. "Education, Confession, and Pious Fraud: Jean Gerson and a Late Medieval Change." *The American Benedictine Review* 47 (1996), pp. 310–38.

————. "Sexual Control and Spiritual Growth in the Late Middle Ages: The Case of Jean Gerson." Pages 123–52 in *Tradition and Ecstasy: The Agony of the Fourteenth century,* ed. Nancy van Deusen. Ottawa, Canada: The Institute of Mediaeval Music, 1997.

————. "Late Medieval Care and Control of Women: Jean Gerson and His Sisters." *Revue d'histoire ecclésiastique* 92 (1997), pp. 5–36.

Masson, A. L. *Jean Gerson. Sa vie, son temps, ses oeuvres.* Lyon: Emmanuel Vitte, 1894.

Morrall, John B. *Gerson and the Great Schism.* Manchester: University Press, 1960.

Mourin, Louis. *Jean Gerson. Prédicateur Français.* Brugge, Belgium: De Tempel, 1952.

Oakley, Francis. *The Western Church in the Later Middle Ages.* Ithaca, N.Y., and London: Cornell University Press, 1979.

Oberman, Heiko Augustinus. *The Harvest of Medieval Theology: Gabriel*

Biel and Late Medieval Nominalism. Originally published in 1963 by Harvard University Press; reprinted Durham, N.C.: The Labyrinth Press, 1983.

OCD = *The Oxford Classical Dictionary.* Oxford: Clarendon Press, 1961.

OCT = Oxford Classical Texts.

Ouy, Gilbert. "Une lettre de jeunesse de Jean Gerson." *Romania* 80 (1959), pp. 461–72.

————. "La plus ancienne oeuvre retrouvée de Jean Gerson: le brouillon inachevé d'un traité contre Juan de Monzon (1389–90)." *Romania* 83 (1962), pp. 433–92.

————. "Humanism and Nationalism in France at the Turn of the Fifteenth Century." Pages 107–25 in *The Birth of Identities: Denmark and Europe in the Middle Ages,* ed. Brian Patrick McGuire. Copenhagen: C. A. Reitzel, 1996 (distributed in North America by Cistercian Publications).

————. See also under Calvot, Danièle.

Pascoe, Louis B. *Jean Gerson: Principles of Church Reform.* Studies in Medieval and Reformation Thought 7. Leiden: E. J. Brill, 1973.

PG (with volume and column number) = *Patrologia Graeca. Cursus Completus.* Paris, 1817–66.

Pinet, M. J. *La vie ardente de Gerson.* Paris: Librairie Bloud & Gay, 1929.

PL (with volume and column number) = J. P. Migne, *Patrologia Latina. Cursus Completus.* Paris, 1844–64.

PMT = *Practical Mystical Theology* (*Theologia Mystica Practica*). Text in Combes; translated here.

Rashdall = Hastings Rashdall, *The Universities of Europe in the Middle Ages.* F. M. Powicke and A. B. Emden, vols. 1–3. Oxford: Oxford University Press, 1936.

RHE = *Revue d'histoire ecclésiastique.* Louvain, 1905–.

ABBREVIATIONS/SELECT BIBLIOGRAPHY

RTAM = *Recherches de Théologie ancienne et médiévale*. Louvain, 1929–.

SBO = *Sancti Bernardi Opera* 1–8, ed. Jean Leclercq and Henri Rochais. Rome: Editiones Cistercienses, 1957–77.

SC = Sources chrétiennes. Paris: Les éditions du Cerf, 1942–.

Schmiel, David. *Via Propria and Via Mystica in the Theology of Jean le Charlier de Gerson*. Graduate Study no. 10. St. Louis, Mo.: School for Graduate Studies, Concordia Seminary, 1969.

Schwab, Johann Baptist. *Johannes Gerson. Professor der Theologie und Kanzler der Universität Paris*, 1–2. Würzburg, 1858; reprinted New York: Burt Franklin, no date.

SMT = *Speculative Mystical Theology (Theologia Mystica Speculativa)*. Text in Combes; translated in part here.

Stenzenberger, Johann. *Die Mystik des Johannes Gerson*, Breslauer Studien zur historischen Theologie 10. Breslau: Verlag Müller & Seiffert, 1928.

Tentler, Thomas. *Sin and Confession on the Eve of the Reformation*. Princeton, N.J.: Princeton University Press, 1977.

Tuchman, Barbara W. *A Distant Mirror: The Calamitous Fourteenth Century*. New York: Alfred A. Knopf, 1978.

VP = *Vita Prima* of Bernard of Clairvaux, compiled by Geoffrey of Auxerre, William of Saint Thierry, and Arnold of Bonnevaux, in PL 185:225–368.

FINAL BIBLIOGRAPHICAL NOTE

As this book goes to press, professor André Vauchez, director of the Ecole Française de Rome, has been kind enough to send me a new edition and translation of the visions of Ermine of Rheims: *Entre Dieu et Satan: Les visions d'Ermine de Reims* (d. 1396), présentées, éditées et traduites par Claude Arnaud-Gillet. Préface d'André Vauchez (Firenze: SISMEL, Edizioni del Galluzzo, 1997). Gerson was asked, as we can see in his Letters, to evaluate the authenticity of Ermine's visions. Until now it has been almost impossible to find the original edition of these visions.

Index

(References in **boldface** are to material in Introduction)

Other Volumes in This Series

Other Volumes in This Series

Other Volumes in This Series